BASIC REAL ESTATE APPRAISAL
THIRD EDITION

RICHARD M. BETTS
Appraiser
Merritt College, Oakland, California

SILAS J. ELY
Certified General Real Estate Appraiser
and
Community College Instructor/Consultant
Real Estate Education

DENNIS McKENZIE
Series Editor

PRENTICE HALL CAREER & TECHNOLOGY
Englewood Cliffs, NJ 07632

333.332
Bet

Library of Congress Cataloging-in-Publication Data

Betts, Richard M
    Basic real estate appraisal / Richard M. Betts, Silas J. Ely.—
3rd ed.
      p.   cm.
    Includes index.
    ISBN 0-13-075987-2
    1. Real property—Valuation. I. Ely, Silas J. II. Title.
HD1387.B43   1994
333.33'2—dc20   93-5466
                                       CIP

Acquisitions Editor: Catherine Rossbach
Editorial/production supervision: Tally Morgan, WordCrafters Editorial Services, Inc.
Buyer: Ilene Sanford

© 1994, 1990, 1982 by Prentice-Hall Career & Technology
Prentice-Hall, Inc.
A Paramount Communications Company
Englewood Cliffs, New Jersey 07632

Printed in the United States of America
10 9 8 7 6 5 4 3 2 1

ISBN 0-13-075987-2

Prentice-Hall International (UK) Limited, *London*
Prentice-Hall of Australia Pty. Limited, *Sydney*
Prentice-Hall Canada Inc., *Toronto*
Prentice-Hall Hispanoamericana, S.A., *Mexico*
Prentice-Hall of India Private Limited, *New Delhi*
Prentice-Hall of Japan, Inc., *Tokyo*
Simon & Schuster Asia Pte. Ltd., *Singapore*
Editora Prentice-Hall do Brasil, Ltda., *Rio de Janeiro*

Contents

Meeting the Authors

RICHARD M. BETTS Mr. Betts is a California Certified General Real Estate Appraiser and consultant in Berkeley, California. He was educated at the University of California, Berkeley, where he earned a B.S. in Business Administration and an M.B.A. degree in Real Estate. Subsequent educational work includes a Real Estate Certificate; AIREA courses/exams I, II, IV, and VIII; SREA Course 301; and Educare Course I. Mr. Betts has extensive experience as a fee appraiser, including expert-witness appraisal before various superior courts and assessment appeal boards. He has taught extensively for Merritt Community College; the University of California, Berkeley, Extension Division; AIREA; SREA; and the Appraisal Institute. He also taught for IAAO (Courses 1, 2, and 3); the University of Southern California College of Continuing Education; and the University of California, Berkeley, School of Business. Mr. Betts holds the professional designations MAI, SRA, and ASA (Real Estate) and is a past president of both the Northern California Chapter 11 of AIREA and the East Bay Chapter 54 of SREA. For some years, Mr. Betts served on national committees of AIREA, including the National Editorial Board, *The Appraisal Journal*. He co-authored *The Essentials of Real Estate Economics*, 3d ed., published by Prentice Hall, Inc., New Jersey, in 1992.

SILAS J. ELY Mr. Ely is a California Certified General Real Estate Appraiser, instructor, and educational consultant. He resides in San Luis Obispo County, California. He is a graduate of the University of California at Los Angeles, where he earned a B.A. degree in Political Science and a Certificate in Real Estate. He also holds a full-time California Community College Instructor Credential. For many years, Mr. Ely was a principal appraiser and regional manager for the Los Angeles County Assessor. Most recently an instructor at the College of the Canyons, Mr. Ely was an appraisal instructor at both Los Angeles Valley and Santa Monica colleges, where he taught the beginning as well as the advanced appraisal courses for many years. Also, he was once a senior faculty member in appraisal for the University of Southern California College of Continuing Education. Mr. Ely was the 1978 chairman of the California Association of Real Estate Teachers and a past president of the Los Angeles County Chapter of the IAAO. A current member of the Real Estate Educators Association and 1994 director of its California Chapter, Mr. Ely holds the RECI designation of the latter group. He was a recipient of the Teacher of the Year Award for 1979 from the California Association of Real Estate Teachers. He is co-author and "1991 Revision" author of the California Community College Instructor and Student Guides for Real Estate Appraisal, and a contributing author of the *Real Estate Handbook*, published by McGraw Hill in 1993.

Preface

This third edition of *Basic Real Estate Appraisal* provides an up-to-date, practical guide to real estate appraisal for students and real estate professionals as well as for consumers. Importantly, this edition of the text now references and explains the Uniform Standards of Professional Appraisal Practice, recently endorsed by most government and industry groups. Conformity with USPAP is now required in most federally related appraisals.

Based on the authors' years of teaching at both the community college and university levels as well as their years of practical appraisal experience, *Basic Real Estate Appraisal* is a thorough outline of generally accepted appraisal theory and practice today. Both simple and complex subjects are covered in terms that are easy to understand yet accurate. Although this is an entry-level text, all of the appraisal-related topics listed in the educational requirements for appraiser licensing and certification have been introduced here.

As to the format of the book, the chapters are subdivided into sections, usually three or four. Each chapter starts with a preview paragraph and statement of learning objectives. These should help the reader to identify the important elements in the chapter. The major sections of the text material follow. Each chapter concludes with a comprehensive summary and a list of important terms and concepts. A group of chapter review questions is provided to help the reader review his or her understanding. The answers to these questions are provided at the end of the book.

Finally, we would like to point out that the appraisal concepts and techniques covered in this book are important tools that are useful to people in every field of real estate. We hope that our presentation will provide many helpful ideas and skills for use in your daily real estate endeavors.

Richard M. Betts
Silas J. Ely

Acknowledgments

Over the years, many people have played a part in the preparation of this book. To each one we express our deep appreciation. Valued technical contributions were made by Lowell Anderson, Department Chairman of Real Estate, Cerritos College; Marjory Reed, former Coordinator of Real Estate Programs, San Diego Community College District; Leon Mochkatel, independent appraiser and appraisal instructor at Mount San Antonio Community College; Dr. Stanley S. Reyburn, instructor at UCLA and several California community colleges; Robert Mason, MAI, consulting appraiser, Mason & Mason; James Goodhue, MAI; Noland Cavey, SRA, Supervising Real Property Appraiser, Sacramento County Assessor's Office; and James Palmer, MAI, independent appraiser. Of the above, Dr. Stanley Reyburn and Mr. Leon Mochkatel were principal reviewers of this third edition.

Many other people have helped in the formulation of *Basic Real Estate Appraisal:* the students in our appraisal classes who have shared their insights with us over the years, the appraisal colleagues and friends with whom we have exchanged and debated ideas, the authors of earlier appraisal texts from which we have learned, and the lecturers at the appraisal courses and seminars at which we have been students. Our special thanks go to the many instructors of real estate appraisal classes who have participated with us at instructor workshops sponsored by the California Community College Real Estate Education Center and the California Real Estate Educators Association. We hope that we have adequately incorporated and passed along all of their good ideas.

R.M.B.
S.J.E.

Chapter 1
Real Estate Appraisal and You

Preview   Well-founded appraisals are a vital part of most real estate decisions, particularly those that involve the listing, financing, sale, and purchase of real estate. What is an appraisal? If you have had other courses in real estate, or have worked in the field, you will know that an appraisal can be defined simply as an *informed* estimate of value.

Most of us make decisions in our everyday lives that use appraisal-related skills, whether in buying consumer goods or in serving as real estate professionals. The goal of this book is to help you develop these skills so that you can make more productive and rewarding real estate decisions.

This first chapter will explain what an appraisal is, who makes appraisals, and how appraisals are used in our society. Brief outlines of the current standards of appraisal practice and typical state requirements for licensing and certification are included.

When you have completed this chapter, you should be able to:

1. *Define the term* appraisal.

2. *Explain the difference between a formal and an informal appraisal.*

3. *List the main uses of appraisals.*

4. *Outline the Standards of appraisal practice.*

5. *List the reasons for studying appraisal.*

1.1 WHAT IS AN APPRAISAL?

Very simply, *an appraisal is an estimate of value*. It is defined as an estimate because it is neither a statement of value nor a fixing of value. An appraisal is only one person's opinion based on whatever skills, training, data, dedication, and/or objectivity that person possesses.

What do we mean by value? Value means the *worth, usefulness, or utility of an object to someone for some purpose*. Under this definition, the value of any object can vary, depending on the purpose for which it is to be used or the person seeking to use it. Thus, there are actually many different types of values, each appropriate to a particular appraisal purpose or need. (The common types of value will be explained in Chapter 3.)

Most often, questions concerning the value of real estate involve estimating its market value, which is defined simply as its most probable selling price. Accurately estimating what real estate should sell for is the focus of this book.

Informal Appraisals

Have you ever estimated what price to pay for an object at a garage sale or auction? If you have, then you have made a type of appraisal. Such an *informal appraisal* is a common part of our lives. Whenever we buy groceries, household appliances, or automobiles, we usually make an informal appraisal to judge if the prices are reasonable. We do this by consciously or unconsciously comparing one product to another, or by matching the price of one item against that of a similar one. As we become more experienced in comparing items and prices, we develop an intuitive understanding of the value of things. Such an intuitive knowledge of value can also be applied to real estate.

Informal appraisals are made by almost everyone working in the field of real estate. For example, the "market analysis" made by brokers and salespeople when listing or selling property can be described as an informal appraisal. Experienced sales agents can very often closely estimate the eventual selling price of a house after only a quick walk-through. To be reliable though, informal appraisals depend on an active and competitive market in the kind of property being analyzed as well as on the knowledge, experience, and judgment of the sales agent or appraiser.

Formal Appraisals

Both real estate practitioners and consumers frequently need to estimate the value of things that they have had little experience buying or selling. Without recent experience, their intuitive judgment about prices may be unreliable. In the case of a real estate consumer, an example is an employee transferring to a new town. This person may be quite familiar with housing prices in the old neighborhood, and therefore feels comfortable selling his or her old residence without outside advice. However, lack of knowledge or experience in the new town would likely present a dilemma when buying the relocation house.

When intuition is inadequate, there are only three alternatives: (1) to guess, (2) to go to someone with adequate intuition, or (3) to deliberately develop the information needed to make good price estimates.

The last of these three choices has led to formal appraisal, or appraisal by a system of logic.

A formal appraisal is an estimate of value that is reached by the collection and analysis of relevant data. Most often reported in writing, formal appraisals are usually made by people specially trained for this work. Since the value conclusion is based on the analysis of factual material, a client or disinterested party can easily review the appraisal and understand how the conclusion was reached. This is in contrast to the informal appraisal, where the conclusion is reached by using intuition, past experience, and general knowledge, which cannot easily be reviewed. To better understand the difference between formal and informal appraisals, see Figure 1.1.

In practice, formal and informal appraisals share some common ground. Although formal appraisals are based primarily on supporting data, in practice, they must also rely to a degree on the appraiser's judgment and intuition. On the other hand, informal appraisals are based mainly on intuition but may also include some data that supports the value estimate. Appraisals by professional appraisers are for the most part formal; those by experienced salespeople are for the most part intuitive and informal.

The Appraisal Report

Formal appraisals are communicated to the client by what is known as the *appraisal report*. Reports may be either oral or written. Written reports may vary in length from a short form or letter to a detailed narrative document. The length of an appraisal report does not necessarily reflect the complexity or quality of the appraisal. However, professional and legal standards often govern the form and content of appraisal reports. Formal appraisal reports will be described in more detail in the chapters that follow.

1.2 HOW APPRAISAL SKILLS ARE USED

Appraisals serve two important functions in our society. The first function is to assist the public by advising them on questions of property value. Many people do not have the skills, the time, or the knowledge to make good value estimates on their own; instead, they turn to professionals for formal or informal appraisals.

The second social function that appraisals perform is to provide an unbiased and disinterested estimate of value, where total objectivity is

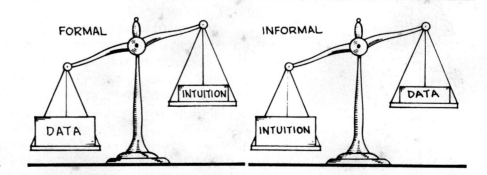

Figure 1.1
Formal and informal appraisals.

required by business practice or the provision of law. Appraisals in such situations must be formal, capable of being reviewed, and presented in written form. Like the notes of the certified court reporter or the signature of the notary public, the formal appraisal made by an unbiased appraiser is an important document in business and legal affairs.

Occasions Requiring Appraisals

In our complex society, there are countless occasions when formal or informal appraisals are necessary. Such occasions can be divided into two major categories: market transactions and legal transactions. As we will see, parties to these transactions might include buyers, sellers, agents, lenders, landlords, and tenants, as well as various agencies of government.

Market Transactions

Most of the market transactions requiring appraisals are connected with the sale, purchase, finance, management, and use of real estate.

As we have already seen, buyers, sellers, and sales agents need formal or informal appraisals to guide them in establishing the price and terms of the real estate transaction being contemplated. When the terms are finally agreed on, some financing is typically involved; this usually means that a formal appraisal will also be required for loan purposes. In cases where there are multiple buyers and sellers (as with some investment properties), several separate appraisals may be involved in a single transaction.

Various kinds of appraisals are also required in the management and use of real estate. For example, an appraisal is sometimes needed to estimate the proper rent level at the time a new lease is negotiated. Usually, an appraisal is also needed to estimate the values of property being exchanged. Or one may be required to estimate proper insurance coverage, based on the kind of coverage in the insurance contract. Appraisals may also be used to see whether the cost of proposed remodeling is justified, considering the probable increase in a property's value. Finally, a formal appraisal may be necessary to estimate which of several possible uses of a vacant land parcel will prove to be the highest and best use, that is, the most profitable use of the land.

Legal Transactions

Legal transactions are defined here as government actions involving real estate and those private actions that take place in legal settings or are otherwise regulated by law. When appraisals are required, they usually must be formal and in writing.

Government actions requiring appraisals are mainly in two areas of public control: eminent domain (the right to acquire private property for a public purpose) and the various forms of taxation. Under the law of eminent domain, condemnation appraisals determine what "just compensation" or payment to the owner should be made for any property acquired for public use or in the public interest. Condemnation appraising is a highly specialized field to be further discussed in Chapter 17 of this book.

Property taxation is perhaps the largest area of public control involving appraisals. In thousands of jurisdictions across the country, the property tax appraiser or assessor must estimate a value to be used as the basis for the tax. In turn, the taxpayer may have the property privately appraised to see if the agency valuation is reasonable or whether it should be appealed. (Appraisals for property tax purposes will be discussed later in this book.) Public or governmental appraisals may also be necessary to establish the basis for inheritance, estate, or gift taxes.

Various types of appraisals are made in conjunction with income tax reporting or appeal. For example, appraisals may be required to support an income tax claim for a casualty loss. An appraisal may be needed to allocate the purchase price of property between the land and the improvements, in order to set up income tax depreciation. On occasion, appraisals are needed to establish historical values so that capital gains can be calculated. As the various tax laws become more complicated, formal appraisals may come into greater demand.

Personal and corporate actions in a variety of legal settings also give rise to appraisals. For example, there is an occasional need for appraisals to accompany environmental impact reports required in many property use and development situations. Appraisals are often needed to set the value of property involved in divorce situations. When lawsuits between building owners and tenants revolve around questions of property value or rental amounts, appraisals may be required. Also, legal actions arising over damages to real estate may require appraisals, usually to estimate the loss in value from such damages.

Another occasion for appraisals arises when loans are in default. Here, lenders need to know the market value of any real estate security while commencing the foreclosure process. Bankruptcy actions may also call for appraisals. If real estate is offered as security for bail bonds, appraisals might be required, too. Appraisals for legal purposes often require the appraiser to act as an expert witness. Such assignments are among the most challenging work appraisers undertake.

Many of the occasions when appraisals are needed are shown in the following list. Most of these occasions will involve at least one formal appraisal.

---

1. **Market Transactions**
    (a) Purchase, sale, and exchange
    (b) Financing
    (c) Leasing
    (d) Management
    (e) Insurance
    (f) Remodeling and development
    (g) Feasibility and highest and best use studies
    (h) Exercise of purchase or lease options.

2. **Legal Transactions**
    (a) Eminent domain—condemnor and condemnee
    (b) Property tax assessment, and tax appeals cases
    (c) Estate, inheritance, and gift tax
    (d) Income tax—casualty loss, depreciation basis, and capital gains reporting

---

(e) Personal and corporate legal actions
(f) Environmental impact reports
(g) Marital and partnership dissolutions
(h) Landlord–tenant, and property damage lawsuits
(i) Loan foreclosures
(j) Company liquidation, merger, and bankruptcy
(k) Security for bail bonds

1.3 STANDARDS OF APPRAISAL PRACTICE

We can see that appraisals are an important part of the social, business, legal, and governmental fabric of our society. How is the public protected against nonprofessional or unethical appraisal practice?

Professional appraisal groups have long sponsored and promoted strict standards of ethics and practice among their members. Several groups continue to award professional designations to those members who distinguish themselves with knowledge, experience, and demonstrated ability. Examples include the MAI (Member, Appraisal Institute) and SRA (Senior Residential Appraiser) designations of the Appraisal Institute.

In 1987, nine leading appraisal groups banded together to formulate uniform appraisal standards that were eventually recognized throughout the United States by government and industry alike. Now published and maintained by the Appraisal Foundation, the Standards set by the Uniform Standards of Professional Appraisal Practice, known informally as USPAP, have been adopted by all major appraisal groups. USPAP imposes both ethical obligations and minimum appraisal standards which must be adhered to by all state licensees and certified appraisers.

Ethics Standards

The Ethics Provision of USPAP places ethical obligations on the appraiser in the following general areas of practice.

1. Conduct—requires that the appraiser perform all assignments with the highest standards of professional ethics, impartiality, objectivity, and independence.

2. Management—requires that the appraiser have no undisclosed interest in the appraisal outcome, in the property, or in the appraisal fee; allows no false or misleading advertising.

3. Confidentiality—requires that the appraiser not reveal the value conclusion to anyone (except a duly authorized professional practice committee) unless authorized by the client or pursuant to court order.

4. Record Keeping—requires that the appraiser prepare and keep written records on all assignments for at least five years.

5. Competency—requires that appraisers accept only that work that they have the experience necessary to perform (either individually or, if needed, in association with others).

Appraisal Standards

The Uniform Standards of Professional Appraisal Practice include the following general standards:

Standard 1. In developing a real estate appraisal, an appraiser must be aware of, understand, and correctly employ those recognized methods and techniques that are necessary to produce a credible appraisal.

Standard 2. In reporting the results of a real estate appraisal, an appraiser must communicate each analysis, opinion, and conclusion in a manner that is not misleading.

The complete text of USPAP standards current at date of this publication may be found in the back of this book. They cover detailed ethics provisions and standards for the entire appraisal process and report. The procedures and techniques presented in this book are a reflection of these standards. More detailed perspectives of professional appraisal groups and of the standards of appraisal practice are provided in Chapters 16 and 18 of this text.

Appraiser Licensing and Certification

By state and federal laws effective in 1993, appraisals made in support of certain federally related financial real estate transactions (federally insured loans, for example) must be performed by licensed or certified appraisers. (Some states had earlier effective dates.) With regulated exceptions, such appraisals must conform to the Uniform Standards of Professional Appraisal Practice outlined above. State license and certification requirements are outlined in Chapter 18 of this text.

1.4 DEVELOPING APPRAISAL SKILLS

We believe that appraisal skills are important to everyone who is, or wants to be, involved with real estate. These skills are particularly important to real estate agents, who have a fiduciary responsibility to their clients. Improved appraisal skills can help salespeople improve their listing skills. For example, suggesting a reasonable asking price can avoid the problems associated with either too high, or too low, asking prices. Either could result in no sale, an unhappy client, and a waste of otherwise productive time.

It is also important for people working in other real estate areas to study appraisal and develop appraisal skills. For example, investors must use appraisal skills to estimate the right price at which to buy or sell property. Lenders rely upon appraisal skills every day when reviewing loan appraisals to ensure that each loan has adequate security.

A second important reason for studying appraisal is to acquire basic knowledge that will help you in any future real estate course. Beginning and advanced real estate finance, real estate investment analysis, and advanced appraisal courses all rely on the information and ideas presented in this book.

Third, studying this book can also help you pass the real estate sales agent's or broker's license test, or prepare for appraiser licensing and certification exams.

Finally, a fourth reason for studying appraisal is to improve your understanding of the way appraisers work and converse. This will help you communicate with appraisers, intelligently evaluate their work, and improve your understanding of appraisal reports. Learning how to explain appraisal procedures for valuing property to your clients is another important benefit.

How Will the Format of This Book Help You?

The format of this book has been developed to simplify your study of the material presented. First, each chapter has a brief introduction that highlights the material to be covered and points out key learning objectives. Since appraising is a process that follows a series of steps, we have provided a diagram of this process in the front of the chapter, where relevant. The step to be covered in that chapter is highlighted. A full explanation of the appraisal process and the first diagram will be given in Chapter 3.

At the end of each chapter, there is a summary, so that you can again review what you have read and reinforce your understanding. The chapter summary is followed by a list of important terms to help you develop an appraisal vocabulary and remember which terms are important. Review questions at the end of each chapter also reinforce your understanding.

Of course, the learning objectives, chapter summary, and review questions will help you most if you put them to work. So take the time to read each chapter carefully and thoughtfully. When you finish, if you can answer the questions without looking back, you are doing fine. If you do need to look back, don't feel upset; looking up the answers will aid your learning considerably. Remember, you only get back from a book what you put into it. Appraisal skills can measurably contribute to your success, so your effort *will* be rewarded.

The Chapters Ahead

This book outlines the entire formal appraisal process and explains the various skills that comprises it. In general, the sequence of the chapters matches the steps in the appraisal process. Chapters 2 and 3 introduce the vocabulary and definition of terms you must be familiar with before the actual appraisal starts. An overview of the entire appraisal process is also provided.

Chapters 4 and 5 outline the major forces that influence value and point out how these forces can be interpreted. Chapters 6 and 7 detail the tasks of the actual property inspection. Chapters 8 to 15 show you the actual analytical techniques that are considered when valuing the property. Chapter 16 outlines the structure of the appraisal report, detailing information that needs to be included in order to satisfy the Uniform Standards of Professional Appraisal Practice. Chapter 17 introduces a number of advanced appraisal topics that will help you build upon your basic appraisal skills as well as prepare you for the advanced appraisal course. Chapter 18 turns your attention to appraising as a profession. It details the typical education and experience requirements for state licensing and certification of appraisers. Chapter 18 also lists several leading national appraisal organizations and describes their activities. The chapter closes with a brief description of professional appraisal work.

SUMMARY   In this chapter, we found that an appraisal is simply an estimate of value. Value generally means the worth or usefulness of something to someone for some purpose. Although there are many types of value, the purpose of most appraisals is to estimate market value, or the price at which something should sell.

Estimating the selling price of things is a process that everyone performs at one time or another. People do this by relying on their prior experiences with selling or buying an item. Such a value estimate is an informal or intuitive appraisal. When people have accumulated a lot of recent experience buying or selling an object, their intuitive appraisals may be very good. However, it is difficult for someone else to judge whether an intuitive appraisal is accurate or not.

Many people do not have the experience or judgment that is needed to make good, intuitive real estate appraisals. They can nevertheless learn to logically gather and analyze data that is relevant to market value. Once acquired, such skills can be used to make formal appraisals. The quality of formal appraisals does not depend on intuition to the degree that informal appraisals do. Formal appraisals also have the advantage of presenting data and analyses that can be reviewed easily. This allows a client or reviewer to consider objectively whether the appraisal estimate seems reasonable. However, in practice, the appraisal report does not always contain all of the information and calculations that were developed during a formal appraisal. Hence, the length of the report does not necessarily reflect the complexity or quality of the appraisal.

Appraisals are a vital part of real estate. Every real estate transaction involves informal appraisals by the buyer and seller. One or more formal appraisals may also be needed, especially to meet the lender's requirements. In addition, the legal framework of our society requires many appraisals, including appraisals for eminent domain, for various taxation purposes, and for use as evidence in civil lawsuits involving real property.

State and federal license and certification laws as well as leading appraisal groups have endorsed and adopted what is now known as the Uniform Standards of Professional Appraisal Practice (USPAP) in order to ensure professionalism in appraisals and thereby protect the public interest. The appraisal procedures and techniques presented in this book reflect these standards.

The study of real estate appraisal is important to all involved in real estate. Whether you are a real estate consumer or real estate professional, having appraisal skills will make your real estate decisions better, more profitable, and more error-free. Another reason for studying real estate appraisal is that this material can assist you in taking future real estate courses or in preparing for real estate sales, broker or appraiser licensing exams. Studying appraisal also enables you to communicate better with appraisers. By learning their language and techniques, you will be able to review their work intelligently. A knowledge of appraisal skills also helps you to communicate clearly to others the way in which your own value decisions are reached.

Important Terms and Concepts

Appraisal (formal and informal)

Appraisal process

Appraisal report

Appraisal standards

Ethics standards

Independent appraisal

Intuitive appraisal

Legal transactions

Market transactions

Uniform Standards of Professional Appraisal Practice

Usefulness

Value

Worth

REVIEWING YOUR UNDERSTANDING

1. The general term *value* means:
   (a) The function of an object
   (b) The average use of an object to all people
   (c) The worth, usefulness, or utility of an object to someone for some purpose
   (d) A good buy

2. An appraisal is:
   (a) A fixing of value
   (b) An estimate or opinion of value
   (c) A statement of value
   (d) A value determination

3. The two types of real estate appraisals are:
   (a) Formal and informal
   (b) Informal and intuitive
   (c) Structural and formal
   (d) None of the above

4. Informal appraisals are performed:
   (a) Only by appraisers
   (b) Only by skilled real estate people
   (c) By all consumers
   (d) Without the use of instinct

5. Informal appraisals rely *mostly* on:
   (a) Intuition and experience
   (b) Facts and figures
   (c) Supporting data
   (d) A value formula

6. Formal appraisals rely primarily on:
   (a) A secret value formula
   (b) Intuition and experience
   (c) Analysis of supporting data
   (d) Facts and figures

7. Besides assisting the public by advising them on questions of value, appraisals serve to:
   (a) Provide unbiased and objective opinions of value

(b) Make market transactions conform to economics
(c) Prove or disprove value estimates made by others
(d) None of the above

8. *Legal transactions* that often require appraisals include all of the following *except*:
   (a) Income tax casualty loss estimates
   (b) Property damage lawsuits
   (c) Company liquidation or merger
   (d) Loan foreclosure
   (e) Private feasibility studies

9. Some of the important reasons for studying appraisal are:
   (a) To improve your value estimation skills
   (b) To help you pass the real estate agent, broker, or appraiser examination
   (c) To help you understand other real estate courses
   (d) To improve your ability to communicate with appraisers
   (e) All of the above

10. State and federal laws require the licensing or certification of appraisers:
    (a) Who do any type of appraisal work
    (b) Who perform loan appraisals
    (c) Who perform appraisals for federally related transactions
    (d) Who are involved in legal transactions

Chapter 2
Legal Considerations in Appraisal

Preview   In Chapter 1, we described what an appraisal is and how it is used in our society. We pointed out that having a knowledge of appraisal is important to people working in *all* areas of real estate. Before going on to the actual appraisal process, we need to carefully define real estate and real property and describe their physical and legal characteristics. We also explain how individual parcels of real estate are legally identified.

When you have completed this chapter, you should be able to:

1. *Define real estate, real property, and personal property; give examples of these; and describe their differences.*

2. *Define and give examples of the bundle of rights.*

3. *Explain and provide examples of the three broad categories of restrictions on the use of real property.*

4. *Define four governmental restrictions on the private ownership of all property.*

5. *List and provide examples of the major types of legal descriptions.*

2.1 PHYSICAL AND LEGAL CHARACTERISTICS OF REAL ESTATE

What is real estate? Understanding this term is very important. People involved with real estate transactions can see, walk on, or go through the physical property in which they are interested. However, the property itself is *not* what they always get! Instead, they get *documents* that convey only specified and limited rights to the physical property.

Real Estate, Real Property, and Personal Property

In order to understand the meaning of real estate, we must first define *property*. Property consists of rights that have value, or, in more legal terms, "valuable rights held to the exclusion of others." For example, the right to occupy a house is a valuable property right. When property rights concern physical objects, such as a house or a car, the rights to these objects are called *tangible property*. If there are no physical objects but just valuable rights or obligations, these rights are called *intangible property*. A company's trademarks constitute one example of intangible property; a patent is another.

Another classification of property divides all property into either *real property* or *personal property*. Real property refers to the land and everything that is permanently fastened to the land. Personal property consists of property that is movable; more accurately, it refers to all property that is not real property.

Originally, the term *real property* referred only to the rights that one gained by owning land. In many states, real property by statute now includes the physical object (that is, the land itself), as well as the rights that go with it. In other states, the physical object is still described by the old technical term, *real estate*. Today, real estate and real property are usually used interchangeably, which is how they will be used in this book.

The Components of Real Property

The term *real property* refers to more than just the land. Actually, real property comprises four components, as shown in the following list.

---

1. The land.
2. Objects permanently affixed to the land.
3. That which is appurtenant to, or legally accompanies, the land.
4. That which is immovable by law.

Examples of real property are given in Figure 2.1.

The Land

The land includes the surface, the soil and rocks beneath, and the space above. In the past, these rights extended "for an indefinite distance upward as well as downward." Now, however, ownership of the space over the land—the airspace—has been limited to that which the landowner can reasonably use and enjoy. Similarly, the ownership of liquids and gases (oil, gas, water, steam, etc.) below the surface has also been limited in several ways. Since these liquids and gases move

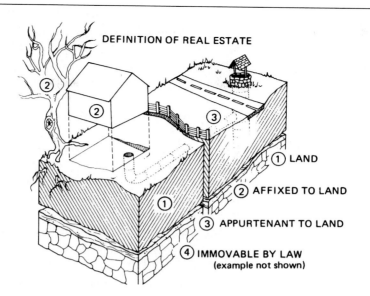

DEFINITION OF REAL ESTATE

① LAND
② AFFIXED TO LAND
③ APPURTENANT TO LAND
④ IMMOVABLE BY LAW
(example not shown)

Figure 2.1
(Courtesy of the California
Department of Real Estate)

naturally through the ground, they do not belong to a particular parcel of land, even if located under it, until they are physically "seized" by the landowner (for example, by being pumped out). The ways in which rights to underground liquids and gases are determined are especially complex and are not covered in this book. Generally, however, in real estate, the term land is easy to define.

Permanently Affixed Objects

When an object is permanently fastened to the land, it is legally considered to be a part of the land and thus a part of the real estate. Clearly objects such as trees, bridges, or buildings are permanently attached to the land and are easily identified as real property. Objects such as doors, which are permanently attached to a permanent building, are also real estate. However, when objects are not clearly attached to the land in a permanent way, their classification as either real or personal property can be difficult. A garden statue is an example. To make things even more complicated, objects that were once considered personal property can become permanently affixed objects. When this happens, the object is called a *fixture* and becomes part of the real estate. The courts have developed a series of tests to determine whether items of personal property have become fixtures. These are listed below. In addition, state legislatures have adopted rules for deciding if an object is to be classified as a fixture or as personal property in different circumstances.

Appurtenant Rights

The third component of real property consists of *appurtenant rights*, or appurtenances. An appurtenance is a right giving the owners of one property (called the dominant tenement) a right to use another property (called the servient tenement) in a specific way that benefits their property. One type of appurtenance would be the continued rights to enjoy the benefit of natural features (such as water courses or drainage channels) that extend beyond the property. Another category consists of an appurtenant easement, which may be established by an agreement between the property owner and the easement owner-user, or by other legal means. The most common easement is for an access right-of-way across another owner's land. Other easements may protect a view or protect exposure to sunlight. A third category of appurtenance is the occasional situation in which ownership of a mutual, or community, water or telephone company is appurtenant to the land. In this instance, the shares of stock are tied to the land and can only be sold with the land. They cannot be sold separately, as normal stock shares can.

That Which Is Immovable by Law

Many laws (for example, the California Civil Code, Section 658) list this as a fourth component of real property. This component is similar to the category of objects that are affixed to the land, but it does not require permanent physical attachment. This fourth category functions as a catchall. Any objects that do not fit into the first three categories and are not clearly movable (i.e., are not clearly personal property) fall in this catchall category. The classification of these objects as being real or personal is up to the legislature and courts.

Property: Is It Real or Personal?

Real estate cannot be moved. It is permanently fixed in its location. Personal property, on the other hand, is movable. Fixtures are personal property items that have become attached to the real estate and converted into real estate.

The Law of Fixtures

The courts have established five tests to determine whether an object is a fixture or personal property. These five tests are weighed collectively.

1. The *intention* of the person incorporating the personal property into the land. For example, clear evidence that a dining room chandelier installed by a tenant in his or her present residence had previously been installed in and removed from the tenant's prior residence might be convincing proof of the tenant's intention to remove it from the current residence at the end of the lease.

2. How permanently the property is *attached* to the land and building. A built-in stove is considered real property; a freestanding stove can be judged as personal property. The courts sometimes refer to this test as the *degree of annexation*.

3. The extent to which the property is *uniquely adapted* to be used with the land. A loose throw rug, if cut to fit an odd-shaped room, might well become a fixture. However, a rectangular throw rug, even if tacked down, probably would not be considered a fixture. Adaptation to use is commonly tested by the object's function. For example, a chalkboard attached to the wall of a classroom serves as a functional part of the building and thus should be classified as a fixture; however, the same chalkboard in a home might not be.

4. The existence of any *agreement* between the parties involved that defines ownership of the property and whether it is to be considered as real estate. Many leases contain such provisions.

5. The *relationship* between the person putting in the personal property and any other person with a claim to the real estate. For example, in a dispute the courts might classify an object differently, depending on whether the dispute is between an owner and tenant or owner and lender.

Why should you be concerned with fixture definitions? You need to be able to determine which objects are to be included in the appraisal as real estate and which are to be excluded. It will often be necessary to find out what items the present occupants expect to take as their personal property when they vacate. These items can be individually evaluated by the five tests (listed above) to determine if the personal property has become a fixture. In some cases, the appraisal may also include personal property left with the realty (for example, the refrigerator). Usually, we can simply specify which questionable items have been included in the evaluation. In some circumstances, we may want to compare lists obtained from opposing parties, such as the owner and the tenant.

A variety of problems can crop up when you are trying to decide whether a particular object is real or personal property. Here are a few examples:

Carpets, drapes, and blinds. Classification depends on the intentions of the parties who installed the items, whether they were cut or tailored to fit, how they are fastened, and in the case of carpeting, whether there is a finished floor or just subflooring underneath.

Cabinets and kitchen equipment. These items are generally held to be realty when they are built into residential structures. They may qualify as personalty in commercial situations, depending on the agreement or intentions of the parties.

Chandeliers. Resolution depends on intentions and who installed the chandeliers. Valuable antiques are often considered personalty (i.e., personal property).

Garden decorations (driftwood, statuary, stone lanterns, etc.). Resolution depends on intentions, how the objects are fastened down, and whether they were modified for use in the specific location. These are often held to be personalty.

Real Property Rights

As noted earlier, the term real estate originally referred to the object itself: the land and what was attached to it. As time went by, a second term, real property, was added to refer solely to the ownership rights to the object. This new term was added to express a new concept, that of dividing the rights to the property without breaking up the physical property itself.

Today, we recognize that the rights to the ownership of land actually consist of many different rights. Included in these are the right to occupy the property, the right to sell it, the right to exclude others from it, the right to borrow against it, and the right to convey ownership by inheritance.

Fee Ownership   The highest form of ownership one can have in real property is called *fee, fee simple, or fee simple absolute*. Of course, such ownership is always subject to applicable zoning and environmental restraints imposed by government. Property owned in *fee simple qualified* means that its use is subject to certain conditions or limitations, such as deed restrictions. Historically, property ownership rights have been compared to a large bundle of sticks, with each stick representing a different portion of the rights of ownership. From this idea came the phrase *bundle of rights*. This concept has been carried further: now, when the rights are divided, people speak of "breaking up the bundle of sticks" among more than one owner, and creating what are now known as partial interests. (See Figure 2.2.)

Partial Interests   Partial interests are created when an owner decides to keep certain property rights but to give or sell other rights to another party. For example, a tenant under a lease has been granted the right to occupy or possess the real estate for the stated term of the lease. This amounts to a partial interest referred to to as a *leasehold estate*. The partial interest remaining with the landlord is called a *leased fee*.

A property owner may also keep the right of possession but surrender the right to "will" the property away. In this event, the rights that you have left are called a *life estate*. A life estate is the right to live on the property or control its occupancy during your lifetime only. You have agreed to surrender the property to another (called the *remainderman*) upon your death but without involving an inheritance or will.

Real property rights may be shared in other ways. For example, the common areas of condominium projects (for example, the parking, storage, and recreation areas) are shared or jointly owned. For each unit, such "undivided interests" are typically joined with the fee ownership of a defined "airspace" to form the total ownership unit. The sharing of

(a)   (b)

Figure 2.2
(a) Dividing the property.
(b) Dividing the rights.

property rights may take many legal forms that will be further discussed in Chapter 17 of this text. Here are examples of partial interests, including those that we have cited above:

1. Leased fee estates
2. Leasehold estates
3. Life estates
4. Undivided interests in commonly held property
5. Easements appurtenant to other properties
6. Timeshares
7. Cooperatives
8. Ownerships subject to financial obligations
9. Air rights

The concept of real property as a collection of rights and of partial interests in real estate is important to real estate evaluation. Ownerships that include all the property rights are obviously worth more than those that include only a portion of these rights. It is vital, then, to *define the property ownership rights to be valued* in the appraisal, and to *clearly identify the rights that are to be excluded.*

2.2 USE RESTRICTIONS

Meaning and Importance of Use Restrictions

When people want to acquire real estate, it is not simply the physical object that they seek. More precisely, they want the benefits that accompany the ownership. Such benefits may come either from an immediate use, or from some anticipated future use. In either case, the purchase is motivated by the expectation of future benefits.

Realistically, what property uses are available? The uses of a property are not determined just by an owner's whims. Instead, the possible uses are dictated by a large number of public and private restrictions that affect the value of property. This is why it is particularly important that use restrictions be understood in appraisals. Use restrictions fall into three broad categories, to be discussed next. (See Figure 2.3.)

Categories of Use Restrictions

Government Restrictions

The government restricts the right to use real property in four ways, as shown below. The authority to make these restrictions exists because, historically, all private ownership of real estate originates from a grant of title given by the sovereign body—the person or organization that is the central or principal authority of a country. In the United States, the sovereign body is "we, the people," collectively acting through our government. The laws of our country limit the ownership rights belonging to private owners of property.

Four specific rights are retained by the sovereign. Thus every aspect of one's right to use a property is limited by these four restrictions. (As a way to remember these four powers, think of the name PETE, which has the first letter of each power: **P**olice, **E**minent domain, **T**axation, and **E**scheat.)

Figure 2.3
Types of restrictions.

1. **Police power**. The sovereign body has the right to regulate property as necessary to promote the safety, health, morals, and general welfare of the public. The police power forms the basis of the controls that directly restrict the use of all property.

2. **Eminent domain**. The sovereign body may take the property back at any time if it is in the public interest to do so (such as for roads, schools, etc.). When this is done, the sovereign body must pay the owner a "just compensation."

3. **Taxation**. The sovereign body may impose any level of taxes needed to raise funds so long as the taxes are fairly imposed.

4. **Escheat**. The sovereign body will take back the title to the property if the owner dies or disappears and leaves no relatives or heirs.

How Police Power Affects Real Estate

Of the four government restrictions listed, police power has the most obvious effect on the use and value of real estate. Under the authority of police power, local government agencies adopt zoning ordinances which specify where various land uses can be located, as well as the type and density of occupancy allowed. Zoning can regulate the height and size of buildings; the extent of yards, decks, parking, and other features; and the appearance, exterior materials, and architectural detailing of buildings. Zoning ordinances can also regulate noise levels allowed, hours that stores can operate, the amount of light, vibration, or odor permissible, and even the type and size of business signs.

Under the police power, the government can also pass building, housing, electrical, and plumbing codes. These codes define in great detail minimum room sizes and heights, restrictions on the materials used, and floor-plan layout restrictions. The types of heat may be defined, as well as allowable systems for plumbing, waste, and electricity. These ordinances extend to regulating types and sizes of windows and doors, as well as types of finish. Minimum maintenance standards are often set by these codes, usually with penalties for violations. In short, almost no detail of a building is exempt from some form of control, regulation, or prohibition.

Numerous types of use restrictions are based on the police power of government. Here are some examples:

Air and water pollution

Building, housing, and electrical codes

Coastal preservation zones

Condominium conversion ordinances

Endangered species acts

Environmental controls

Flood zones

Historical preservation acts

Master plans

Park dedications

Public utility easements

Rent control

Scenic corridors

Seismic safety study areas

Sign abatement ordinances

Solid waste disposal

Strip mining rehabilitation acts

Subdivision requirements

Underground utility requirements

Wild river protection acts

Zoning ordinances

The importance and effect of government restrictions will be further discussed in Chapter 6.

Private Restrictions   The government is not alone in restricting the use of land. When people sell real estate, they sometimes impose conditions that restrict the future owners or users. For example, at one time many properties were sold with a clause prohibiting the sale of alcoholic beverages on the property.

More recently, most condominiums and planned unit developments with common areas utilize recorded CC&Rs (Conditions, Covenants, and Restrictions) to regulate their use, operation, and control. Usually, the existence of CC&Rs, or other private deed restrictions connected with the property, is revealed in a preliminary title report or title search. It is often advisable to inquire about the possible effects of such restrictions and, if necessary, to review the actual documents.

Restrictions on the use of property can also be imposed by private easements and contracts. For example, the owners could grant an easement for an electric power transmission line which could restrict building any structures under the power lines. An easement for a buried gas pipeline could bar any structures over the pipeline. A view easement granted to a neighbor could limit the height of any building to one story and perhaps require a flat roof. A lease could restrict the use of the property to a specific purpose (a high-priced retail shoe store, for example). A mortgage note could also contain provisions limiting the uses of the property. In other words, nearly every contract that a real property owner signs involving the property can impose limits on its use.

The importance of private restrictions will be further discussed in Chapter 6.

Market Restrictions

In an economic sense, neither the government nor the property owner really determines the ultimate use of land. Instead, the eventual use of land depends on the restrictions imposed by the market which operates within the limits set by the government and by private restrictions.

How does the market restrict the use of land? Each proposed land use must appear to be financially satisfactory or investors will not choose that use. Proposed uses of land must earn enough money, or create enough benefits at that location, to justify the cost of the land and buildings. Thus the market encourages uses of land that are *economically feasible*, that is, those uses that are able to pay at least all the costs of using the site and any necessary improvements. If a use is economically feasible but forbidden by zoning and/or deed restrictions, there is an economic incentive for someone to have the restrictions removed. Otherwise, nothing will be done with the land until some allowable use becomes economically feasible.

The Results

It is the combination of the three types of restrictions (government, private, and market) that determines how land will be used. The government limits uses by zoning; the private owners limit uses through deed restrictions; and the marketplace dictates what uses are economically feasible at a particular location. The real estate appraiser must be aware of these restrictions and their impact on current use, as well as their possible impact on future uses of land and buildings. Knowing how real estate can be used will result in better evaluations.

2.3 PROPERTY DESCRIPTIONS

When real estate is sold, leased, or borrowed against, legal documents must spell out the transaction. In each case, the property involved will be identified in these documents by its legal description.

Many people do not realize the importance of legal descriptions. For example, an error might cause a prospective buyer to look at a different property than the one covered by the legal description. What they may buy is the legally described property. What they wanted was the property they looked at. In other words, what you see may not always be what you get.

Most of the time, minor errors in legal descriptions can easily be corrected. On occasion, however, an error can result in confusion and ultimately a lawsuit. In one instance, a contractor built an office building on the wrong lot! Everyone in the real estate industry should know how to read the various types of legal descriptions and compare them with the physical property observed. Such knowledge can resolve many common questions such as: Who owns the vacant lot next door? Who owns the common driveway between the houses? Who owns that overgrown area at the rear of the lot?

Three Basic Types of Legal Description

There are three basic types of legal description: (1) the *recorded lot, block, and tract* (also known as the recorded map or subdivision map) description, (2) the *metes and bounds* description, and (3) the *government (or rectangular) survey* description. Some valid legal descriptions use combinations of these types. It should be noted here that the Assessor's Book, Page, and Parcel identification is *not* a valid legal description.

Recorded Lot, Block, and Tract

Recorded maps can include *licensed surveyor* maps, *parcel* maps, and other maps that serve to subdivide the property. In most states, however, the most common type of legal description is based on subdivision maps that divide the land into *lots, blocks, and tracts*. When a developer buys acreage and subdivides it into lots and streets, the local government, in the process of giving its approval, requires that a map of the division be drawn by a licensed surveyor. The surveyor first checks the legal description used in prior transfers of this parcel and the parcels around it to be sure that they do not have conflicting boundaries. Then the surveyor stakes out the new subdivision boundary lines, using established government survey markers in the area as starting points. Existing markers from previous surveys of the property may be used instead. Finally, the surveyor produces a scale map drawing that satisfies local agency requirements. Figure 2.4 is an example of a subdivision map.

The subdivision map divides the property into lots and, for larger subdivisions, into blocks of lots. Each block and each lot is labeled on the map with a number or letter. The map itself is identified with the name or number of the subdivision and is registered in the public records. Public recorders' maps are usually indexed by volume, book, and page.

With a recorded map on file, a written legal description of a lot need contain only the lot number, the block number if any, the subdivision name or number, and the map record volume and page number. With this legal description, another surveyor, years later, can look up the map and, by a field survey, accurately stake out boundaries of the described lot. The legal descriptions of subdivision maps (also called tract maps) are among the shortest and easiest to understand. A sample might read:

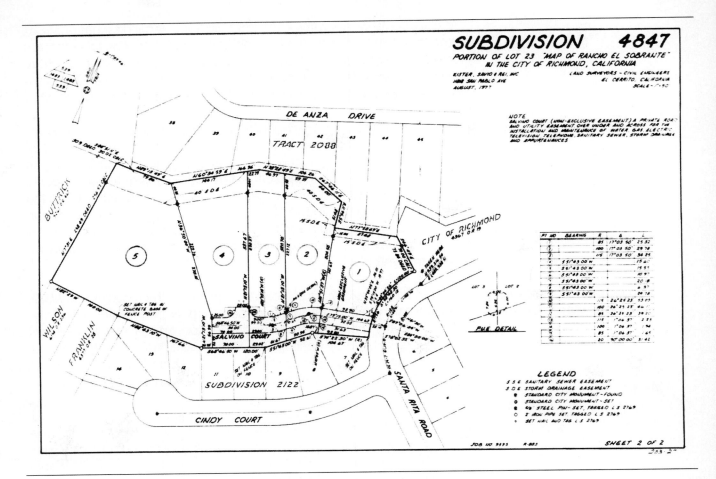

Figure 2.4
An example of a subdivision map.

Lot 37 of block A of Greenhill Estates, Tract 2314, as recorded November 11, 1946, in Book 23 of Maps, Page 318, official records of Washington County.

Metes and Bounds

The earliest legal descriptions of property were by metes and bounds. Many legal descriptions today are also of this type, particularly descriptions for large and irregular parcels. A metes and bounds description simply gives the distance and direction of each boundary line of the property. It starts at a point of beginning and goes around the perimeter of the property, back to the point of beginning. Early metes and bounds descriptions often started at a well-known natural feature, such as a large oak tree by the Jones farm, and went from tree to rock to boulder to tree. Figure 2.5 contains the actual wording from such a deed. As the trees died of old age and the rocks were bulldozed away, such descriptions became unusable. Today, more durable legal descriptions usually start at governmental survey monuments or other known points and proceed by very accurate direction bearings and distances around the property and back to the point of beginning. *Any* parcel, even a lot in a recorded subdivision, could be described by a metes and bounds description. An example of such a description is shown on the next page.

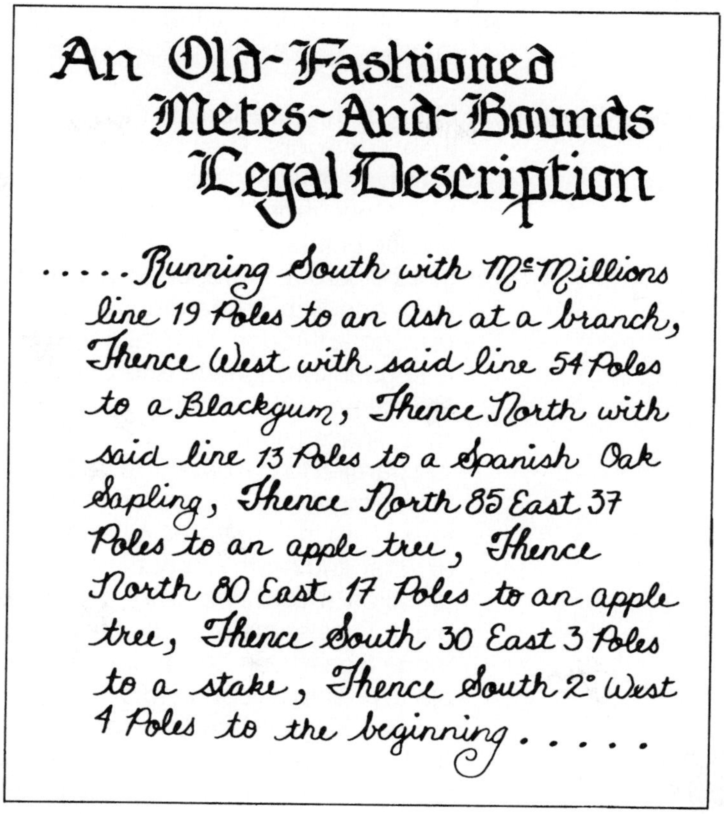

An Old-Fashioned Metes-And-Bounds Legal Description

.....Running South with McMillions line 19 Poles to an Ash at a branch, Thence West with said line 54 Poles to a Blackgum, Thence North with said line 13 Poles to a Spanish Oak Sapling, Thence North 85 East 37 Poles to an apple tree, Thence North 80 East 17 Poles to an apple tree, Thence South 30 East 3 Poles to a stake, Thence South 2° West 4 Poles to the beginning.....

Figure 2.5
From a deed recorded in the Book of Deeds, Book C-1, page 462, on the 6th day of March, 1907, with the Office of the Registrar of Deeds, in Ashe County, North Carolina.

Beginning at a point on the southerly line of Henry Street, 100 feet east of the southeast corner of Henry Street and 35th Avenue; running then due south 100 feet; then due east 75 feet; then due north and parallel to the first course 100 feet to the southern line of Henry Street; then due west along the southern line of Henry Street, 75 feet to the point of beginning.

Modern metes and bounds legal descriptions can describe lines that do not run exactly north, east, south, or west ("a line north 1 degree, 46 minutes, 30 seconds west 209.71 feet"). Such descriptions can also define lines that curve ("then along the arc of a curve to the right, of radius 203.3 feet, for a distance of 37.63 feet"). From this combination, almost any shape of a parcel can be described. However, metes and bounds descriptions can be pages in length. They are sometimes difficult to understand. Typing errors are an occasional problem as well. Despite these disadvantages, metes and bounds descriptions are necessary for some parcels and are a valuable cross-check for others.

Today, appraisers often calculate the area of a parcel by feeding the metes and bounds description into a program in a desktop computer. The computer can also be used to simulate a survey around the perimeter or boundary of the property to see if the description ends at exactly the point of beginning. If it does not, there may be an error in the description. In order to have an unquestionable description, some legal documents will include both the parcel or tract map description and the metes and bounds description. Figure 2.6 shows an example of an irregular parcel map.

Government Survey Much of the rural land in this country was first surveyed by U.S. government surveyors. Their basic survey system became the foundation for the third type of legal description, which is really just another type of map system. Government (or rectangular) survey legal descriptions start with reference points, often a point on a large mountain. For example, there are three different reference points in California, labeled Humboldt, Mount Diablo, and San Bernardino. A north-south line, called the *principal meridian*, goes through each reference point. An east-west line, called the *base line*, goes through the reference point as well. Figure 2.7 shows the reference points, meridians, and base lines in California. A series of range lines, spaced six miles apart, parallel the principal meridian. Township lines run parallel to the base line and are also six miles apart. The series of intersecting *township* and range lines, as shown in Figure 2.8, set up a pattern of six-mile squares of land each one, two, three, or more lines east or west and north or south of the reference point. Each six-mile square is called a township and is identified by counting from the reference point. One sample township would be identified as "township 3 north, range 2 east, San Bernardino Base and Meridian." In Figure 2.8, this sample township is identified by an "X" in the proper township square.

Each six-mile square township is further subdivided. North-south and east-west lines, one mile apart, divide the township into 36 parcels, each part being one mile square. These are called *sections*. Each section is numbered, in a back-and-forth or serpentine system, as shown in Figure 2.9. Thus, each section is described by its number and appropriate township.

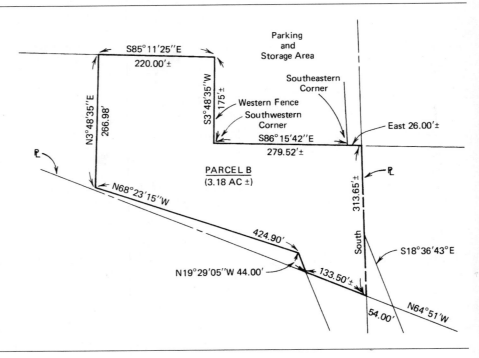

Figure 2.6
An example of an irregular
parcel map.

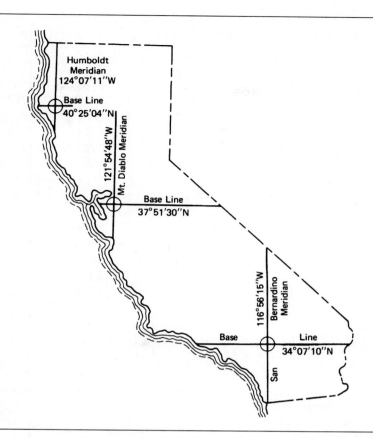

Figure 2.7
California base lines and meridians. (Courtesy of the California Department of Real Estate)

A section is one mile in each direction, with an area of one square mile, or 640 acres. Sometimes, it is necessary to describe smaller portions of a section. This is usually done by dividing the section into halves or quarters, or lesser amounts. Figure 2.10 shows how the section could be subdivided and how the parts would be labeled.

As precise and predictable as the government survey may look, there are complications. The first complication is that the survey grid is square but the earth is round. Consequently, parallel sets of range lines and base lines must be tapered to match the shape of the earth. This taper causes the north 6-mile boundary of each township to be about 50 feet shorter than the south boundary. Thus each township north of the reference point shrinks in width by 50 feet, and each to the south grows by 50 feet. To compensate for this, correction lines, both north-south and east-west, are run every 24 miles from the reference point. The result is that the actual dimensions and acreage area of a particular section can vary considerably from the "standard" 1-mile-square section. A second complication is that some early surveys contained actual errors, so that a given section might be quite different in size from what it was supposed to be.

Because of the importance of identifying the property being studied, real estate professionals must be able to read and understand the legal descriptions of property. Otherwise, neither they nor their clients will know for sure what property they are considering.

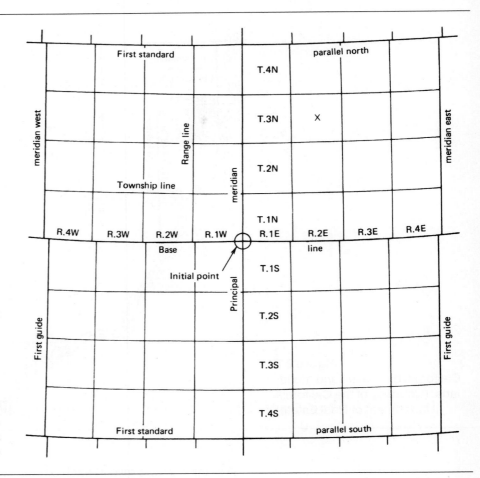

First standard parallel north

T.4N

meridian west

T.3N   X

Range line

T.2N

Township line

meridian

T.1N

R.4W   R.3W   R.2W   R.1W   R.1E   R.2E   R.3E   R.4E

Base   line

Initial point

Principal

T.1S

First guide

T.2S

First guide

T.3S

T.4S

First standard   parallel south

Figure 2.8
Map of township lines.
(Courtesy of the California
Department of Real Estate)

SUMMARY

In this chapter we explained the distinction between real estate and real property. When making an appraisal, it is not enough just to look at a property and appraise what you see. Rather, you must first establish what legal rights exist for the property and then identify which rights are to be included in the appraisal.

Real estate is defined as the physical object, whereas *real property* refers to the rights gained by owning the object. *Personal property* includes all objects on the property that are not real estate. Real property is made up of four elements: the land, the objects permanently affixed to the land, the rights that are appurtenant to the land, and that which is immovable by law.

When personal property has been permanently affixed to the land, it changes into a category of real property called a *fixture*. To determine whether a particular object is a fixture depends on legislative statute and five different court-applied tests. These are: (1) the *intention* of the person installing the object, (2) the *permanence* of the installation, (3) the *modification* of the object to fit or work uniquely with the real estate, (4) any *agreement* of the parties, and (5) the type of *relationship* (one created by a lease or mortgage, etc.) between the parties interested in owning the object. Numerous problems concerning fixtures and personal

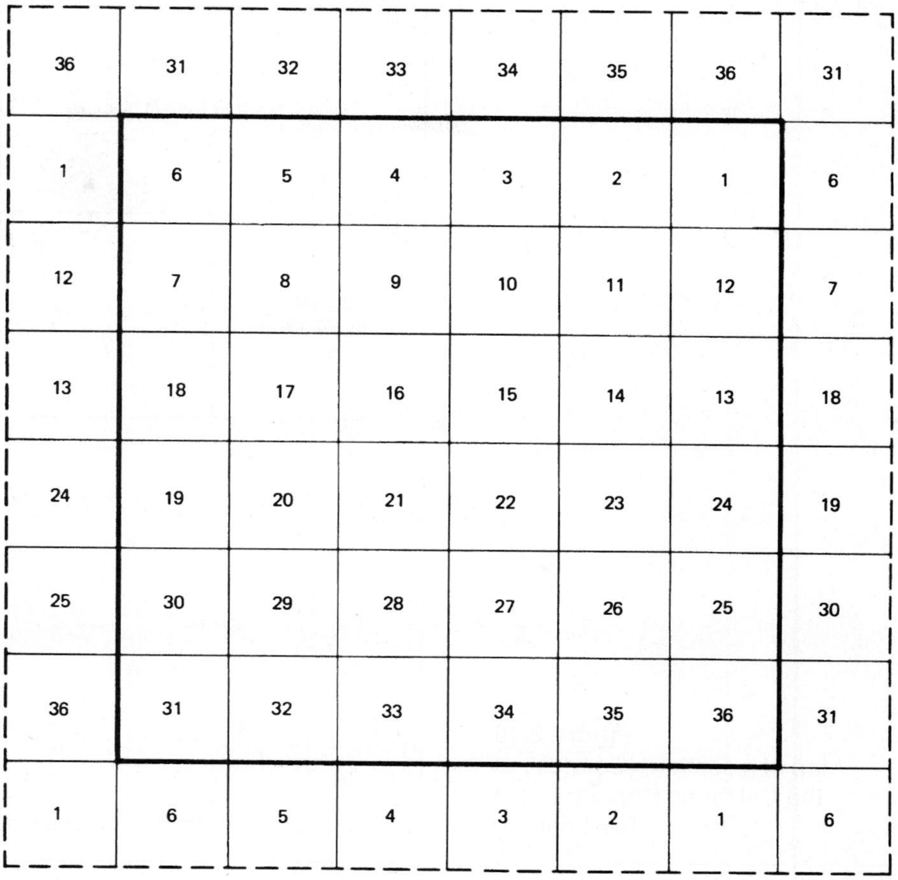

Figure 2.9
Map of a township. (Courtesy of the California Department of Real Estate)

property can arise in an appraisal unless appraisers are careful to distinguish one from the other and define what is being appraised.

Next, the chapter noted that real property refers to the many rights associated with real estate. The fact that this "bundle" of rights may be broken up, with different parties holding different parts of the bundle, or different rights, is very important. Partial rights to a property, such as those established by leases and mortgages, are very common. Thus, there are many occasions when you may have to examine or appraise portions of the bundle of rights.

We went on to point out that the value of land depends on what it can be used for. This is restricted by three types of limitations: *government, private*, and *market*. The government limitations consist of four restrictions: police power, eminent domain, taxation, and escheat. Most governmental restrictions on land use, such as zoning and building codes, are based on the police power. Private restrictions, often in the form of deed restrictions (or CC&Rs), are encountered less often than government restrictions but, on occasion, they are significant to the appraiser. Market restrictions have a powerful influence on value, since only economically feasible uses—ones that have a strong enough market demand—can be financially successful.

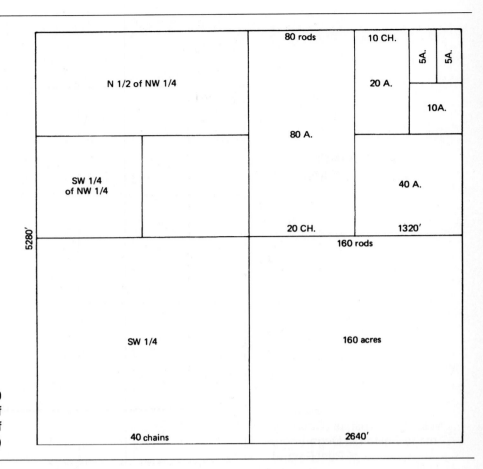

Figure 2.10
Map of a section. (Courtesy of the California Department of Real Estate)

Finally, we noted that the buyer does not really buy just the physical object but, rather, he or she buys specified rights to the property that are legally described in the purchase documents. The legal description of the property is needed to identify, with certainty, what real estate to appraise; hence, it is important to understand this description. The three common description types—recorded lot, block, and tract, metes and bounds descriptions, and government surveys were explained and illustrated. With a good understanding of legal descriptions, you will be able to review a particular legal description, have its accuracy checked, and use it to calculate land areas or dimensions.

Important Terms and Concepts

Appurtenance

Bundle of rights

Fee simple estate

Government survey

Intangible property

Legal descriptions

Life estates

Market restrictions

Metes and bounds

Partial interests

Personal property

Police power

Power of
    eminent domain
    escheat
    taxation

Private restriction   Rights

Real estate   Sovereign

Real property   Subdivision map

Recorded map   Tangible property

REVIEWING YOUR UNDERSTANDING

1. What are the two categories of tangible property?
   (a) Real property and personal property
   (b) Intangible property and real property
   (c) Real estate and intangible property
   (d) None of the above

2. Real property includes all the following *except*:
   (a) The land and objects permanently affixed to the land
   (b) Bank accounts for purchase of land
   (c) Appurtenant rights
   (d) That which is immovable by law

3. List and define the five tests for a fixture.

4. Types of use restrictions include all *except*:
   (a) Government
   (b) Fee simple
   (c) Private
   (d) Market

5. The sovereign holds four specific rights relative to private real estate, grouped under the authorities known as:
   (a) Appurtenances, eminent domain, police power, and escheat
   (b) Police power, taxation, ordinances, and bundle of rights
   (c) Taxation, escheat, police power, and eminent domain
   (d) None of the above

6. Give six examples of government regulations based on police power.

7. The three common types of legal descriptions are:
   (a) Metes and bounds; recorded lot, block, and tract; and government survey
   (b) Government survey, private survey, and county survey
   (c) Metes and bounds, acreage blocks, and government survey
   (d) Legal, informal, and house number

8. What is the shape, size, and area of a standard section?

9. What is the shape, size, and area of a township?

10. How many sections are there in a township?
    (a) 48
    (b) 36
    (c) 360
    (d) 100

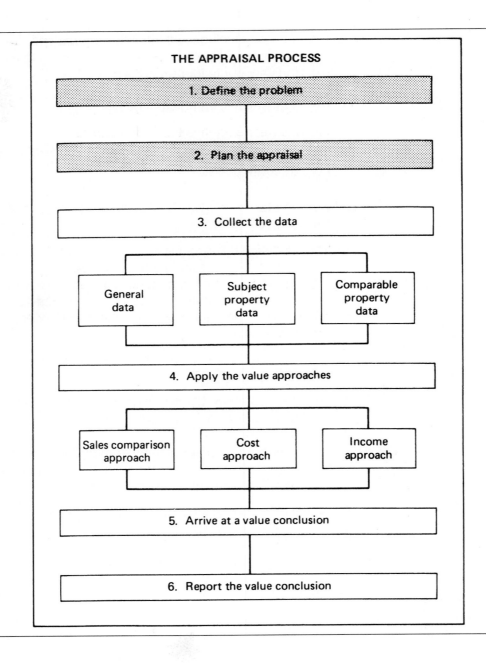

THE APPRAISAL PROCESS

1. Define the problem

2. Plan the appraisal

3. Collect the data

| General data | Subject property data | Comparable property data |

4. Apply the value approaches

| Sales comparison approach | Cost approach | Income approach |

5. Arrive at a value conclusion

6. Report the value conclusion

Chapter 3
The Formal Appraisal Process

Preview   This chapter outlines the formal appraisal process, stressing the systematic and orderly process needed to meet the highest appraisal standards. The three traditional approaches to value are introduced here, along with a formal definition of market value as set forth in the Uniform Standards of Professional Appraisal Practice.

When you have completed this chapter, you should be able to:

1. *List the six steps in the appraisal process.*

2. *Name the seven elements that define the appraisal problem.*

3. *Explain the difference between "value in use" and "value in exchange."*

4. *Define the term market value and explain how it differs from market price.*

5. *Outline the three approaches to value and explain how they are used in appraisals.*

3.1 THE APPRAISAL PROCESS

The appraisal, or valuation, process is the orderly procedure that appraisers use to help solve a valuation problem. Over a period of time, well-defined ground rules have been established by professional appraisers for this procedure.

The appraisal process consists of:

> 1. Clearly defining the appraisal problem.
>
> 2. Formulating an efficient appraisal plan.
>
> 3. Collecting and analyzing the pertinent data.
>
> 4. Applying the appropriate value approaches.
>
> 5. Arriving at a conclusion of value.
>
> 6. Reporting the conclusion of value.

These six steps in the appraisal process are shown in the flowchart at the beginning of this chapter and are further developed in the following discussion.

Defining the Appraisal Problem

The beginning of any formal appraisal requires a clear and concise statement of what the appraisal is to accomplish. By clearly defining the questions to be answered in the appraisal, the appraiser can better plan the appraisal and seek out the exact information required by the client and the appraisal assignment.

In order to define the appraisal problem, seven specific elements must be examined.

> 1. Identification of the property.
>
> 2. Property rights to be appraised.
>
> 3. The purpose and intended use of the appraisal.
>
> 4. The extent of the data collection process.
>
> 5. Any special limiting conditions.
>
> 6. The effective date of the appraisal.
>
> 7. Definition of the value being considered.

Identification of the Property

The property to be appraised must be precisely located and identified. Although a complete legal description is required for federally related appraisals, and is generally preferred, a less formal street address identity, such as that used in a sales listing contract, may be acceptable for other appraisals. In the latter case, the property identification may read, "the property under appraisal is that which is known as 1714 Mountain View Road, Pasadena, California. It consists of a 50 × 100 foot parcel of land improved with a single-family residence and garage." Note that in *all* cases, the property identification must leave no doubt as to what land and improvements are included in the appraisal.

Property Rights to Be Appraised

The typical appraisal assignment is to value all the rights of ownership of a property, commonly referred to as the *fee simple* or *fee simple estate*. However, appraisals involving less than all the property rights are not uncommon. The evaluation of the leased fee, the leasehold estate, the subsurface mineral rights, and other partial interests are examples of such assignments. A clear statement of the property rights to be appraised is a necessary part of defining the appraisal problem.

The Purpose and Intended Use of the Appraisal

The usual *purpose* of an appraisal is to estimate what is known as market value, the value most often sought in the sale and financing of a home. However, appraisals can be made for many other purposes, for example, to estimate the replacement cost or perhaps the liquidation value of a property. Other appraisals may seek to estimate the insurable value, "going concern" value, assessed value, or rental value of a property.

The *intended use* of the appraisal and the report is also part of defining the appraisal problem. Buyers and sellers, banks, institutions, and public agencies each use appraisals for their own unique purposes, whether for sale, financing, property taxation, or public acquisition. Each of these users has different requirements as to the type of appraisal report and the information required. Thus the intended use may dictate specific appraisal standards that must be met, as well as the type of appraisal report that must be used. For example, if the appraisal is to be used in a federally insured loan transaction, the Uniform Standards of Professional Appraisal Practice must be adhered to by the appraiser.

The Extent of the Data Collection Process

The extent of the data collection process can vary with the intended use of the appraisal report as well as the type of property being appraised. An assignment to estimate the market value of an income property for purposes of a lease renewal might require a detailed analysis of each tenant space, suggesting a need for more data than usually required. The appraisal of a unique property such as a large resort hotel could involve a search for comparables reaching over a broad region around the subject property. A condemnation appraisal could require a detailed narrative report designed to analyze the subject property from several perspectives, depending upon the type of public action involved. When the extent of the data collection process is fully outlined, the appraisal can be planned more efficiently.

Special Limiting Conditions

Generally, appraisal reports must include a statement of qualifying and limiting conditions. Such a statement serves to detail the assumptions made by the appraiser, limit his or her liability, and define the right of disclosure of the appraisal report contents. These and any other special conditions should be defined at this initial stage of the appraisal process.

The Effective Date of the Appraisal

Defining the appraisal problem also requires a statement pinpointing the date as of which the value estimate applies. A specific date is important because real estate values are constantly changing. An appraisal conclusion will be valid *only* as of a particular point in time. For this reason, the date of value should be agreed on in advance between the appraiser and the client. When a current value is sought, the date of the appraiser's last field inspection is often selected as the date of the value estimate.

Sometimes, appraisals are needed to estimate value as of a past or even a future date. Appraisals for inheritance tax, divorce, condemnation, and other legal purposes often must estimate value as of an earlier date than the date of the appraisal report. On occasion, the assigned date of value may coincide with a future event, as in the completion of a construction project. When either a "retrospective" (date in the past) or "prospective" (date in the future) appraisal is made, the report must clearly specify the historical or future date, so as not to mislead the reader into thinking that the stated value is the current market value. (See Figure 3.1.)

Definition of the Value Being Considered

Whatever the appraisal assignment, the type of value stated as the purpose of the appraisal must be given a precise and formal definition.

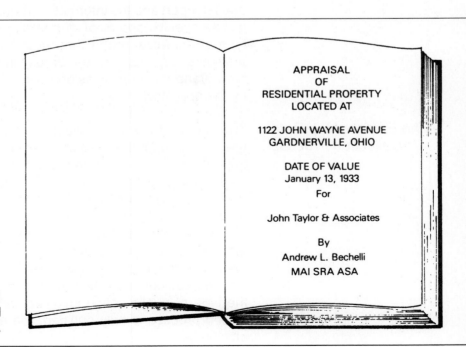

APPRAISAL
OF
RESIDENTIAL PROPERTY
LOCATED AT

1122 JOHN WAYNE AVENUE
GARDNERVILLE, OHIO

DATE OF VALUE
January 13, 1933
For

John Taylor & Associates

By
Andrew L. Bechelli
MAI SRA ASA

Figure 3.1
Title page of a historical
appraisal report.

Market value has its own special definition, which will be discussed in section 3.2 of this chapter.

Formulating the Appraisal Plan

The second step in the appraisal process is to develop an appraisal plan. A well-organized plan increases efficiency by scheduling the various tasks in the sequence in which they are to be done, with the time required for each. A good plan can also help reduce the chance of oversight or errors when collecting necessary information. The appraisal plan may take the form of a simple checklist of tasks to be performed, or it may become an elaborate work schedule, designed to organize and expedite a complex assignment. Whatever the format, a workable appraisal plan should include the following steps:

1. *Preliminary inspection of the property.* Often termed the preliminary survey, this preview of the subject property and its neighborhood helps to size up the appraisal assignment. The preliminary survey will help the appraiser refine any tentative plans he or she may already have made for getting the job done.

   In some cases, a preliminary inspection may be unnecessary if the appraiser is familiar with the neighborhood and the type of property under appraisal.

2. *List of needed data.* All general and specific data needs should be itemized during the planning stage. Neighborhood and community particulars, in addition to all factual data required for the subject and comparable properties, belong on this itemized list. If special reports such as engineering or geological surveys are needed, these should also be noted.

3. *Outline and work schedule.* An appraisal outline should be used to plan the sequence of points to be covered in the appraisal report. The outline is essentially a flowchart of the order in which the work is to be done. Although not always necessary, a time schedule of all the work required to complete the appraisal is also a helpful tool.

Collecting and Analyzing the Data

As we learned in Chapter 1, a formal appraisal is not a wild estimate of value; rather, an appraisal should be an estimate of value based on, and supported by, information and facts gathered in the real estate market. These market-derived facts are commonly called "market data," and they form the backbone of all formal appraisals. Collecting and analyzing data forms the third step in the appraisal process.

Most market value appraisals require:

1. **General data on the region, city, and neighborhood.** Includes data on population, employment, income, and price levels, as well as data on the availability of financing and on current construction costs.

2. **Specific data on the subject property**. Includes detailed legal and physical data on the land and the existing buildings.

3. **Specific data on comparable properties**. Includes detailed legal and physical data on comparable land and buildings, as well as detailed information on the terms and sales prices of the comparable properties considered.

Highest and Best Use Analysis

The kind of data required for any appraisal depends in large part on what is known as a "highest and best use" analysis. To be more fully discussed in Chapter 6, a highest and best use analysis is a study of how well suited the property is to its physical, legal, and economic environment. To illustrate, an appraiser might conclude that a single-family house on a commercial lot is not the most beneficial use of the land. A well-prepared highest and best use study suggests the preliminary data on the region, city, and neighborhood that needs to be gathered at this point. Once the highest and best use has been established, the collection of more detailed property data can begin. Figure 3.2 points out a humorous aspect of a highest and best use analysis.

How Much Information Is Needed?

The amount and kind of data required in an appraisal also depend on the type of property being appraised, the purpose of the appraisal, and the type of appraisal report required. Let us examine these points.

The type of property and the purpose of the appraisal may suggest the most appropriate value approaches, hence the kind of data needed. A single-family home being appraised for a loan would usually emphasize the cost and sales comparison approaches. Thus cost and sales data will certainly be part of the specific information required

Figure 3.2
Highest and best use?

in the appraisal. Later on, we shall discuss the importance and application of each valuation approach.

The type of appraisal report and its intended use may govern the degree of detail needed when data are collected. The data needed in a longer form appraisal may be more detailed than that required in a short letter report. Also, appraisals made for legal purposes generally require more supporting detail than those made for purchase and sale. *Comparable properties are the key*. Regardless of the type of property or the type of report, most appraisals require sales information on comparable properties fitting the general description of the property being appraised. For instance, if several newer three-bedroom homes of approximately 1,800 square feet in the same area have recently sold for prices ranging from $200,000 to $250,000, then a newly constructed three-bedroom property might be valued by comparing it with the sold properties. Specific data on the size, quality, age, and general amenities of the comparable homes could suggest a reasonable value for the subject property. However, it would be logical and prudent to consider additional data before settling on a conclusion of value. What if the sold properties had better financing than currently available? What if market conditions have changed since the recent sales as a result of serious unemployment emerging in the community? What if the new house under appraisal recently cost the owner $300,000 to develop, including land and building? Should this cost govern the estimate of value? Each question suggests a need for additional data. Of course complex assignments, such as the appraisal of income or commercial properties, call for considerably more market data than single-family home appraisals.

Techniques for locating and analyzing both general and specific data required for appraisals will be discussed in subsequent chapters.

Using the Value Approaches

The fourth step in the appraisal process is to group the collected market data for further analysis, using one or more of the three approaches to value (see Figure 3.3). The *sales comparison approach* uses data on current sales of comparable properties. The prices people are willing to pay are usually a good indication of the value of any commodity. The *cost approach* relies on the appraiser's estimate of the amount required to buy vacant land and the cost to construct the desired buildings and structures on it. Any loss in value from age or other causes is subtracted. Last, the *income approach* analyzes the income-producing capability of rental investment property to indicate its market value.

The approach, or approaches, to value that clearly appear to be the most pertinent should be applied at this point in the appraisal process. Depending on the appraisal assignment, one, two, or all three approaches to value may be required. An outline of the three value approaches is included in section 3.3.

Arriving at a Conclusion of Value

When two or more approaches have been used by the appraiser to estimate value, the fifth step in the appraisal process is to review the es-

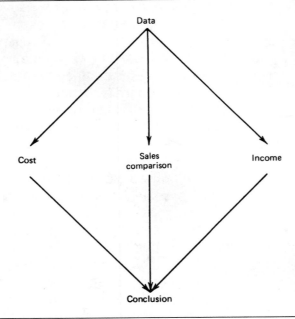

Figure 3.3
Flow of market data.

timates produced by the approaches and arrive at a final conclusion. This procedure is referred to as the *reconciliation* (previously called correlation) process. Three primary considerations are involved in this reconciliation:

1. The appropriateness of each approach in view of the purpose of the appraisal.

2. The adequacy and reliability of the data and the validity of any assumptions made in its analysis.

3. The range of indicated values and the position of each value within that range.

If the purpose of the appraisal is to estimate market value (as opposed to liquidation value, for example), the sales comparison approach is often the most persuasive because it is the most direct and it is also the approach with which most people have experience. It is generally the preferred method in single-family residential appraisals, as we shall explain. Where there are unique property characteristics or insufficient sales data, the cost and/or income approach may be emphasized, depending on the type of property under appraisal. The income approach is usually emphasized in the appraisal of commercial and income properties.

Appraisers often rely on the placement (high, low, or middle) and range (amount of spread) of the values indicated by each approach to help suggest the weight, or importance, to be assigned to each indicated value. In other words, each approach is used as a check on the others.

Although the appraisal process is designed to be as objective and factual as possible, the appraiser still must use personal judgment to reach a conclusion of value. The final value is dependent on factual market information and the judgment and experience of the appraiser. The value conclusion is rarely ever based on a simple averaging of the three value estimates.

Reporting the Conclusion of Value

The sixth and last step in the appraisal process is reporting the appraisal conclusion. On occasion, only an oral report is required, but most often the client wants some form of written report. The content of all appraisal reports should follow the Uniform Standards of Professional Appraisal Practice (USPAP).

There are three traditional types of written reports: the letter report, the form (or short-form) report, and the narrative report. The type of appraisal report to be used depends on the amount of information and detail required by the client, the intended use, and the appraisal standards to be met. A brief description of these reports follows. An expanded discussion will be presented in Chapter 16.

The Letter Report

The least formal appraisal report is the letter report. Typically only one to five pages long, this report sets forth the conditions of the assignment, a summary of the nature and scope of the appraiser's investigation, and an opinion of value. The letter form is used most often when the client is already familiar with the property and appraisal details are not needed. Professional standards strictly limit the use of letter reports.

The Form Report

As the name implies, the form report uses a printed sheet to organize and standardize appraisal report content. A checklist is often used for describing and rating property characteristics. Institutions and government agencies that handle large quantities of appraisals use forms designed to suit their special needs. Separate forms are usually available for all the major property classifications, that is, single-family residential, multifamily residential, commercial, industrial, and so on. This is the most common type of report used for real estate loan appraisals.

The Narrative Report

The narrative appraisal is the longest and most formal of the appraisal reports. It is a step-by-step summary of the facts used by the appraiser to arrive at a value. The report also contains a detailed discussion of the methods used to interpret these facts. Narrative appraisal reports are preferred when the client needs to review each logical step taken by the appraiser.

Narrative reports may also be needed when the elements of the report are strictly regulated by law, as is the case in most federally-related appraisals, and appraisals that are to be used in court (as in eminent domain cases). Narrative reports are also common in the appraisal of major investment properties.

3.2 TYPES OF VALUE

In this section, we will discuss the various meanings and types of value, the basic economic ways of measuring value, and finally, the market value concept itself.

Why Value Concepts Differ

While value is generally defined as the dollar worth of a thing, it is a word that has many different meanings. For example, the value of a parcel of real estate may be different to a buyer or seller than to a lender, an insurance adjuster, or an accountant. This difference exists because value can be very subjective. For example, some real estate buyers and sellers have a tendency to measure value only by their personal desires and needs. On the other hand, the lender's concept of property value is most often related to an objective view of the market, where value is related to the listing and sales prices of similar properties and the most likely selling price of the subject property. The insurance adjuster's idea of value (depending on the policy) might be strictly related to the cost of replacing the improvements in case of fire or other disaster. The accountant may think of value in terms of the original acquisition cost, the cost basis, or so-called *book value* of the property.

In the examples given above, each interested party has a different concept of value in mind, each that is quite limited in purpose and in definition. There are literally dozens of value types and concepts, each carrying its own identifying name. Here are some of the value labels you might encounter:

Assessed value	Lease value
Book value	Liquidation value
Capitalized value	Listing value
Cash value	Loan value
Depreciated value	Market value
Economic value	Nuisance value
Exchange value	Potential value
Face value	Rental value
Fair value	Salvage value
Going concern value	Use value
Inheritance tax value	Value in foreclosure
Insurance value	

Contrasting *Value in Use* and *Value in Exchange*

Economic theory suggests that most types of value fit into one of two basic categories. These categories are known as *value in use* and *value in exchange*.

Value in use refers to the value of an item or object to a particular user. For example, a single-family home located next to a bakery might have a higher value to the family operating the bakery than to the public in general. Its higher value is a unique value to that user. This is often described as a *subjective* value concept.

Value in exchange describes the value of a thing to people in general. This can be termed *objective value*. Value in exchange can be estimated only for items or properties that are commonly bought and sold in the market, that is, "exchanged" for money or its equivalent. (See Figure 3.4.)

Almost 2,400 years ago, Aristotle (Figure 3.5) said:

> All things which are exchanged must be comparable to one another. Money measures and compares; it states whether and by how much the value of one thing exceeds another.

The vast majority of real estate holdings are indeed bought and sold on the open market at prices that are measured and compared by that market. Under the right conditions, we refer to this kind of price as market value.

Defining Market Value

Most formal appraisals are made for the purpose of estimating market value, as opposed to the other types of value discussed above. It is important to understand how market value differs from other types of value and why it is sought in appraisals.

Market value is broadly understood to mean "what property should normally sell for, assuming a willing buyer and a willing seller." However, economic and legal definitions have been developed that imply some important additional criteria. As defined by our federal financial institutions (and required for appraisals made in connection with federally related real estate transactions), market value means:

> . . . the most probable price which a property should bring in a competitive and open market under all conditions requisite to a fair sale, the buyer and seller each acting prudently, knowledgeably, and assuming the price is not affected by undue stimulus.

Figure 3.4
Market value = value in exchange.

Figure 3.5
Aristotle. (Alinari-Art
Reference Bureau)

Implicit in this definition is the consummation of a sale as of a specified date and the passing of title from seller to buyer under conditions whereby: (1) buyer and seller are typically motivated; (2) both parties are well informed or well advised, and each acting in what he or she considers his or her own best interest; (3) a reasonable time is allowed for exposure in the open market; (4) payment is made in terms of cash in U.S. dollars or in terms of financial arrangements comparable thereto; (5) the price represents the normal consideration for the property sold, unaffected by special or creative financing or sales concessions granted by anyone associated with the sale.

In other words, market value is a price arrived at in the market under certain prescribed conditions, regarding (1) the terms of sale, (2) market exposure, and (3) informed parties, not under duress.

Terms of the Sale   There is a saying in real estate that the price depends on the terms: how much cash down and how much per month. Two identical houses will probably sell at different prices if each deal involves markedly different financing. This teaches us that price differences do not necessarily indicate value differences. If prices of comparables are to be taken as indicative of value in an appraisal, financing terms must be considered. Terms of sale will be discussed in Chapter 9.

Market Exposure   Market exposure means making the potential buyers of a property aware that the property is available for sale. Some form of advertising is usually necessary to meet this condition. Figure 3.6 represents one possible form. Prices resulting from sales lacking adequate *open market exposure* do not typify the market and therefore do not represent

Figure 3.6
An example of market exposure. (Photograph courtesy of Doug Frost)

market value. Family transfers and business expansion sales are usually not "open" or "arm's length" transactions. Not only are they not advertised, but family sales are often available only to a select few family members. Lack of market exposure also invalidates many forced sales that result from job transfer, threat of foreclosure, or family breakup. What is adequate market exposure? There is no set standard; however, it is generally assumed that unique properties require a greater market exposure because they are of interest to a narrower market. For example, a rambling five-bedroom house may take two or three times as long to sell as a standard three-bedroom house in the same neighborhood.

Informed Parties

For a parcel of real estate to command a price matching its utility and value, the property's uses and purposes must be known to the potential buyers and sellers. Even in a normal market, buyers and sellers sometimes lack adequate information about the property. However, sellers are often more familiar with specific features of the sale property than the prospective buyer. The sellers may know about certain property defects or neighborhood nuisances not fully understood by the buyer. Without expert advice from real estate brokers, salespeople, and appraisers, parties on both sides of a given transaction may have a mistaken view of value, and the price agreed on may not represent market value.

The concept of market value is important in appraisals because it clearly distinguishes between price and value. Price reflects not only the terms and conditions of sale but the unique and sometimes subjective motives of buyers and sellers. Most appraisal purposes are best served by relating value to a more precise standard than price alone. Thus, market value refers to the value of real estate to people in general, its value in terms of money, and its value between informed and knowledgeable people who are buying and selling on the open market. In summary, then, market value can be referred to as the most likely sale price when the conditions referred to above have been met.

3.3 THE CLASSICAL APPROACHES TO VALUE

As indicated in section 3.1, the appraisal process requires the application of one or more of the three classical approaches to value. The sales comparison, cost, and income approaches are considered classical in the appraisal field because they incorporate time-tested techniques for valuing real estate. In early appraisal theory, all three approaches were required in every formal appraisal. Today, they are usually required only if they relate to the value problem at hand. Each approach has its own unique importance. The three approaches are briefly outlined below and will be covered in greater detail in later chapters.

The Sales Comparison Approach

The sales comparison approach, also known as the market approach, is the most direct of the three approaches and usually the most reliable. Simply stated, the sales comparison approach compares the property being appraised to similar properties that have recently sold in the open market. From the prices paid, the appraiser estimates a probable selling price or value for the subject property by making a careful analysis of differences in sale conditions and property characteristics. Example 3.1 uses the sales comparison approach.

Example 3.1 Using the Sales Comparison Approach

Assume that the subject property is a medium-quality, 20-year-old, three-bedroom home, which has a two-car garage. The square footage of the home is 1,800 square feet. The appraiser locates three similar homes that have sold in the neighborhood at fair market prices. All have similar square footage and number of rooms.

Comparables

Data	Comparable A	Comparable B	Comparable C
Price Paid	$250,000	$240,000	$200,000
Location	Better than subject property	Equal to subject property	Equal to subject property
Lot size	Equal to subject property	Larger than subject property	Smaller than subject property
Overall condition	Better than subject property	Equal to subject property	Worse than subject property

Dollar Adjustment Factors Indicated by Market Study

For illustration purposes, assume the sales analysis suggests the following adjustments:

Location difference = $25,000
Lot size difference = $15,000
Overall condition difference = $10,000

Adjustments

Data	Comparable A	Comparable B	Comparable C
Price paid	$250,000	$240,000	$200,000
Location	−25,000	0	0
Lot size	0	−15,000	+15,000
Overall condition	−10,000	0	+10,000
Price comparables would have sold for if they were like the subject home	$215,000	$225,000	$225,000

Conclusion

Subject property's indicated value is about $220,000.

In application, the sales comparison approach involves the following steps:

1. Investigating sales of comparable properties; ascertaining motives of buyers and sellers; and determining conditions of the sale as to date, price, terms, and market exposure.

2. Analyzing and comparing the sales with the subject property, considering the time of sale, location, and other factors affecting market value.

3. Judging how the observed differences affect prices paid for the properties under study. These differences are normally treated as "adjustments" to the prices paid.

4. Arriving at a conclusion of value for the subject property based on the most comparable sales.

Comparing the sales of comparable properties with the subject property involves first listing desirable features that are found in the comparable properties but are not present in the subject property. Their estimated dollar values must be *subtracted* from the respective selling prices of the comparables. Next, features found in the subject property that are not found in the comparable properties must be noted. The estimated dollar value of these features must be *added* to the prices of the comparables to "improve" their comparability. It is important to remember that the appraiser must adjust the sale to be more like the subject. Another way to say it is to "adjust *from* the sale, *to* the subject."

In deciding how much to adjust for differences in the properties being compared, appraisers often rely on techniques "borrowed" from the cost (or even income) approach. For example, a new house with a fireplace might be appraised at $5,000 more than a comparable sale lacking this feature if that amount represents the current cost of installing a fireplace. Sales comparison approach techniques will be more fully discussed in Chapters 8 and 9.

The Cost Approach

The cost approach is based on the principle that property is worth what it would cost in money to duplicate. (See Figure 3.7.) Adjustments to cost are made to allow for any loss in value due to age, condition, and other factors reducing market appeal. Thus the cost approach involves adding the depreciated replacement cost of the improvements to the value of the land as estimated from a market or economic study. Because of this *addition* step, the cost approach is also known as the *summation* approach.

Applying the cost approach requires an appraiser to:

1. Estimate the value of the land as if vacant and available for use.

2. Estimate the total cost to build the existing structure, figured at today's construction prices.

3. Estimate the appropriate amount to allow for accrued depreciation, that is, the loss in value of the subject building as compared to a new structure.

4. Subtract the estimated depreciation from the cost of the hypothetical new structure, giving a depreciated cost estimate.

5. Add the value of the land to the depreciated cost of the new structure. The result is the indicated property value by the cost approach.

Figure 3.7
Value is related to the cost of development. (Photograph courtesy of Doug Frost)

Example 3.2 illustrates how to use the cost approach.

Example 3.2 Using the Cost Approach

Given

Cost new
  Home: $78 per sq ft
  Garage: $30 per sq ft

Depreciation
  Recent comparable sales prices decline about 0.5% for each year of age. Present age is 20 years.

Land Value
  $120,000, based on recent comparable sales

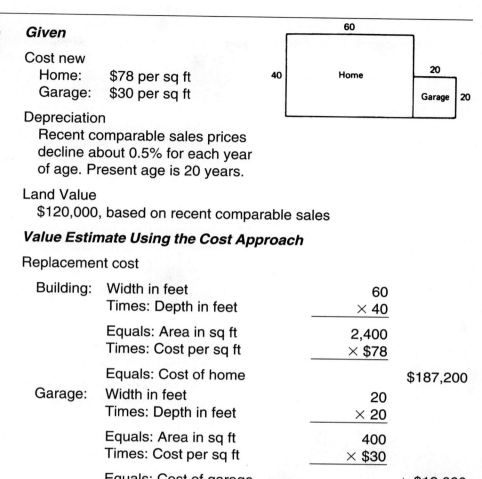

Value Estimate Using the Cost Approach

Replacement cost

Building:	Width in feet	60	
	Times: Depth in feet	× 40	
	Equals: Area in sq ft	2,400	
	Times: Cost per sq ft	× $78	
	Equals: Cost of home		$187,200
Garage:	Width in feet	20	
	Times: Depth in feet	× 20	
	Equals: Area in sq ft	400	
	Times: Cost per sq ft	× $30	
	Equals: Cost of garage		+ $12,000
Total improvement replacement cost			$199,200
Less:	Depreciation: Age in years	20	
	Times: Annual depreciation	× 0.5%	
	Equals: Total percent depreciation	10%	
	Times: Total cost new	× $199,200	
	Equals: Depreciation amount		− 19,920
Replacement cost less depreciation			$179,280
Plus land value:			+120,000
Equals:	Indicated value by the cost approach (rounded)		$299,000

Since the cost approach requires an estimate of depreciation, or loss in value, it is unreliable where buildings show major losses in value because of old age or substantial obsolescence. Realistic amounts of value loss from these causes are very difficult to estimate. The cost approach is normally given more weight in the appraisal of new buildings and in service-type or special-use properties which are not frequently bought or sold (eg., churches and schools).

The Income Approach   The income approach (or capitalized income approach) is used to appraise commercial, industrial, and residential-income properties according to their ability to produce net income. Where the cost and sales comparison approaches are being emphasized in an appraisal, the income approach is often used to test the results. A building such as the one in Figure 3.8 is a typical income-producing property.

Basically, the income approach involves estimating what the market will pay for the property's expected income. Six steps are involved:

1. Obtain annual rent schedules for the subject property and compare them with the competition to arrive at a projection of reasonable gross rents for the subject.
2. Estimate annual vacancy and collection losses.
3. Subtract these from the gross income to arrive at the effective gross income.
4. Estimate the annual expenses and subtract them from the effective gross income to arrive at the net income. Net income is sometimes called net operating income.
5. Analyze comparable investments in order to arrive at a capitalization method and rate.
6. Capitalize the projected net income into an estimate of value.

There are a number of capitalization methods in common usage, each designed to handle a specific type of appraisal problem. In the case of single-family homes, the gross rent multiplier method is often

Figure 3.8
An example of an income-producing property. (Photograph courtesy of Doug Frost)

used instead of income capitalization. Both income capitalization and the gross rent multiplier method will be defined and discussed in Chapters 13 and 14. Example 3.3 illustrates how to use income capitalization.

Example 3.3 Using the Income Approach

A 20-unit apartment building has market rents of $800 per unit per month, or $192,000 per year. The estimated factor for vacancies and collection losses is 6% of the potential income. Projected annual operating expenses are:

Property taxes	$15,000
Insurance	3,500
Management	10,500
Utilities	6,500
Maintenance and miscellaneous	7,000
Total	$42,500

The capitalization rate selected by the appraiser is 10%.

Solution, Using the Income Approach

Gross annual income		$192,000
Less:	Vacancies and collection loss	−11,520
Equals:	Effective gross income	$180,480
Less:	Annual expenses	−42,500
Equals:	Net operating income	$137,980
Divided by:	Capitalization rate	÷ 0.10
Equals:	Indicated value by income capitalization (Rounded)	$1,380,000

SUMMARY

A formal appraisal is usually a written estimate of value that results from following an orderly and well-established procedure known as the *appraisal process*. This involves (1) defining the appraisal problem, (2) planning the appraisal, (3) collecting and analyzing the data, (4) applying the appropriate value approaches, (5) arriving at a value conclusion, and (6) reporting the conclusion of value.

An estimate of market value is the object of most appraisals. Market value differs from other types of value primarily in that it attempts to measure *value in exchange* rather than *value in use. Value in exchange* means value to people in general rather than to a specific user.

The formal definition of market value attempts to remove any element of subjectivity (or personal bias) from the value question by requiring that the price paid be (1) in terms of money, (2) upon adequate market exposure, and (3) between knowledgeable parties not under duress.

Three classical approaches are used for valuing real estate: sales comparison, cost, and income. The sales comparison approach is often the most reliable because it is the most direct. It involves comparing the property under appraisal with similar properties that have recently been sold. The cost approach estimates the value of a property by adding its land value to the estimated current cost of existing structures, less depreciation. The cost approach tends to be more relevant to the appraisal of newer properties and of single-purpose properties. It is based on the principle that property is worth what it would cost in money to duplicate. The income approach compares the income-producing capability of the property with that of properties that have been sold. The net income projected for the subject property is then translated into an indication of value by a process known as capitalization. The income approach is used to appraise property that generates income. For single-family homes, an alternate gross rent multiplier method can be used.

Important Terms and Concepts

Appraisal process	Market value
Appraisal report	Purpose of the appraisal
Comparison, market	Reconciliation
Income approach	Sales comparison approach
Intended use of the report	Value in exchange
Limiting conditions	Value in use
Market exposure	Worth
Market price	

REVIEWING YOUR UNDERSTANDING

1. The appraisal process involves six steps, the first of which is to:
   (a) Define the appraisal problem
   (b) Choose an appropriate value approach
   (c) View the property
   (d) None of the above

2. In appraisals, the effective date of value is:
   (a) The date of the property inspection
   (b) The date agreed upon in advance with the client
   (c) The day the appraisal is completed
   (d) The date the appraisal is signed

3. The typical appraisal assignment is to appraise the:
   (a) Value of the mining rights
   (b) "Fee simple" ownership
   (c) Value subject to an existing loan
   (d) Leased fee estate

4. The form and supporting data in an appraisal vary mainly with the:
   (a) Preferences of the appraiser
   (b) Purpose and intended use of the appraisal

(c) Legal restrictions on use
(d) The type of value sought

5. The cost approach is based upon:
(a) Market data on comparable sales
(b) Data on sales listings
(c) The income-producing capability of the property
(d) The depreciated cost of improvements plus land value from comparables

6. The appraiser's conclusion of value should be based on:
(a) An averaging of the three value conclusions indicated by the three approaches to value
(b) A weighing of the values indicated by each of the three approaches according to their appropriateness and the reliability of the data used in each
(c) The most recent selling price
(d) None of the above

7. An objective kind of value that can be assigned to items and properties bought and sold in the market is called:
(a) Value in use
(b) Value in exchange
(c) Economic value
(d) Potential value

8. Subjective value can be defined as:
(a) Value in exchange
(b) Assessed value
(c) Listing value
(d) Value in use

9. The concept of market value in appraisal practice does *not* include:
(a) Most probable price
(b) Competitive and open market
(c) A good buy
(d) Buyer and seller each acting prudently

10. The cost approach is normally given more weight in the appraisal of:
(a) Old and substantially obsolete buildings
(b) Single-family tract houses over 10 years old
(c) New buildings and special-use buildings
(d) None of the above

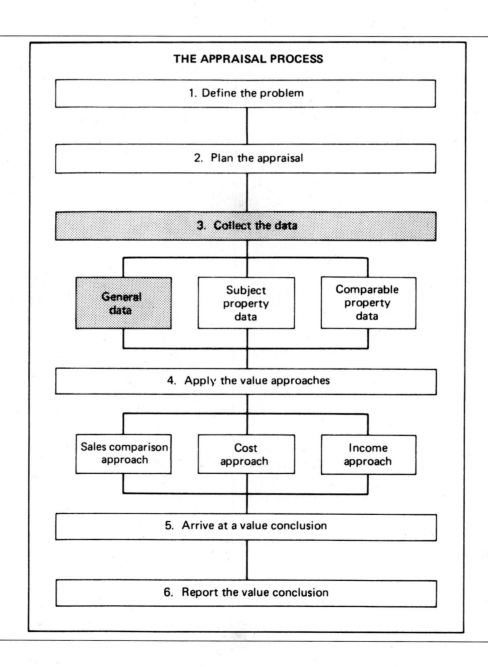

THE APPRAISAL PROCESS

1. Define the problem

2. Plan the appraisal

3. Collect the data

| General data | Subject property data | Comparable property data |

4. Apply the value approaches

| Sales comparison approach | Cost approach | Income approach |

5. Arrive at a value conclusion

6. Report the value conclusion

Chapter 4
Focus on Neighborhood, Community, and Market

Preview In the previous chapters, we explained the necessity of defining the appraisal problem and planning the appraisal. In Chapter 4, we now turn to the gathering of data for the appraisal. The first phase of the data program is to examine the neighborhood and community around the property and to note the influences that have the most important effect on the property's value. Since property value must always be understood in the context of the market, this chapter concludes with an analysis of real estate markets.

When you have completed this chapter, you should be able to:

1. *Describe the neighborhood concept and how neighborhood boundaries are defined.*

2. *Explain how you can use information from a neighborhood study in the appraisal process.*

3. *Explain the economics of community origins and growth.*

4. *Name four different physical patterns of community land use.*

5. *Define a perfect market and explain why real estate markets are not perfect.*

6. *Discuss the real estate market actions that you should study and why.*

4.1 NEIGHBORHOOD ANALYSIS

No other aspect of appraising is as difficult to define as neighborhood analysis. As a result, its meaning and usage have often been misinterpreted. Each person, community group, and organization have certain ideas as to what a neighborhood is and how it affects property values. People concerned about allegations of discrimination in housing have questioned how and why appraisers use neighborhood information. In fairness to all, it is essential for those in real estate to understand the concept of the neighborhood as it is used in appraisals and be able to objectively analyze the neighborhood around a subject property. In this section, we shall explain the concept of the neighborhood and show how to use neighborhood information.

Defining the Neighborhood

The term *neighborhood* has been defined as follows:

> A neighborhood is a cluster of properties (most of which are) of relatively similar land use and value.*
> A portion of a larger community . . . in which there is a homogeneous grouping of inhabitants, buildings, or business enterprises.†

More broadly, a neighborhood is an area whose occupants and users share some common ties or characteristics. Thus some form of *shared identity* creates a neighborhood and binds it together. From this larger definition, we can see that one neighborhood may be residential, another commercial, another industrial, and so on.

What is the meaning of the term *shared identity?* Simply stated, shared identity can be defined economically, by the land uses; physically, by the buildings; or sociologically, by the occupants. It refers to whatever characteristics are shared in common that create a positive bond, or so-called "linkage" among the occupants. There can be many types of positive bonds. In an office neighborhood, for example, the bonds might include the sharing of a common work pool, similar surroundings, and accessibility to nearby services. Sometimes the nature of the bond is difficult to see. For example, in a very diverse residential-commercial neighborhood, the most powerful bond could be the desire to live in such a diverse and varied environment. Greenwich Village in New York City has been considered such a neighborhood.

Boundaries of the Neighborhood

Neighborhood boundaries are influenced by a wide variety of factors, usually *economic, physical,* or *legal* in character. *Economically,* such boundaries are determined by where the benefits of the location seem to change. Evidence of such a boundary can be seen in the changes in the types of buildings or land uses, or changes in the shared characteristics of the occupants. *Physical* features often define the boundaries of a neighborhood. Examples include rivers, lakes, and moun-

---

*D. J. McKenzie and R. M. Betts, *The Essentials of Real Estate Economics,* 3rd. ed. Prentice Hall, New Jersey, 1992.
†B. N. Boyce, *Real Estate Appraisal Terminology,* rev. ed., Ballinger Publishing Co., Cambridge, Mass., 1981.

tains, as well as freeways, railroads, and other man-made structures. City, school district, and/or zoning boundaries are commonly noted by appraisers as *legal* factors establishing neighborhood boundaries.

The boundaries of a neighborhood are not always obvious. Property features often change gradually as one moves from one neighborhood to the next. When this is the case, neighborhood boundaries are difficult to establish. Sometimes, however, the neighborhood boundary can be very precise. For example, the boundaries of commercial neighborhoods are often precisely defined by zoning laws and by where the commercial buildings are located. Also, industrial neighborhoods most often have boundaries that are precisely defined by zoning.

Adjacent neighborhoods may have similar characteristics. When adjacent neighborhoods lack noticeable physical boundaries and have important features in common, it is possible to combine them for study purposes and treat them as a *larger neighborhood.* On the other hand, almost every neighborhood can also be divided up into *smaller neighborhoods,* by emphasizing minor differences in the common bonds that define the neighborhood as a whole. So we can call the one the larger neighborhood and the other the immediate neighborhood.

In summary, neighborhood boundaries may be set by economic factors, physical features, or legal boundaries or by changes in the characteristics of occupants, buildings, and/or uses.

Neighborhood Profile

The neighborhood analysis should begin with a factual description of the significant characteristics of the area. This may be in the form of a short profile of the location, housing, and market trends. Typical features described for a residential neighborhood include:

1. *Location*—Classified as urban, suburban, or rural.

2. *Development and growth rate*—The percentage of available land that has been built up or developed. Growth rate may be described as rapid, static, or slow.

3. *Trend of property values*—Whether values are increasing, stable, or declining.

4. *Demand/supply*—Whether housing supply is short, in balance, or in oversupply compared with current demand.

5. *Marketing time*—The average time needed to sell a reasonably priced property in the neighborhood.

6. *Present land use*—The relative percentage of single-family, two- to four-family, multifamily, commercial, or industrial buildings and vacant land in the defined neighborhood.

7. *Land-use change*—Whether change in land use in the near future is not likely, likely, or in process.

8. *Predominant occupancy*—Whether owner or tenant occupancy predominates; show approximate vacancy percentage.

9. *Single-family housing price and age*—The range of housing prices in the neighborhood and the predominant price; also the age range and typical age of existing homes.

FACTORS AFFECTING NEIGHBORHOOD QUALITY

Since every neighborhood offers different advantages to its inhabitants, neighborhoods are said to differ in quality. Although it may seem a complex idea, the quality of a neighborhood can best be judged in terms of the needs and standards of its occupants. For example, the desirable features of a residential district would be different from those of a commercial or industrial district. Appraisers often rate the various aspects of a neighborhood by comparing them with features of competing neighborhoods.

The major factors that affect the quality of any neighborhood can be grouped as physical, economic, social, and political in nature.

Physical and Locational Factors

The physical factors that affect neighborhood desirability and quality include the natural features of location, as well as those created by people. Natural features include topography, trees, lakes, and other visual amenities. Desirable views in a residential neighborhood are often the result of these things. Natural features that affect neighborhoods also include climate and geological conditions such as weather, soil quality, flood, slide, and earthquake zones. Examples of neighborhoods with negative value influences from such conditions include some in the fog belts in San Francisco, the smog areas in Pittsburgh, and those in the flood zones of the central riverways of the country.

Physical features that have been created by people are also part of the locational attributes of a neighborhood. Thus, the desirability of a neighborhood depends in part upon its present land uses, development and growth rate, and the quality, age and style of its housing. Other factors related to location include:

---

1. Convenience to schools, employment, transportation routes, shopping, public health and medical facilities, religious and recreation centers.

2. Adequacy of utilities and other public services.

3. General appearance and compatibility of properties.

4. Appeal to the market.

5. Absence of toxic wastes and other adverse environmental conditions.

Economic Factors

The first important economic factor to consider is whether the income level of the neighborhood occupants is sufficient to maintain existing structures. This strongly relates to employment opportunities available, as well as the stability of existing employment.

In residential neighborhoods, for instance, you might study housing costs as a percent of household income. In commercial neighborhoods, you might study store sales volume per square foot size of building floor area. Generally, the greater the economic strength, the greater the neighborhood quality.

Other economic factors to consider include those just described in the neighborhood profile: growth rate, trend of property values, supply and demand, marketing time for properties, and land-use changes in evidence.

Social Factors

Neighborhood desirability is influenced by the many social characteristics of the occupants. This is because people often seek to be in a neighborhood whose occupants have interests similar to theirs. For example, people with young children often want to live in a residential neighborhood where there are children of the same age as their children. Significant social factors include life-styles or standards, education, occupations, ages, and family makeup of neighborhood occupants. The predominant occupancy (whether renters or owner-occupants) and the rate at which occupants move (the turnover rate) also affect how a neighborhood is viewed.

The presence of neighborhood groups and organizations taking an active role in community affairs can be an important factor. For example, homeowners' associations such as those found in condominium and planned unit developments can be a positive feature in a neighborhood, as can neighborhood watch organizations.

Neighborhood desirability is also dependent on the effort and money that neighborhood occupants put into building maintenance and modernization. Community support for the existing legal and political order is also a factor, since neighborhood attitudes can influence political decisions, such as the amount of city services provided, tax rates, and the quality of the schools. Another neighborhood attitude that the appraiser might study is how the occupants rate the desirability of the neighborhood relative to other neighborhoods.

Political Factors

The level of taxes, assessment fairness, police and fire protection and other city services provided, public education, and protective zoning or planning all have an effect on neighborhood desirability. Governmental positions on air, soil, and water pollution, job safety, social programs, and noise, odor, and ecological controls can also be noted. Many political factors are the ultimate result of social attitudes, either in the neighborhood the appraiser is studying or in the city as a whole.

Neighborhoods and Change

Every neighborhood, regardless of land use, goes through a series of changes over the years. These changes usually follow a pattern. The first phase occurs when the vacant land is subdivided, streets and utilities are installed, and the first buildings are constructed. Over time, most of the available land is built upon. This first phase in the cycle of a neighborhood is called the *development phase.*

The second phase gradually begins as development slows down. It is called the mature or *stable phase.* The most significant feature of this phase is the relative stability of the existing buildings and occupants. This phase usually lasts for an extended period of time.

During the stable years, building maintenance and renovation generally keep up with the normal deterioration from weather and usage. In time, however, neighborhood occupants may postpone needed repairs; then the third phase, *decline* or *decay,* begins. Regardless of the type of building or use, the effects of age continually attack the stability apparent in the second phase. The elements, insects, pollution, and use of the building all cause wear and tear to the interior and exterior of structures. Over time, there is competition from newer neighborhoods and from new building designs, decorative finishes, or building layouts, which make the older neighborhood less desirable. The degree of neighborhood decline varies, as does the length of time until the beginning of the fourth phase.

The fourth phase of neighborhood change is called the *renaissance:* the transition to a new sequence of life for the neighborhood. Neighborhood renaissance can occur slowly or rapidly and may have either private or government sponsorship or a mixture of the two. This renaissance phase will involve either of the following events:

---

1. Demolition or relocation of the existing buildings and development of the land with new buildings, often for different uses.

2. Major renovation of the existing buildings to correct maintenance problems and obsolete features. The buildings may continue in the same uses or be converted to new uses.

The four phases of neighborhood change shown in Figure 4.1 form a cycle that occurs in every type of neighborhood. In older, more stable cities, there is evidence to suggest that this neighborhood cycle has been repeated several times and often involves renovating the same buildings for similar uses over and over again.

Evidence of Neighborhood Change

As a neighborhood passes through each of the four phases of the neighborhood cycle, there are clear signs of transition. The transition from the growth phase to the stable phase, for example, is identified by a reduction in available vacant land and a decline in the construction of new buildings.

The transition from the stable phase to the declining phase is identified by marked changes in existing buildings. One common change is a decrease in the amount of building maintenance, with noticeable deterioration resulting. Often, there will be a change in the density of use, with more people occupying the same space. In commercial or industrial property, this increase in density often means that there will be smaller firms occupying a given building than in earlier years.

The transition to neighborhood renaissance is usually marked by the renovation of individual structures. Improved maintenance and in-

Figure 4.1
The four phases of neighborhood change. (*a*) Development. (*b*) Stable. (*c*) Decline. (*d*) Renaissance. (Photographs courtesy of Doug Frost)

creased remodeling are first noted at scattered locations and then gradually become more common.

The neighborhood renaissance phase may also involve demolition of old buildings and the construction of new ones. The transition into this phase is often marked first by changes in the uses of existing buildings. As the new, higher-priced uses begin to prosper, deteriorated buildings will be demolished and replaced. Substantial physical deterioration must be present if this phase is to be carried out by private capital because well-maintained structures are usually too valuable to be demolished.

Neighborhoods as Barometers of Change

Why should you learn about the neighborhood cycle or about neighborhood changes? The value of a property is influenced by the neighborhood around it. So, we study neighborhood changes in order to understand how and why a property's value is changing. Often, too, some other location in a neighborhood will show changes before similar changes actually reach the property being appraised.

The immediate neighborhood has the most impact on the subject property. For most land uses, this immediate area will include the properties in the same block, on both sides of the street, plus those "across the back fence" and even those on the cross streets. Figure 4.2 shows the neighborhood locations that are likely to have the greatest impact on the property being appraised. Neighborhood locations that are farther away have a gradually diminishing impact on the value of a particular property.

Every neighborhood is *always* changing, no matter how stable it may seem. Normal wear and tear from age, the elements, and neglect continually act to reduce a declining neighborhood's condition, desirability, and value. As the occupants work to delay or halt such decay, they can often reverse the decline, improving the desirability and value of the neighborhood. All the positive and negative forces present in the neighborhood eventually lead either to the renovation of the existing structures or to their demolition.

These changes in the neighborhood affect every property but usually at differing times. Noticeable change usually starts at the edge of a neighborhood, where land uses conflict with, or are different from, those of the adjoining neighborhood. Depending on the community reaction, the good or bad change may disappear or may spread to the rest of the neighborhood. For this reason, appraisers look beyond the immediate area of the subject property to the fringes of the neighborhood. They want to see what kinds of changes are occurring and how the neighborhood is meeting these changes. See Figure 4.3 for an example.

In summary, appraisers study neighborhoods and their changes in order to see physical evidence of what forces are affecting the neighborhood. These same forces are at work on the property being appraised but can often best be seen through their effect on other prop-

Figure 4.2
The immediate neighborhood—
one version.

erties elsewhere in the neighborhood. As we shall see, the appraiser uses this understanding of neighborhood change throughout the appraisal process.

Using Information About Neighborhoods

Why do appraisers need neighborhood information? One reason is to include an objective picture of it in the description section of the appraisal report. A second and key reason is to define the geographic area that will be the center of the market-data search area. Whether one looks for land sales, improved-property sales, leases, costs, depreciation or income capitalization rates, the neighborhood around the property is the *starting point* in the search.

A third reason for studying neighborhoods is that it will assist you in defining the highest and best use of the property. (There are many possible uses of a property, varying in their legal and economic feasibility.) Recent history and trends in uses in a neighborhood tell the appraiser much about the feasibility of various uses as well as the legal, social, and political problems that may block the success of a particular use. The term *highest and best use* will be more fully developed in later chapters.

The fourth reason for studying neighborhoods is to find out whether, and by how much, to adjust market data for differences. Comparable sales might have occurred too many months ago to be useful, or might

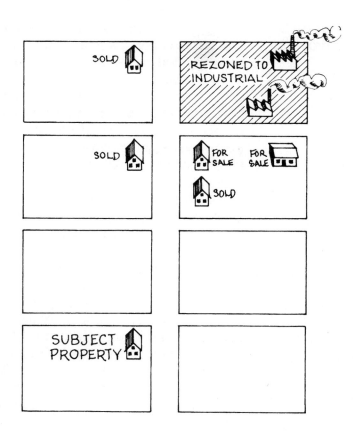

Figure 4.3
One reason for studying the neighborhood.

represent smaller or older structures than the subject property, or might be too far away. As a result, market data must often be adjusted to reflect the differences. The amount of such adjustment must be based on the importance of those differences in the particular market area or neighborhood. In home sales, for example, the price of a property lacking a basement should be adjusted if the subject property has a basement. This adjustment must be based on the importance of a basement in that market. In an industrial neighborhood, the absence of an office area in a warehouse must be considered in light of warehouse office usage in that neighborhood. In considering the sale of a large house, the appraiser must keep in mind the general range of house sizes in the neighborhood as well as trends in family sizes and incomes.

Neighborhood properties are rarely identical from one end of the neighborhood to the other. It is therefore important to understand how the various locations within the neighborhood may differ. Such knowledge helps the appraiser correctly use and adjust market information coming from different places within the neighborhood.

A significant problem arises when adequate information cannot be found within the subject neighborhood. When you lack sales of properties similar to the subject, you may need to use sales or information from other neighborhoods, communities, or even other states. Then you must try to understand each neighborhood in order to adjust for the difference in location.

The Neighborhood Controversy

In the past, appraisers have been accused of using neighborhood analysis to collect information that is entirely irrelevant to the appraisal or is intended to prejudice. Some have even suggested that neighborhood analysis should be eliminated from the appraisal process. The controversy arises, it seems, from appraisers' failure to define clearly how certain neighborhood information is to be used. When its purpose is not clear, certain information collected may be challenged as irrelevant or no longer important. Reporting the race, creed, sex, handicap, familial status, or national origin of occupants is an example of information irrelevant to nearly all appraisal assignments.

The study of neighborhoods is at the heart of appraising and the estimation of market value. It is the study of the neighborhood that helps the appraiser discover what property characteristics are important to buyers and sellers and suggests the relative importance of such characteristics at any particular time.

4.2 UNDERSTANDING COMMUNITIES AND HOW THEY GROW

All neighborhoods exist in relation to the social, economic, and political environment of a community. Understanding the origin, location, and layout of cities helps us understand the land uses within the community and the patterns of land use that tend to form. The factors that contribute to economic growth are especially important. As communities grow, they change in layout, and these changes affect value.

Community Origins and Growth

Each community is located where it is for specific social, political, physical, or economic reasons. The town's original location strongly influences its early physical layout. This early layout strongly influences how the town changes as it grows. For this reason, it is helpful for you to study community origins and growth.

Townsite Selection Factors

Historically, town locations were often selected because food and water were accessible and the site could easily be defended against enemies. Some townsites were chosen for religious purposes. In America, most townsites were selected because of their commercial benefits. Often, the choice of a site was determined by the *topography* of the land, the availability of *raw resources,* and the *transportation systems* in use at the time.

Topography has always been one of the most important factors in the selection of a townsite because it usually determined where the existing transportation routes would be. In turn, these routes influence the accessibility of the land for habitation. Topography has particularly influenced the location of towns whose major function was to provide services along transportation routes.

The availability of *raw resources* has long been a major factor in choosing the location for a townsite. Resources with a *low* value for their bulk, such as copper ore, were usually processed near the mine, creating an industry. This processing industry often grew into a townsite. Resources that had a *high* value per ton, or per unit of size, could be shipped without processing. Thus some processing towns did not need to be as close to the mine. The total number of mines in an area also determined where processing was to take place, so the townsite remained just a mining town or grew into a larger village.

Finally, the choice of location, especially for water transport towns, depended on the form of *transportation system* in use at the time of the town's founding. If shallow-draft paddlewheel schooners were in use, a shallow, sheltered dock was sufficient for the site. When oceangoing steamers came into use, deep-water docks became necessary. Wind shelters were also critical for protection from storm waves. These examples show how the requirements for success as a townsite constantly change.

Types of Towns

In America, towns and cities usually fit into one of three types, depending on the major functions they serve. The *central town* is one that performs a variety of services for a surrounding area. The area is first developed, usually for farming, with widely scattered residences. The need for a place to buy supplies and locate churches and schools soon leads to the formation of a town. The town grows in population as a result of the expansion and profitability of the farming. Figure 4.4 shows a map of three central towns and their respective trade areas.

The *transporation service town* is one that is selected to provide services along a transportation route, as noted earlier. Usually, these towns are situated at points called *nodes.* These are points where transportation routes split or shift, or where a change in the type of transportation occurs. Typical nodes include ports, major rail intersec-

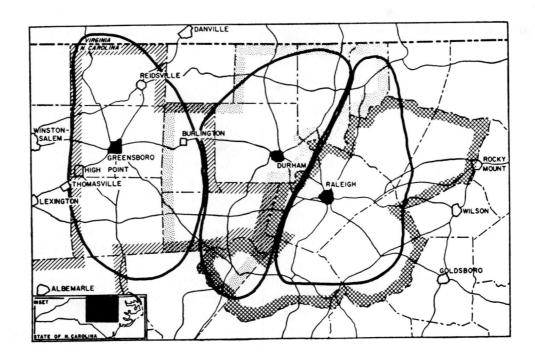

Figure 4.4
Three central towns in North Carolina and their trade areas. (Courtesy of the University of Illinois Press. From F. Stuart Chapin, Jr., *Urban Land Use Planning.* New York: Harper and Row Publishers, 1957. Copyright assigned in 1963 to the Board of Trustees of the University of Illinois Press)

tions, freeway intersections, navigable river forks, and mountain passes. Figure 4.5 shows San Francisco when it was a port town. Transport service towns may also develop at a place where transportation systems must be maintained. Some railroad water stops in the western United States have become cities, including San Bernardino, California, and Logan, Utah.

Special-function towns are those that concentrate on one special service or purpose, such as a mining town, a government seat, or a retirement community. Other examples include resort towns and university towns. Figure 4.6 displays some examples of special-function towns.

Changes in City Function

As a town grows, it can change from one functional type to another. Pittsburgh, Pennsylvania, was first founded at Fort Pitt, beside a major river fork, as a point of control over the commercial transportation in the area (then consisting entirely of riverboats). It was first a transport service town. Because of the mining of nearby coal and iron ore deposits, Pittsburgh later became a resource-oriented iron mill town. The nearby iron and coal are now exhausted, but the workers' skills and huge mills allow Pittsburgh to continue as a special-purpose, resource-oriented manufacturing town.

Economic Growth

Once a town comes into being, its continued existence depends on whether the town is an economic success. No town or community today is self-sufficient. The cars, radios, food, and other commodities we use come from other towns, and we must pay for them. It follows that the many costs of imported goods and services must be earned by

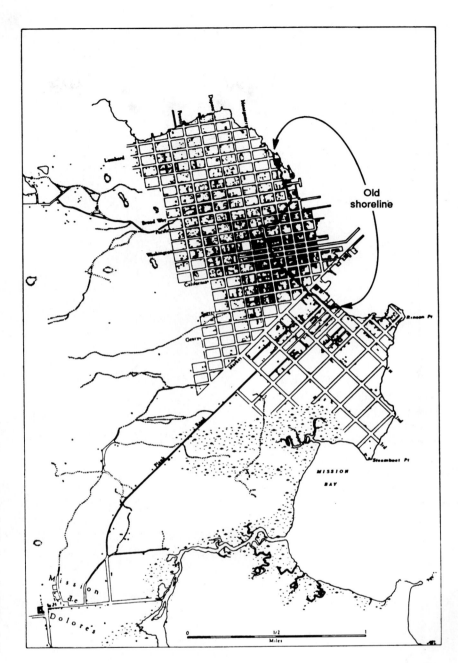

Figure 4.5
A transportation service town—San Francisco in 1853. (From U.S. Coast Survey Map No. 627, 1853. Key—Original high water line, Eddy Survey, 1852. Courtesy of the Berkeley Institute of Governmental Studies, F. K. Lane Series. From James E. Vance, Jr., *Geography and Urban Evolution in the San Francisco Bay Area,* Berkeley Institute of Governmental Studies, University of California, 1964)

sales of the town's own products and services to other towns. Each town must perform some economic function: make products, mine a natural resource, or perform a service. Usually, whatever this economic function is, a portion of the product or service will be for sale or for use in the town. This is called *local production.* More important, however, is the surplus production that is sold to other towns and called *export production.* An example of local versus export production is shown in Figure 4.7. The latter economic activity forms the economic base of the town. The growth of towns, then, depends on the

Figure 4.6
Special-function towns.
(*a*) University town. (Photograph
courtesy of Doug Frost) (*b*) Mining
town. (Earl Dotter/Magnum)

Figure 4.6 (*continued*) (*c*) Retirement community, Sun City, Arizona. (Georg Gerster/Rapho-Photo Researchers) (*d*) Government town. (Photograph courtesy of Doug Frost)

richness of the town's basic resources (e.g., ore bodies, timber stands, and agricultural fields) plus the skills, creativity, and industriousness of its workers.

Each community tends to develop a specialty, usually related to the town's origin. This specialty can be a product or a skill. When we compare one town with another, or one region with another, we can see

Figure 4.7
Local and export production.

differences in the products that are made in each town and in how the population is employed. These differences *reveal* the special products or skills that provide the economic base for the town or region. We use this knowledge of the economic-base activities to study the possibility of population growth or decline, the relative stability of employment, or the future of particular neighborhoods economically tied to the area's exports. See Figure 4.8.

Physical Patterns of the Community

As towns grow, the different land uses in the community form patterns. As we noted in our discussion of neighborhoods, each use often concentrates at one location because the various users choose the most advantageous location for each use. The various neighborhoods, each with their characteristic uses, make up the land-use pattern of the community. It should be remembered that the pattern may change over the years in response to changing social and economic influences.

Major Factors in Land Use

A number of factors influence the land-use patterns and the location of new buildings in a community. Four factors are especially important. Each, however, is to some extent connected to the other.

1. **Topography:** the shape and slope of the land, and its natural features such as rivers, swamps, and lakes. Topography usually determines transportation routes and good building sites.

2. **The town's origin:** where the town started and why. Both the functional origin and the point of origin of a community are determined by topography, transportation, and natural re-

Figure 4.8
Growing communities. (By Henry R. Martin, from *The Rotarian,* April, 1978)

"Say, were those houses there last night?"

sources. In turn, the town's origin is a major factor in the subsequent development of the townsite.

3. **Transportation systems:** how people and goods move around. Early transportation systems, such as walking, pack animals, and carts, allowed random movement in any direction, which contributed to the circular shape of towns. But as transportation systems became more sophisticated, the shape of towns changed. Of all four factors, transportation is the most important in creating change in the pattern of land use, as you will see in our discussion of current trends in the following pages.

4. **Major existing uses:** the presence of major buildings or concentrations of buildings continues to attract people, even when the original reason for selecting the location of these buildings no longer exists.

Typical Patterns

The most common land-use pattern is the cluster of commercial uses at the intersection of major transportation routes (again, the *node* idea). In small villages, commercial buildings at the crossroads become the downtown area. In towns larger than a small village, the number of land uses in the downtown area increases to the extent that the area around the crossroads becomes divided up into different zones of uses. Although the prime commercial uses remain at the main intersection, the pressures of the town's growth eventually drive residences to the outskirts of town. High rents and values in the prime commercial area tend to cause offices, government buildings, schools and less profitable commercial uses to move away from the main intersection and gradually fill in the intermediate area of the town. As this process continues, the town pattern begins to look like a series of rings around the downtown area. The prime commercial zone forms the inner ring, followed by a ring of office, government, and wholesale buildings. This ring, in recent years, has included a growing number of apartment buildings. The next ring contains older houses with some conversions to offices or boardinghouses, and some new structures moving out from the second ring. The fourth ring consists of single-family residences, with the newer homes on the outer circumference. Figure 4.9 shows this pattern of concentric rings.

As concentric rings form around the downtown section of many cities, various factors often cause the rings to become segmented. Depending on the existing uses and the topography of the ring, each segment will have some different uses from the other segments in the ring. Often service, retail, wholesale, and manufacturing uses will concentrate in segments on one side of the downtown, with offices and higher-priced commercial stores on the other. Particular segments on the outer rings will be favored for high-priced new homes, perhaps because of good views, favorable surroundings, or close proximity to older luxury homes. Mid-priced new homes will usually be located on the remaining segments of the outer ring. Usually, the high-priced commercial ring segment will line up with the high-priced home segment, as Figure 4.10 demonstrates.

The concept of perfect concentric rings is somewhat oversimplified, but it still serves as a good analytical tool. Land-use patterns can be so dominated by topography (as in the San Francisco Bay area) that the ring looks more like a cucumber. Economic-use patterns are also altered by personal motives. People sometimes hold on to their old family homes despite economic pressures to sell or to convert to commercial uses. In general, however, the pattern of land uses shows a strong concentric ring relationship, which is especially noticeable in small cities.

Current Trends   The early transport systems (walking or horse-drawn) were replaced by streetcars traveling fixed linear routes. This change caused urban land-use patterns to change gradually from concentric to linear, as city

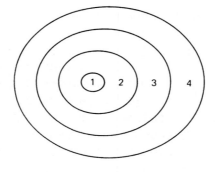

Figure 4.9
Typical patterns of land use: concentric rings. (From Dennis J. McKenzie and Richard M. Betts, *The Essentials of Real Estate Economics,* 3rd ed., New Jersey: Prentice Hall, 1992, p. 102)

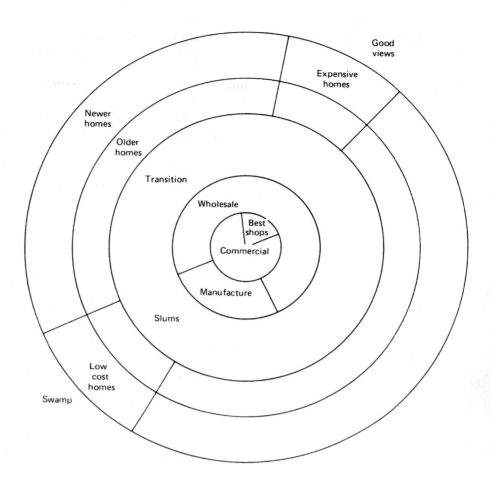

Good
views

Expensive
homes

Newer
homes

Older
homes

Transition

Wholesale

Best
shops

Commercial

Manufacture

Slums

Low
cost
homes

Swamp

Figure 4.10
Segmented rings. (Courtesy of
the California Department of
Real Estate)

growth began to follow the fixed-rail lines. Although automobile transportation at first encouraged a return to the earlier patterns of random
movement and circular cities, arterial roads and freeways soon took
the place of the familiar fixed-rail routes, and cities developed an even
more linear pattern.

As the arterial roads and freeways of large cities intersect, each major road intersection forms a node, and a commercial cluster often de-
velops. In turn, small concentric rings often form about the cluster.

To summarize, in modern cities locations for new developments are
chosen more by proximity to transportation lines than by the distance
from the downtown. Thus the concentric circles that we discussed earlier are altered in larger cities that have freeways, thruways, express-
ways, arterials, streetcars, subways, and so on. Now, commercial uses
often form linear strips instead of rings. Each major intersection devel-
ops its own minor ring. Service industries and warehouses often adjoin
the linear strip or occupy districts far removed from the old warehouse
district. So, we can understand why the pattern of uses in most of the
larger modern cities does not look like a series of concentric rings but
rather like an irregular spiderweb or a tangled pattern of yarn. The outline of the city itself, instead of being circular, is likely to look more like
a star with a number of points. Figure 4.11 is an example.

Using Information About Communities

As the appraiser looks at the community and region surrounding the property being appraised, the scope and amount of information may appear to be staggering. Countless data about political, social, economic, and physical aspects of the community might be collected. In order to select the most relevant information, the appraiser must have a clear concept of how and why this information is to be used.

The appraiser uses regional and community information for several reasons. The first is that some community forces and trends affect the trends in the neighborhood. For example, if the town is growing, residential neighborhoods close to downtown could be under pressure to become locations for stores or offices. Understanding these community trends helps you to interpret what is happening in the neighborhood.

Second, some community trends can affect all the real estate markets in the community. For example, prices of all types of property in all neighborhoods in a town may decline if a dominant employer shuts down, or prices may increase if a large factory opens up. Understanding this second type of community trend helps you decide which sales occurred in comparable market conditions as of your date of value. For instance, in the case of an unexpected factory closure, sales prices for homes sold prior to the factory closing may differ from prices after the closing.

In summary, understanding community origin and patterns of growth helps the appraiser to analyze the economic and political factors affecting the subject property and its neighborhood. Some of these factors affect the entire community. Other influences may affect properties and values over a smaller area. Notice that as the area you study gets smaller, the focus on the community gradually changes to a neighborhood study, as discussed earlier in this chapter.

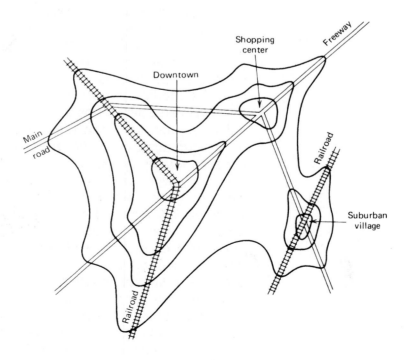

Figure 4.11
The modern star-shaped city. (From Dennis J. McKenzie and Richard M. Betts, *The Essentials of Real Estate Economics,* 3rd ed., New Jersey: Prentice Hall, 1992, p. 112)

4.3 REAL ESTATE MARKETS AND THEIR ANALYSIS

Since appraisals usually involve estimating market value, appraisers must understand real estate markets. Knowing the condition of the market will help you in different ways. It will help you when you select the market data to use in the appraisal. Sometimes the market data that are selected may have defects. Frequently, such defects are caused by market imperfections. If appraisers have a solid grasp of what is going on in the market, they can often detect these imperfections and thereby reduce the possibility of error.

What Is a Market?

Most of us have some impression of what a market is. We have seen an auction, a farmer's market, or pictures of the trading floor of the stock market. These are general examples of a market: a place where buyers and sellers meet to exchange goods or services. The concept of a market also has an exact technical definition based on seven criteria.

The Perfect Market

From the study of markets has come the concept of the perfectly competitive market, or *perfect market.* It is a standard against which all other types of markets are compared. The perfect market is defined as one that meets each of the following criteria:

---

1. There are numerous buyers and sellers.

2. All parties are knowledgeable.

3. All parties are free to trade or not trade.

4. All products are similar and interchangeable.

5. All products can be transported to better markets.

6. Items are small, inexpensive, and frequently purchased.

7. The government plays a very minor role in pricing.

Markets such as the stock market come close to being perfect markets. In such markets, prices move continuously up and down, and neither seller nor buyer can control the price movement.

Imperfect Markets

Many markets cannot meet the seven tests of a perfect market that we have listed. These markets are referred to as *imperfect markets.* For example, in some imperfect markets, such as uncut diamonds, there are very few sellers. These sellers tend to fix prices and there is little price fluctuation. A limited number of sellers is one type of problem that causes imperfect markets.

Another common feature of imperfect markets is the inadequate knowledge of buyers and/or sellers, either about the product itself or, more often, about true conditions in the market. The lack of adequate knowledge means that buyers and sellers are not able to make good decisions so that when added information is finally obtained, price or location decisions turn out to have been wrong. When more information about a product becomes available, prices change. Some people get information ahead of the general market and use this information to their advantage and profit. When this occurs, the profits are made at the expense of those who lack full information.

Real Estate Markets

We can see, from reviewing the definition of a perfect market, that real estate markets are *not* perfect markets. In fact, real estate markets are often used by economists as examples of imperfect markets—the other extreme—because real estate markets do not meet *any* of the seven requirements for a perfect market.

At any one time in real estate markets, there are relatively few buyers and sellers of one type, price range, and location of real property. Neither buyer nor seller is very knowledgeable because the product, real estate, is complex and not as commonly bought and sold as other commodities. Both seller and buyer are often anxious to complete the deal in order to get housing or buy another property. Available properties are not very similar or interchangeable. Practically speaking, they cannot be transported to a better market, should the local market be poor. The properties are not small or inexpensive and are not frequently purchased by most market participants. Surveys of buyer characteristics reveal that few people have made more than a half-dozen real estate purchases. Finally, real estate pricing is strongly influenced by government actions. The FHA financing and income tax benefits, for example, tend to help buyers; at the same time, property-use controls, such as zoning, building permits and so on, tend to restrict the activity of buyers and sellers alike.

Because of the imperfection of the real estate market, prices for real estate do not rise or fall smoothly or rapidly as do, for example, stock prices. Thus, in the real estate market, individual sales can occur well above or below the prices that would occur with a more perfect market. A unique price can result when there is a poorly informed buyer or seller, or when there is some unique characteristic of the property from the point of view of the typical buyer. To illustrate the latter, there are relatively few buyers willing to pay a proportionately high price for a large house (3,500 square feet, say) with only one bedroom. To the right buyer, a relatively high price could be reasonable. To most buyers, however, the price would have to be considerably lower to be attractive.

Since real properties are so complex, there are many factors that can influence prices. These factors vary in importance, depending on the place, time, or property type. Consequently, real estate markets are more varied and unique than, say, bond markets.

In the real estate market, each subcategory of property is somewhat distinct from the others. Homes in Michigan may not sell at the same price as identical homes in California, for example. Even within California, prices in the community of Alturas (in the northeast corner of the state in remote Modoc County) will have limited connection to prices in Sacramento, about 200 miles away.

Market Analysis and Interpretation

Why does the appraiser need to analyze and interpret the market? Fundamentally, it is to find out what is happening in the marketplace surrounding the subject property. In the appraisal process, the appraiser uses the knowledge and understanding of market activity in three critical ways: (1) to help decide what kinds of market data to collect and what adjustment to make, (2) to estimate a reasonable marketing time for the subject property, and (3) to report on current marketing conditions and trends that may affect projected or forecasted income and/or the absorption period for income producing or multiple-unit properties.

For study purposes, market behavior can be divided into three parts, namely, (1) price levels, (2) price movement and trends, and (3) the levels of market activity.

Price Levels

The most obvious aspect of market activity to be examined is the level of prices. By comparing prices with current costs for new construction and lot prices, we can see how the market may eventually increase or deflate the value of older homes. We can also see whether this change varies with the type of building, location, or market. Studying such market information helps us interpret market data.

We can also compare prices for other reasons. For example, within a neighborhood, we could compare and see the effects of age, size, an added half-bath, a swimming pool, or a view on sales prices. On the other hand, by comparing prices paid for similar properties in different locations, we can learn how the market views the desirability of these locations.

Price Movements

The appraiser can learn even more by studying price movements rather than just price levels. In studying price movements, we see which way prices are changing, how fast, and whether there are differences between various markets. The direction and speed of price movements tell us how strong or weak a particular market is. We can also compare the strength of the market with our knowledge of the community's economy. This sharpens our understanding of what economic forces may be causing prices to change.

For example, we might find that a city has two high-priced, residential neighborhoods, but one has declining prices while the other has stable or increasing prices. As a result, market data from these two markets will have to be interpreted differently. Upon further study, we may be able to develop an idea of why the difference is occurring. Perhaps the declining neighborhood previously catered to wealthy central-city commuters who are now residing farther out. Perhaps the other neighborhood attracted local professionals who have not been as quick to move to the distant suburbs.

We might also want to compare the direction and speed of current price changes with past price changes or with price movement in other price ranges and in other types of real estate. Is the rate of price change speeding up, slowing down, or staying the same? Answers to such questions may shed additional light on the appraisal problem at hand.

How do price changes compare with construction cost changes? If the price changes are greater, then we can see that either builder profits or land prices may be going up. If they are less, then land prices and builder profits may be under pressure.

This study of the direction and speed of price movements will demonstrate again and again a need to compare real estate trends to trends in the general economy. Are real estate prices going up faster than general prices? Than new construction costs? What about lot prices? Raw land prices? As we develop an understanding of the cost approach, we shall see that a change in the price of a completed house *must* involve changes in the prices of some or all of the elements that go into making up the house.

Levels of Activity The appraiser should also study how active the market is. In real estate markets, we noted earlier that prices do not always respond smoothly to minor shifts in seller supply or buyer demand. Prices may move smoothly upward, as the general real estate price increases of 1976 to 1978 demonstrated, or they may literally jump, as they did in many areas in the west in 1989 to 1990. However, when real estate prices are under pressure to move downward, an irregular pattern is more typical.

When downward pressures develop, what usually happens first is that buyers refuse to buy at the old prices. In a more perfect market, prices would slowly start to fall. In real estate markets, however, what often happens is that sellers try to wait this period out, hoping for an offer every day. Many eventually withdraw their property from the market rather than sell for less. As a result, the volume of sales may fall off dramatically.

In a stagnant market, the first clue to where the market is heading is the declining number of sales, rather than a decline in prices. In time, either buyers will return to the market at old price levels, or else the more anxious sellers will cut prices and entice a buyer into purchasing. If buyer resistance continues, then sellers may go through a wave of repeated cuts in listing prices without tangible results. When the sales finally do occur, they often will be a step lower than prior sales. Therefore, we might want to compare the current volume of sales with the volume in the past for that type of property. Is the volume up or down and by how much? How does the sales volume compare to the number of listings? Has this relationship changed?

The patterns of listing activity can also help us decide what is happening in a market. How long is it taking to sell property? Are many listings expiring, unsold? Have there been many asking price reductions for the current listings? Have owners of current listings received any offers? How low were the offers relative to the listing price?

Finally, we are interested in the buyer activity just as much as the listings. What is happening to the number of lookers? How many people are showing up for open houses compared to earlier times? Are people coming back for a second look?

There are several unusual patterns of activity levels of buyers or sellers that you might find. One pattern consists of increasing numbers of lookers, sometimes also with declines in the numbers of listings or with listings being withdrawn by the sellers. These signs can indicate a market condition in which an upward price jump could be forthcoming. This would be a different pattern of activity than for a stable market or one with smoothly moving gradual price changes.

The third pattern is the troubled market, as generally experienced in the early 1990s. As we observed earlier, when a real estate market turns downward, prices usually do not smoothly turn downward. Instead, list prices are often maintained at the old levels while buyer activity declines, often substantially. When sales finally occur, they are often at lower prices.

In the absence of recent sales, then, the appraiser may not want simply to use earlier sales. What may be needed is a careful study of recent listing activity and the reasons behind the absence of recent sales. Activity levels are perhaps the most sensitive measure of the state of real estate markets.

SUMMARY

In the first section of this chapter, we discussed the concept of the neighborhood and its importance to appraisers. Although the neighborhood can be defined in a number of ways, it is, in general, an area whose occupants or users share some common ties or characteristics. Economically, neighborhood boundaries are set by where the characteristics and benefits of a location change. The neighborhood's quality depends on how the neighborhood serves the land uses and how the occupants maintain the neighborhood.

Neighborhoods go through a series of changes over the years, starting with the development of the initial buildings, then a phase of stability, which is followed by a third phase of decline. The fourth phase, called the renaissance, is the transition to a new life sequence, either by rehabilitation or by demolition.

Appraisers study the neighborhood because it leads to an understanding of the forces affecting the values of the subject properties. The locations immediately around the property being appraised are the most important to study because they will have the most direct impact on the subject property. Locations at the periphery of the neighborhood are also important to study because changes in a neighborhood tend to start at one edge and move inward.

The neighborhood study is used to define the center of the market-data search area. It helps estimate the highest and best use of the property and establish what types of adjustments to the market data will be necessary.

This chapter then discussed the study of community trends. The influence that the town's origin plays in its future growth was the first topic. Origins of American communities were usually commercially motivated. Growth of the town depended on its commercial success in developing some resource, product, or skill to trade to other communities for goods which the local town could not produce.

As towns grow in size, predictable patterns emerge for the various land uses. The major influences affecting these patterns are the town's origin, its topography, the transportation systems in use, and the attraction of existing major buildings. The simplest pattern is the cluster of commercial uses at the main intersection. As towns become bigger, the cluster becomes a series of rings around the major downtown intersection, and the rings of similar uses then break up into different segments. Depending on transportation systems, the circles can be distorted by linear strip–commercial zones, making larger cities more star-shaped.

This study of the community enables the appraiser to better understand trends in the community that are affecting property and its value. The third section of the chapter focused on markets. First was a definition of the elements of a perfect market, followed by a description of the flaws that produce imperfect markets. Real estate markets were shown to be almost classic examples of imperfect markets.

The appraiser studies real estate markets for information to help interpret current market data. Price levels, for example, are compared to estimate the price difference between properties of different sizes, ages, and so on. Price movements tell even more about the market. We can compare prices at different times, for different areas or types of property or against changing prices in other parts of the economy. In some cases, levels of sales activity can be the most significant factor if there are no recent sales. All this information helps the appraiser to correctly understand and adjust the many types of market data and to report on market trends and likely marketing time as required in the appraisal.

Important Terms and Concepts

Central town	Neighborhood boundaries
Competing neighborhoods	Neighborhood cycle
Decline phase	Perfect market
Demand-supply balance	Present land use
Development phase	Price levels
Development rate	Renaissance phase
Economic base	Sales volume
Imperfect market	Shared identity
Growth rate	Special-function town
Land-use change	Stable phase
Land-use patterns	Topography
Marketing time	Town origin
Neighborhood	Transportation-service town
Neighborhood bonds, or linkage	Trend of property values

1. A neighborhood can be defined as:
   - (a) A group of properties with very dissimilar land uses
   - (b) An area in which the occupants and users share some common ties and characteristics
   - (c) An area of a city that contains similar land uses within a defined location or boundary
   - (d) Both (b) and (c)

2. "Shared identity" can mean:
   - (a) Some characteristic of a neighborhood that is common to most of the inhabitants, land uses, or buildings
   - (b) Some common characteristic of the occupants
   - (c) Whatever shared characteristics create a common bond
   - (d) All of the above

3. The boundaries of a neighborhood might be determined by:
   - (a) An economic change in use
   - (b) Physical features such as lakes, rivers, or freeways
   - (c) Zoning or city limits
   - (d) Two of the above
   - (e) All of the above

4. The four stages of the neighborhood cycle are:
   - (a) Development, stable, decline, and renaissance
   - (b) Development, stable, demolition, and renaissance
   - (c) Demolition, decline, renaissance, and stability
   - (d) Renaissance, stability, decline, and demolition

5. The three most common types of towns and cities in America include all of the following *except:*
   - (a) The central town
   - (b) The shopping town
   - (c) The transportation-service town
   - (d) The special-function town

6. The interrelated factors that have the most influence on the patterns of land use of a community include all the following *except:*
   - (a) The town's original location
   - (b) The social systems
   - (c) The transportation systems developed
   - (d) The natural topography

7. A perfect market occurs when:
   - (a) There are numerous buyers and sellers who are knowledgeable and are free to trade or not trade
   - (b) All products are similar and interchangeable and can be transported to better markets
   - (c) The items are small, inexpensive, and frequently purchased, and the government plays no role in pricing
   - (d) Two of the above
   - (e) All of the above

8. Real estate markets are imperfect because:
   - (a) Real estate markets can be easily exchanged

(b) They meet none of the criteria of a perfect market

(c) They meet some of the criteria of a perfect market

(d) Most real estate sales are resales of used property

9. Appraisers use all except one of the following to study and interpret market activity:

(a) Price levels

(b) Margin of profits

(c) Price movements

(d) Levels of market activity

10. Appraisers study neighborhoods for the following reason(s):

(a) To give an objective account of the neighborhood in appraisal reports

(b) To define the geographic area that will be the center of market data

(c) To assist in the highest and best use study

(d) All of the above

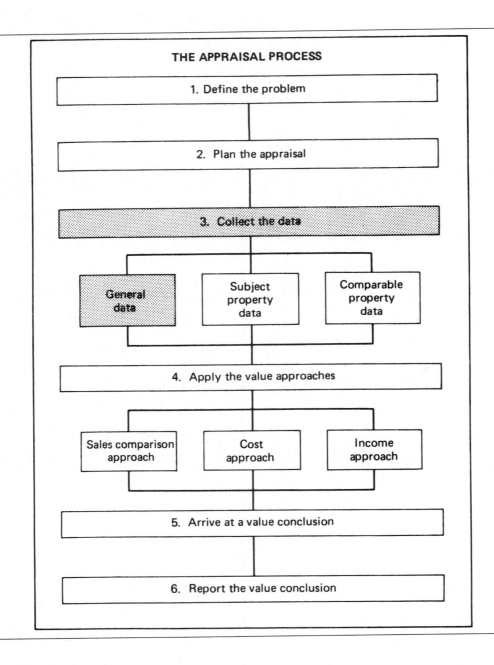

THE APPRAISAL PROCESS

1. Define the problem

2. Plan the appraisal

3. Collect the data

| General data | Subject property data | Comparable property data |

4. Apply the value approaches

| Sales comparison approach | Cost approach | Income approach |

5. Arrive at a value conclusion

6. Report the value conclusion

Chapter 5

Real Estate Economics and Value

Preview   Real estate is a basic and fundamental form of wealth. All material possessions of people can be traced to their beginnings in the land. To understand how real estate is produced, adapted, distributed, and utilized is to understand the economics of real estate and to gain insight into its value.

The value of real estate is created and modified by the many physical, economic, social, and governmental forces that act on it. In this chapter we describe these basic forces, discuss economic trends affecting real estate, and outline the economic principles that govern appraisals.

When you have completed this chapter, you should be able to:

1. *List the four basic elements of value.*

2. *List and give examples of the broad forces that affect value.*

3. *Define real estate cycles.*

4. *Name the major supply and demand factors that are involved in economic trends affecting real estate.*

5. *Describe the federal government's role in the economy.*

6. *Explain how the principles of value relate to the marketability and productivity of real estate.*

5.1 THE BASIC VALUE INFLUENCES

Real estate has no intrinsic value. That means it has no value in and of itself. Instead, the monetary value of real estate is derived from the rights and benefits that come from its ownership, possession, and use. As we learned in Chapter 2 of this book, such rights are referred to as real property rights. When real property rights are bought and sold in the market, the value of such rights is measured by the prices that are paid for them.

For any object to have market value, certain essential elements must be present. A review of these elements is necessary if we are to understand the basic forces that influence the value of real estate.

Four Essential Elements of Value

In the context of the market, there are only four basic elements of value. Sometimes referred to as prerequisites, these elements are:

1. **Utility:** usefulness; ability to arouse a desire for possession.

2. **Scarcity:** in relatively short supply; lack of abundance.

3. **Demand:** desire to possess plus the ability to buy; effective purchasing power.

4. **Transferability:** ability to change ownership or use; marketable title.

All the listed elements must be present before an object can have value in the marketplace. An object must be useful, and at the same time scarce, for there to be any measurable benefits from owning it. For example, desert sand and ocean water are useful for certain purposes, but because they lack scarcity, they have little value. Modern new houses and office buildings are extremely useful objects for human activity, but a serious oversupply of such buildings would without question reduce their market price. Why? Because oversupply is the opposite of scarcity.

Where does demand fit in? For any item to have value, there must be people ready, willing, and able to buy it at some price. Utility and scarcity cannot create a market unless there is demand and the purchasing power to implement it. And if an object does not have transferability, the demand is ineffective. For example, a parcel of real estate that lacks marketable title can have no value in the market because rights to its use cannot be transferred. In summary, utility, scarcity, demand, and transferability interact in combination to create the condition that we refer to as *market value,* which is demonstrated in Figure 5.1.

Broad Forces Influencing Value

As we have seen, real estate has value because it meets the four tests listed above. Four broad forces increase or decrease that value; they are physical, social, economic, and political in nature. (See Figure 5.2.) In their many combinations and forms, these forces involve all aspects of human behavior. When understood at the national, regional,

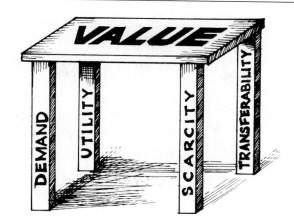

Figure 5.1
Basic elements of market value.

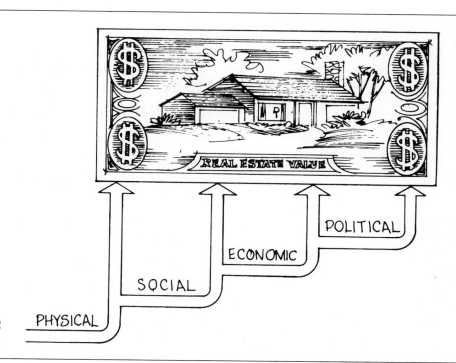

Figure 5.2
Forces affecting value.

community, and neighborhood levels, they help to explain why the nature and value of real estate are constantly changing.

Physical Forces   Because they are the most visible, the physical forces (or factors) affecting value are perhaps the easiest to understand. Some of them are natural and others are man-made. Examples include:

1. **Natural resources:** the land itself, its topography, soil, access, and location; climate, air, and mineral resources

(including water); plant and animal life; and scenic beauty and ecological balance.

2. **Developed resources:** the size and shape of land parcels; structures for human occupancy, commerce, and industry; public utilities, environmental controls, and health and safety facilities; street and road improvements, highways, airports, waterways, and harbors; public transportation, communication, and recreation systems; and facilities for education and cultural pursuits.

Social Forces

The social forces affecting values include all of the characteristics and customs of the people that make up the community. Here is a partial list:

1. Family sizes and age-group distribution in the neighborhoods and communities.

2. Neighborhood stability and attitudes about property.

3. Population growth, decline, or shifts at the community, regional, and national levels.

4. Life-styles and living standards, often combined with other forces.

5. Attitudes about law enforcement, the role of government, and individual responsibility.

6. Attitudes about development, growth, and ecology.

7. Attitudes toward public education.

Economic Forces

Our earlier discussion of the essential elements of market value mentioned various interactions among utility, scarcity, and demand. These elements are, to a large extent, the products of our constantly changing economic climate. Thus the major economic forces affecting real estate include:

1. Income levels of neighborhood and community residents.

2. Employment opportunities and trends.

3. Level of wages.

4. Availability of money and credit, and interest rate levels.

5. Price levels and property tax burdens.

6. Personal savings levels and investment returns.

7. General business activity.

8. Supply and demand in housing.

9. Production of goods and services.

Real estate appraisers and analysts often study statistics from many of these areas to help identify economic trends.

Political Forces   In Chapter 2, you learned about the authority of the government to restrict the use of property, to impose taxes for government expenditures, and to regulate property in promotion of the safety and welfare of the general public. Besides the limitations and burdens placed on property by police power and taxation, there are many government programs that stimulate private enterprise and help create a healthy business climate. High employment, general economic stability, and business opportunity are partially the result of government involvement in our economy.

Whether regarded as positive or negative, the various government actions can be classified as political forces. They have a far-reaching effect on the value of real estate.

A partial list of political forces affecting value includes:

1. Zoning and land-use regulations.

2. Building and safety regulations.

3. Environmental protection laws.

4. Endangered species acts.

5. Police, fire, and health protection services.

6. Crime prevention, education, and recreation services.

7. Public works: power, water, transportation, sewers, and flood control.

8. Fiscal policy and taxation.

9. Monetary policy and controls.

10. Government-sponsored urban redevelopment and housing finance programs.

11. Regulation of industry and business.

In summary, the four great forces that maintain, modify, or destroy real estate value are known as physical, social, economic, and political forces. As you can see, these forces overlap; many factors appear under more than one category. For example, "availability of money" is listed under economic forces. Note that this same factor is heavily influenced by what is called "monetary policy and controls," under the category of political forces. Even though the factors overlap and the forces interplay, carefully itemizing all relevant factors within each force can help the appraiser better understand the conditions affecting each property to be appraised.

5.2 HOW ECONOMIC TRENDS AFFECT REAL ESTATE

It is difficult to overstate the importance of real estate in the national economy. First, it represents two-thirds of the net worth of the country. Second, it is an essential part of the production process, since money or rent is universally paid for its use. Third, real estate is a major employer. Real estate development, construction, finance, management, and brokerage provide employment for a large segment of the population, accounting for billions of dollars of national income.

It is obvious that real estate does not exist in a vacuum. In today's space age, national and international events constantly change the social, economic, and political climate in which real estate functions. Economic trends are an important part of this climate.

Economic Trends and the Business Cycle

An economic trend is a pattern of related changes in some aspect of the economy. The most important national economic trends are those that affect the supply of, and demand for, goods and services. Examples include the balance of foreign trade, commodity price levels, and change in the annual gross domestic product.

National trends in the economy often help explain trends we can observe at local levels. Understanding economic trends at the regional, community, and neighborhood levels helps the appraiser interpret the market, cost, and income data that are pertinent to a particular appraisal. The local trends important to real estate include such factors as plant production, employment, construction activity, deed recordings, and the general volume of business. Changes in employment, income, price levels, and production have the greatest effect on real estate activity. Real estate price trends, such as those shown in Figure 5.3, are the result of these local economic trends.

Some economic changes repeat in a seasonal pattern. Whether at the national, regional, or local levels, these usually are caused either by weather or social customs. For example, construction activity declines during the winter in many parts of the country. Travel and recreational activities typically increase during the summer. Retail sales volume often experiences a surge during the "back-to-school" and Christmas seasons.

Information relating to economic trends is available from many banks, savings and loans, trade associations, and private research organizations. However, most statistical information on the economy is derived from the United States Printing Office, Superintendent of Doc-

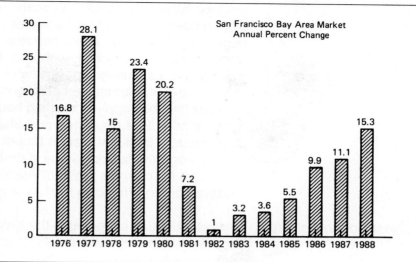

Figure 5.3

Annual percent change in estimated value of sample properties, San Francisco Bay Area market. (From *Northern California Real Estate Report,* Vol. 40, No. 1, April 1988. Courtesy of the Real Estate Research Council of Northern California)

Cycles

uments, in Washington, D.C. (See its publication *Economic Indicators.*) Government agencies such as the Federal Reserve, the Department of Commerce, and the Bureau of the Census are also major sources of such data.

Many important changes are cyclical in nature. The well-known business cycles are made up of expansions and contractions of general business activity that repeat on an average of every four years or so. Business cycles involve a series of stages. Prosperity increases to a point of stability, then declines, and a recession of the general economy follows. Finally, a recovery leads to growing prosperity, starting the cycle again. The length of the cycle is the time between one peak and the next.

The real estate cycle refers to the repeating changes noticeable in many areas of real estate, including the number of new subdivision lots, amount of new construction, and volume of sales. Some economists have contended that there are long real estate cycles lasting about 18 years. Recently, however, recurrent changes in real estate seem to involve a shorter cycle of three or four years in duration. Although our understanding of the real estate cycles is incomplete, we note that the short cycle often relates most directly to the cost and availability of money. Even so, a reduction in the cost of money does not always stimulate a flagging real estate market.

Real Estate Supply Factors

In order to understand the supply of real estate, we must study both existing and new facilities. Usually, we must consider residential property separately from commercial and agricultural property. Some of the more important factors in this supply are listed and briefly discussed here.

Housing Supply

There are approximately 105 million housing units in the national supply. This existing supply continually changes because of: (1) decreases caused by disasters, abandonment, demolition, and conversion to other uses, and (2) increases resulting from new construction, conversion from other uses, and remodeling. To allow for new family formations and building demolitions, the annual construction of new dwelling units should be approximately 3% of the existing inventory. In recent years, the annual net additions have been below this amount.

Protecting the supply of existing housing is a matter of national concern. Hundreds of neglected and abandoned inner-city homes have been brought back into use in recent years by neighborhood revitalization programs subsidized by state and federal funds. Examples include San Francisco's Western Addition and the Pico and Normandy Redevelopment Project in the Los Angeles area.

New Construction Activity

New construction spending in the United States is a good measure of conditions in this industry and the changing supply of real estate. In recent years the annual new construction spending has amounted to over $400 billion, representing about 9% of the value of all goods and services produced in the nation.

Historically, the cost of construction has followed general price levels, increasing during inflation and declining somewhat during recessions. Added costs for labor and materials that are used in energy-efficient heating, cooling, and insulating systems are adding to the upward trend. Construction costs increased by about 8.2% per year between 1971 and 1981, but only about 3% per year since that time. Product substitution (e.g., the trend toward replacing traditional wood framing material with less costly steel studs) plays a role in helping to keep costs under control. Higher construction costs tend to discourage development.

The Supply of Vacant Land

Political and social changes have greatly influenced the availability and cost of vacant land for real estate development. For example, as important as they were, many environmental protection and subdivision reform laws, starting with the Federal Clean Air Acts of the early 1970s, had the effect of decreasing the supply of buildable land and increasing the price. So did "open-space" and scenic easement agreements, wherein landowners agreed to restrict land to agricultural use in exchange for preferential property tax treatment (in California and a number of other states). "No-growth" or limited-growth local planning, coupled with time-consuming public approval procedures, has also increased the cost and reduced the supply of subdivided lots in many areas.

Real Estate Demand Factors

Earlier in this chapter, we described *demand* as one of the essential elements of value. The two dominant factors that affect the real estate market are population and purchasing power. Although these two factors are obviously related, we shall try to look at them one at a time.

Population

All other things being equal, the demand for housing and the other forms of real estate increases in direct relationship to our population growth. Since there is a limited supply of land on earth, an increase in demand for real estate usually results in higher land prices. Thus population increases usually mean higher real estate values.

Our interest in population change is not just in the numerical increase or decrease that may occur at a particular location. In projecting housing needs, we study the composition and makeup of households. Thus certain population characteristics like birthrates, age, sex, occupation, and family income are important. Known as demography, the study of such characteristics makes it possible to estimate the rate of formation of new families and the likely changes in household composition. From this information, we can predict specific demands for various types of housing, in terms of size, desired features, and price range. Figure 5.4 is an example of a study of changes in the number of persons per household.

Americans are often on the move—from city to suburb, country to city, or city to country; North to South or East to West, and so on. The resulting migratory shifts continually affect the growth or decline of population in many communities. Population studies must therefore consider migration patterns as well as the national population growth factors already mentioned.

Purchasing Power

Population increases mean higher real estate demand only to the degree that the population has purchasing power. One measure of purchasing power is the size of the national labor force. The Bureau of Labor Statistics (BLS) makes long-range predictions in this area. These are based on birthrates, mortality rates, and worker-participation rates, all of which can be estimated from the national census information and other statistical data. According to BLS estimates, the labor force is expected to grow from 1986 through 2000 at an average yearly rate of around 1.4%, slowing from the higher rate of 2.5% per year for the period 1972–1986, when unusually large numbers of both young people and women were entering the work force.

Another important influence on purchasing power is the annual change in the value of the gross domestic product (GDP). A gauge of the strength of our economy, the GDP measures the value of all

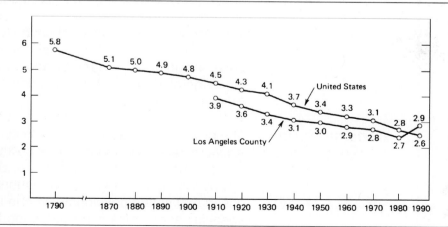

Figure 5.4
Persons per household: United States, 1790–1990; Los Angeles County, 1910–1990. (From Department of Regional Planning, County of Los Angeles)

domestic goods and services produced in the country. After allowances for inflation, the annual variations in the GDP have ranged from a 2% decline to a 9% increase in the years since World War II. Economists estimate that the average annual growth rate of the GDP is between 1.5% and 2.5%, figured in constant dollars (i.e., adjusted for inflation).

Statistics on employment, wage levels, and family income relate even more directly to the purchasing power of the American consumer. These figures allow economists to estimate the amount of money the average family has available to spend after paying taxes. This is often called "disposable income" or "per-capita spendable income." Since the major share of it is spent on living necessities, including housing, disposable income is significant to the potential demand for real estate. Other statistical figures used to study purchasing power include consumer-price-level indexes, land-use and city-growth figures, and industrial-expansion rates. Many economists pay close attention to the relative rates of increase between inflation and disposable income. When disposable income increases faster than inflation, the real estate demand tends to be strong.

Purchasing power is also dependent on the availability of money for mortgage financing, usually arranged by savings and loan associations, banks, or insurance companies. The supply of money is largely dependent on the annual amount of personal savings and the general prosperity of the nation. As we shall see, the supply of money is also greatly affected by the monetary policy of the Federal Reserve System and the fiscal policy of government.

Federal Government Activity

Since real estate is our greatest national resource, the government makes use of programs involving real estate to pursue many of its social and economic goals. The areas of federal government activity that most directly affect privately owned real estate include housing and urban development, environmental protection and energy, monetary policy, and fiscal policy. We shall discuss these programs individually.

Housing and Urban Development Programs

Through the Department of Housing and Urban Development (HUD), the U. S. government encourages low-rent housing and urban renewal projects. By stimulating new construction, the government helps create jobs, trying to attack social and economic problems at the same time. Figure 5.5 is an example of a HUD program.

A number of federal agencies fall within the HUD sphere of influence, including the Federal National Mortgage Association (FNMA), the Federal Housing Administration (FHA), and the Urban Renewal Administration.

Energy and the Environment

The government has vested authority in the Environmental Protection Agency (EPA) to enforce federal pollution standards. The government also attempts to control the quality of air, water, and coastal-zone ecology by the requirement of environmental impact studies for major proposed real estate developments and uses. State and local regulatory agencies sometimes carry out federal mandates in this area through

Figure 5.5
An example of a government housing project. (Photograph courtesy of Doug Frost)

their own elaborate regulatory activities. The Department of Energy was formed by Congress in 1977 to develop and carry out an overall plan to encourage the efficient use of existing energy sources and develop new ones. One of the more direct effects of the program has been felt in the housing industry, where solar-energy systems, electronic pilot lights, and minimum insulation standards were promoted. Income tax credits and preferential loan incentives have also been used in order to increase the demand for energy-efficient homes.

Governmental Banking and Monetary Policy

The Federal Reserve System was established in 1913 as a semi-independent government agency. The function of the Federal Reserve Bank ("The Fed") is to regulate banking and the flow of money and credit. Today, the Federal Reserve System's goals are to stabilize the economy and control inflation, recession, and unemployment. The actions that the Federal Reserve Bank takes are called *monetary policy* actions.

An economic theory called the *monetary theory* holds that the supply of money in circulation influences the level of the economy—too much money leads to rapid expansion and resulting inflation; too little money causes contraction and recession or depression. The Federal Reserve Bank seeks to control the supply of money by buying and selling government securities, changing the discount rate (the interest rate the Federal Reserve Bank charges member banks for loans), and changing the amount of cash reserves that the Federal Reserve Bank requires member banks to hold. Because the Federal Reserve Bank controls the supply of money, this affects the supply of money for financing real estate and changes the cost of money—the interest rate. Changes in interest rates, in turn, change the market price of real estate. High rates tend to depress prices; low rates tend to increase them. The Federal Reserve Bank's Board of Governors and its Open Market Committee are constantly fine-tuning the money supply as they try to maintain a stable economy.

In an indirect way, the regulatory activities of the Federal Deposit Insurance Corporation help to assure the availability of funds at its member banks and thrifts and other covered lenders. FDIC insurance is critical to real estate financing.

Fiscal Policy
Our government also uses its taxation and spending powers to moderate recession, inflation, and unemployment and to further the aims of various social reform programs. In recent years, the annual federal government expenditures have exceeded one trillion dollars, up from $479 billion in 1979. In times of recession, increased government spending and reduced taxation act to stimulate the economy and increase the demand for land, labor, and capital. During periods of inflation, reduced government expenditures and increases in taxes tend to reduce demand, thus reducing the pressure on prices and cooling inflation.

Real estate and business have long been favored areas for government programs designed to stimulate the economy. Home ownership has been encouraged by allowing the mortgage interest and property taxes to be deducted for income tax purposes. Real estate and business investments sometimes benefit from various income tax advantages, including some interest and depreciation deductions for real estate holdings.

The fiscal policy of government works parallel to its monetary policy. For example, the government provides money for private real estate loans (through Federal Reserve money supply actions) besides insuring FHA loans and guaranteeing Veterans Administration (VA) loans. As the state of the economy dictates, our federal government modifies its fiscal policy in well-publicized "tax-reform" acts that have become a familiar part of our economic system. Since the government budget has generally operated at a deficit in recent years, fiscal policy has had inflationary effects, which monetary policy has attempted to counteract completely with varying degrees of success.

In summary, it might be said that our economic environment is increasingly the result of governmental laws, regulations, controls, and policies intended to benefit the general public and to promote social equality. Although economists may disagree on the effects, and therefore the desirability, of such extensive government involvement, it appears that government laws and regulations will continue to shape and reshape our real estate economy.

5.3 THE ECONOMIC PRINCIPLES OF VALUATION

The economic principles of valuation are based on time-tested theories about real estate as both a form of, and a source of, wealth. As a *form* of wealth, real estate competes in the market with other goods and services. As a *source* of wealth, real estate combines with other economic forces and agents to produce income and other amenities for its users. Economic principles define and predict basic market patterns in both the consumption and development of real estate.

The principles of value covered in this section are the foundation for all appraisal methods and procedures. The principles apply collectively; none is independent. However, those that relate to real estate *marketability* help us understand the procedures and methods of the sales comparison and cost approaches. Those principles that relate to real estate *productivity* assist us primarily in understanding the various techniques of the income approach to value. Again, be aware that the principles often interrelate, as do the three value approaches. (See Chapter 3.)

Principles of Real Estate Marketability

Real estate marketability is based on the following principles:

1. Principle of substitution.
2. Principle of conformity.
3. Principles of progression and regression.
4. Principle of change.
5. Principle of supply and demand.
6. Principle of competition.

Principle of Substitution

When a property can be easily replaced by another, the value of such property tends to be set by the cost of acquiring an equally desirable substitute property. A house listed at $250,000 will tend to sell for only $200,000 if there are others with the same amenities available for $200,000 in that neighborhood. On the other hand, this same house might be worth only $185,000 if a similar one could be constructed nearby for that figure (including house and lot) with no unusual delay. Because it is a comparing tool for either market price, cost, or income, the principle of substitution is basic to each of the three approaches to value.

Principle of Conformity

In many markets, maximum value results when properties in a neighborhood are relatively similar in size, style, quality, use, and/or type. This depends primarily on market attitudes but is particularly true in a relatively stable area of average homes. The rule of conformity predicts that a five-bedroom home in a neighborhood of three-bedroom homes, for example, would probably be an overimprovement. This means that its value would be less than if it were in a neighborhood of similar five-bedroom homes.

For high-valued homes or other types of properties, or in a high demand market, much less importance is placed on the conformity of physical features. In some markets, a greater amount of conformity is demanded than in others.

Principles of Progression and Regression

Lower-valued properties generally benefit (increase in value) from close proximity to many properties of higher value. This illustrates the principle of progression. Conversely, higher-valued properties tend to suffer (decrease in value) when placed in close proximity with lower-valued properties, following the principle of regression. The principles of progression and regression, which are related to the principle of conformity, assist us mainly in the analysis of sales in the sales comparison approach.

Principle of Change

Change is eternal. Changes in physical, social, economic, or political conditions constantly modify real estate use and value patterns. As suggested in Chapter 4, economists have a theory that neighborhoods, cities, and nations experience change in four stages, not surprisingly described as development, stability, decline (or old age), and renaissance (or rebirth).

    The appraiser must view real estate and its environment as always in transition. Since important changes might be sudden or gradual, current market conditions cannot always be measured by assuming that past trends will continue unchanged. All things change, even the *rate* of change!

Principle of Supply and Demand

Prices and rent levels increase when demand is greater than supply and tend to decrease when supply exceeds demand. In real estate a strong demand for housing, for example, if coupled with effective purchasing power, can logically lead to a short supply and higher prices. When builders and developers increase production to meet demand, the new supply tends to force prices back to "normal." If severe competition among builders occurs during the shortage, oversupply often results, leading to a weakening of prices. In time, attractively low prices serve to bolster demand until the new supply has been absorbed. Theoretically, when supply and demand are in balance, market prices reflect the cost of production when you include a reasonable profit. As we saw earlier in this chapter, a large number of factors affect the supply and demand of real estate.

Principle of Competition

Market demand generates profits, and profits generate competition. When there is a strong demand for any form of real estate (as in houses, apartments, and commercial or industrial facilities), developers and builders will compete for the profits that are available by constructing new units for sale or rent. Competition usually holds down profits and keeps them stabilized. However, if excess profits are available, "ruinous" competition sometimes leads to oversupply and the collapse of prices.

Principles of Real Estate Productivity

The following principles relate most closely to the productivity of real estate:

1. Agents of production.
2. Principles of surplus productivity, balance, and contribution.

3. Principle of increasing and decreasing returns.

4. Principles of highest and best use and consistent use.

5. Principle of anticipation.

Agents of Production

The benefits produced by real estate come in many forms. These may be intangible amenities, as is true in the case of certain benefits of home ownership, or they may be tangible, as in the case of dollar return on real estate investments. In economic terms, all such benefits are labeled as real estate production. Such production always requires the use of *labor, coordination, capital,* and *land.* These are known as the four agents (or factors) of production. The balance between these factors critically affects the ability of any property to serve the purpose for which it was intended. To understand the potential value of real estate, we must define the four agents of production and understand their economic priorities. (See Figure 5.6.)

Labor includes the cost of all operating expenses and all wages except management. In theory, it has the first claim on all money generated by production. *Coordination,* or management, includes charges for management and entrepreneurial effort. Such services have the second claim on returns of the enterprise. *Capital* includes all construction and equipment costs. Capital charges include return on, and repayment of, such investment monies. Capital charges have the third priority on production returns. *Land* includes the land, minerals, and airspace. Economically, it has the last claim on production revenues. This is why returns to the land are sometimes called "residual," because they refer to the residue remaining after all other claims have

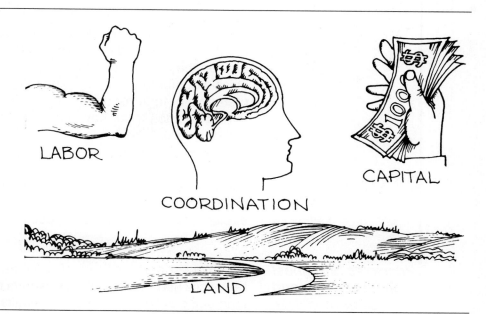

Figure 5.6
The agents of production.

been satisfied. The concept of economic agents of production underlies many of the principles that follow.

Principles of Surplus Productivity, Balance, and Contribution

The net income or other benefits that remain after the cost of labor, coordination, and capital have been satisfied has been described as "residual" returns to land. These same returns are often referred to as the *surplus of productivity.* Since the value of land depends on its own earning power, the dollar amount of this surplus becomes a basis for land value.

According to the *principle of balance,* a proper balance in the agents of production is required if the maximum value is to result from the costs invested. Consistent with the principle of conformity, an overly expensive home built on a low-valued lot in a low-income neighborhood could probably *not* be sold for the full amount invested. A less expensive home is more likely to sell for its full cost and would represent a better investment. In a similar way, the value of any individual agent of production depends, not on its cost, but on how much it contributes to the value of the whole. This is the *principle of contribution.* A swimming pool that adds $10,000 to the value of a home would be said to have a value of $10,000 even if it recently cost $25,000 to build.

The principle of surplus productivity forms the basis for the principle of increasing and decreasing returns and the principle of highest and best use.

Principle of Increasing and Decreasing Returns

It is possible to increase the value and potential income of real estate by adding appropriate improvements. However, there is a theoretical point of balance. Beyond that point, additional expenditures will not result in proportional added value or income. This general rule is important in understanding the economics of development and investment for profit. If a builder can make a 20% profit by developing a small tract of large houses, such a project would be preferred to a larger tract of small houses where only a 15% profit might be made. Even if the larger subdivision promised a greater dollar profit, the higher percentage profit would generally be favored. In actual practice, the investment decision would probably be based on a careful market study and also on the number of other investments available to the builder. The classic illustration of decreasing returns is in farming, where added increments of fertilizer do not result in equal additions to crop yield. After a point, no matter how much fertilizer is added, no added production can be obtained.

Applied to existing properties, the principle of increasing and decreasing returns helps property owners make decisions about adding improvements or remodeling. If the market value of a home can be predicted to increase in proportion to the cost of a bedroom and bath addition, for example, the needed changes can be economically justified.

Principles of Highest and Best Use and Consistent Use

The highest and best use of a property means its most profitable or beneficial use. Such a use represents the theoretical balance between land and building investment. It results in the greatest present value of the land, during the economic life of the improvements or structures. The principle of highest and best use is helpful in the estimation of land value and in making land-development feasibility studies.

In appraisal, the highest and best use usually must be estimated both for the land as if it were vacant and also for the property as improved. Whether the two uses are different or the same will have a major impact on all three value approaches, both as to the data selected and also how they are analyzed.

As a corollary to the principle of highest and best use, the *principle of consistent use* requires that land and improvements be appraised on the basis of the same use. As a matter of economic consistency, it might be improper, for example, to add the "value" of a single-family structure to the value of the lot as if vacant, where the lot in question has an obvious highest and best use as an apartment site.

Principle of Anticipation

Property has value according to its expected or anticipated use, as measured by the benefits that should result from such use. A buyer with full knowledge of "the uses and purposes to which a property may be put" is concerned with future use and not just previous use. The price he or she is willing to pay, then, is said to be equal to the present worth of such future benefits. Some of the benefits may be in the form of intangible amenities—as in the case of home ownership and use—or they may be in the form of tangible benefits such as rental income or capital gain. The principle of anticipation underlies the income approach to value.

SUMMARY

Although real estate is a basic and fundamental form of wealth, it has no intrinsic value. Its market value is a measure of the rights that owners control. Such rights are valued at prices set in the market, but in order to enter the market, the rights must have the four elements of utility, scarcity, demand, and transferability.

Four broad forces maintain, modify, or destroy real estate value. These important forces are physical, social, economic, and political in nature. In their many combinations and forms, these broad forces account for the dynamic nature of real estate value.

National and international events constantly change the social, economic, and political climate of our country. An understanding of real estate and its position in the national economy can help us understand the effect of these events.

We know that real estate is affected by changing business conditions such as employment, income and price levels, production volumes, and building construction costs. Thus it is possible to analyze and better understand real estate by observing key supply and demand factors in the general economy. Economic trends tend to be cyclical in nature.

We have seen that the federal government is heavily involved in areas vital to real estate. These include finance, housing, and urban development, as well as environmental protection and energy.

In this chapter, we also discussed in detail the economic principles that form the basis of most of the methods and procedures we use in appraisal. To summarize here, the principles that relate primarily to the marketability of real estate include the following concepts.

Substitution   The value of any replaceable property tends to equal its cost of replacement. As a tool for comparing market price, cost, or income, this principle underlies all three approaches to value.

Conformity   A reasonable degree of conformity is required for maximum value to result. A serious lack of market conformity in size, style, quality, or use type can be detrimental to value, particularly in single-family residential properties.

Progression and Regression   When a property does not conform in size or quality, its value tends to seek the level of the surrounding properties.

Change   Real estate values are constantly changed by the many social, economic, and political changes that occur in our society.

Supply and Demand   Real estate prices tend to increase when effective demand exceeds supply, and tend to decrease when supply is greater than demand.

Competition   Market demand creates profits, and profits generate competition. In turn, competition decreases profits because new supply tends to overshoot demand.

The valuation principles that relate mainly to the productivity of real estate primarily help the appraiser understand the income approach. We summarize them here:

Agents of Production   All real estate production depends on the use of labor, coordination, capital, and land.

Surplus Productivity, Balance, and Contribution   Income that is available to land after the other economic agents have been paid for is known as the "surplus of productivity." A proper balance of the agents maximizes the income available to land. The value of any agent is determined by its contribution to the whole.

Increasing and Decreasing Returns   Income and other benefits from real estate may be increased by adding capital improvements, but only up to the point of balance in the agents of production. Beyond that point, the increase in value tends to be less than the cost increase.

Highest and Best Use, Consistent Use   The most profitable, likely use of a property is its highest and best use. If the existing use does not qualify in this respect, consistency requires that the appraiser recognize this fact in the method used to value the existing structures.

Anticipation   Value is the present worth of future benefits, whether they be in the form of income or intangible amenities. The principle of anticipation is fundamental to the income approach to value.

Theory is no substitute for practical experience. But neither can any appraiser always expect his or her intuitive knowledge to suggest or recall just the right approach or procedure for every valuation problem. When properly applied, the economic principles can suggest ways to solve the typical problems encountered by the real estate appraiser.

Important Terms and Concepts

Agents of production

Amenity

Cycle, business, and real estate

Demography

Economic forces

Fiscal policy

Gross domestic product (GDP)

Monetary policy

Physical forces

Political forces

Principle of:
   anticipation
   balance
   change

competition
conformity
consistent use
highest and best use
increasing and decreasing
   returns
progression
regression
substitution
supply and demand
surplus productivity

Purchasing power

Scarcity

Social forces

Transferability

Utility

REVIEWING YOUR UNDERSTANDING

1. One of the essential elements of value is:
   (a) Highest and best use
   (b) Transferability
   (c) Location
   (d) Environmental control

2. Which of the following is ineffective without purchasing power?
   (a) Utility
   (b) Supply
   (c) Demand
   (d) Level of wages

3. The broad forces affecting value do *not* include:
   (a) Physical
   (b) Price trend
   (c) Political
   (d) Social

4. Political forces affecting value may include:
   (a) Life-styles and living standards
   (b) Topography
   (c) Education and recreation services
   (d) None of the above

5. The real estate supply factors include:
   (a) Housing supply
   (b) New construction activity
   (c) Both of the above
   (d) None of the above

6. Environmental protection and subdivision reform laws affecting the availability and cost of vacant land include:
   (a) The Federal Clean Air Acts of the early 1970s
   (b) "Open-space" and scenic easement agreements
   (c) Zoning changes to reduce the density of use
   (d) All of the above

7. Areas of government activity that directly affect privately owned real estate include:
   (a) Housing and urban development
   (b) Environmental protection laws
   (c) Monetary and fiscal policy
   (d) All of the above

8. The fiscal policy of government is concerned primarily with:
   (a) Urban development
   (b) Interest rates
   (c) The gross domestic product
   (d) Government spending and taxation

9. The four agents of production do *not* include:
   (a) Land
   (b) Waste
   (c) Coordination
   (d) Labor
   (e) Capital

10. The principle that would prevent an appraiser from appraising a lot for its commercial value and the improvement thereon for residential value is the:
    (a) Principle of increasing and decreasing returns
    (b) Principle of consistent use
    (c) Principle of highest and best use
    (d) Principle of anticipation

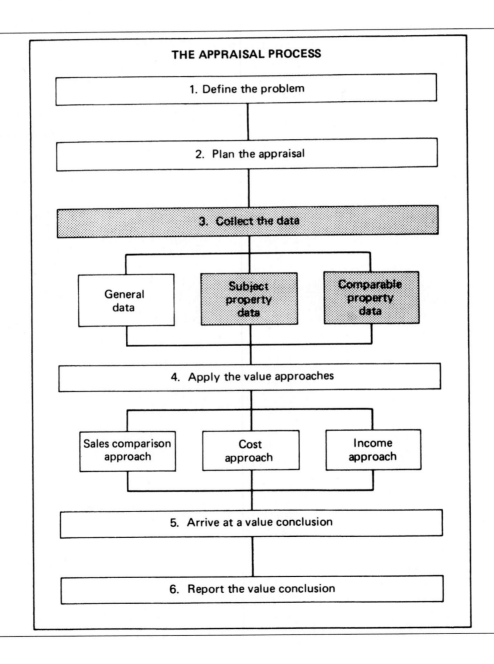

THE APPRAISAL PROCESS

1. Define the problem

2. Plan the appraisal

3. Collect the data

General data | Subject property data | Comparable property data

4. Apply the value approaches

Sales comparison approach | Cost approach | Income approach

5. Arrive at a value conclusion

6. Report the value conclusion

Chapter 6
Property Inspection and Analysis: The Site

Preview   This chapter takes you through the actual site inspection by describing how each step is performed. You will learn how to prepare for the inspection, why a highest and best use analysis is critical to the appraisal, and what categories of site information are the most important in estimating site value. Finally, this chapter shows how to calculate the area of lots and buildings, a skill that is essential in both site and building analysis.

This chapter may be seen as an introduction to the appraisal of the site, which is covered in Chapter 10.

When you have completed this chapter, you should be able to:

1. *List three reasons for making site inspections.*

2. *List the four criteria for highest and best use.*

3. *List the three main categories of site information.*

4. *Calculate the area of a square, rectangle, triangle, trapezoid, and circle.*

6.1 PREPARING TO INSPECT THE SITE

Before performing the site inspection, you should ask yourself two questions: "Why am I inspecting the site?" and "What information do I need to gather?" Answering these questions in advance allows you to plan your site inspection, look for any special site problems, and do a faster and better job.

Reasons for Inspecting and Analyzing the Site

Overall, there are three reasons for inspecting and analyzing the site.

---

1. To estimate the highest and best use.

2. To identify key features.

3. To identify possible legal or physical problems.

Highest and Best Use Estimate

The most important reason for inspecting and analyzing a site is to collect information that you will need in order to estimate the *highest and best use* of the land. Highest and best use is generally defined as:

> that reasonable and probable use that will support the highest present value of the land, as of the date of value of the appraisal.

The importance of highest and best use and techniques for its analysis will be covered in section 6.2.

Before estimating the highest and best use, the appraiser must identify the key features of the property, and then gather other preliminary data.

Identify Key Features

The appraiser should identify and note all of the significant characteristics of the property under appraisal. Although there are many factors to be considered in the site analysis, they may be grouped as follows:

---

1. Physical characteristics.

2. Site location elements.

3. Public and private restrictions.

To be further discussed in Section 6.3, the listed site characteristics are key to its possible uses, and to the selection and adjustment of comparable sales.

Identify Possible Legal or Physical Problems

Another reason for inspecting and analyzing the site is to help identify possible legal or physical problems that may be present. Appraisers are not trained to be experts in every problem that may exist; however, it is helpful to be aware of the most common site problems and to recognize clues to their existence. Any unresolved issues can then be referred to qualified experts for their analysis.

Site problems may be of a legal nature. For example, an apartment building located on land zoned for single-family homes could logically represent either a legal or illegal non-conforming use. The close proximity of a neighboring structure to the property line of the subject could suggest an unauthorized encroachment. As we will see in section 6.3, site problems could also be physical ones such as flood risks, poor soils, or the existence of actual or potential environmental hazards. (See Figure 6.1)

Real estate is subject to many problems that can have a negative effect upon market value. While not expected to be an expert in highly technical problems, the appraiser does have the responsibility of noting in the appraisal report any adverse conditions that are evident or that have been revealed during the appraisal. Estimating the effect of legal or highly technical land problems on market value, however, may not be possible without the advice of a trained specialist. When serious problems are found in the course of an appraisal, the appraiser should notify the client and request that an expert's opinion or study be furnished. If the client is unwilling to supply such a study, the appraiser should clearly note in the report that a specifically described deficiency in knowledge on the part of the appraiser could reduce the reliability of the appraisal.

What Data and Tools are Needed?

It is wise to gather certain basic information about the site before the actual inspection. Having information in advance can make the field work more efficient and can prevent accidentally overlooking an important property detail during the inspection.

Figure 6.1
Identify possible problems. (By Bill Shelly, from *Shopping Center World,* May 1, 1980)

"Gentlemen, I have some bad news about your proposed site."

Sales History of Subject   Industry standards generally require that a sales history and any known current agreement of sale, option, or listing of the subject property be considered and analyzed by the appraiser. Such data may be collected either before or after the site inspection. (Refer to Chapters 8 and 10 for further discussion of this topic.)

Site and Neighborhood Data   Factual information about the site and its environs should be assembled for the inspection. The appraiser should take a plat map or drawing of the site to the field as an aid to the inspection. Such a map should show the location, boundary dimensions, and size and shape of the site. For improved parcels, the location of buildings and structures can be noted and sketched on the map for future reference. When indicated, special flood and geologic maps should also be acquired and taken to the field.

Information on such legal characteristics as ownership, assessed value, zoning, and recorded easements and encumbrances should also be gathered in advance. Knowledge about the availability of utilities is also useful prior to inspection, particularly when a vacant site is being appraised. With such data, a more intelligent site inspection is possible.

Certain data on the neighborhood and city should also be known in advance. Examples include population demographics and the location of schools, churches, and public offices. Appraisers often like to get an overall picture of the site and its surroundings by driving several blocks in each direction around the site to observe nearby shopping areas, major transportation routes, and areas of possible conflicting land uses.

Appraisers may also collect tentative market data prior to making a field inspection. When preliminary facts suggest the highest and best use, advance data could include vacant land sales, improved property sales, and/or market rent comparables. Collecting this information in advance allows comparables to be inspected on the same field trip as the inspection of the subject property. However, collecting the sales in advance is recommended only when the appraiser has a good idea of the type of comparables that will be needed.

Data Sources   The data necessary for site inspection can come from a number of sources. Lenders and other clients often furnish the appraiser with a subject property profile, acquired from a local title company. Such a profile can include a plat map, information on ownership, property taxes, recent sales, recorded easements, and encumbrances of record. Most of this information is also available from city or county assessors' offices. Many appraisers subscribe to data services that provide public information on microfiche or by computer access.

Official zoning information and pending public actions affecting the site may usually be acquired from city or county planning offices; community demographics are available from census reports and chambers of commerce. Information on flood-prone areas is found in the 100-year flood maps produced for FEMA (the Federal Emergency Management Agency) and is available from county engineering departments. Figure 6.2 shows one such map. Geologic and seismic-fault maps are produced by the national and state topographic and geologic agencies. The best place to inspect these maps is at city and county engineering departments, safety offices, or permit bureaus. Information on radon gas and toxic waste is available from the local office of the state or federal Environmental Protection Agency. Other site data may be obtained from the various sources noted in Chapter 8.

Tools and Equipment

Since various tools and equipment are used during the inspection, it is a good idea to accumulate them in advance. Some appraisers use a standard checklist to ensure that they collect all needed information during the inspection. Others use the actual form on which the appraisal is to be presented. The URAR (Uniform Residential Appraisal Report), also known as the Freddie Mac form 70 or Fannie Mae 1004, is an example. A copy of the site description portion of the FHLMC 70 is shown in Figure 6.3. These forms will be discussed later.

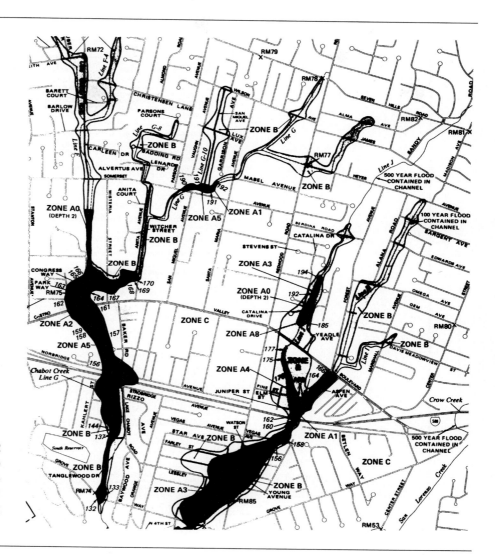

Figure 6.2
Flood map. (Courtesy of the National Flood Insurance Program of the Federal Emergency Management Agency)

KEY TO MAP

500-Year Flood Boundary

100-Year Flood Boundary

Zone Designations

ZONE B

100-Year Flood Boundary

500-Year Flood Boundary

ZONE B

Base Flood Elevation Line
With Elevation In Feet** ~~~~~ *513* ~~~~~

Base Flood Elevation in Feet
Where Uniform Within Zone** (EL 987)

Elevation Reference Mark RM7×

Zone D Boundary

River Mile ●M1.5

**Referenced to the National Geodetic Vertical Datum of 1929

EXPLANATION OF ZONE DESIGNATIONS

ZONE	EXPLANATION
A	Areas of 100-year flood; base flood elevations and flood hazard factors not determined.
A0	Areas of 100-year shallow flooding where depths are between one (1) and three (3) feet; average depths of inundation are shown, but no flood hazard factors are determined.
AH	Areas of 100-year shallow flooding where depths are between one (1) and three (3) feet; base flood elevations are shown, but no flood hazard factors are determined.
A1-A30	Areas of 100-year flood; base flood elevations and flood hazard factors determined.
A99	Areas of 100-year flood to be protected by flood protection system under construction; base flood elevations and flood hazard factors not determined.
B	Areas between limits of the 100-year flood and 500-year flood; or certain areas subject to 100-year flooding with average depths less than one (1) foot or where the contributing drainage area is less than one square mile; or areas protected by levees from the base flood. (Medium shading)
C	Areas of minimal flooding. (No shading)
D	Areas of undetermined, but possible, flood hazards.
V	Areas of 100-year coastal flood with velocity (wave action); base flood elevations and flood hazard factors not determined.
V1-V30	Areas of 100-year coastal flood with velocity (wave action); base flood elevations and flood hazard factors determined.

NOTES TO USER

Certain areas not in the Special Flood Hazard Areas (zones A and V) may be protected by flood control structures.

This map is for use in administering the National Flood Insurance Program; it does not necessarily identify all areas subject to flooding, particularly from local drainage sources of small size, or all planimetric features outside Special Flood Hazard Areas.

Coastal base flood elevations apply only landward of the shoreline shown on this map.

For adjoining map panels, see separately printed Index to Map Panels.

INITIAL IDENTIFICATION:
NOVEMBER 1, 1974

FLOOD HAZARD BOUNDARY MAP REVISIONS:

FLOOD INSURANCE RATE MAP EFFECTIVE:
APRIL 15, 1981

FLOOD INSURANCE RATE MAP REVISIONS:
Map revised February 19, 1986 to change flood plain boundaries, zone designations, base flood elevations, corporate limits, scale, cultural features, or map format.

Map revised **December 17, 1987** to show detailed flooding. Zone AO (Depth 1) and Zone B, from Line A (Zone 2) in the reach downstream of the Western Pacific Railroad to approximately the Southern Pacific Railroad. This added flooding data is not reflected in the revised Alameda County Flood Insurance Study dated February 19, 1986.

Figure 6.2
(continued)

Dimensions	90 x 145.2						Topography	Up, Level pad
Site area	13,068			Corner Lot [X] Yes [?] No			Size	Typical
Specific zoning classification and description	R-1-10; Single Family						Shape	Rectangular
Zoning compliance [X] Legal	[ ] Legal nonconforming (Grandfathered use) [ ] Illegal			[ ] No zoning			Drainage	Appears Adequate
Highest & best use as improved: [X] Present use	[ ] Other use (explain)						View	Minimal

Utilities	Public	Other	Off-site improvements	Type	Public	Private		Landscaping	Average Quality
Electricity	[X]		Street	Asphalt	[X]	[ ]		Driveway Surface	Asphalt
Gas	[X]		Curb/gutter	Concrete	[X]	[ ]		Apparent easements	None
Water	[X]		Sidewalk	None	[ ]	[ ]		FEMA Special Flood Hazard Area [ ] Yes [X] No	
Sanitary sewer	[X]		Street lights	Electric	[X]	[ ]		FEMA Zone ___ Map date ___	
Storm sewer	[X]		Alley	None	[ ]	[ ]		FEMA Map No. Not mapped	

Comments (apparent adverse easements, encroachments, special assessments, slide areas, illegal or legal nonconforming zoning use, etc.): No adverse conditions are present. Site has a steep upslope back yard.

Figure 6.3

Site description section of the Uniform Residential Appraisal Report (URAR, or Freddie Mac form 70/Fannie Mae form 1004).

Here is a list of tools commonly used during the site inspection.

1. Checklist or appraisal form and clipboard.

2. A note pad or small tape recorder; sheets of graph paper for making sketches of the property.

3. A measurement device, such as a reinforced cloth tape (usually 50 or 100 feet long), or a measuring roller, as shown in Figure 6.4. A shorter steel tape may also be useful.

4. An ice pick in a sheath is a common tool in many field kits. It may be used to anchor the end of the tape or to test for possible wood rot.

5. A camera to take photographs of the property either for the report itself or for the appraiser's files.

6. A plat map of the site, as described above; a street map of the area may also be helpful.

In addition to a plat map of the subject site, other kinds of official maps may be helpful in the site inspection. County maps and United States Geological Survey topographical maps are helpful in rural areas. The latter show land contours and other important geographic features. As already mentioned, geologic maps can help you locate earthquake faults and other significant land features, and official flood maps can reveal whether the subject property is located in a flood hazard area.

6.2 HIGHEST AND BEST USE ANALYSIS

Whether land is improved or vacant, its value is economically a function of its highest and best use. As introduced in section 6.1, the highest and best use represents "that reasonable and probable use that will support the highest present value . . . as of the date of value for the

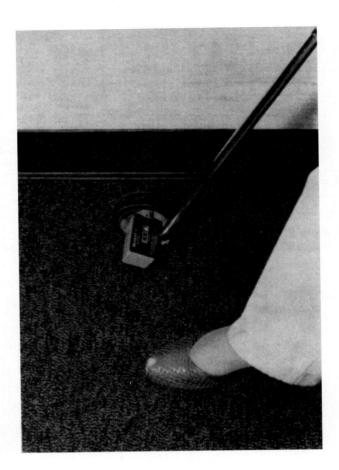

Figure 6.4
Measuring roller. (Photograph courtesy of Doug Frost)

appraisal." Required by the Uniform Standards of Professional Appraisal Practice in all written appraisal reports, an opinion of highest and best use should be based upon a thorough analysis of the property and its environs.

In this section we will cover the purpose, alternative use assumptions, and criteria of highest and best use as it applies to appraisals.

Purpose   An opinion of highest and best use defines the use of the property that will become the basis of both the data collection process and the appraisal methodology. Let us look first at the question of data collection.

The collection of market data in an appraisal relies strongly upon comparability. Because of complex market factors, land often has different values for different potential uses. For example, property zoned for income or commercial use often has a higher value than that zoned for single residential use.

Assume that you are appraising a small commercial building and that you intend to estimate land value in order to apply the **cost** approach to value. Realizing that land may have a different value for different uses, you will understand that the vacant land comparables selected should each have a potential use that agrees with the highest and best use of the subject land. When the market approach is being applied in that same appraisal, the potential use of the underlying land in each improved sale should, for the same reason, be comparable to the land of the subject property. Both examples show the importance of making an analysis of highest and best use *before* the collection of market data.

The question of highest and best use also affects the appraisal methods to be used. For example, the cost approach would not be reliable in the appraisal of a single-family home that has been misplaced on commercial land. In all cases, the highest and best use analysis is critical to the value approach and appraisal method to be emphasized.

Alternative Use Assumptions

The appraiser's opinion of highest and best use must recognize and address two alternative use assumptions:

> 1. The highest and best use of the land *as if vacant.*
>
> 2. The highest and best use *as presently improved.*

The importance of estimating the highest and best use of land *as if vacant* derives from valuation theory. The value of land is presumed to be a function of its potential use, rather than its actual or present use. Most of the economic principles of valuation discussed in the previous chapter are based upon this assumption. The appraiser's estimate of the highest and best use as if vacant requires a consideration of the feasibility and profitability of alternative uses. When the most profitable use is found, such use forms the basis of value for the land.

The appraiser's opinion of the highest and best use of the property *as presently improved* recognizes that the land is committed, at least for now, to the existing use. Existing improvements may contribute to the property value even when they don't represent the land's highest and best use as if vacant. The appraiser should explore alternative uses and management methods that can be used to maximize the benefits, or theoretical return, on the property. Ultimately, the appraiser will suggest the ideal use or occupancy for the property as presently improved. If such use is different from the highest and best use as if vacant, it is often referred to as an *interim* use. To reflect the disadvantage attached to a use that does not represent the highest and best use, the appraiser must then assign an *interim use value* to the improvements based upon their contribution to the total property value.

Highest and Best Use Criteria

The appraiser's opinion of the highest and best use of a property should be based upon a careful consideration of all the physical, legal, and economic factors affecting the land and the property. Here are the commonly accepted tests (or criteria) of highest and best use. To be eligible, the suggested use must be:

1. Physically possible.

2. Legally permissible.

3. Economically feasible.

4. Maximally productive.

A projected use would be *physically possible* or practical if the site's location, access, size, shape, topography, soil type, and other characteristics are amenable to such use. Uses that require a larger or more level site than the subject, for example, can be eliminated from consideration.

A suggested use is *legally permissible* when such use is allowed under present zoning, reasonably expected future zoning, or other entitlement. However, if any required conditional use permit, variance, or environmental approval would likely be denied for a particular use, such use would not qualify.

To be *economically feasible,* a projected use must be viable in terms of cost and economic demand. For example, a suggested use should not involve excessive costs of development, either in terms of money or time required for completion. If the acquisition and development costs promise to exceed the value of the end product, the use would not be economically feasible. In a similar way, a property use projected as the highest and best use must be a use that is needed at that location and a use that would provide a fair return on the investment.

To be *maximally productive,* a use that is suggested must provide more return or income than any alternative use, i.e., the greatest net return that can be attributed to the land. To test this, a number of possible uses are projected and analyzed. In each case, the potential net income should be estimated, then that amount should be reduced by the income required for a fair return on the projected cost of improvements. The particular use that promises the greatest "residual" return to the land would be suggested as the highest and best use.

Feasibility studies and the analysis of highest and best use are further discussed in Chapters 10 and 14 of this text.

6.3 MAJOR CATEGORIES OF SITE INFORMATION

The appraiser should identify and record all significant aspects of a site and its environs. These aspects fall into three main categories. (See Figure 6.5.)

1. Physical characteristics.

2. Site location elements.

3. Public and private restrictions.

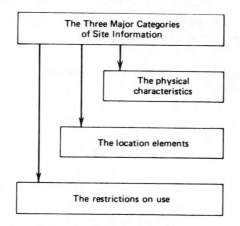

The Three Major Categories
of Site Information

The physical
characteristics

The location elements

Figure 6.5

The restrictions on use

Important Physical Characteristics

The physical features most important to the site's overall utility should be carefully noted in the site inspection. These can be divided into the following five main topics:

1. Size and shape.

2. Topography, soil, and drainage.

3. Form of ownership.

4. Lot type and orientation.

5. On-site and off-site improvements.

Size and Shape

Aside from location, the most important detail of the site is its overall size. The minimum legal size of a parcel generally depends upon its zoning and projected use. However, in most jurisdictions, the size of the lot also determines the size of allowable construction in terms of floor area, and/or the number of residential or commercial units allowed. Thus, lot size greatly influences the site's utility.

The size, or area, of the lot is usually expressed in terms of square feet or acres, although other measurements are sometimes used. If we ever convert to the metric system, appraisers will measure in square meters, or hectares. One hectare is about two and one-half acres. Often, the area of a site is shown on the local assessor's maps. If not, it can be calculated from the dimensions of the property as shown by the maps.

When the size of a parcel limits its utility, the disadvantage may sometimes be overcome. In larger residential-income and commercial properties, two or more small sites are often combined before development to create the desired size parcel. The process is referred to as *assemblage,* or *plottage.* Any increase in unit or square-foot value that results is often referred to as *plottage value.* The subdivision of large acreage parcels into smaller, more marketable parcels is yet another example of changing the size of land parcels to improve the overall utility.

In some cases, the *gross* area of a site is not as important as its *useful* or net area. Depending on topography, shape, zoning, soil type, and so on, some lots may have a useful area considerably smaller than the gross area. Indeed, the useful area could change with different uses. This difference could be great enough to influence the estimate of highest and best use.

Shape is a particularly important characteristic of the site. Shape generally refers to the relationship between the parcel's width and depth. Some lots are too narrow for ideal use, and others are too shallow. Shape can also refer to the configuration of the lot. Property with an ideal shape on a map may be found upon inspection to have features (such as a swamp or a cliff) that alter the shape of the usable area of the parcel, making it less useful. (See Figure 6.6.)

The length of the property's "frontage" should also be recorded. Frontage is the boundary or lot side that faces, or is adjacent to, a street or highway. The amount of frontage often affects the utility and value of a site.

The depth of the parcel is also significant. The projected use of a parcel can determine its ideal dimensions. A deep lot, that is, one that extends far back from the street, may be efficient for one type of use and not for another. When the rear portion of a lot is significantly less useful than the front portion, the lot has what is known as "excess depth."

Figure 6.6
Be sure to check the useful
shape of the lot.

The usefulness of relative depth in a parcel can vary not only from use to use but also from time to time and from community to community. This makes it difficult to accurately evaluate deeper parcels. Over the years, studies have been made to see how lot values vary with depth. Some of these studies have produced *depth tables*. Used primarily for mass appraisal work, depth tables are available for general use. However, since depth tables have usually reflected only one time period, one land use, or one location, their reliability is generally limited by their lack of connection to the particular market under study. Nonetheless, some interesting ideas are presented. One well-known depth table suggests that for the standard depth lot in a particular location, 40% of the value lies in the first one-quarter of the depth, 30% of the value is in the second one-quarter of the depth (making 70% of the value in the first one-half of the depth), 20% for the third one-quarter, and 10% for the last, or back, one-quarter of the depth. If the standard depth in one community is 200 feet and the going market price for lots in this location is $100,000, a lot that is 50 feet deep would be considered to be worth 40% × $100,000, or $40,000. A lot that is 100 feet deep, or one-half of the standard depth, would be considered to be worth 70% (40% + 30%) × $100,000, or $70,000. Of course the type of use projected, minimum lot size and set-back requirements in a particular location are more likely to govern market demand, utility, and relative site value for depth than published tables.

Topography, Soil, and Drainage

After examining the size and shape of the parcel, the appraiser should look at the topography, soil, and drainage of the site. *Topography* (or contour) refers to the surface of the parcel and its particular features. These features may include hills, valleys, creeks, ravines, cliffs, and slopes. Although land with irregular topography is generally more costly to build on, certain features can be assets or liabilities, depending on the use and size of the parcel and the location of roads and utilities. For instance, slopes may command a premium when developed to take advantage of a good view of the surrounding area. However, if they cause problems with providing utilities or gaining access for building materials during construction, slopes can cause substantial value penalties. The pros and cons of any land feature must be carefully evaluated and compared. While looking at the topography of the parcel, the appraiser should also look at the surroundings. What might be an impressive view may be obstructed by a roof or tree on a neighbor's property. Usually, the highest knoll in the area has the greatest value as a homesite because lower knolls may have others looking down on them. Do surrounding parcels pose threats of landslides or rock falls? This too can seriously affect the value of the subject property. View lots are to be further discussed under Lot Type and Orientation section below.

Soil and geology are other important aspects of land utility and value, particularly as these features affect the ability to support structures. A steep slope in rock is more stable than a steep slope in sand. Clays that expand when wet may make construction impossible without expensive footings. Soils may be of such poor composition that deep pilings are necessary, or soil may be too dense or moist for septic tanks to work. Public maps may indicate that the site is situated in a soil liquefaction or earthquake hazard area. Certain geologic factors may preclude *any* building on the site.

A number of environmental factors may also limit building on the site under study. Of most recent concern are areas of high concentrations of either radon or methane gas, and/or proximity to toxic waste sites. Radon and methane are odorless gasses occurring naturally in the soil. Many areas across the country have been found to have dangerously high concentrations of radioactive radon gas, according to standards published by the federal Environmental Protection Agency. In the West, however, methane gasses are more commonly found than radon. Areas with hazardous levels of gasses or toxic wastes are currently being listed or placed under study by local health services and environmental protection agencies.

A feature closely related to topography and geology is water drainage. The topography of land creates its own drainage through natural systems of rainwater runoff, such as valleys, creeks, and rivers. People modify the natural runoff when the land is used or developed. Ideally, this is done by constructing drainage systems such as underground drains, culverts, and lined ditches. When surveying the site, the appraiser must consider how present and future drainage systems will affect the planned use of the site. It may be found that the property is located in a mapped flood plain or flood zone, and that excessive soil erosion could result from uncontrolled water runoff. These and other factors can obviously influence the value of the site.

Form of Ownership

Important site characteristics also involve the form of real estate ownership. The form of ownership refers to the physical and legal form of the parcel. The most common entity is the conventional detached lot, where the site is the entire lot with ownership in fee. Its frontage will be on either a street or a permanent access easement.

A second common form of ownership involves a subdivided lot on which the improvements sit, plus an undivided interest in appurtenant common areas. These common areas may include recreational facilities, parking areas, driveways, walks, lawns, open space, and so on. This second type of ownership or legal entity is known by a number of names. Perhaps the most common of these is the *Planned Unit Development (PUD),* named after the zoning category under which it is often developed. The term *townhouse* is also sometimes applied, named after the townhouse building design style frequently used (see Figure 6.7). In some jurisdictions, this second type of legal entity is referred to as a *condominium,* or "condo." More commonly, the term *condo* is used to refer to the third type of legal entity, to be discussed next.

Condominiums, or *airspace condominiums,* involve the ownership of a defined block of airspace in a building, plus an undivided interest in the common areas. (See Figure 6.8.) The difference between the planned unit development (PUD) type and the airspace condominium is that a PUD is built on a separate wholly owned lot; in a condo-

Figure 6.7
Townhouse. (Photograph courtesy of Doug Frost)

minium, the dwelling is one of a number of units that share one piece of ground. Both the PUD and condominium typically include an undivided interest in common areas, as described earlier. Of course, condominium ownership includes an undivided interest in the structural support and the building systems such as the pipes and drains necessary for the unit to function.

Since both PUDs and condominiums have common areas that are part of the total "site," the appraiser's site inspection should review

Figure 6.8
Airspace condominiums. (Photograph courtesy of Doug Frost)

both the unit site and the common areas as well as the various association agreement documents. The latter may include the current budget as well as the CC&Rs, bylaws, and articles of incorporation.

At one time, lenders and the Federal National Mortgage Association (FNMA) created a special category of PUDs known as a *De Minimus PUD*. Used mainly to qualify certain projects for insured loans, the term described a PUD in which the owner (1) actually owned the fee title to the land; (2) was responsible for maintaining the unit interior and exterior; and (3) was motivated to purchase the unit primarily for housing needs, rather than for recreation benefits or other amenities. In 1990, FNMA eliminated these restrictions and dropped the term from its regulations.

Lot Type and Orientation

Another physical characteristic to consider is the type of lot and its relationship to other lots and streets that surround it. The major types of lots are shown in Figure 6.9. The most common type of lot is the interior lot. This is a lot that "fronts" on only one street. Another common type is the corner lot, which has frontage (and usually access) on two intersecting streets. In the past, corner lots often sold at a premium over interior lots because people with home offices (e.g., doctors and lawyers) needed a separate side entrance for the office. Today, residential corner lots often command a premium because of the easy ac-

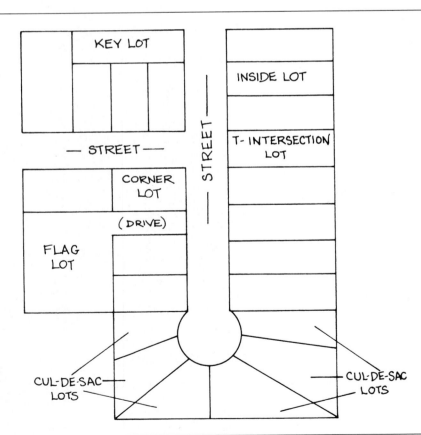

Figure 6.9
Common types of lots.
(Courtesy of the California
Department of Real Estate)

cess to the rear yard. Such access is very desirable in communities that prohibit the parking of mobile homes or trailers on streets or in the front driveways of houses. When residential lots have wide frontages, the corner premium may disappear. Side yards on such lots are sometimes wide enough to allow easy parking for recreational vehicles. However, commercial corner lots nearly always sell for a premium price because of the increased frontage or "showcase" space. In summary, corner premiums today depend on the use of the lot, its location, and its size.

A less common type of lot is the *key lot.* This is a lot that has several other lots backing onto its side yard. A key lot is often considered a less valuable lot than other types because of a loss of privacy.

A cul-de-sac lot is one that is located at the end of a dead-end street. Because most cul-de-sacs are now made with a curved turnaround, the lots taper and have very little street frontage. Although this may make guest parking difficult, the disadvantage is usually counterbalanced by large backyards, extra privacy, and reduced street traffic. Cul-de-sac lots are usually considered especially desirable for family housing because of the large rear play area and the relatively greater traffic safety from reduced auto traffic.

Another type of lot is the *flag lot.* This is a rear lot, behind other houses or lots, with a long narrow access. The lot and access route resemble a flag and flagpole. Flag lots usually have excellent privacy but may be inconvenient for visitors, since street numbers are hard to find. In snow country, the long driveway is a drawback. The flag lot is also less desirable than other lots for people who prefer that their attractive house be visible to the public.

Still another type of lot is the *T-intersection lot,* which is a lot at the end of a T intersection. In some cases, T-intersection lots suffer from the danger of speeding cars failing to turn the corner. However, T-intersection lots seldom sell for a lower price. They may even sell for a premium because the site can be seen from a long distance down the intersecting streets. This is particularly true of commercial parcels.

Just as important as the relationship of the lot to surrounding streets and other lots, is its orientation to sun, wind, climate, views, and surrounding land features. For example, a lot with desirable views of land or sea commands a higher selling price. Generally, water views are worth more than land views.

Views and exposure may depend on whether a lot slopes uphill or downhill from the street access. Upslope lots are generally more expensive to build on than downslope lots and therefore may sell for less if there are no compensating factors.

Orientation to the sun is becoming more important as we consider the utilization of solar energy. For maximum solar efficiency, houses should have the glassed areas facing south and the windowless areas facing north. If the best views are to the north, however, only careful design will produce an energy-efficient house that also benefits from the good view.

The appraiser should check to see if any orientation advantages of an existing house can be considered permanent. New construction on the lot across the street or the growth of vegetation may destroy advantages of view or of sun exposure. Protection is sometimes provided by view easements across adjacent properties, by tract restrictions that require regular tree topping, or simply by the natural topography of the land.

For any site to be utilized, it must have convenient access. Access depends on the type of lot as well as the street and traffic patterns. Lots that are accessible only by circuitous travel routes normally sell for less than competing lots located on more direct routes.

Physical access is also affected by the topography of the area. Access routes in hilly, older neighborhoods or areas with banks, ravines, slopes, and creeks can be so winding and narrow as to block fire trucks or other emergency vehicles. In such neighborhoods, the narrow streets often increase the costs of new construction by limiting space for the delivery of lumber and other materials. (Figure 6.10 humorously notes this problem.)

Some land parcels are completely inaccessible, surrounded by other parcels, and "landlocked." When physical access is sought for a parcel, it is usually necessary to obtain an easement and construct an access road. Access easements can be very expensive to purchase, develop, and maintain.

On-Site and Off-Site Improvements

Improvements to the site represent another important part of the physical characteristics of a site. On-site improvements may consist of earth leveling, grading, filling in, compaction, or excavation. The property may be landscaped with trees, lawns, and shrubs, and may also have a sprinkler or drainage system. In addition, there may be retaining walls or fences, walks, paths, or patios. Because some of these

Figure 6.10
A question of access.

features may eventually be appraised as improvements instead of as land, they must be inspected and noted in the same manner as the main building improvements (to be discussed in Chapter 7).

Adjacent off-site improvements include the width and paving of streets and the presence or absence of curbs, gutters, sidewalks, alleys, street lighting, and parking facilities. Some appraisal books include utilities as part of the off-site improvements. Here utilities are considered as part of the characteristics of that location.

In some states, many of the off-site improvements in new subdivisions are financed by municipal bonds, to be paid off by special assessments imposed on the eventual owners. (California's so-called "Mello-Roos" law provides for such financing.) By this device, land developers are sometimes able to pass the costs of street improvements, utilities, and the like on to future buyers without such costs reflecting in the selling prices. Bonded indebtedness assessments may not only increase annual costs of ownership, but they can also reduce the purchase financing available. Appraisers need to identify and consider the source of funds for off-site improvements in new subdivisions.

Analysis of Site Location Elements

There is a humorous saying that there are three important factors in the value of property: location, location, and location! Analyzing the location of a property can be done in three easy steps, as shown in Figure 6.11. The first is to compare the site to the properties around it. The second is to note the availability of utilities to service the site. The third is to look at the transportation systems or facilities that link this location to the greater metropolitan area.

Comparison with Neighborhood Properties

In the analysis of the site, it is important to see how the site conforms to the average site characteristics in the neighborhood. Whatever the size, shape, topography, and overall utility of the property being appraised, it must be put into the scale of those characteristics in its own

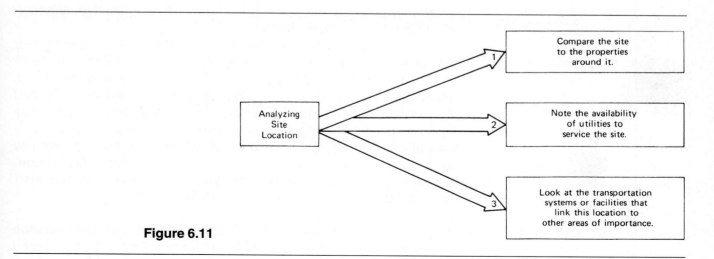

Figure 6.11

neighborhood. A one-acre site, for example, may pose a special appraisal problem when surrounded by standard-sized city lots.

Consider the impact of the neighboring properties on the value of the subject property. How are they maintained, judging by the standards of the neighborhood? Is there evidence of renovation or remodeling? Does the immediate area have a history of high, average, or low crime rates or of family or civic disturbances? Obviously, you must also consider whether the past record may be changing.

When comparing the site to neighborhood properties, you should note whether there are nearby properties with conflicting uses. Are neighboring properties being used in such a way that they will interfere with the usefulness of the subject property? Use conflicts may result from unwanted noise, odors, or other negative characteristics referred to above. Next, note the property's amount of privacy. Privacy may be measured simplistically by what other people hear or see of you and by what you hear or see of them. However, the standards of the local market will judge its importance. In some markets, privacy is more highly valued than in others.

Utilities   The availability of utilities is the second element to consider in rating location. Cost, restrictions on service, reliability, and the sources of each utility are all pertinent considerations. This review should focus not only on water supply, trash collection, and electricity service, but also on telephone, cable TV, natural gas, or propane service. Provisions for either septic tank systems or public sewers, as well as storm runoff systems, should be carefully noted.

The absence of municipal water supply in an area would suggest a reliance on private wells. Observing the location of existing wells will give you an idea of the chances of drilling a successful well on the subject property. Similarly, the absence of city sewer lines may mean that a sewer line extension is needed or that a septic tank and drainfield must be installed before development can occur. The appraiser usually cannot tell with certainty whether septic tanks will be permitted unless an official percolation test has been performed and the site is large enough for any required drainfield. However, a check of public records for such permits issued nearby might be indicative, although certainly not conclusive evidence.

Since the services provided by utility companies are available over wide areas, the appraiser may not need to research utility company information for each and every appraisal assignment. It is worth noting, however, that many assignments include land parcels that are located beyond municipal boundaries, where the availability or cost of utility services must be thoroughly investigated. When utility services are inadequate or absent, the possible cost of providing the required new services has a direct impact on land value, and therefore must be considered in the rating of site location. Vacant sites are often considerably more difficult to analyze than improved parcels.

Transportation   The third element of site location is transportation and transportation access. In modern living, any site has value only if it can be connected to other sites where we live, work, shop, and play. Generally, the poorer the transportation and accessibility, the lower the value of the property. When reviewing transportation, the appraiser should be sure to consider both public and private systems. With public transportation, check to see how close the property is located to public transportation systems and loading points. How well does the local system connect to the main travel points? Find out the cost of fares, the frequency of schedules, and the travel time between the property and the places to which users of this property might travel.

The appraiser's concern for transportation services differs depending on the type of property under appraisal. With a residential site, for example, you should check the availability, cost, and convenience of the public transportation system for commuting and shopping. When appraising a commercial location, on the other hand, the concern is for midday shopping travel, easy access to working people, and access to those transferring between different transportation routes or lines.

In the review of private transportation, there are other things to consider. How close is the subject property to freeways or arterial streets? How convenient is it to get on and off the freeway or throughway from this property? Is it convenient from both directions? Consider the time of travel and direction of travel the users of this property are likely to take. It should vary, depending on the peak traffic hours and the destination of the commuters.

Public and Private Restrictions

Nothing can be more important than understanding the public and private restrictions on the use of property. As detailed in Chapter 2, such restrictions have a notable impact on value because they help to determine the highest and best use. To be able to compare properties and judge the feasibility of different uses, the appraiser's analysis of the site must therefore include an investigation of public and private restrictions.

Public Restrictions

There are many categories of public restrictions, and the importance of these restrictions is increasing. Public restrictions include community master plans and regional plans that control land use and development. Importantly, these plans usually control the content of zoning ordinances.

Common zoning regulations cover permitted uses, the density or intensity of use, setback or yard requirements, height restrictions, and parking requirements. Among such controls, use density seems to play the most familiar role in land development. Typical zoning regulations, for example, classify residential land in categories such as R-1, R-2, R-3, etc., and allow development in each category according to the square-foot land requirements for each residential unit to be built. On standard-sized lots, R-1 land generally allows only single-family homes; R-2 and R-3 zoned land may permit or allow two or more units on such lots, with additional units allowed on larger sites. Residential-income and commercial zoning usually include parking requirements that vary with the size, number, and type of units. Parking requirements often combine with the coverage requirements in a way that further restricts the size of the project that can be built on any given lot or site.

Requirements for obtaining variances from zoning restrictions will differ by jurisdiction. However, variances are typically granted only where the strict application of the zoning ordinance deprives a property of privileges that are enjoyed by nearby properties. Zoning regulations will also vary in how they handle a *nonconforming use.* This term refers to a use that is not allowed under the current zoning, but one that was legal on this site before the current ordinance was adopted. The appraiser should be familiar with zoning laws, and be alert to their impact on property values.

Subdivision laws also restrict the development and use of real estate. State and local requirements for subdivision maps, off-site improvements, utilities, and public reports generally depend on the proposed use, the size and number of lots, and whether the new parcels will be offered for sale. Subdivision requirements are particularly important in the appraisal of vacant or under-improved land, as they greatly affect its highest and best use and value.

Building and safety regulations represent another category of public restriction. The housing, building, plumbing, and electrical codes are examples. Because such codes differ from place to place, there can be circumstances in which a particular type of construction is economically feasible in one town and not in an adjacent town. As we have seen, such factors as soil type, local geology, and proximity to earthquake faults can also affect the feasibility and type of construction for a site.

Another type of public limit on the use of property arises when the rights of access to a property are restricted. A common example is when access rights alongside a freeway are purchased and extinguished. Adjacent lands must then rely on other access routes. Sometimes, access restrictions simply limit the location of driveways, which often restrict the use and value of the property particularly when applied to commercial land. Gas stations and drive-in restaurants are prime examples of properties needing driveway access that may be unavailable for such reasons as the proximity of freeway ramps.

In the current era of environmental protection and concern, many new types of governmental restrictions are important in the analysis of vacant land. State and federal laws require that special studies (e.g., *environmental impact reports,* or *EIRs*) precede certain types of new development. Studies are also required where potential or actual environmental hazards exist. Examples of listed hazards include toxic wastes, methane or radon gas, and abandoned munitions.

Local ordinances, also designed to protect or to preserve the environment, may include moratoriums on new water or sewer hookup permits. This can mean that construction is prohibited until problems with water supply or the quality or capacity of water or sewer treatment plants can be resolved. In some "slow-growth" areas, there is an increasing tendency to ration building permits in ways that can temporarily prohibit development, even in the case of subdivided land.

Federal flood zones can also severely affect the ability to use property. In other cases, however, several feet of relatively inexpensive fill can serve to flood-proof the property and restore the land's usefulness. Still another public restriction results from state or local geologic hazard zones. These include earthquake fault-rupture zones, areas where soils are likely to liquefy in the event of an earthquake, or areas where an earthquake could generate a tsunami (earthquake sea or tidal wave) that could endanger property. Building restrictions in such areas can vary from a total banning of development, to moderate increases in structural strength requirements. Whatever the type or reason, public land-use restrictions can seriously impact the value of land.

Property Taxes

As a form of public restriction on the use of land, property taxes deserve special attention here, as they can often notably affect the value of a site.

Historically, property taxes in this country have been based upon an *ad valorem,* or according to value, formula. In theory, this makes the tax burden proportional to the benefits received. However, in some states, including California (via the well-known "Prop. 13"), a public revolt against county and municipal spending practices led, in the late 1970s, to drastic assessment "reforms." Under California law, property assessments are now based *not* upon current market value, but on historic value. A 2% maximum annual increase is allowed for change in the consumer price index. Reassessments at market value are allowed only with (1) change of ownership, (2) a new long-term lease agreement, or (3) new construction. Because of the inequities between the tax burden of the newly acquired properties and those that have remained in the same ownership for a number of years, some lawmakers are now suggesting remedial reforms.

Besides ad valorem taxes, direct (or "special") assessments also affect the total tax burden, and therefore the market value of land. Often collected with regular property taxes, direct assessments are increasingly imposed by local government entities to replace revenue lost to ad valorem tax limits. Municipal street lighting, water supply systems, sewage treatment plants, and public landfills may be financed by special assessments, as can flood and water runoff control services. As mentioned in our earlier discussion of off-site improvements, direct assessments are sometimes imposed to reimburse developers of new subdivisions for the cost of streets, curbs, and utilities. If two properties are otherwise equal but one has a large annual special tax assessment to pay, it is logical that the one without the assessment would sell at a higher price.

Property tax exemptions and preferential tax laws make the analysis of tax burden even more complex. Certain religious and charitable exemptions have long shielded some properties from property taxation. Now, many laws provide reduced assessments to certain lands restricted to agriculture or recreational use, and also to land set aside as scenic corridors.

For the reasons cited above, the existing taxes on a property are not a good indication of the future tax burden for the property. The appraiser should become familiar with local property tax laws and practices and consider their effect on property value from one location to another.

Finally, another tax that is levied on property is the property transfer tax. At one time, this was a federal tax, collected from revenue stamps placed on various types of deeds, and called a documentary tax. Transfer taxes are now imposed by local jurisdictions. The most common transfer tax is at the rate of $0.55 per $500 of cash consideration. In the usual ordinance, assumed trust deeds or mortgages are not included in the calculation of tax, whereas new mortgages and equity cash payments are considered. A number of cities are increasing transfer tax rates to raise revenues in support of local services.

Private Restrictions

Private restrictions take many forms, ranging from simple deed restrictions to complex agreements between groups of owners. The most simple deed restriction may specify the minimum size of structures. For example, in a residential subdivision, houses may be required to have a certain minimum-sized living area. Some older deed restrictions prohibited the sale of alcoholic beverages. There are deed restrictions that forbid commercial use of the property and some that restrict the property to only commercial or industrial uses. Restrictions against race, color, religion, sex, handicap, marital or familial status, age, or national origin are generally prohibited by law.

The most complex private restrictions include those typical of planned unit developments and condominiums. These are known as *association* or community agreements. Here each property is part of a larger group of parcels and is bound by the "Conditions, Covenants, and Restrictions" that apply to all properties within that association. Such agreements may mandate paint colors, degree of maintenance, type of landscaping, type of shades, awnings, and drapes, and so on. Association restrictions should be reviewed by the appraiser and discussed with the community association manager before a judgment is to be made as to their effect on the value of the property.

Another type of possible restriction is a public or private easement. Easements can include utility easements for underground gas or water lines, or for power and telephone lines or poles. Air and light easements are also common. There could be drainage easements that allow water to flow from a nearby property onto the property being appraised, flood easements that allow the federal government to flood portions of the property from time to time, or aviation easements that allow aircraft to fly low over the parcel while using a nearby airport. Figure 6.12 shows a typical private road and utility easement. Clearly, such easements have some impact on the use of the property and its value.

Leases are another example of private restrictions. Depending on the length of the lease, the rent to be paid, and other terms, the impact on property use and value can be significant. Appraisals made of a property which is subject to an existing lease must consider all landlord and tenant covenants that affect the benefits received by the owner. This topic will be discussed further in Chapter 17.

As this section suggests, there are a large number of factors that can influence the value of a site. The appraiser seeks to be aware of them in order to properly consider those that are significant to the value of the property being appraised.

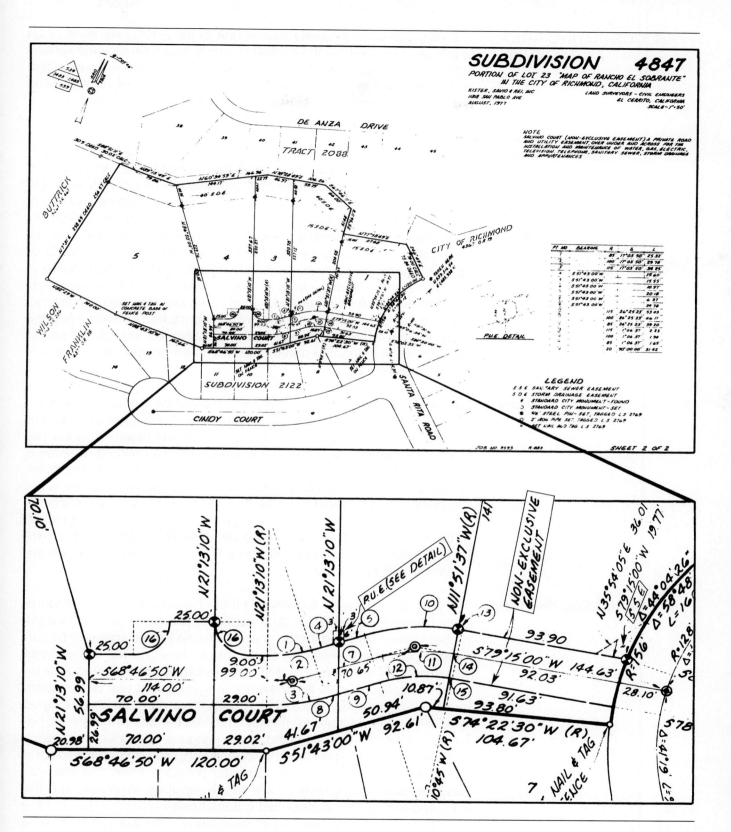

Figure 6.12
An example of a private road and utility easement.

6.4 COMPUTING AREA AND VOLUME

The ability to do basic arithmetic is one of the necessary skills of an appraiser. This section demonstrates how to make simple calculations that assist the appraiser in estimating lot and house areas, room sizes, and surface areas of walls as well as measurements of volume. Area and volume measurements are often important in the sales comparison approach and also in the cost and income approaches to value.

Definition of Terms

Area

The *area* is the space or the size of an object on a flat surface. A surface or plane has no more than two dimensions of measurement. The area of an object is calculated as the product of multiplying its length and width. In real estate, circumstances calling for the calculation of area include finding the area of a lot or parcel of land, typically measured in square feet or acres of land area. In larger land parcels, area could be described in sections (as discussed in Chapter 2) or even in square miles. Area is also calculated to find the floor space in a building or the surface area of the roof cover (which, on a sloping roof, will be greater than the floor area of the building the roof covers). In some cases, you may need to know the kitchen counter area; the areas of individual rooms, garages, and finished versus unfinished basements; the sleeping porch area; the average area per apartment unit; and so on.

Volume

The *volume* relates to size in three dimensions, that is, to the measurement of the content of a certain space within a three-dimensional object. The most common example in real estate appraisal is the calculation of the airspace, or cubic volume, within a building. Volume is sometimes used in estimating construction costs. One can see, for example, that in calculating the cost of a silo or a grain storage elevator, the cubic volume would be a helpful measure for cost calculations. Some complicated building code regulations also require calculation of the room volume in order to compare the volume with the square feet of usable window area. However, this is a calculation that an appraiser would not normally do.

Computing the Area

The calculation of area requires (1) that only one system of measurement be used (all in feet, or all in yards, for example), and (2) that the proper formula be used for the shape or figure whose area is to be calculated. The importance of a single measurement scale is that if one dimension is given in feet and another in yards, the two cannot be directly multiplied to give an answer either in square feet or in square yards. Consequently, the measurement in yards must be translated into feet, or the measurement in feet must be translated into yards, before the area can be calculated. If the distance and direction of each perimeter line of a figure are known, one very modern method to compute area is with a surveyor's computer program. Here, the line "values" (distance and direction) are simply input as variables, and the area and/or diagram is produced automatically.

The most common method of computing the square-foot or acre size of a figure is to prepare a scale drawing with a ruler or straight-edge and calculate the area based on dimensions and shape. Following are the formulas for calculating some of the more common figures or shapes that an appraiser might encounter. These include the square, the rectangle, the triangle, the trapezoid, and the circle. The formulas for other types of figures are not used as often. If needed, they can be located in a geometry text or mathematical reference book. An alternative is to have a surveyor calculate the area or to use a survey computer program.

The Square

A *square* is defined as a closed figure with four equal sides and four right angles. A right angle is one-fourth of a full circle. The formula for the area of a square is as follows ("length" refers to the length of a side):

$$\text{Area of a square} = \text{length}^2 \text{ (or length} \times \text{length)}$$

The concept of multiplying a number times itself is called the square of the number. Thus we could say that the area of a square equals the length squared. Let us calculate the area of a lot that is square in shape, with four equal sides and four right angles, having a street frontage of 100 feet and a depth of 100 feet. By using the given formula, the area can be found to be 100×100, or 10,000 square feet.

The Rectangle

A *rectangle* is defined as a closed four-sided figure with four right angles, with its opposite sides equal and parallel. The formula for the area of a rectangle is

$$\text{Rectangle area} = \text{width} \times \text{length}$$

Thus the area of a lot with a street frontage of 75 feet and a depth of 100 feet would be 75×100, or 7,500 square feet. Notice that a square is a special type of rectangle, and its area is the same using either formula.

The Triangle

A *triangle* is defined as any closed figure with three sides. We could create a triangle by first drawing a square and then connecting any two opposite corners with a diagonal line. This allows us to see that the two triangles created must have the same total area as the area of the square. The formula for the area of a triangle is as follows:

$$\text{Triangle area} = \text{height} \times \text{base} \times \tfrac{1}{2}$$

In calculating the area of a triangle, be sure to determine the base and the height. By convention, the base is taken as the lower or bottom line of the triangle; however, any of the three sides can be used as the base if it makes calculation easier. Height is defined as the length of the line that is perpendicular to (i.e., at right angles to) the base line, and connecting the base line with the opposite point of the triangle. See the examples shown in Figure 6.13.

The appraiser will find a variety of situations in which the formula for the area of a triangle can be used. The most common use is in calcu-

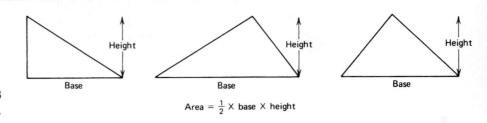

Figure 6.13
Examples of triangles.

Area = $\frac{1}{2}$ × base × height

lating the area of a lot that is wider at the rear than at the front (or vice versa). Such lots are common at the end of cul-de-sac streets. The area of such lots can be calculated by dividing the lot into a series of rectangles and triangles. The area of each rectangle or triangle is calculated. If necessary, missing dimensions can be scaled on a map. The areas of the several rectangles and triangles are then totaled to give the area of the total parcel. This method is not as accurate as the calculations performed by surveyors or by modern computer survey programs but is adequate for most appraisal purposes if more accurate calculations are not available.

The Trapezoid

The *trapezoid* is defined as a closed four-sided figure that has two parallel sides. The two other sides are usually not parallel. From what you have already studied, a little doodling will show you that it is possible to calculate the area of a trapezoid by breaking the figure up into a rectangle and one or two triangles, calculating the area of each, and adding the areas together. However, it is quicker to use the formula for the area of a trapezoid because it takes fewer calculations. The formula for the area of a trapezoid is

$$\text{Trapezoid area} = \frac{(\text{side 1} + \text{side 2}) \times \text{height}}{2}$$

In this formula, the two sides mentioned are the two parallel sides. The height is the perpendicular distance between them, just as in the formula for a triangle (see Figure 6.14). In a common real estate example, you might need to calculate the area of a lot that had a street frontage of 100 feet. Both sidelines go back at right angles to the street, with one sideline being 110 feet deep and the other 130 feet deep. The rear line, as you can see from the following drawing of the lot (Figure 6.15), slants at a diagonal to the street, making the lot

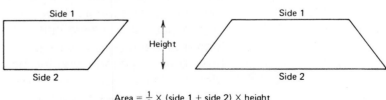

Figure 6.14
The area of a trapezoid.

Area = $\frac{1}{2}$ × (side 1 + side 2) × height

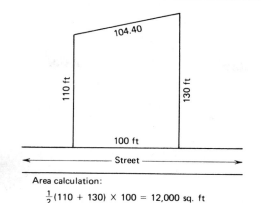

Figure 6.15
Example of a trapezoid-shaped lot.

Area calculation:
$\frac{1}{2}$(110 + 130) × 100 = 12,000 sq. ft

deeper in one corner. This lot is in the shape of a trapezoid. The height (the perpendicular distance between the sides) is the 100-foot frontage on the street. The area would be ½ (110 + 130) × 100 = 12,000 square feet. Lots that are somewhat trapezoidal are common, so this formula is one that appraisers often use.

The Circle

The *circle* is defined as a curved line that forms a closed figure which has a center that is of equal distance from all points on the curved line. A straight line joining two points on the circle and passing through the center is called the *diameter*. A straight line joining the center point to one point on the curve is called the *radius* of the circle and is, of course, one-half of the length of the diameter. The distance around the circle is called the *circumference*. The formula for the area of a circle is

Circle area = pi × radius² (or pi × radius × radius)

This calculation involves a new feature: the constant *pi*. A *constant* is something that has the same number value at all times. The value of pi is 3.1416+. Whenever you calculate the area of a circle, whether large or small, pi will always be the same, 3.1416. It should be remembered that a number squared means that the number is multiplied by itself. A circle is shown in Figure 6.16.

If the appraiser is seeking to calculate the area of a house built as a geodesic dome and finds that the distance across the house from one outside wall to the opposite outside wall is 100 feet, then the area of the structure would be 50 × 50 × 3.1416 = 7,854 square feet—a substantial floor space! The formula for the area of a circle is useful not only under rare circumstances when you are appraising a geodesic dome but also for homes that have half-circle bay windows. In this case, the area of the bay window would be one-half of the area of the circle. Similarly, there can be round swimming pools, round gazebos, round commercial buildings, and even half-circle sections of lots where the appraiser can use the formula for the area of a circle.

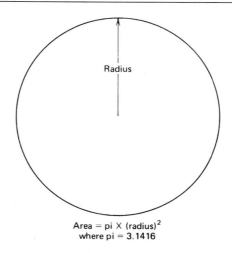

Figure 6.16
The area of a circle.

Area = pi × (radius)^2
where pi = 3.1416

Using Area Formulas

However irregular or unusual the shape of the object, the same procedure is used to calculate its area. The first step is to prepare a scale diagram of the shape of the object. This might be taken from existing drawings or maps or might require measuring the object itself. The second step is to analyze the figure that is before you and decide how it can be broken down into a series of regular geometric shapes such as rectangles, triangles, trapezoids, half-circles, and so on. The third step is to determine the dimensions of each of the subdivided shapes. This may require scaling the known distances on the map and using this calculation to estimate the length of unknown distances or lines. In some cases, it is also possible, using formulas in geometry books, to calculate some unknown distances from others that are known. The fourth step is to compute the area of each of the geometric shapes that were developed. The final step is to total the areas of each of the shapes. A practical example of this process is shown in Example 6.1.

Example 6.1 Using Area Formulas

Steps

1. Prepare a scale diagram.

2. Decide how to break it down.

3. Determine the dimensions.

4. Compute the area of each shape.

5. Total the areas of each shape.

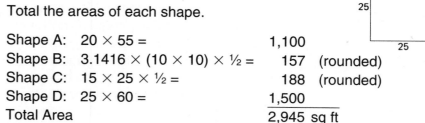

Shape A:	20 × 55 =	1,100
Shape B:	3.1416 × (10 × 10) × ½ =	157 (rounded)
Shape C:	15 × 25 × ½ =	188 (rounded)
Shape D:	25 × 60 =	1,500
Total Area		2,945 sq ft

Computing Volume Volume is calculated by multiplying the three dimensions of an object. All three must be the same scale, that is, they must all be measured in feet, all in yards, or all in inches. The formula for calculating volume is as follows:

$$\text{Volume} = \text{area} \times \text{average height}$$

The use of this formula requires that the area be calculated first. Once the area is calculated, it is multiplied by the average height. In a building with flat ceilings or a flat roof, the average height would not be hard to determine. With pitched or sloping ceilings, however, the average height (the average of the lowest and highest height) must be calculated. In multiple-story buildings, the average height is calculated using the distance from the floor level to the next floor level up. For an example of the use of volume calculations in real estate appraisal, assume you are appraising a single-family residence with a living area of 2,340 square feet. The ceiling height is 10 feet including the ceiling joist and roof structure. You are using a cost manual that reports building costs only in the cost per cubic foot and, for your building, the cost per cubic foot is $7.00. You calculate the cubic volume of the structure to be $2,340 \times 10 = 23,400$ cubic feet and multiply it by $7.00 to estimate its replacement cost new of $163,800. The use of cubic costs is less common now than it once was, so the calculation of volume is of less practical use today than earlier.

SUMMARY

The actual site inspection is one of the most important parts of the entire appraisal process. Therefore, the inspection should be planned well in advance.

The three major reasons for inspecting the property are:

1. To estimate the highest and best use of the site. The highest and best use generally means the legal and feasible use that will support the highest land value. The use must be physically possible, legally permissible, economically feasible, and maximally productive. The value of a property will vary depending on its uses. An estimate of highest and best use is required in almost all written appraisals, by the Uniform Standards of Professional Appraisal Practice.

2. To identify the key site features. These may be grouped as physical characteristics, site location elements, and public and private restrictions.

3. To identify possible problems. Although you may not be experienced in all the areas in which a problem can exist, there are potential legal and physical problems to be noted.

It is desirable to have certain kinds of information before the actual site inspection begins. Data on the size and shape of the parcel, its legal characteristics, and the availability of utilities generally should be known beforehand. Information on comparable properties may also be useful. With this information, the site and comparables can be inspected on the same field trip.

The tools and equipment necessary to perform the inspection were then outlined. Many appraisers use a checklist during the actual inspection to make certain that they gather all the necessary information.

A great variety of information about the site and its surroundings can be noted during the inspection. This information is divided into three categories:

---

1. The physical characteristics of the site.

2. The locational features of the site.

3. Public and private restrictions on the use of the site.

During the inspection, the appraiser should first investigate the physical characteristics of the site, which include the size, shape, and frontage of the site, and the depth. The topography, soil, and drainage of the site are also important. Land with irregular topography may be more costly to build on but may contain advantageous features such as a sweeping view. Is the soil of good quality? Will it support the uses being considered for this site? The type of water drainage systems, whether they are man-made or natural, should also be inspected.

Physical characteristics also include the form of ownership, type of lot, its orientation, and physical access. There are several forms of ownership, ranging from the conventional detached lot, to the planned unit development (PUD), to the airspace condominium. The conventional detached lot is a site that is the entire lot. The PUD is a site that involves ownership of a subdivided lot on which the owner's unit is built, plus an undivided interest in the common areas. A condominium unit includes the fee ownership of a block of airspace (within which the unit sits), plus an undivided ownership in the common areas and the building's supporting walls.

There are a variety of lot types that you should be familiar with. These include the key lot, the cul-de-sac lot, and the flag lot. It is also important to note the lot's orientation to the sun, climate, and view. In recent years, utilization of the sun's energy has become more important.

The property must also be reasonably accessible. Properties situated in areas less accessible to large emergency vehicles, such as fire trucks, could face a reduction in value.

The improvements made to the site or on areas surrounding it should also be examined. Such improvements include landscaping, grading, excavation, and the width and paving of streets and sidewalks.

The second category of information to note during the site inspection is the location of the site. Analyzing the location involves three steps:

1. Compare the site to the properties around it.

2. Note the availability of utilities.

3. Examine the transportation systems that connect the site to nearby shopping and jobs.

The third category of information to consider during the site inspection includes public and private restrictions. Public restrictions are becoming more complicated and influential in our sophisticated society. Examples include zoning regulations, building and safety code regulations, and health and environmental protection laws. Another form of public restriction is the property tax. Property taxes are a burden on property, reducing the profitability of any use. While property taxes were historically imposed according to value, state and local laws and practices now vary as to the basis. Related to the property tax are taxes collected by special assessment districts. Such taxes are used to pay for a particular public improvement such as street lighting. Special assessments are generally based on the benefits that the project provides to the properties in the district.

A variety of private restrictions can affect the property's use. These range from simple deed restrictions to complex agreements between owners, as found in condominiums and in planned unit development projects.

Since public and private restrictions have a direct influence on the use and value of real estate, it is important that they be carefully considered during the site inspection and analysis.

In section 6.4, we discussed the importance of having some basic arithmetic skills. These mathematical skills are required throughout the appraisal process in measuring the area of lots, building floor areas or volumes, and so on.

Some buildings and lots have very irregular shapes so that calculating their areas may seem impossible. However, complex shapes can usually be broken into simple squares, rectangles, triangles, trapezoids, and circles (or half-circles). The area of each of these shapes is easily calculated using the proper formula.

The volume, or cubic area, of a building can also be easily calculated by a formula. Such a volume calculation is sometimes used in the cost approach.

Important Terms and Concepts

Access

Area

Assemblage

Association agreement

Condominium

Corner lot

Cul-de-sac lot

Depth

Easement

Environmental impact report (EIR)

Flood map

Form of ownership

Frontage

Highest and best use

Interior lot

Location

Lot orientation

Lot shape

Methane gas

Off-site improvements

Planned Unit Development
  (PUD)

Plottage

Plottage value

Private restrictions

Public restrictions

Radon gas

Site features

Site improvements

Topography

Toxic waste

Transportation

Utilities

Volume

REVIEWING YOUR UNDERSTANDING

1. Before performing the site inspection you should:
    (a) Gather basic information about the site
    (b) Be sure you know the reasons for the site inspection
    (c) Have a map or drawing of the site
    (d) All of the above

2. The first important reason for inspecting and analyzing the site is to:
    (a) Estimate the highest and best use
    (b) Note any unusual characteristics
    (c) Find comparable sales
    (d) None of the above

3. An appraiser should identify and record the physical characteristics, the public and private restrictions, and the locational elements of a site. Which of the following is considered an aspect of location?
    (a) Topography
    (b) Neighborhood conformity
    (c) Deed restrictions
    (d) Size and shape

4. Which best describes the site in a planned unit development?
    (a) Subdivided lot plus appurtenant interest in the common areas
    (b) Defined block of airspace, plus an undivided interest in the common areas
    (c) Townhouse
    (d) None of the above

5. The criteria that define the highest and best use include all of the following *except:*
    (a) The use must be physically possible

(b) The use must be legally permissible and economically feasible
(c) The use must be low density
(d) The use must be maximally productive

6. Public restrictions on the use of land include all the following *except:*
   (a) Zoning regulations
   (b) Deed restrictions
   (c) Subdivision laws
   (d) Environmental protection laws

7. The appraiser's opinion of highest and best use should include:
   (a) The highest and best use as if vacant
   (b) The highest and best use as presently improved
   (c) Both a and b above
   (d) None of the above

8. A key lot is:
   (a) A lot that is shaped like a key
   (b) A lot that has several other lots backing onto its side yard
   (c) A lot that is located at the end of a dead-end street
   (d) None of the above

9. What is plottage value?
   (a) The value of land between the subject property and another property
   (b) The increase in value that may be obtained from combining parcels
   (c) The price of land per plot
   (d) The depth divided by the frontage

10. The formula for the area of a trapezoid is:
    (a) $\dfrac{(\text{side 1} + \text{side 2}) \times \text{height}}{2}$
    (b) $\dfrac{(\text{side 1} + \text{side 3}) \times \text{height}}{3}$
    (c) $(\text{side 1} + \text{side 2}) \times \text{height}$
    (d) $\dfrac{(\text{side 1} + \text{side 2}) \times \text{height}}{4}$

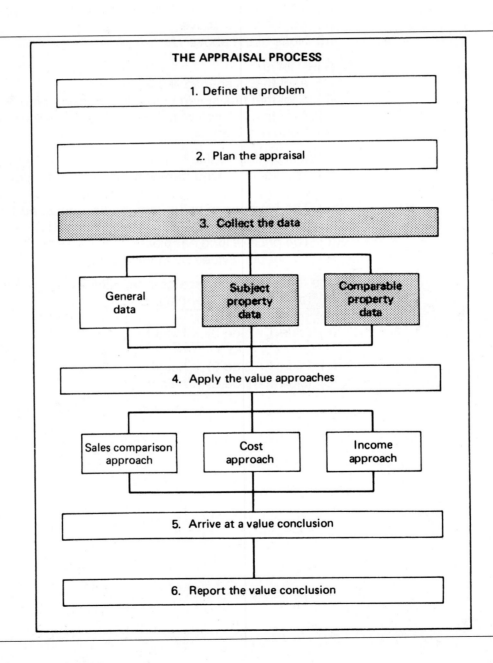

THE APPRAISAL PROCESS

1. Define the problem

2. Plan the appraisal

3. Collect the data

General data

Subject property data

Comparable property data

4. Apply the value approaches

Sales comparison approach

Cost approach

Income approach

5. Arrive at a value conclusion

6. Report the value conclusion

Chapter 7

Property Inspection and Analysis: The Improvements

Preview   In the last chapter, we discussed the inspection and analysis of the site and its surroundings. Now we shall cover what is involved in the inspection and analysis of the improvements. As used in appraisal terminology, improvements include everything attached to the vacant lot, that is, the building, swimming pool, shed, patio, fence, and whatever other structures are to be found.

When you have completed this chapter, you should be able to:

1. *Describe what tools are required to make a field inspection of the improvements.*

2. *Describe the data emphasized in each of the three approaches to value.*

3. *Name the major items of a structure that the appraiser seeks to describe and rate.*

4. *Describe four construction classification types.*

5. *Explain what is meant by functional utility.*

7.1 PLANNING THE BUILDING INSPECTION

Any appraisal will go more smoothly if you prepare for the building inspection. This means assembling the tools necessary to perform the inspection and planning what data to collect.

Equipment Needed

The building inspection requires a few special tools in addition to the clipboard and pencil, measuring tape or roller, ice pick or nail, and camera which you have already assembled for the inspection of the site. The most important of these is a checklist or appraisal form for recording your data in an organized manner. Appropriate checklists include the standard FNMA appraisal forms and forms developed by many savings and loan associations, banks, and mortgage and insurance companies. The property description section of the FNMA Uniform Residential Appraisal Report (referred to as URAR) is shown in Figure 7.1. Methodical use of a standard checklist avoids having to return to the site for details overlooked at the first inspection. Some appraisers carry a pocket tape recorder and dictate building details for later transcription and completion of appraisal forms.

To help in the building inspection, you may also want to carry a pocket flashlight for looking under houses and into dark corners. A marble is handy for testing surfaces to see if they are level. For difficult jobs, take along plot plans and blueprints if they are available. These plans can help you verify the location and dimensions of the improvements, and spell out important structural and mechanical details.

What Information Should You Collect?

The information collected for an appraisal varies with the purpose of the appraisal and the intended use of the report. Also, some special data may be necessary to support the particular value approach that is being emphasized.

IMPROVEMENTS

GENERAL DESCRIPTION		EXTERIOR DESCRIPTION		FOUNDATION		BASEMENT		INSULATION		
No. of Units	One	Foundation	Concrete	Slab	Yes	Area Sq. Ft.	None	Roof		☐
No. of Stories	One	Exterior Walls	Stucco	Crawl Space	None	% Finished		Ceiling	G	☒
Type (Det./Att.)	Detached	Roof Surface	C/Shingle	Basement	None	Ceiling		Walls		☐
Design (Style)	Modern	Gutters & Dwnspts.	Yes	Sump Pump	No	Walls		Floor		☐
Existing/Proposed	Existing	Window Type	Sld.Alum.	Dampness	No	Floor		None		☐
Age (Yrs.)	22	Storm/Screens	Yes	Settlement	None Noted	Outside Entry		Unknown	AVG	☒
Effective Age (Yrs.)	17	Manufactured House	No	Infestation	None					

ROOM LIST

ROOMS	Foyer	Living	Dining	Kitchen	Den	Family Rm.	Rec. Rm.	Bedrooms	# Baths	Laundry	Other	Area Sq. Ft.
Basement												None
Level 1	1	1	Area	1				4	2			1,768
Level 2												

Finished area above grade contains: 6 Rooms; 4 Bedroom(s); 2 Bath(s); 1,768 Square Feet of Gross Living Area

DESCRIPTION

INTERIOR	Materials/Condition	HEATING		KITCHEN EQUIP.		ATTIC		AMENITIES			CAR STORAGE:	
Floors	Carpet/Good	Type	F.A.U.	Refrigerator	☐	None	☒	Fireplace(s) #	1	☒	None	☐
Walls	Plaster/V.Good	Fuel	Gas	Range/Oven	☒	Stairs	☐	Patio	Concrete	☒	Garage	# of cars
Trim/Finish	Stock/Good	Condition	Good	Disposal	☒	Drop Stair	☐	Deck	Wood	☒	Attached	two
Bath Floor	Ceramic/Good	COOLING		Dishwasher	☒	Scuttle	☐	Porch		☐	Detached	
Bath Wainscot	Tile Shower	Central	None	Fan/Hood	☒	Floor	☐	Fence	Wood	☒	Built-In	
Doors	Wood/Good	Other	None	Microwave	☐	Heated	☐	Pool		☐	Carport	
		Condition		Washer/Dryer	☐	Finished	☐			☐	Driveway	Asph

COMMENTS

Additional features (special energy efficient items, etc.): Kitchen and bath have skylights. Master bath has double pullman lav. (mirrored). Covered patio and 7 foot heated spa in rear yard.

Condition of the improvements, depreciation (physical, functional, and external), repairs needed, quality of construction, remodeling/additions, etc.: No physical, functional or external inadequacies noted; kitchen and baths redecorated six months ago.

Adverse environmental conditions (such as, but not limited to, hazardous wastes, toxic substances, etc.) present in the improvements, on the site, or in the immediate vicinity of the subject property: None in evidence.

Freddie Mac Form 70 6-93 PAGE 1 OF 2 Fannie Mae Form 1004 6-93
Software by Dynamic Computing (314) 644-1802

Figure 7.1 Improvement description sections of the URAR form.

Consider the Appraisal Purpose

The purpose of most appraisals will be to estimate market value. An inspection for this purpose usually requires a detailed and accurate description of the physical structures and a rating for market acceptability. Conformity to building codes, deed restrictions, and zoning regulations should also be reviewed. In this regard, any nonconformity should be carefully noted so that its influence on market value can be considered. Finally, the highest and best use of the property as presently improved should be analyzed. If the present use differs from the highest and best use as if vacant, the building inspection should be designed to explore alternative uses. As suggested in Chapter 6, maximizing the contribution of the improvements to the total property value is the goal.

The type of appraisal assignment also affects the building inspection. For example, if the assignment calls for a preliminary appraisal with only exterior inspection, the work would be very different from another assignment for which the assignment requires a full appraisal and a full narrative report.

Appraisals made for purposes other than market value may also demand more specialized data. For example, appraisals made for the purpose of estimating insurable value would probably emphasize such data as construction costs, rating of the structure's fire resistance, and the physical condition of the building.

Consider the Intended Use of the Report

The intended use of the appraisal report also determines its form and content, and therefore the data to be collected. When the appraisal report is to be used by the seller of a single-family dwelling to determine a realistic price, a brief set of comparable sales with a short discussion as to comparability may be all that is required to satisfy the client. However, if the appraisal is being made for loan purposes, the lender may require completion of a specific form, such as the URAR shown in Figure 7.1. (A detailed description of URAR and its requirements may be found in Chapter 16.) Besides specific physical details, loan appraisals usually require measured judgment on such factors as conformity to neighborhood, market acceptability, compatibility with surrounding land uses, and the marketable physical condition of the subject property. Generally, lenders require that appraisals of one- and two-family dwellings contain enough data to show that they conform to the following requirements:

1. Safe, secure, healthful, and attractive living facilities.
2. Ease of circulation and housekeeping.
3. Visual and auditory privacy.
4. Appropriate light and ventilation.
5. Fire and accident protection.
6. Economy of maintenance.
7. Adequate sanitation facilities.
8. Accessory services.

Lender requirements may be quite detailed, covering specifics as to acceptable room sizes, door and window placement for cross ventilation, heating, plumbing, finish materials, storage, access, and privacy. As you can see, physically measuring room sizes and noting door openings could take more time and effort than you might have allowed if you just planned a quick measure of the outside dimensions. When an appraisal report is prepared for court proceedings, more specialized information and added documentation are also necessary.

Special Limiting Conditions

The presence or absence of special limiting conditions as understood at the outset of an appraisal assignment may also influence the detail required in a building inspection. For example, if an appraisal is being made subject to the completion of remodeling in progress, the exact nature and extent of the proposed changes to the improvements must be obtained in advance, then kept in mind during the building inspection.

What Value Approaches Are to Be Emphasized?

The information that you gather during the visual inspection will be influenced by the value approach you expect to emphasize. Generally, the cost approach requires the most descriptive detail. Besides the appraiser's rating for age, condition, and the utility of the improvements, the data collected must be adequate to allow you to calculate the building cost estimate. Cost estimates often rely on the use of published cost manuals. Here are some of the factors that cost manuals usually consider as determinants of cost.

---

1. Design or use type.
2. Construction classification.
3. Rating of quality.
4. Size, shape, and height.
5. Special equipment.
6. Yard or site improvements.

Some cost-estimating methods (such as the segregated method that is an option in the Marshall Valuation Service) utilize detailed measurements of individual building components. This might call for the dimensions of the floors, exterior walls, interior partitions, storefronts, roof structure and cover, and so on. The rating for age, condition, and utility strongly affect the allowance for depreciation in the cost approach, so close attention to details of property maintenance and repair is also important.

The sales comparison approach requires improvement details that can be compared with the features of similar properties that have sold. So, again, familiarity with the type of data to be compared is important to avoid a second inspection to fill in the gaps. Here is a list of the typical property characteristics to be noted in single-family home appraisals. Most of these items are also included in the various computerized residential sales lists reports by appraisers.

Architectural style	Total number of rooms
Construction type	Square feet of living area
Type of exterior	Basement area
Type of roof	Type of heating and cooling
Number of stories	Fireplace(s)
Floor plan	Built-ins
Overall quality	Any remodeling
Condition	Parking accommodations
Year built	Outside improvements (such as pools and patios)
Number of bedrooms	
Number of bathrooms	

If the income approach is to be emphasized, the appraiser should be aware of the property characteristics that have the greatest effect on the income potential and the probable expenses. For example:

1. Number and types of units.

2. The ratio of rentable areas to the total area.

3. Quality of the tenant space.

4. Recreation, parking, services, and other amenities available.

5. Durability of the structure and materials.

6. Physical condition of the structure and equipment.

Now that we have assembled the necessary tools and made appropriate plans for the task, we are ready to begin the building inspection.

7.2 PERFORMING THE BUILDING INSPECTION

The purpose of the building inspection is to identify the condition, quality, features, and problems of the property being appraised. In this section, we shall describe the building inspection techniques most appraisers use.

When you have your equipment in order, your checklist in hand, and have made an appointment with the owner, manager, or tenant of your subject property, you are ready to begin the building inspection.

Recording and Rating Improvement Characteristics

As you start noting the physical features of a property, be prepared to follow the checklist or appraisal form you have selected for the job. Most checklists suggest a logical sequence of observations which, if followed, prevents the oversight of important data. It is desirable to use correct construction terminology in your descriptions. Structural components and finish materials will be discussed in the next section.

The exterior is often inspected first, starting with the foundation and basement (if any), then the exterior finish, and finally the roof. Be sure to note the type, style, materials used, and condition of each of the parts of the exterior. Now, outside structures and landscaping should be described.

Next, the interior is inspected. The number and type of rooms and their arrangement are noted. The interior finish is rated as to type of materials and quality of workmanship.

Finally, the built-in kitchen equipment (such as range and oven) as well as the heating, air conditioning, and other systems are inspected and rated as to their type and adequacy. The presence and adequacy of insulation in the roof, ceiling, walls, and floor must be checked, noting the R-factor, if available. (See the heading, Typical Residential Specifications, in section 7.3.) Also, note any special energy-efficient equipment, such as solar heating. Lastly, some recent state and local laws require (upon sale) that all houses have, or be retrofitted with, smoke detectors and/or water conservation devices. Some now require safety glass in shower and patio doors. Be sure to note the presence or absence of such items.

Rating for Appeal and Marketability

As you walk through the building, you should be able to get some idea of the general marketability and appeal of the property. Be aware of the demands and tastes of the specific market in the neighborhood of the property. Do the features of this house fit in with others in the neighborhood? If you were buying here, would you like this house?

It is generally agreed that the marketability and appeal of a single residential property depend on:

1. Construction quality, materials, and finish.

2. Physical condition of structure, finish, equipment, and floors.

3. Room size, layout, and privacy.

4. Closets and other storage areas.

5. Energy efficiency.

6. Adequacy and condition of plumbing and bath facilities.

7. Adequacy and condition of electrical system.

8. Adequacy of heating equipment and any air conditioning.

9. The adequacy, condition, convenience, and quality of kitchen cabinets and equipment.

10. Type and adequacy of car storage facilities.

11. Landscaping and outdoor improvements.

12. General livability and appeal.

Every person has an ideal home in his or her imagination. While inspecting a residence, the appraiser tries to "wear the shoes" of the typical buyer of the particular property in order to see the faults and advantages of a home. A certain "quiet quality" may increase the marketability of a home far more than extra equipment, whereas other factors such as a pervading musty odor in the bathrooms and closets or poor room arrangement may seriously detract from the appeal of an otherwise sound building.

Evaluating Construction Quality

Quality can be a very subjective word. However, in appraising, it is used to describe the basic structural integrity, materials, finishes, and special features of the building. The quantity and type of fixtures, cabinets, and built-in equipment are considered to be part of the quality rating, as is the level of overall workmanship.

Quality is also relative; that is, we can judge it only by comparison with a given standard. Most appraisers attempt to rate buildings according to typical specifications provided in published cost-estimating guides. Generally, these guides use the four ratings of (1) good, (2) average, (3) fair, and (4) poor. These quality ratings will be discussed in detail in section 7.3.

Evaluating Physical Condition

Although the physical condition of a building is often closely related to its age, each aspect is of concern to the appraiser. Has the house generally been kept in good repair or allowed to run down? When rating a building for condition, any deferred maintenance or structural defects found should always be examined and described. It is also appropriate for the appraiser to try to identify and note any probable asbestos-containing material. Asbestos-containing materials are most commonly found as insulating materials in older structures. If the inspection suggests the presence of any of the environmental hazards described in Chapter 6 (methane or radon gas, for example), an official environmental report should be requested or made.

Note the condition of paint, floor and wall coverings, kitchen counter tops, shower walls, hardware, equipment, and fixtures. Describe any remodeling or renovation you may find, as well as any abnormal neglect or wear.

Are there any signs of water leakage or moisture inside the house? These may be caused by roof or plumbing leaks, inadequate seals or flashing at windows or doors, or improper ventilation. Look for discolored or peeling paint on the walls or ceilings. Notice recently patched spots, discolored or moldy seams, or a musty odor in bathrooms and kitchens. Any of these conditions may indicate problems.

Pay special attention to whether additions, major repairs, and remodeling conform to the building codes. Sometimes you will find garage conversions and even more ambitious structural work that has been done without a building permit. If you suspect such a condition, you should investigate and report your findings in the appraisal.

Every building inspection should include a check for any possible structural problems or foundation settling. Any such problem could reduce both the marketability and value of a property. Therefore, it is very important to note such telltale signs as large cracks or fresh patchwork in the foundation, walls, and ceilings. Structural cracks caused by a sagging foundation most often show up at the door and window openings, as demonstrated in Figure 7.2. Cabinets that have pulled away from the wall or that are no longer plumb (vertical); doors that stick or have been trimmed out of square; floors that hump, dip, or are not level (see why you needed that marble?) all suggest either a settling of the foundation or a shifting of the structure. Sometimes evidence of property damage may be found after earthquakes such as those occurring in 1971 and 1990–92 in California. However, the most common cause of settling is either poor soil compaction under the foundation or inferior construction of the improvements.

Part of the appraiser's job is to estimate the cost to cure any deferred maintenance or structural defects. Depending on his or her cost-estimating experience, the appraiser may need to consult contractors or engineers before making a *cost-to-cure* estimate or before completing the report. Sometimes the owners have already consulted such experts and have obtained a written estimate.

Effective Age   Some appraisal procedures require the assignment of an "effective age" to a building. *Effective age* is usually defined as the relative age

Figure 7.2
An example of structural damage. (Photograph courtesy of Doug Frost)

of a structure considering its physical condition and marketability. Thus a very old building that compares in these respects with similar buildings that are, say, 10 years old may be said to have an effective age of 10 years. In assigning effective age, appraisers usually consider historical age and degree of maintenance, as well as room additions and remodeling.

Often the first step in an effective age analysis is to calculate the average age of a remodeled structure. For example, if a 30-year-old house was remodeled 10 years ago, and about 80% of the original structure remained un-remodeled, then the average age, (based solely on the physical elements) would be 26 years. Here is how that would be figured:

$$
\begin{aligned}
80\% \times 30 \text{ years} &= 24 \text{ years} \\
+20\% \times 10 \text{ years} &= \underline{2 \text{ years}} \\
\text{Average age} &= 26 \text{ years}
\end{aligned}
$$

In actual practice, remodeling may or may not extend the useful life of a structure. Thus effective age need not agree with average age. It is the market that really determines the effect of age on value.

Thus the second step in estimating the effective age of the property is to judge the market reaction to the property's standard of maintenance, for example, how recently major areas of potential obsolescence such as kitchens and baths have been remodeled. Often this analysis can be bolstered by examining the sales to see if the prices of remodeled property are noticeably higher.

Measuring Improvements and Preparing Drawings

Most appraisals call for information on the area (and sometimes the volume) of the buildings. Necessary dimensions are usually included on a diagram prepared by the appraiser. Sometimes you will need to include a floor plan of the rooms. Traditionally, building measurements are expressed in feet and inches (as opposed to metric measures).

For most detached residential structures, the "total living area" or "floor area" is measured on the exterior of the building and includes the exterior walls and finish. These measurements are usually rounded to the nearest foot, half-foot, or inch. However, condominium units are often measured using interior rather than exterior measurements, since the airspace is what is bought and sold. In commercial buildings, interior measurements of room size, or tenant space, may be required. These measurements are also taken between the finished wall surfaces.

It is easier to record your field measurements on a rough sketch as you work (graph paper of the proper scale helps). Later you can draw a final sketch when you have a better writing surface and your hands are cleaner (handling a measuring tape can make them grimy). One-tenth or one-twentieth inch to the foot are the most commonly used scales, the choice depending on the size of the building.

Have you ever wondered how to measure a building? It is really quite simple. Just start at one right-angle corner, usually the front left corner as you face the building. Using the hook on your tape or an ice pick stuck into a crack (or on the ground), attach your tape and measure across the front of the building to the other corner. Move your tape hook to the second corner and continue the same procedure along one side, then the back and the other side, until you return to your starting corner. Be sure to pick up any special measurements you might need, such as patio dimensions, while you are there. Your plane geometry from high school will come in handy if you run across angles that are not right angles. Be sure the building outline is in "balance." Horizontal measurements across the front must add up to equal the horizontal measurements across the back; also the right and left side measurements must equal each other when totaled. Example 7.1 may help you see what is meant by "balancing" the building diagram.

When you have completed your diagram, you must compute the building areas. Divide the living area into "natural rectangles" by sketching light broken lines horizontally or vertically across the diagram. Compute each of the areas separately by multiplying the length by the width of each rectangle. Add these areas together for your total living area. Methods of computing areas of irregular building shapes may be found in Chapter 6.

Open porches, garages, carports, and other outside areas are figured separately, since they are not a part of the living area. Small entryways and bays are usually counted as part of the living area.

7.3 UNDERSTANDING CONSTRUCTION DETAILS

It is important for the appraiser to understand the basic principles of construction and be familiar with typical structural details. (Figure 7.3 shows examples of wood framing details.) This section will cover (1) the classification of basic construction, (2) the selection of building materials, (3) typical building specifications, and (4) the standards used for judging the quality of a building.

Construction Classification Systems

Historically, most systems for classifying types of construction were based on the structure's resistance to fire. For this reason, buildings are generally classified into four or five classes according to their particular type of basic frame, wall, and floor construction.

In most building codes and construction cost manuals, basic construction types are classified by either an "A, B, C, D" or a "1, 2, 3, 4" designation system. Details of Class A, B, and C construction are shown in Figure 7.4; Class D details were given in Figure 7.3. The typical specifications for all four classes follow.

Class A buildings have fireproofed structural steel frames and reinforced concrete or masonry floors and roofs. Major institutional buildings as well as high-rise office and hotel buildings are usually Class A construction. Class A construction is the strongest for its weight but is the most expensive.

Class B buildings have reinforced concrete frames and reinforced concrete or masonry walls, floors, and roofs. The typical Class B building is a three- to five-story office building or a heavy industrial plant. Class B construction is second only to Class A in cost and fire resistance.

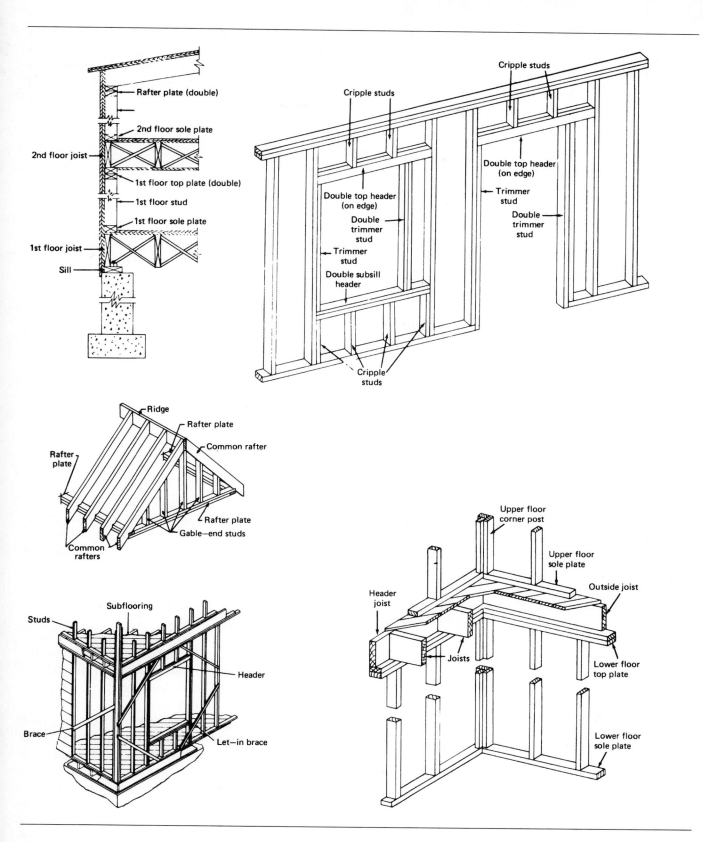

Figure 7.3
Structural detail: Wood framing. (From *Builder 3 & 2,*
Bureau of Naval Personnel, 1965)

Class C buildings have masonry exterior walls, and wood or exposed steel floor and roof structures. Many one- and two-story commercial and industrial buildings fall into this category. Also, many residential buildings in colder climates belong in this classification.

Example 7.1 Example of a Building Diagram

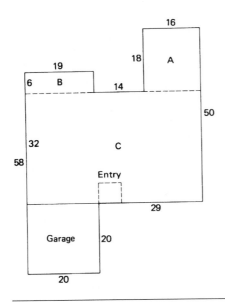

Area Calculations

Floor area:

Shape A:	16×18	=	288
Shape B:	6×19	=	114
Shape C:	32×49	=	1,568

1,970 sq ft

Garage:
$20 \times 20 = 400$ sq ft

Proof That Drawing "Balances"

Front (house and garage):	$20 + 29$	=	49 ft
Rear:	$19 + 14 + 16$	=	49 ft

Front and rear are in balance.

Left side:	$58 + (18 - 6)$	=	70 ft
Right side:	$50 + 20$	=	70 ft

Left and right sides are in balance.

Class D buildings have wood or light steel frames and roof structures. Most residential buildings in the West and South fall into the Class D construction classification. Basic construction features of Class D construction include concrete or concrete-block foundations; concrete slab or raised wood floors; wood frame; stucco and/or wood siding exterior; drywall or plaster interior; and tar and gravel, composition shingle, wood shingle, or shake roofing.

Choice of Materials

Traditionally, the materials used for structural and mechanical components, as well as the "finish" of buildings, are dependent on the climate, availability, cost, style, durability, and building code requirements.

The climate can dictate the type of foundation, walls, insulation, roof pitch, and finish material. In the moderate climate of America's West and Southwest, stucco and wood structures prevail. Insulation is needed primarily against the summer heat. In colder climates, extensive insulation may be needed to provide better protection from the elements. Heating and air-conditioning systems should be designed to meet climatic conditions. In today's energy-conscious economy, such systems need to be energy-efficient: hence the trend toward solar heating and design features that minimize energy loss.

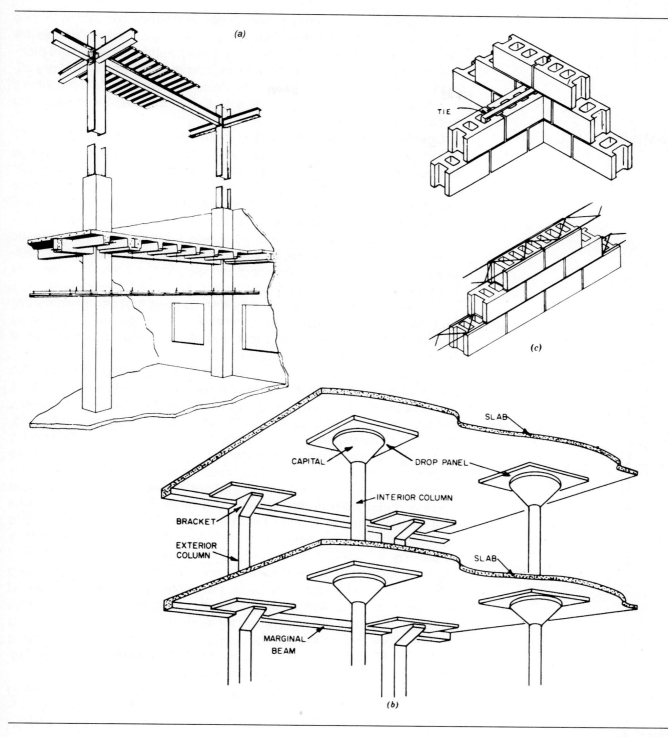

(a)

TIE

(c)

SLAB

CAPITAL — DROP PANEL

INTERIOR COLUMN

BRACKET

EXTERIOR COLUMN

SLAB

MARGINAL BEAM

(b)

Figure 7.4
Construction class details. (*a*) Class A. (Courtesy of Marshall & Stevens Publication Company) (*b*) Class B. (From *Design Manual Structural Engineering.* Department of the Navy, Naval Facilities Engineering Command, October 1970) (*c*) Class C. (From *Builder 3 & 2,* Bureau of Naval Personnel, 1965)

The selection of materials also depends on their availability. Since the earliest times, mankind has used readily available materials for shelter. Adobe was used in the early Southwest because it was plentiful, easily made into building blocks, and suitable to the hot, dry climate. Wood is used where forests are found, and clay is used where it is readily available and of a quality that is suitable for making into bricks.

Cost is also a factor in the use of materials. Custom homes may still incorporate expensive marbles and rare woods, but the average builder must think twice about the comparative cost of the materials used. As wood is becoming more and more costly and scarce, some builders are beginning to experiment with plastic, steel, and fiberglass walls, prefabricated to meet the building specifications. We are already conditioned to the use of fiberglass tub enclosures and plastic counters in bathrooms. Plastics and polymers have also replaced expensive metals in rough plumbing and electrical building components in many areas of the country.

The style of the construction will often suggest that certain materials be used. Traditionally, shingles and shake roofs "go with" ranch-style and Cape Cod houses. Tile roofs and textured stucco are typical of Spanish- or Mediterranean-style houses.

The durability of materials must also be taken into consideration when deciding on the materials to be used in a structure. Durability is partly dependent on climate. Most exterior woods deteriorate in areas of high temperature or humidity. One exception to the rule is redwood. Although more expensive than many other types of wood, redwood is quite impervious to weather, does not require paint, and may in the long run be more economical for exterior siding. Durability also depends on usage. Interior finishes that are subject to heavy wear must meet a reasonable durability test. The modern vinyl floor coverings and plastic laminate counter tops that increasingly replace hardwood and ceramic tiles are not quite as resistant to wear, but they are less expensive.

Local building code requirements are also important in determining the materials to be used. The stress and load requirements for wood framing in construction eliminate many varieties of forest products. Douglas fir is most often preferred for its relative strength. Many codes do not allow any wiring except copper for the electrical circuits in a structure. Plastic pipes and sewers are not allowed in some areas. Each locality has its own fairly rigid building code.

Although they often contribute to high housing costs by restricting the types of materials to be used, for the most part, building codes offer the community protection from fire, health hazards, insect and rodent infestation, and unsafe buildings.

Typical Residential Specifications

As already noted, residential structures differ widely in materials and specifications. Examples of the range of choices are shown in Figure 7.5. Typical features found today are listed on the following pages.

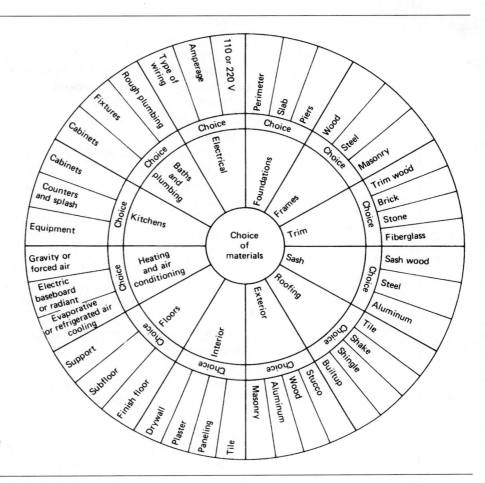

Figure 7.5
Choice of materials.

Foundations:
    Concrete or block piers.
    Perimeter foundation walls of reinforced concrete or concrete block.
    Reinforced concrete slab foundation and floor.
Frames:
    Wood, steel, or masonry.
    Douglas fir, cypress, or hemlock preferred as framing lumber.
Trim and Sash:
    Trim: wood, brick, stone, or fiberglass simulation.
    Sash: wood, steel, or aluminum (double-hung, casement, or sliding), sliding glass doors to privacy areas (such as backyards).
Roofing:
    Built-up composition or fiberglass felt, covered with hot-mopped asphalt and gravel. Asbestos felt may still be found in older structures.
    Shingles: composition, wood, concrete, or clay tile. Asbestos tile shingles were used at one time.
    Shakes: split cedar.
    Other: Spanish or Mission tile, concrete tile, or slate.

Exterior:
  Stucco, wood or aluminum shingles or siding, hardboard, wood or plywood batten and board, or brick or stone veneer.
  Types of wood: pine, Douglas fir, spruce, cypress, hemlock, cedar, redwood, or prefinished hardboard.
  Masonry walls: adobe, stone, concrete block, slumpstone, brick, or precast concrete panels (usually reinforced for bearing walls).
Interior:
  Wallboard, sheetrock (drywall) or lath and plaster; special finishes may include plywood, hardwood veneer, Douglas fir, redwood or hardwood plank (tongue and groove), ceramic tile, plastic, or marble.
  Unfinished or painted masonry walls, sometimes furred out and finished as above.
Insulation:
  Roof, ceiling, walls, or floor: aluminum foil, fiberglass, polystyrene, or other synthetic. Asbestos-containing materials may still be found in older structures. Typical R-factor, or rating, varies from about R-10 to R-20 for good ceiling and wall insulation. (The higher number indicates better heat/cold insulating qualities.)
Floors:
  Concrete slab.
  Raised subfloors of plywood, particle board, or lightweight concrete.
  Finished flooring of tongue and groove (or parquet) hardwood, asphalt tile, linoleum, sheet vinyl or vinyl tile, ceramic tile, terrazzo, or carpeting.
Heating and Air Conditioning:
  Gravity or forced-air circulation:
    Gas-fired floor, wall, or central furnace.
    Oil or wood-burning furnace.
    Solar-heating system.
  Baseboard or radiant:
    Electric or hot water, using various fuels, including solar heat.
  Wood-burning fireplaces.
  Air cooling:
    Individual through-wall unit or central ducted unit.
    Evaporative or refrigerated.
Kitchens:
  Cabinets: pine, particle board, plywood, hardwood, plastic laminate veneer, or baked-enamel prefabricated steel.
  Counters and splash: ceramic tile, stainless steel, laminated wood, or plastic laminates.
  Equipment: sink, garbage disposal, vent-fan and hood over stove; built-in range and oven, grill, barbecue, dishwasher, mixer-blender, or trash compactor.
Baths and Plumbing:
  Rough plumbing: of polyvinyl chloride or other plastic, galvanized iron, or copper pipe.
  Plumbing fixtures: vitreous china toilet; bathtub of porcelain-enameled cast iron, steel, or fiberglass; enameled cast iron or molded plastic basin (sometimes integral with pullman counters).

Enclosures, counters: plastic laminate, fiberglass, ceramic tile, cultured marble, quarry marble, and mirrored vanities.

Electrical:

Older systems: 110-volt system with fuse box or circuit-breaker overload control, 70 to 100-ampere capacity (Figure 7.6*a*).

Newer systems: 220-volt circuit-breaker system, 100- to 150-ampere capacity (Figure 7.6*b*).

Type of wiring varies from "Romex" plastic-coated with plastic receptacles to metal flex conduit, metal outlets.

Outlets vary from one to five or more per room.

Building Quality

The published cost-estimating guides most often used by appraisers provide guidelines for rating the quality of most types of buildings. Typical standards for single-family residential structures are as follows:

1. *Good:* To achieve this rating, the building must incorporate better than average architectural design, materials, and workmanship. A residence receiving this rating usually has at least two bathrooms, some form of central heat, and built-in kitchen appliances.

2. *Average:* This rating stands for a medium-quality standard. Acceptable to FHA and VA standards with no extras.

Figure 7.6
Electrical systems. (*a*) Old-type fuse box. (*b*) Modern circuit-breaker box. (Photographs courtesy of Doug Frost)

3. *Fair:* This refers to a minimum-quality building with limited equipment, plain exterior and interior, and low cost.

4. *Poor:* This quality is assigned to a substandard building with poor structure, interior and exterior finish, and/or inadequate bath/kitchen facilities.

7.4 FUNCTIONAL UTILITY AND ARCHITECTURAL STYLES

It is often said that good architectural design is the use of appropriate materials in a proper scale and in harmony with the setting. Good architectural design and functional utility work together.

Defining Standards of Functional Utility

Functional utility consists of the combination of the usefulness and attractiveness of a property. Functional utility measures the livability of a house in terms of how well it is placed on the site, the general suitability of the floor plan, and the comfort and convenience of the equipment. A functional design provides the most benefits for a given cost. Some design features that contribute to functional utility in homes are contained in the typical minimum property standards already discussed in section 7.1.

In income-producing properties, functional utility is often measured by using economic standards. Design features that are in demand by tenants, and at the same time help maximize investment return, are the functional ideal. The open and bold styles found in the newest shopping centers, office and industrial complexes, and apartment projects are reflective of these goals.

Orientation and Floor Plan

Ideally, any residential structure should be oriented or placed on the site to take advantage of the view, sun, weather, and natural topography. Such orientation should also provide adequate front, back, and side yards as well as light, air, privacy, and access to the street. Provisions for parking, storage, refuse areas, and recreational facilities also contribute to property acceptability.

Inside the residence, the floor plan is considered an important factor in determining functional utility. Easy access to each room, a good flow of traffic, separation of areas of different use, cross ventilation, wall space for the placement of furniture, and adequate storage space are sought. Efficient and pleasant layout of the kitchen and a convenient access to yards and utility areas also affect the usefulness and marketability of a home, whether it is a conventional freestanding house or a condominium unit. See Figure 7.7 for typical differences in floor plans.

Architectural Styles

Historically, architectural styles sprang up in diverse geographical locations of the world. Now, the traditional styles are named after the location of their origin or by the historical period during which they were most popular. The combinations and modifications of various styles lend spice and variety to our neighborhoods. Examples of some common styles are shown in Figure 7.8 and described here.

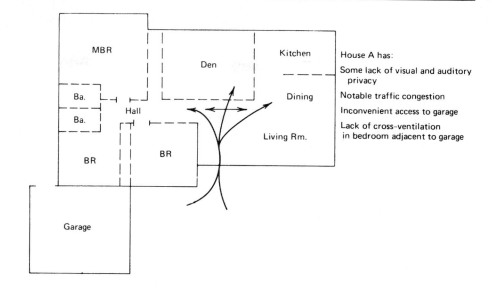

House A has:

Some lack of visual and auditory privacy

Notable traffic congestion

Inconvenient access to garage

Lack of cross-ventilation in bedroom adjacent to garage

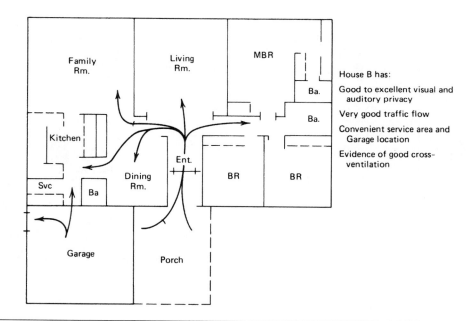

House B has:

Good to excellent visual and auditory privacy

Very good traffic flow

Convenient service area and Garage location

Evidence of good cross-ventilation

Figure 7.7
A study in floor plans.

Contemporary styles, sometimes called modern, feature a low, flat roof, a low outline or profile, and a floor plan that is oriented to the outdoors. Often, these homes are designed with extensive glass areas. Many residential tracts in the Southern California and Arizona areas are of the contemporary style.

The California ranch style is closely related to the contemporary style but precedes it historically. The main elements are a low, rambling profile, with a gable roof, wide roof overhang, and lots of heavy wood trim. The ranch style also shows some relationship to the Spanish style of architecture through the use of brick or stone trim and design elements.

Figure 7.8
Some examples of architectural styles. (From *Reference Book,* California Department of Real Estate, 1989)

The Spanish style is popular in the western states. It is characterized by its thick-appearing stucco walls (whether adobe or simulated), wood beam trim, and red tile roof.

The Monterey or Monterey-Spanish style is a modification of the Spanish style. The addition of a wood-beamed, second-story porch or balcony in the front of the house is its distinguishing feature.

The Colonial style includes several types of early American architecture, including New England, Cape Cod, Dutch, Southern, and Georgian. These are recognized by square or rectangular, stately, and symmetrical buildings, with steep gable roofs, shutters, and dormer windows. Each locality added individual variations that set them apart from their neighbors.

The English half-timber style looks like many of the "Squire" houses of the English countryside. The key features are the half-timber walls with masonry or stucco between the timbers, steep-pitched roof, and casement windows.

Because it was so widely copied at the turn of the century, the Victorian style is still apparent in almost every city in America. It is typified by a roof with many gables and a wood exterior. The elaborate wood trim designs around windows, roof eaves, rails, doorways, and ceilings have given this style the description of "gingerbread" architecture.

French Provincial, also known as French Country, is usually a large house on a large land parcel. It is identified by its very high, steep-pitched hip roof, dormers, and overall formal, balanced appearance.

By no means are today's architectural styles "pure." Most modern construction actually incorporates features from two or more traditional building designs. Nor is it always possible to judge the market acceptability of a particular style. The many different tastes in architecture suggest that a variety of styles is more important than purity of styles.

SUMMARY

The inspection and analysis of real property improvements require preparation and planning. The appraiser should prepare to arrive at the field inspection with the equipment and tools needed for an efficient physical inspection of the building. The most important tool is the checklist or appraisal form for recording data. The amount and kind of data to be collected depend on the purpose of the appraisal, the intended use of the report, and the value approach to be emphasized; therefore, the appraisal should be planned in advance. In this way the appraiser is alerted to note the relevant information at the time of the inspection.

The purpose of most appraisals is to estimate market value. This requires a detailed and accurate description of the physical structures and a rating for market acceptability. Appraisals made to estimate some other type of value require more specialized data.

The intended use of the report greatly affects the amount and kind of data required in the inspection and analysis of improvements. The seller of a single-family dwelling might be satisfied simply with a set of comparable sales and a short discussion of comparability. A lender's appraisal report requirements are usually much more detailed and demanding.

If the cost approach is to be emphasized, the data collected must support the building cost estimate and the rating for age, condition, and utility. If the sales comparison approach is to be stressed, the data required will include items such as the architectural style, number of rooms, and parking accommodations, which can be *compared* with features of similar properties that have sold. If the income approach is to be emphasized, the appraiser should record the features that most affect the income potential and probable expenses.

Regardless of the approach to be emphasized, the building inspection should accurately describe and rate the physical features of the structure for marketability, quality of construction, and physical condition. Measuring and diagraming the subject property are usually required.

Last but not least, the inspection and analysis of improvements require a working knowledge of structural detail. Industry standards should be understood by the practicing appraiser.

Since market acceptability is the ultimate test of value, it is important that the appraiser have a basic knowledge of design principles in construction. Good architectural design incorporates not only the building style but also those features that contribute most effectively to the utility of the building.

Important Terms and Concepts

California ranch style

Class A, B, C, or D construction

Colonial style

Condition

Construction classification

Construction specifications

Contemporary style

Effective age

English half-timber style

French Provincial style

Functional utility

Inspection checklist

Living area

Monterey style

Quality rating

Spanish style

Victorian style

REVIEWING YOUR UNDERSTANDING

1. The most important tool you will need for recording your data during the building inspection is:
   (a) A plat map
   (b) A measuring tape
   (c) A checklist or appraisal form
   (d) A marble

2. The building inspection must be geared to:
   (a) The purpose of the appraisal
   (b) The use of the appraisal report
   (c) The value approach to be emphasized
   (d) All of the above

3. Minimum property standards may include:
   (a) Ease of circulation and housekeeping
   (b) Adequate sanitation facilities
   (c) Both (a) and (b)
   (d) None of the above

4. Some of the factors usually considered as determinants of cost are:
   (a) Design or use type
   (b) Construction classification
   (c) Rating of quality
   (d) All of the above

5. The major items to describe and rate in a structure include:
   (a) Foundation, exterior, and roof
   (b) List of rooms
   (c) Interior and built-in kitchen equipment
   (d) All of the above

6. Rating a single-family residence for market appeal considers:
   (a) The demands and tastes of the market in the neighborhood of the subject property
   (b) The quality of construction, materials used, and their finish
   (c) General livability and condition of the property
   (d) All of the above

7. "Effective age" refers to:
   (a) Original age
   (b) Average age
   (c) Relative age considering the physical condition and marketability of a structure
   (d) All of the above

8. The "total living area" of a residential structure is measured by:
   (a) Exterior measurements including walls and finish
   (b) Interior measurements only
   (c) House and garage area combined
   (d) None of the above

9. Classification of basic construction refers to:
   (a) Type of use
   (b) Type of basic frame, wall, floor, and roof construction
   (c) Quality of construction
   (d) All of the above

10. The criteria used in the selection of building materials include:
    (a) Climate
    (b) Availability
    (c) Durability
    (d) All of the above

11. Good architectural design consists, in part, of:
    (a) A unique floor plan
    (b) Functional utility
    (c) The use of expensive materials
    (d) All of the above

12. The architectural style that uses elaborate wood trim designs around windows, doorways, and roof eaves is:
    (a) English
    (b) California-Monterey
    (c) Victorian
    (d) French Provincial

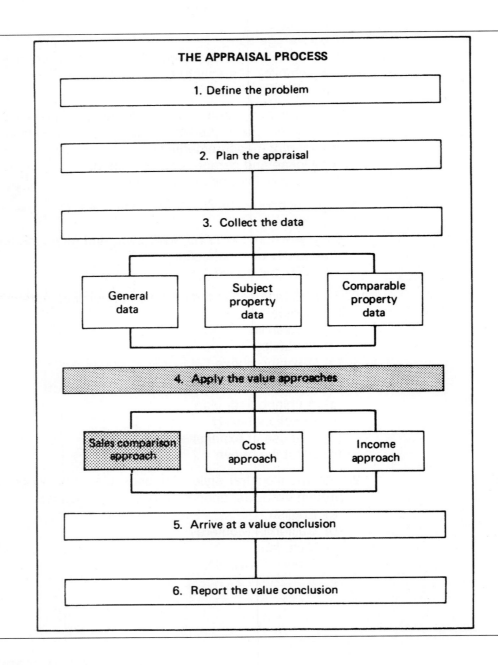

THE APPRAISAL PROCESS

1. Define the problem

2. Plan the appraisal

3. Collect the data

| General data | Subject property data | Comparable property data |

4. Apply the value approaches

| Sales comparison approach | Cost approach | Income approach |

5. Arrive at a value conclusion

6. Report the value conclusion

Chapter 8
The Sales Comparison Approach

Preview   Perhaps the most important approach used by appraisers to estimate value is the sales comparison approach. In brief, this approach involves analyzing recently sold properties and comparing them to the property being appraised. Chapter 8 first outlines the steps in the sales comparison approach and then describes the important process of collecting comparable sales data. Finally, this chapter outlines the appraisal statistical concepts most commonly used in appraisals.

When you have finished this chapter, you should be able to:

1. *List and explain the four steps in the sales comparison approach.*

2. *Explain the several important concepts behind the approach.*

3. *Explain how to decide if a sale is comparable.*

4. *Discuss what information about a comparable sale should be collected.*

5. *Identify the major sources of market data.*

6. *Outline the statistical techniques appraisers use in the analysis of sales.*

8.1 INTRODUCING THE SALES COMPARISON APPROACH

The sales comparison approach (also called the market approach) is a process that analyzes and compares sales to the property being appraised. This process is based on the principle of *substitution.* In order to understand and use the sales comparison approach and the principle of substitution, a thorough understanding of the neighborhood, city, and region, as well as a complete inspection of the property, is needed. You should review Chapters 4 through 7 if you have any questions concerning this material.

Outline of the Sales Comparison Approach

The sales comparison approach involves four steps, which are summarized in Figure 8.1. *The first step is to seek out recent sales of properties that are comparable to the subject property.* This requires understanding the meaning of the word *comparable,* identifying comparable properties, and collecting the necessary information about each property.

Once the necessary information about comparable sales has been obtained, *the second step is to analyze these sales and compare them with the subject property.* The purpose of analyzing the sales is to identify which features or characteristics are important in establishing prices. The process has two parts. The first is to identify the ways in which the sales differ from each other and from the subject property. Important differences often include the terms, conditions, or dates of sale. Physical differences such as location, age, and/or size almost always exist. The second part of sales analysis is to compare the differences in the sale prices of the comparables with the differences in property features. We are trying to find out what causes the price of this type of property to vary. If the available sales are essentially iden-

Figure 8.1
Steps in the sales comparison approach.

tical to the subject property, the prices should be in a very narrow range. However, the sold properties often differ in various ways, with a wider range of prices.

The third step in the sales comparison approach is to adjust for the differences between the sales and the subject property. The purpose of this step is to adjust the price of each comparable to reflect what the price would have been if that sale had been more nearly identical to the subject property. To carry out this step, you will select and use one or more of the adjustment techniques discussed in the next chapter.

After the sales have been located, analyzed, and adjusted, *the fourth step is to arrive at a value estimate as indicated by the adjusted sales.* This final step in the sales comparison approach is also covered in Chapter 9.

Key Concepts of the Sales Comparison Approach

Several concepts are needed to understand the sales comparison approach, its significance to appraisers, and its strengths and weaknesses. These concepts are described as the importance of substitution, the simplicity of market comparisons, the relationship to statistics, the relevance of adjustments, and the significance of market data. A discussion of each concept follows.

The Importance of Substitution

The principle of substitution (Chapter 5) is particularly important to the sales comparison approach. If a well-informed buyer is interested in a particular property, he or she will generally pay no more than the cost of acquiring another property that is a satisfactory substitute. This process of substitution is commonly used by buyers and sellers: Buyers compare a number of competitive listings and select the one that they like best, considering the features and the list prices. Sellers, in turn, set these list prices by seeing what buyers have paid for similar property in recent transactions.

Simplicity

Generally, the sales comparison approach is simpler and more direct than the other two approaches, and it often requires fewer calculations. Consequently, there is less possibility of either an error in appraisal judgment or a mathematical error. Since the sales comparison approach is often the easiest approach to understand, it is usually the easiest to explain to clients. In summary, the simplicity and directness of this approach may produce a more reliable value conclusion than could be obtained by other approaches.

Statistical Connections

Another aspect of the sales comparison approach is its use of concepts from the field of statistics. For example, when we obtain information about recent sales transactions, the latter represent only a portion of the total activity occurring in the market at that time. Thus, we are making use of the statistical concept called *sampling.* Appraisers seek to find out, through sampling and market analysis, how buyers and sellers behave in a particular real estate market. Estimating market value as "the most probable selling price . . ." is a task similar to the work of statistical economists.

Bracketing is another concept employed by appraisers that is derived from statistics. Statisticians try to make predictions only within the range of the data they have studied. For example, a consumer goods marketing study would likely use data that included both extremes of the market or industry being studied. Gathering data that brackets known consumption would give an economist a more accurate understanding of the market than just a random sample. (See Figure 8.2.)

Appraisers apply the same concept of bracketing when selecting market data (such as home sales, rent comparables, or land sale comparables). If the comparable sales differ in any major way from the subject property, sales should be selected to reflect both better and worse features from the subject property. For example, if comparable sales differ from the subject property in building size, comparable sales of *both* larger and smaller buildings should be obtained. Differences such as age and location should be treated in the same way. By including some sales that are better than the subject property and some that are worse, you develop a better view of the range of market reactions.

An outline of appraisal statistical concepts is presented in section 8.3 of this chapter.

Adjustments

As mentioned in Chapter 1, people with expertise in a market can estimate sales prices by intuition. Such appraisals, however, provide no specific analysis of relevant property differences. In contrast, the adjustment techniques contained in the sales comparison approach enable you to *specifically* identify property differences that are important in a given market or neighborhood. Sales comparison approach techniques can also indicate how much to adjust prices for any particular difference. Once an adjustment for a single factor is accurately estimated, you may be able to identify smaller adjustments that you might have missed before. Finally, using specific adjustments allows the appraisal to be objectively reviewed by the client. For these reasons, adjustment techniques are one of the most important contributions that formal appraising offers to the broker or salesperson.

Market Data as the Foundation

Market data are essential to *each* of the three value approaches. (See Figure 8.3.) For example, the sales comparison approach is used to

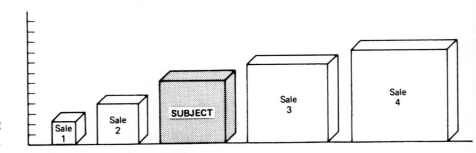

Figure 8.2
The concept of bracketing.

Figure 8.3
Market data is key to
all approaches.

estimate land value in the cost approach. Similarly, one of the best ways to estimate accrued depreciation in the cost approach is by the analysis of market sales. In the income approach, market rents are estimated by analyzing market rental transactions. Vacancy and expense information for the income approach is often obtained from competitive buildings. Usually, income approach capitalization rates are obtained by analyzing market sales or other market data.

The relationships between the three approaches will become clearer to you as you read the following sections. For now, remember that when you estimate market value, by whichever approach, *the market is the support for that estimate.* If your opinion of value is to be based on objective analysis instead of subjective intuition, you must obtain and analyze some type of market data.

8.2 COLLECTING COMPARABLE SALES DATA

As we have already stated, the sales comparison approach depends on comparing the subject property with current sales of similar properties. In this section, we discuss the first step in the sales comparison approach, which involves (1) selecting the comparable sales and (2) locating the appropriate information about the sales.

Selecting the Comparable Sales

A sale must meet three criteria to be considered a valid comparable. First, the property should be a competitive property. Second, the sale should qualify as an open market transaction. Third, assuming a current date of value, the sale will have occurred recently. Where listings are used, these criteria still apply, with open market exposure substituting for open market transaction. Let us take a closer look at these three criteria, which are summarized in Figure 8.4.

The Competitive Property

To be a competitive property, a sale property (or listing) should be a reasonable substitute or alternative for a potential purchaser looking at the subject property. A competitive property is located in an area that a buyer of the subject property would also consider. The comparable must be similar enough to the subject property in size, shape, and fea-

Figure 8.4
What is a comparable?

tures to satisfy the requirements of the buyer. In general, a competitive property should appeal to the same group of buyers. In economics this group of buyers is called a *submarket.* Thus, you should consider to which submarket the subject property is likely to appeal.

In residential property, the different owner-occupancy submarkets are identified by such important characteristics as family size, age, and economic status. Each group of buyers will have its own housing needs. For example, families of different sizes would seek homes of different sizes. Thus a two-bedroom home would not usually qualify as an appropriate comparable for a four-bedroom home under appraisal. Such a home clearly would be sought by buyers in a different submarket in terms of family size. Note, too, that in owner-occupied residential property, family incomes of the buyers of the comparable properties should be similar to those of likely buyers of the subject property. For residential property purchased as an investment, on the other hand, the buyer submarket will be different because the buyer's motives are different.

In nonresidential property, the submarket may have other characteristics that are important. For example, among potential buyers of small neighborhood stores, one buyer submarket may consist entirely of local investors. Another buyer submarket may be people who intend to have their business occupy the store. Since the two groups of buyers have different motives for purchasing the property, the factors that they consider important could vary.

Open Market Transactions

The second criterion for comparability is that a sale must be an open market transaction. This test seeks to eliminate sales that are *not* "arm's length" market sales. For example, an income property that has been sold directly to a tenant may or may not have been at the market price. In such a transaction, the sale price might represent either a bargain given by an uninformed seller or a premium offered by a tenant seeking to avoid the cost and uncertainty of relocation. Adequate exposure to a number of prospective buyers is essential to establish a market-determined price.

Further, when applying this test for an open market transaction, consider if the sale involved any unusual conditions. At times, personal property is included in the sale price, or there is seller financing at favorable interest rates. Transfers between relatives may result in favorable prices. In short, you must consider whether there are unusual circumstances about any particular sale that could have distorted its price. In some cases, the appraiser may simply discard a sale where the sale price is not in line with that of the other sales. If the sale is important, however, a careful investigation and an interview with the parties involved in the transaction may be necessary.

Date of Sale

The third criterion for a comparable sale is that the date of sale must be relatively close to the date of value. The supply and demand, and thus the value, of real estate changes with time. These changes can be rapid, as with a sudden shift in interest rates, or the announcement that a major factory is to be built in the area. If certain sales occur before such a change and you are appraising a property after that time, such sales are unlikely to be comparable. Over a longer period of time, more subtle changes in market attitudes may not shift prices but may shift the importance of particular property features or locations. For example, a long-lasting gasoline shortage could increase the values of properties close to public transportation routes. Consider any circumstances or events that might have had an effect on market attitudes. Be wary of using comparables that reflect earlier market attitudes toward particular features or locations.

When deciding upon the relevance of earlier sales, the appraiser must also consider general market trends. All sales prices are affected by the underlying *inflation, or deflation,* in the economy. However, real estate is affected by *local* influences much more than by *national* ones. Even during a period of inflation, prices will be going down for some locations and property types. Similarly, during a depression prices might be going up in some locations and for some property types. Real estate price trends are somewhat unpredictable. They may change from month to month or may remain stable for months at a time, in the same manner as general economic price indexes.

How Comparable Must a Comparable Be?

Every property is unique in some way. As a result, the appraiser may not find enough recent market sales of completely comparable properties. The appraiser should try to collect sales that are as similar as possible in time of sale, location, and important characteristics. However, the appraiser should **not** use sales that do not meet the criteria for an open market transaction. On occasion, it may be necessary to widen the standards of comparability in order to obtain an adequate number of sales. For example, if the subject property is a house built in 1962, we would probably prefer to find comparable sales that were built between, say, 1955 and 1970. As Figure 8.5 indicates, annual price changes can vary for homes of different age categories. However, if we can only find one such sale, then we have to widen the range of acceptable ages to houses built between, say, 1950 and 1975.

			Price Range in 1967		Year Built		
	Overall Index	Percent Change	Under $27,500	Over $27,500	Before 1941	1941-1955	After 1955
1967 Apr.	100.0	——	100.0	100.0	100.0	100.0	100.0
1968 Apr.	103.2	3.2	103.8	102.2	102.9	103.8	103.1
1969 Apr.	109.1	5.7	110.4	106.9	108.6	109.3	109.6
1970 Apr.	114.4	4.9	116.4	111.7	113.2	115.0	115.3
1971 Apr.	120.4	5.2	123.3	116.3	118.4	122.2	120.8
1972 Apr.	126.1	4.7	129.0	121.8	124.0	126.9	127.5
1973 Apr.	134.7	6.8	137.2	131.2	131.6	136.2	136.6
1974 Apr.	150.0	11.4	152.2	147.2	145.5	152.3	152.7
1975 Apr.	170.2	13.5	172.2	167.8	166.4	173.1	172.1
Oct.	182.1	7.0	183.4	180.7	181.0	183.9	182.9
1976 Apr.	195.4	7.3	195.3	195.8	194.3	197.7	195.8
Oct.	212.7	8.9	212.6	213.0	211.7	216.5	212.0
1977 Apr.	241.8	13.7	240.3	244.0	239.9	243.9	243.2
Oct.	272.5	12.7	272.4	273.1	267.1	276.6	275.2
1978 Apr.	294.8	8.2	296.7	293.0	289.9	298.9	297.2
Oct.	313.5	6.3	313.9	313.5	312.8	315.6	314.4
1979 Apr.	341.7	9.0	340.0	343.9	342.1	348.1	338.8
Oct.	387.0	13.3	382.5	391.9	396.1	386.9	382.8
1980 Apr.	421.6	8.9	415.3	428.3	434.7	426.9	411.1
Oct.	465.0	10.3	462.2	468.1	481.2	469.6	453.4
1981 Apr.	489.2	5.2	486.2	492.5	502.2	494.6	479.2
Oct.	498.7	1.9	498.6	499.1	508.9	504.2	490.5
1982 Apr.	503.7	1.0	502.7	505.0	516.0	505.8	496.5
Oct.	503.6	——	505.5	501.9	522.2	502.9	494.0
1983 Apr.	511.7	1.6	513.1	510.5	536.1	509.9	499.1
Oct.	519.8	1.6	523.1	516.8	548.4	523.9	506.7
1984 Apr.	530.2	2.0	533.1	527.5	561.0	533.5	516.4
Oct	538.7	1.6	542.5	535.2	574.4	542.2	521.8
1985 Apr.	550.6	2.2	555.0	546.6	593.1	555.4	528.8
Oct.	568.3	3.2	571.9	565.2	615.4	574.5	543.0
1986 Apr.	591.6	4.1	595.9	587.9	649.8	600.1	558.3
Oct.	624.7	5.6	626.3	623.7	696.0	634.8	582.9
1987 Apr.	653.7	4.6	653.9	654.0	734.2	667.3	604.8
Oct.	694.1	6.2	691.0	697.8	783.1	707.8	640.9
1988 Apr.	753.4	8.5	746.4	761.1	865.2	761.2	692.9

Figure 8.5
San Francisco Bay Area market trend index—by age of home. (From *Northern California Real Estate Report,* Vol. 40, No. 1, courtesy of the Real Estate Research Council of Northern California)

Consider the Sales History of the Subject Property

While appraisal tradition does not favor the use of a current sale or prior sales of the subject property as a direct market comparable, such evidence of value must not be ignored by the appraiser. At the present time, the Uniform Standards of Professional Appraisal Practice generally require the appraiser to consider and analyze any known current agreement of sale, option, or listing of the property to be appraised. Prior sales of the subject property should also be considered, when they have occurred within one year, if one- to four-family residential property is being appraised, or within three years for all other property types.

What Information Is Needed?

Once you have investigated the sales and decided which are comparable to the property being appraised, the next step is to collect the pertinent data. General information is needed about each sales transaction: the property's physical characteristics, its legal status, and its location. If located in a speculative market, a sales history of the comparable is generally required.

The Sales Transaction Data

Several items of information about each sales transaction are needed. One is the *date of sale.* Appraisers prefer the actual date that the sales price was agreed on, rather than the date the sale was recorded. Why? Because the sales price is sometimes established by an option or other agreement by the parties well before the actual recording of the sale. While not always available, the date of the "meeting of the minds" is the theoretical ideal for the date of sale. You also need to know the correct sales price and the *terms of sale;* by terms of sale we mean the financing arrangements that were made. You should know if the financing was by the seller or by a third party, and whether it was at market interest rates. Where seller financing was at favorable rates, the advantage to the buyer may have been offset by a higher price. Ideally, you should know the actual interest rate, the payment schedule, amortization period, and due date. You should also know whether the mortgage had a due-on-sale acceleration clause, a variable interest rate clause, or any other special provisions. This information is needed to see if the sales price should be adjusted because of the financing. Unfortunately, complete information on sales terms is not always available.

Depending on the type of appraisal and its intended use, additional sales transaction data may be needed. The property's legal description makes it possible to verify exactly what property was sold. Although required only in the more formal appraisals, obtaining the name of the seller (the grantor) and the buyer (the grantee) can also be useful. This helps to determine whether the sale was a family transfer. Sometimes, you may need to contact one or both parties to verify details of the transaction. Try to find out if there were any items of personalty, such as drapes, kitchen or laundry appliances, rugs, pianos, lawn furniture, and so on, included in the sale price. In large residential-income transactions, for example, some personalty is often included with the sale.

Finally, you must consider the buyer's and seller's motives. Was it a family transfer? Was it a sacrifice sale? Was it a tenant purchase? Was it bought by the adjacent property owner? As already indicated, answers to these questions may be required to determine whether a sale is a valid comparable.

In income and commercial appraisals, the sale transaction data should also include complete tenant rolls and income and expense information for the property. Sometimes available from sales data services, such information is usually sought out from the seller, agent, or property manager. It is common for commercial sales to be subject to an existing lease, and thus represent *only* the value of a leased fee interest. In such cases, the question of comparability must be addressed.

Physical Characteristics of the Sale

After you have collected information about the sales transaction, the next step is to seek out the physical characteristics of the property. Try to identify all of the characteristics that are important to the market being studied. These could include:

1. Land size, shape, topography, soil, and so on.
2. The size and nature of the structure or structures.

3. The age of the structures and the quality of their design and construction.

4. Any special features, such as built-in kitchens, remodeled baths, patios, swimming pools, room additions, air conditioning, electronic air filters, solar heating, insulation, and desirable views.

5. The condition of the structure and the quality of any modernization.

6. Available utilities.

7. Any problems with the property, ranging from small room sizes or poor floor plans to substantial deferred maintenance, inadequate wiring, roof leaks, landslides, and so on.

Legal Data About the Comparable Sale

In addition to the important physical characteristics of the sale, the appraiser should be aware of certain legal characteristics of the comparable property. For example, you should investigate the property's zoning category. Are the uses that are permissible comparable to those of the subject property? Next, note the property taxes that are currently being paid for the property and whether these taxes will likely change upon transfer of ownership. Any special assessment taxes should also be identified. Finally, are there any other public or private restrictions on the property? Any deed restrictions, easements, or leases should be reviewed to see if they have affected the sale price.

Location of the Sale

When investigating a comparable property, the appraiser should watch for any differences between the subject property's location and those of the comparable sales that are likely to be important to people in that market. In urban areas, differences in access to public transportation, the cost of fares, and the ability to transfer to other routes may be important. Are freeways easily accessible? How similar is the proximity to jobs, schools, cultural facilities, local shopping, and recreational facilities? Check for detrimental influences such as traffic noise, incompatible land uses, and/or possible natural hazards. Properties around the sale should be reviewed to see if their age, value, quality, condition, and/or use differ substantially from the properties around the subject. In short, compare the neighborhood around the sale property with the neighborhood around the subject property (Figure 8.6) to see if there are differences that would significantly affect the attitude of prospective buyers.

Market Conditions

For each sale, you must consider what the state of the market was at the time of the sale. Were market conditions at the time of the sale different from those at the date of value? Increased costs of conventional financing or lack of funds for FHA financing in particular areas are examples of changes in market conditions that usually affect prices.

SUBJECT PROPERTY

SALE #1   SALE #2   SALE #3

Figure 8.6
Comparing locations.

Using Listings and Offers

In most appraisal assignments (eg. FNMA loan appraisals), listings and offers are not allowed as substitutes for closed sales. However, in an uncertain market, it is a good idea to cite (in the remarks section, or separate attachment if necessary) several current listings or escrows (unclosed sales) to show current market trends and attitudes, and to support the value evidence represented by closed sales. At times, some lenders require this kind of data in appraisals.

Listings of property currently for sale can also indicate the upper limit, or highest probable market value. Offers that have been refused are helpful too, because they can suggest the lower limit of the value range. It is important to select listings that are current, and have characteristics similar to those of the subject property. When listings are cited, it is helpful to learn from the agent, broker, or other principal party whether there are any unusual conditions in a listing, particularly one where reasonable offers have been refused. Perhaps a personality conflict between the principal parties was the only reason a particular offer did not become a sale.

How Many Sales?

There is no specific number of comparables that is right for every appraisal. The desirable number depends, in part, on how comparable the sales are. For example, if the sales are very similar, located nearby, and fairly close to the date of value, three sales are considered adequate for most appraisal assignments. But where the sales are less comparable or the appraiser has less confidence in the reliability of the information obtained about the sales, a larger number of sales is usually desirable. Sometimes, too, a larger number of sales will be needed to justify the adjustments used.

The desirable number of comparables is also influenced by the techniques that will be used in the sales comparison approach. Some statistical techniques, for example, cannot be performed with only 3 or 4 sales, and might even require 20 or 30 sales, or more. The purpose or use of the appraisal report can also influence the number of comparables needed. An appraisal made for loan purposes usually requires fewer sales than an appraisal for court testimony.

Defining the Sales Search Area

How wide an area should you search for comparable sales? The general rule is that the more sales activity there is in an area, the more geographically restricted the appraiser's search can become. In an active market, it is often possible to find an adequate number of comparable sales within several blocks of the subject property, particularly if the subject is located in a residential tract. On the other hand, in appraising a large, new custom home in the middle of a neighborhood of older, smaller homes, the appraiser would have to enlarge the comparable search area. Similarly, when few sales are occurring because of a market slowdown, the appraiser must widen the boundaries of his or her comparable search area in order to collect adequate sales.

For some types of property, such as large industrial warehousing, buyers are free to select satisfactory substitute properties a considerable distance from the subject. In some markets, they will even buy property in another state. To define the search area for comparable sales in this kind of a market, the appraiser must carefully define comparability of location to suggest where a potential buyer would look for likely substitute properties.

Verification of Data

Perhaps the most important aspect of the sale search is the verification of data. As the appraiser, you must consider whether the sales information you have collected is reliable. You may find that one sale has a price that appears way out of line with the other sales. It is wise to recheck the key information about that sale. There could be a mistake in your information concerning the price, terms, or physical and locational characteristics.

Basically, you have two ways to improve the reliability of the information you obtained. The first is to inspect the sales. In most appraisals, a field inspection of the comparable sales is routine. This customarily consists of viewing the exterior of the property. Such an inspection serves to verify the data collected and to make it possible to evaluate the quality of the property, its condition, and its overall market appeal. Note that in making this survey, you must be careful to identify any work that appears to have been done on the property since the date of the sale. The sale price would have been based on the condition of the property at the time of the sale, and not at the time of your field inspection. Such factors as new exterior paint, new roof cover, or visible remodeling would suggest that you should check with a party to the transaction to verify the condition of the property at the time of sale.

In more complex or controversial assignments, the appraiser might want to view the interior of each comparable sale. This may be difficult since the occupants often resent a stranger knocking at the door. However, a careful explanation of who you are, what is happening, and why an interior inspection is desired can often produce positive results.

The second way to improve data reliability is to cross-check the data already obtained by contacting another information source. When sales data are obtained from a data service, such as the California Market Data Cooperative, or from public records, it may be desirable to verify the price and terms of the sale with a party to the transaction. This could be the real estate broker, a lawyer, the buyer, the seller, or the loan officer involved in the financing. There is no clear rule as to when this should be done. Generally, it depends on the reliability of the source from which the sale was obtained and the type of appraisal assignment involved. Thus, in preparing a residential loan appraisal in a stable market with ample, consistent sales, many appraisers would not verify the data with a party to the transaction. On the other hand, when appraising a unique property for some type of litigation (such as an eminent domain lawsuit), most appraisers try to verify the price and terms with a party to the transaction.

Sources of Market Data

Becoming an efficient appraiser includes identifying the available sources of market data for an area and knowing the advantages and drawbacks of each. Each source may be useful for different types of information. Obtaining information quickly is an important appraisal skill because it affects how much time is used to perform the appraisal.

Public Records

One major source of sales information is public records. Most public records (usually in county seats) include copies of all the deeds transferring ownership to real estate. These deeds are filed by document number on the date that they are recorded at the office. They are usually kept on microfilm and are referenced either by a document number, the microfilm reel and image numbers, or by book and page numbers. Each deed is indexed both by the name of the grantor (seller) and by the grantee (buyer). In large counties, the office where the records are kept is called the recorder's office. Small counties often assign record-keeping functions to the county clerk.

Figure 8.7 shows that the deed contains the name of the grantor and the grantee, a legal description of the property sold, and the date the transaction was recorded. In addition, there will be a documentary transfer tax paid at the time the deed was recorded. Often, this tax is a standard $0.55 per $500 of cash consideration. This means that an assumed mortgage, which does not involve new cash, will not be taxed. A new mortgage, however, will be taxed, whether it is made by the seller or by an independent lender. Nearly all jurisdictions "rubber stamp" the deed with information on the transfer tax. They will fill in the amount of the tax and check whether it is calculated on the full price or whether the tax is on a value reduced by any assumed mortgages or liens (called "less liens").

Some jurisdictions have a different transfer tax rate, and some calculate it differently. If you are going to use this transfer tax information to calculate the purchase price, you should investigate how it is calculated in that jurisdiction. At times, there is no record of the exact tax on the deed. The record is kept separately at the recorder's office, so their

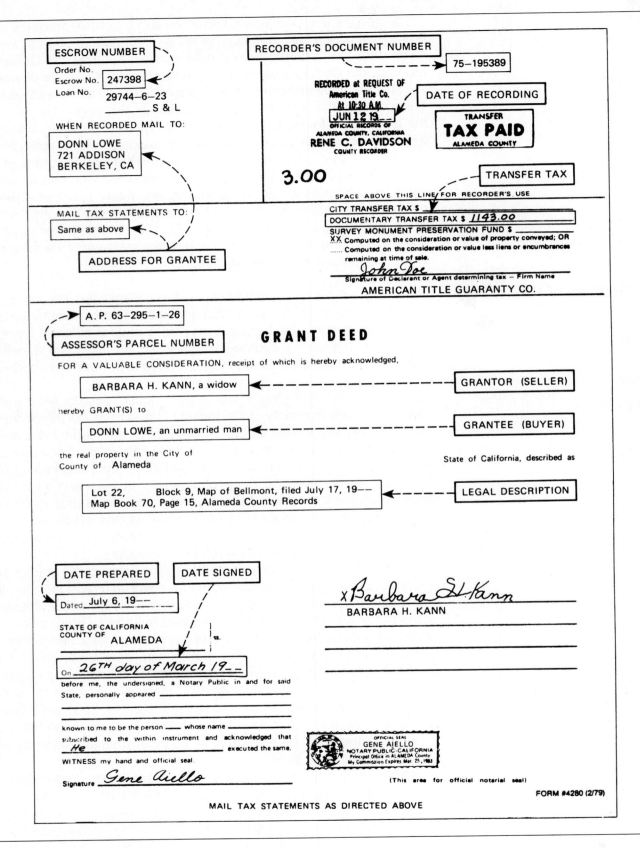

ESCROW NUMBER

Order No.
Escrow No. 247398
Loan No. 29744–6–23
_____ S & L

WHEN RECORDED MAIL TO:

DONN LOWE
721 ADDISON
BERKELEY, CA

MAIL TAX STATEMENTS TO:

Same as above

ADDRESS FOR GRANTEE

RECORDER'S DOCUMENT NUMBER

75–195389

RECORDED at REQUEST OF
American Title Co.
At 10:30 A.M.
JUN 12 19__
OFFICIAL RECORDS OF
ALAMEDA COUNTY, CALIFORNIA
RENE C. DAVIDSON
COUNTY RECORDER

DATE OF RECORDING

TRANSFER
TAX PAID
ALAMEDA COUNTY

3.00

TRANSFER TAX

SPACE ABOVE THIS LINE FOR RECORDER'S USE

CITY TRANSFER TAX $ _____
DOCUMENTARY TRANSFER TAX $ 1143.00
SURVEY MONUMENT PRESERVATION FUND $ _____
XX Computed on the consideration or value of property conveyed; OR
..... Computed on the consideration or value less liens or encumbrances
remaining at time of sale.
John Doe
Signature of Declarant or Agent determining tax – Firm Name
AMERICAN TITLE GUARANTY CO.

A. P. 63–295–1–26

ASSESSOR'S PARCEL NUMBER

GRANT DEED

FOR A VALUABLE CONSIDERATION, receipt of which is hereby acknowledged,

BARBARA H. KANN, a widow

GRANTOR (SELLER)

hereby GRANT(S) to

DONN LOWE, an unmarried man

GRANTEE (BUYER)

the real property in the City of
County of   Alameda

State of California, described as

Lot 22,   Block 9, Map of Bellmont, filed July 17, 19——
Map Book 70, Page 15, Alameda County Records

LEGAL DESCRIPTION

DATE PREPARED   DATE SIGNED

Dated July 6, 19——

STATE OF CALIFORNIA
COUNTY OF   ALAMEDA   } ss.

On 26TH day of March 19__
before me, the undersigned, a Notary Public in and for said
State, personally appeared _____

known to me to be the person ___ whose name _____
subscribed to the within instrument and acknowledged that
He _____ executed the same.
WITNESS my hand and official seal.

Signature Gene Aiello

x Barbara H. Kann
BARBARA H. KANN

OFFICIAL SEAL
GENE AIELLO
NOTARY PUBLIC-CALIFORNIA
Principal Office in ALAMEDA County
My Commission Expires Mar. 25, 1983

(This area for official notarial seal)

FORM #4280 (2/79)

MAIL TAX STATEMENTS AS DIRECTED ABOVE

Figure 8.7
Recording information.

tax books can be properly audited and tabulated. This separate record is sometimes available upon request.

In addition to the above-mentioned information affixed to the deed, you can obtain other types of information from the deed. Some counties will not record a deed unless it has the county assessor's parcel number on it. In California, a "Preliminary Change of Ownership" form must be completed by the seller and forwarded to the county assessor at the time of deed recording. Designed to assist the assessor in the change of ownership reassessment, this form discloses the price and terms of the current transaction. Some assessors' offices and private data banks make this information available to private appraisers.

Usually, the recorded deed contains a mailing address where it is to be returned. Often the mailing address for the buyer or the buyer's attorney or broker is used. Most deeds also contain the new address to which the property tax bill should be mailed. This could be the buyer's address, the buyer's agent (if the property tax is being paid by another party), or the buyer's bank (if taxes are to be paid from an impound account). Either or both of these addresses can lead you to someone who could verify information about the sale.

Most deeds also indicate which party requested that the deed be recorded. This is particularly common when deeds are recorded as part of a title or escrow company closing. Usually, the name of the title company is on the deed as well as the escrow account number and the code letters indicating which title company branch handled the transaction. Title companies will not divulge the details of a transaction but will sometimes disclose the name of the broker(s). The broker, in turn, can provide information about the property. The name of the notary public who notarized the seller's signature can also be helpful. For example, the notary public's seal will state the county in which the notary practices, which could help you locate buyers or sellers who live out of town.

When an institutional lender makes a new loan on the property as part of the sale transaction, the lender's loan number is sometimes typed on the deed. This loan number can prove helpful when discussing the property with the lender or the lender's appraiser, since the loan number enables them to locate the file quickly.

Finally, you should note that the deed contains dates other than just the date of recording. Often the date next to the signatures indicates either the date that the document was signed or the date it was prepared. Another date will be on the notary public's affidavit of signatures. This will be the date the individual sellers had their signatures notarized.

If a new loan was placed on the property at the time of sale, the deed of trust securing that loan will be recorded as the document immediately following the deed. This deed of trust will give the lender's name and the amount of the loan. It may also indicate whether it is a variable interest rate loan and if a clause was included making the loan due in full when the property is resold. The loan number will sometimes be on the deed of trust, as will a mailing address for the borrower, a date of signature, and another notary's signature with the date and county of business. Much of this information may already be on the deed, but occasionally, missing details are found that will be helpful to the appraiser.

Additional documents may also be recorded, such as a chattel mortgage for any personal property, and an assignment of rents if the property generates income. A second mortgage might have been placed by the broker to secure a note for the commission due. This would identify the broker's name and location. There may also be other encumbrances in favor of the seller or a third party, or there may be requests for a notice of default. The recorder must notify the named party if a notice of default is filed for any deeds of trust listed on the request. The seller who has a second mortgage from the buyer or some other party (such as a broker with a loan for a commission) may want to be notified.

A second major public source of information for appraisers is the assessor's office. Although the exact jurisdiction will differ from one location to another, property tax assessment records are usually maintained by the county assessor. The primary document to look for is the assessment roll. Besides showing the assessed value of all privately owned property by assessor's parcel number, the roll shows the current owner of record and an address for tax bill mailing purposes. Most jurisdictions have a standard series of maps, so that each listed parcel can be described by map reference number. Assessment rolls will often show the date of the most recent transfer of ownership and the document number used by the public recorder's office for that transfer. Assessment rolls may also contain a use code (which identifies a category of use for the property, such as residential, commercial, industrial, or vacant land) and may show the age and size of buildings. (See Figure 8.8.)

The assessor's maps include index maps for the entire county, area index maps, and maps showing each of the parcels in a block. These maps give the dimensions of the parcels and usually show major easements, as well as streets and railroads. Often, the area of larger parcels will be calculated and noted on the map.

There are also indexes for the assessment roll. The roll itself usually lists property in parcel number order. One index will list property by address and a second index by the name of the owner. Still another document maintained by some assessor's offices is a list of current sales. Originally prepared for use by the assessor's appraisal staff, these lists have become, by law, public information in some states.

Multiple Listing Services

In many areas, there are multiple listing services (often called MLS). These are usually sponsored by a local board of Realtors or by local brokers. All the property listings submitted by members are combined and made available to subscribers. These current listings are often published in a weekly or biweekly book. Usually at the end of the book you will find an index of listings which have sold in the immediate past. A quarterly book is published summarizing all the sales and expired listings that have occurred during that quarter. In the past many multiple listing services restricted the use of such books solely to their members; however, some states have made licensed and certified ap-

PARCEL BY PARCEL SUMMARY LISTS

	USE CODE	ZONING	YR BLT	#UN	SQ FEET	ASSESSED VAL	PHONE	TFR DATE
(1) 9438-014-007		SITE: 11472 BRIGHT ST*BURBANK CA						91506
OWNR:JONES KENN		MAIL:11472 BRIGHT ST*BURBANK CA						91506
SINGLE RESIDENCE	BUR1YY	83	1		2100	$173,653	555-1234	04/08/93
(2) 9438-014-010		SITE: 11475 BRIGHT ST*BURBANK CA						91506
OWNR:HALLIWELL,ART		MAIL:11475 BRIGHT ST*BURBANK CA						91506
SINGLE RESIDENCE	BUR1YY	83	1		2100	$173,000	555-5678	10/06/91
(3) 9438-014-013		SITE: 11479 BRIGHT ST*BURBANK CA						91506
OWNR:AQUILA,JANE		MAIL:11479 BRIGHT ST*BURBANK CA						91506
SINGLE RESIDENCE	BUR1YY	83	1		2100	$171,000	555-9876	8/07/92

INDIVIDUAL DETAIL PROPERTY LISTING

PARCEL-NO : 423-224-00   USE DESC   : SINGLE FAMILY RESIDENCE
OWNER   : LITTLE CHARLIE &GAYLE   2ND OWNR : NONE
SITE   : 4225 BAY ST   MAIL   : 4225 BAY ST
              : SAN DIEGO CA   92109   : SAN DIEGO CA   92109
PAGE-GRID: 52-A4   PHONE : 555-9085
ASSESSMENT/TAX INFO.   PROPERTY CHAR.   SALE/LOAN INFO.

ASSESSMENT/TAX INFO.		PROPERTY CHAR.		SALE/LOAN INFO.	
ASSESSD VAL	: $289,918	ZONING	: R1 SNGL F	LAST SALE	: 09/05/91
LAND VALUE	: $168,398	EXP ZONING	: R15	AMOUNT	: $284,500F
PERCENT IMP	: 41%	# OF UNITS	: 1	COST/SQ FT	: $144
EXEMPTION	: HOMEOWNER	YEAR BUILT	: 40	DOC NUMBER	: 296811
TAX RT AREA	: 08001	LOT SIZE	: 9147	TITLE CO.	: BISMARCK TITLE
ANNUAL TAX	: $2,983.92	SQ FOOTAGE	: 1976	LENDER	: 2ND FINANCIAL
TAX STATUS	: CURRENT	BEDROOMS	: 4	FIRST TD	: $200,000
MAP	: 1098	BATHROOMS	: 2.0	ADDT'L TDS	:
BLOCK	: 1	GAR SPCS	: 2	PREV SALE	: 06/07/87
LOT	: 3	POOL/VIEW	: Y / N	AMOUNT	: $223,000

Figure 8.8
Assessment roll property listing samples. (Courtesy of DataQuick)

Data Services

praisers eligible for membership. MLS data are usually maintained on a computer and can be accessed by personal computers over a telephone line.

In recent years, the number of organized, private sources of appraisal data has increased. One of the best known of these is the Appraisal Institute Market Data Center, a nonprofit corporation. The sales data are generated by cooperating lenders and appraisers and are made available to Data Center members in several formats. For example, at the time of this writing, listings of single-family sales are available in many areas through a monthly sale book and also by computer terminal. A sample page from the California Market Data Cooperative, a licensed member, is shown as Figure 8.9. Quarterly books of apartment sales are available in the same areas. The majority of the sales data is developed from loan appraisals. Regular sales listings also incorporate current sales transfer information from public records as well as all available assessor's data. This cooperative data coverage for appraisers started in Southern California in 1968 and gradually spread across the United States under sponsorship of SREA Market Data Center, now operating as the Appraisal Institute Market Data Center. The service in each area varies, depending on the participation of local lenders.

A number of other private firms provide some type of data service. Several of these are nationwide. For example, TRW-REDI (headquartered in Riverside, California) offers property data in a broad array of formats and media, including on-line property data with access to eight major databases, as well as CD/ROM (Compact Disc/Read Only Memory) data discs, microfiche, and commercial-industrial transaction reports. Now growing in popularity, CD/ROM discs are inserted into a reader that can be connected to a computer. While the on-line data service is generally available only in California, the others are nationwide. There are a number of local sales services that exist in various

Figure 8.9
Single-family residential sales data. (Copyright 1993 by California Market Data Cooperative, Inc.)

CMDC CALIFORNIA MARKET DATA COOPERATIVE — **SINGLE FAMILY RESIDENTIAL / PUD SALES DATA** — SEB SANTA CLARA

Map Code or City Name or Census Tract	Source	Property Address / Assessor's Parcel Number	Lot/Tract	Recording Number	Clsd Sle	Sales Price	Sales Date	Loan Type / Mrtg % 1st # Oth	Price per SqFt	Year Blt / Style Stories	Rooms Bedrooms / Baths	Sq Feet Liv Area / Basement Sq. Feet	Oth. Rms. / Kitchen Equipmnt	Heating / Air Cond	Fireplace	Utils. / Zoning	Prkg Spaces Type Constr	Property Description Codes	Lot Size or Area	Flood Zone	Other Improvements / Comments	Total Units	Ownership	Pool/Spa	Phys Upd
67 -A4	C	2375 WESTGATE AVE, SAN JOSE 439-30-015	55/1599	11705779	Y	210,000 210,000	110192 122492	90%	123	1947 N 1	6 3 1.50	1713	AFL R	A N	G 1	P P P P R1 SFR	N D A 2 G D	A G C C V	140X75	N	PATSLB FR NEIGHBOOR ACC ST-MIN NOISE DET	1	S		F 1
67 -A5	A	3200 CHERRY AVE, SAN JOSE 451-12-085	1/3470	11702015	Y	210,000	122292	C 90%	143	1963	7 4 2.00	1465				R1	2 G		63X095				S		
	A	3274 CHERRY AVE, SAN JOSE 451-12-082	4/3470	11715257	Y	570,000	123192	C F 32%	389	1963	7 4 2.00	1465				R1	2 G		63X095				S		
	H	3661 CHERRY AVE, SAN JOSE 451-19-008	224/2096	11697267	Y	191,500	121892	C F 85%	150	1959	5 3 2.00	1280		A C	G 1	P P P P R1	A	A A	9120		PATSLB UPDATED KIT, UPDATED BATH	1	S		F 3
	C	4008 ROSS PK CT, SAN JOSE 451-24-115	75/3435	11701738	Y	247,000 247,000	100192 122292	C 80%	149	1964 N 1	7 4 2.00	1657	AF B	A N	G 1	P P P P R1	N D A 2 G A	A A T C V	114X66	N	CVRPAT, FEN	1	S	POOL	F 1
	F	3150 SANTA MARGARITA AVE, SAN JOSE 447-01-051	20/1249		N	225,000	010893	C	167	1954 N 1	6 3 2.00	1349	DY RHS	A N	G 1	P P P P R1	N D A 2 G A	A G A T A	9500	N	FEN, PATSLB REMOD: BTH; W/I CLST	1	S		F 1
	H	3316 THOMPSON AVE, SAN JOSE 447-22-060	66/2425	11723161	Y	295,000	010793	C 80%	169	1960 1	7 3 2.50	1744	DF B	A	G 2	P P R	D G D	G A C W	7071	N	CVRPAT, FEN		S		0
	C	1536 WILLOWBROOK DR, SAN JOSE 447-23-107	20/1998	11698617	Y	210,000 210,000	100192 121892	C F 80%	6000 145	1958 R 1	7 4 2.50	1446	F B	A N	G 1	P P P P R1	N D A 2 G A	A A C C C	62X100	N	CVRPAT, FEN	1	S		F 1
67 -A6	F	1353 BOYSEA DR, SAN JOSE 451-34-021	29/3045		N	208,000	010193	C	173	1962 2	5 3 2.00	1205	AL BM	A N	G	P P P P R1	N A 2 G A	A A C T V	6500	N	CVRPAT	1	S		F 1
	A	4552 CALLE DE FARRAR, SAN JOSE 451-43-007	5/5334	11697858	Y	257,500	121892	C 79%1	146	1973	7 4 2.00	1769				R1B6	2 G		60X100				S	POOL	
	F	1531 CASA DE PONSELLE, SAN JOSE 451-43-071	39/5334		N	285,000	010193		143	1974 2	8 4 2.00	1999	DF B	A N	G 1	P X X X R1B6	N D A 2 G A	A A A C W	6000	N	CVRPAT EXT RE	1	S	BOTH	F 1
	F	1418 GLACIER DR, SAN JOSE 451-35-015	197/3700		N	207,500	011293	C	141	1965 R 1	7 3 2.00	1470	DFLY B	A C	G 1	P P P P R1	V D A 2 G A	A A A T A	56X107	N	CVRPAT CENT BURGLAR ALARM, ADDED FAM RM	1	S		F 1
67 -B1	F	1773 ARBOR DR, SAN JOSE 439-24-071	15/633		N	210,000	010193		207	1950 1	5 3 1.00	1015	D H	A N	G 1	P P P P R1	N D A 1 G A	A A C C A	57X100	N	CVRPAT	1	S		F 1
	F	1822 BIRD AVE, SAN JOSE 439-24-062			N	210,000	120192	C	157	1950 R 1	7 3 1.00	1338	DRLY B	A N	G	P P P P R1	V D A 1 G A	A A C C C	5000	N	REMOD: CONV/GAR; GRG & FAM RM ADDED, COV PCH, VAUL CEIL	1	S		F 1
	A	1742 COASTLAND AVE, SAN JOSE 439-21-065	14/603	11728451	Y	58,500	011293	C	57	1949	5 3 1.00	1030				R1	1 G		58X104				S		
67 -B2	F	2111 COASTLAND AVE, SAN JOSE 439-18-019	9/736		N	269,500	120592	C	147	1950 N 2	5 3 2.00	1838	AL RHS	A C	G	P P P P R1	N D A 3 G D	A G C W V	7140	Y	DEC, FEN, PATSLB EE ITM: GLZD WIN; CEIL FANS	1	S		F 1
	A	877 CURTNER AVE, SAN JOSE 439-17-078	54/LINCOLNH	11730322	Y	208,000	011393	C 90%	158	1945	6 3 2.00	1319				R1	2 G		51X153				S		
67 -B4	H	2930 COTTLE AVE, SAN JOSE 439-44-043	81/1599	11734667	Y	268,500	011593	C F 80%	158	1956 R 1	6 4 2.00	1701	B	A	G 1	P P R	D G A	G A C C	61X108	N	CVRPAT		S		0
	A	1333 CRESTWOOD DR, SAN JOSE 451-03-021	78/1214	11724634	Y	200,000	010893	C F 75%	145	1957	6 4 2.00	1376				R1	2 G		62X100				S		
67 -B5	F	1216 GREENMOOR DR, SAN JOSE 451-39-014	23/4021		N	255,000	010193	C	161	1966 N 1	7 4 2.00	1585	AF B	A N	G 1	P P P P SFR	N D A 2 G A	A G A C V	10605	N	FEN	1	S		F 1
	F	3773 THOUSAND OAKS DR, SAN JOSE 459-32-054	240/5564	11645654	Y	289,250 289,500	100192 111792	C 94%	137	1976 N 2	8 4 2.50	2108	DF B	A N	G 1	P P P P R1 SFR	N D A 3 G A	A G A C V	60X100	N	DEC, FEN TILE ENT, WT BAR, CATH CEIL	1	S	SPA	F 1
	A	3739 WELLINGTON SQ, SAN JOSE 459-32-028	222/5564THOU	11703688	Y	240,000	122392	C 90%	156	1976	7 4 2.00	1540				R1B6	2 G		62X121				S		
67 -B6	A	4374 BALD EAGLE WAY, SAN JOSE 451-37-015	11/5484	11715558	Y	290,000	123192	C F 55%	137	1976	9 4 2.50	2115				R1B6	2 G		58X103				S		
	F	1189 CHERRYVIEW LN, SAN JOSE 569-57-018			N	195,000	122692	C	135	1984	6 3 2.50	1444	DLYX B	A N	G	P P P P APD	V R A 2 G	A A W S	20X54	N	CVRPAT EE ITM: AUTOTHERM, W-STRIP, FURN IG; BONUS ROOM, W/I CLST	22	P		F 1
	H	4331 MONTMORENCY CT, SAN JOSE 451-37-134	32/7007	11715525	Y	299,000	123192	F 80%	174	1983 N 1	7 3 2.00	1716	DFLY BM	A N	G 1	P P P P R1	N D G 2 G A	G G A C C	55X109	N	CVRPAT, FEN TILE ENT, BURGLAR ALARM SYS, VAUL CEIL	1	S		F 3
67 -C3	A	716 CREEKFIELD DR, SAN JOSE 455-30-025	65/6884	11699192	Y	546,000	122192	C F 25%	318	1983	9 4 3.00	1718				APD	2 G		40X085				S		

THE ABOVE DATA IS BELIEVED TO BE RELIABLE BUT ACCURACY IS NOT GUARANTEED. **FEB 1993** – 125 –

MAP / CITY / CENSUS: 67 –A4 THRU 67 –C3
REMEMBER, YOUR APPRAISAL COPIES ARE THE NEXT BOOK.

SINGLE FAMILY / PUD SANTA CLARA

areas. Some services may specialize in just one county, providing microfiche or deed copies as their basic data. In many areas there are local appraisal cooperative data centers. These can range from a large company to informal agreements between two appraisers to share sales data. In many areas of the country, the publicly available assessment and transfer information is available in both the microfiche format and some form of computer format, usually by telephone. In California, the largest on-line and CD/ROM data service is DataQuick, in San Diego. This firm provides comparables from their own complete database, as well as from CMDC ON-LINE.

Finally, sales data information can be provided by title insurance companies. Title companies have extensive microfilm files of public records affecting real estate. Often featuring a computerized index, each file includes assessment and sales transfer records, deeds and other recorded documents. Title companies often provide customers with a property "profile," which may include assessment details of the subject property, along with recent transfers for the surrounding area. Appraisers may be able to obtain copies of such profiles, along with other needed documents. Sometimes, arrangements can be made with the title insurance company to research other specified sales in the area for a reasonable fee. If the research is quite limited, some title companies are willing to provide the information without charge.

Parties to the Transaction

As suggested above, you should consider the possibility of obtaining information from the parties to the transaction. These parties include not only the buyer and seller but their respective agents as well. Other parties that could also have relevant information include any brokers who had offers on the property at the same time or brokers who had prior listings that expired. Any lender involved with the sale can also be a source of information. Sometimes, a particular broker's office, or a particular lender's branch, may have been a party to a large percentage of all the recent transactions in an area, or indeed, may have originated the transaction in question. If so, such an office would be an important resource.

Appraisal Office Data Files

Many appraisers find that the types of properties they appraise will change from time to time. However, houses are the most common appraisal assignment. The information needed to complete single-family appraisals is usually plentiful and easy to find. However, there will be times throughout an appraiser's career when an unusual property will be assigned and the necessary data will not be accessible. Keeping this in mind, many appraisers keep on file much of the market data that were researched, particularly the data collected for unusual assignments. If a similar assignment comes up in the near future, the market data can be reused. Files of this type are also a useful source of information for other appraisers. One appraiser may have information on file that another appraiser cannot find without a major effort. In many areas, appraisers share their sales data with other appraisers, especially local ones. However, a clear policy concerning this type of cooperation does not exist. You may find areas in which no cooperation is given. Thus it is up to the individual appraiser to decide whether to cooperate with other appraisers.

Locating good comparable sales data in an efficient manner is an art. You must be imaginative, resourceful, and, above all, determined. Very often, the most important differences between a fair appraisal and a good one are the several added sale and the several added relevant facts about the sale properties. Like all arts, skill at appraisal improves with experience, so do not be dismayed if it seems difficult at first.

Computer Data Search

As noted previously, the sales data and other information that appraisers need are increasingly stored on a computer, whether at the appraiser's office, at the local multiple listing service or title company, or at a regional or national data service. In turn, this increased computerized data collection has led to a greater use of appraisal office computers to access, sort, and preserve the data. How does computer data search work? Each data service has its own organization of data, rules for access, and search procedures. Nevertheless, there is enough standardization that some generalizations can be made.

Access

First, most computer sales data collections are currently accessed via telephone, using a modem to connect the office computer to the telephone. The data computer will be directly connected to a special telephone number, reachable from anywhere in the country (or perhaps the world) via regular long-distance dialing or, usually, by a local call to a specialized long-distance computer network. In a few cases, some local cooperative data networks exchange updated disks on a periodic basis. As mentioned earlier, data service also includes sales data distribution on CD/ROM discs.

Procedure

Usually, the first step is to connect to the computer through the appropriate telephone network. A customer password is given each subscriber. Next, the appropriate database is selected from the several usually available. The database chosen might depend upon geographical location and type of property (homes vs. apartments vs. commercial, for example) or type of information sought (assessment roll vs. sales data, for example).

Within the appropriate database, the next step is usually to define the search to be performed. This is done by selecting the criteria or property characteristics that are considered most important. One characteristic is nearly always location. The acceptable locations, or search area, must now be identified by a commonly used local map reference, such as Thomas Maps, or by street address. Assessment maps, subdivision map references, federal township and range surveys, and other reference systems are sometimes acceptable to the data bank. In this way, the appraiser is able to eliminate all sales data not meeting the locational search criteria.

Other search criteria might be the use of the property, its physical size (maximum, minimum, or range), the number of bedrooms and baths, age, price, sale date, or any other information stored in the data bank and usable as search criteria.

Clearly, selecting the best search criteria is important if computers are relied on for the sales data search. If the criteria are too demanding, the search might produce only a few sales, or even none. If the criteria are not rigid enough, too many sales in the data collection may qualify. For this reason, many systems allow the user to do a search and get a report back giving the number of sales meeting the criteria. In this way, the user knows whether to change the search criteria before looking at the individual sales more carefully.

8.3 APPRAISAL STATISTICAL CONCEPTS

As was suggested in section 8.1, the use of comparable sales in the sales comparison approach is a "sampling" process, a technique of statistics. The sales selected for analysis constitute the "sample." When applying the sales adjustment methods described above, certain other statistical methods may be useful to validate and interpret data from the sample. However, a fairly large number of comparables are usually required.

One statistical concept helps the appraiser discover the "central tendency" among the sales. *Central tendency* means the numeric value that is suggested as typical, with regard to size, price, or other variable studied. Calculating the central tendency can help in several ways. For example, an analysis of the typical square-foot size of the comparables could help interpret their sales prices, or suggest the weight to be assigned them in the adjustment process. Measures of central tendency include the following:

---

1. **Mean:** the average numeric "value" of the sample (the average price or average size, for example).

2. **Median:** the middle value, that is, the one with as many values above it as values below it in the sample.

3. **Mode:** the most frequently occurring value.

4. **Range:** the difference, or spread, between the highest and lowest value in the sample.

5. **Standard deviation:** a measurement of whether the observations are clustered close to the mean, or, instead, throughout the range; the square root of the sum of the squared differences between each observation and the mean of all observations, divided by the total number of observations. (Here, each sale price, for example, would be considered an observation.)

Used primarily in mass appraisal work, linear and multiple regression represent two additional statistical methods used in valuations. These methods typically calculate the relationship between a series of numbers representing property characteristics and the selling prices of the sample, producing a formula for such relationship. Hence, the significant characteristics of each sale property (price, square-foot area, age, etc.) are entered into the formula. A statistically indicated value of the subject property may then be calculated. Linear and multiple regression techniques will be explored further in Chapter 9.

SUMMARY   The sales comparison approach is one of the three approaches used to estimate value. The main feature of the sales comparison approach is the process of analyzing sales and comparing them to the subject property, based on the principle of substitution. The sales comparison approach consists of four steps.

---

1. Research sales.

2. Analyze sales.

3. Adjust sales for differences between the sales and the subject property.

4. Arrive at a value estimate.

When employing the sales comparison approach, an appraiser should consider the concepts that are fundamental to it. These concepts include the principle of substitution, the importance of simplicity, the connections to statistics, the relevance of adjustments, and the foundation—market data. Each of these concepts is important in understanding how to use the sales comparison approach.

The first step of the sales comparison approach—researching comparable sales—consists of two parts: (1) selecting comparable sales, and (2) seeking out the appropriate sales information. When selecting comparable sales, three criteria should be met for a sale to be considered a comparable sale: The sale must be a competitive property, an open market transaction, and close to the date of value. The ideal is to find comparable sales that meet all three criteria. If you cannot, try to find sales that were open market transactions and are as comparable and as close to the date of value as possible.

Once you have decided on the sales you are going to use, the next step is collecting the necessary information about the sales transaction, the physical characteristics of the property, its legal status, and its location. It is also important to consider whether there were unusual market conditions at the time of sale.

The number of comparables needed varies with each appraisal situation. How comparable the sales are and which adjustment techniques are used will both affect the number of sales needed to support your conclusion. The area of the sales search will vary as well, depending on the type of property being appraised and the amount of market activity.

After deciding on the sales data to be used, you must then decide whether your data are reliable. Inspecting the sales is one good way of ensuring that your data are reliable. Cross-checking your data with another source is another.

Since there are many sources of market data, the trick is knowing where to find the information you need as efficiently and easily as possible. There are a variety of sources with which you should be familiar, ranging from public records at the county assessor's office to private firms that provide information on sales for a fee.

Public records include deeds, which contain such needed information as names of grantor and grantee, a legal description of the property, transfer tax information, a mailing address for the buyer, and the transaction date. The assessor's office contains the assessment roll, which lists privately owned property, its value for property tax purposes, and its tax-bill mailing address. Assessor's maps provide the measurements of parcels and show major easements, streets, and railroads.

One private data source is the multiple listing services (MLS) sponsored by local boards of Realtors. Private data sources are becoming increasingly valuable, particularly those offering services like those of the California Market Data Cooperative (CMDC). Access to central computer databases is a recent trend, allowing rapid, inexpensive sharing of data and easier processing of sales analyses and reports. Whenever possible, the appraiser also seeks out the parties to a transaction—the buyer, the seller, or their agents—to obtain information. If you learn to utilize all these sources, you will master the art of finding good comparable sales.

The sales comparison approach has a connection to statistics, in that the comparable sales represent a "sample" from which we can draw certain conclusions. Appraisers use several statistical methods that can help with the analysis of the sample or with data drawn from the sample. The most useful of these mathematical tools are those that can suggest how typical a price or other variable is in the sample, an idea known as central tendency. The mean, median, and mode are the most common of these statistical measures.

Important Terms and Concepts		
	Adjustments	Linear and multiple regression
	Bracketing	Location
	Buyer's motives	Mean
	Central tendency	Median
	Comparable sales	Mode
	Comparable search area	Open market transaction
	Competitive property	Physical characteristics
	Data reliability	Public records
	Data services	Range

Regression, linear and multiple

Seller's motives

Sales comparison approach

Standard deviation

Sample

Variable

Sales history

Verifying sales information

REVIEWING YOUR UNDERSTANDING

1. The sales comparison approach involves:
   (a) Analyzing sales
   (b) Comparing sales to a subject property
   (c) Both (a) and (b)
   (d) None of the above

2. The first step in the sales comparison approach is to:
   (a) Research comparable sales
   (b) Adjust for differences between the sales
   (c) Arrive at a value conclusion
   (d) Set up an office data system

3. The sales comparison approach is simpler and more direct than the income or cost approaches because:
   (a) Fewer comparable properties are required, so that it is easier to outline the results to clients
   (b) There are fewer mathematical calculations, so that there is less chance of mathematical errors
   (c) Both (a) and (b)
   (d) None of the above

4. Appraisers use bracketing in order to:
   (a) Apply the cost approach to large mansions
   (b) Estimate the upper and lower range of value
   (c) Estimate the adjustment for units of comparison
   (d) Study markets that are better and worse than the market for the subject

5. Market data are used:
   (a) In the sales comparison approach
   (b) In the income approach
   (c) In the cost approach
   (d) All of the above

6. In order for a property to be considered comparable:
   (a) It must have sold within five years
   (b) It must be a competitive property
   (c) It must be an open market transaction
   (d) Both (a) and (b)
   (e) Both (b) and (c)

7. The Uniform Standards of Professional Appraisal Practice provide that prior sales of the subject property:
   (a) Need not be considered in the appraisal

(b) Must be considered when they have occurred within one year for one- to four-family residential properties

(c) Must be considered when they have occurred within three years for all *other* than one- to four-unit residential properties

(d) Must always be considered

(e) Must be considered as suggested in (b) and (c) above

8. The number of comparable sales needed for the sales comparison approach is dependent on:
   (a) How good the comparables are
   (b) The reliability of the data
   (c) The intended use of the appraisal
   (d) All of the above

9. You need to know all the following information about a comparable property *except:*
   (a) The sales price
   (b) The date of sale
   (c) The date legal work began on the transaction
   (d) The type of financing involved

10. In order to improve the reliability of the information about a sale, the appraiser should:
    (a) Make at least an exterior inspection
    (b) Identify changes made since the sale date
    (c) Verify the price and terms of sale
    (d) All of the above

11. Which of the following statistical concepts helps measure central tendency in a sample?
    (a) Mean
    (b) Median
    (c) Mode
    (d) All of the above

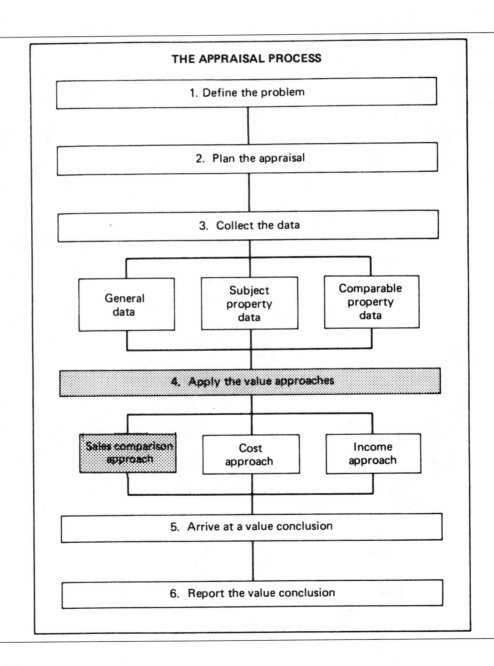

THE APPRAISAL PROCESS

1. Define the problem

2. Plan the appraisal

3. Collect the data

General data

Subject property data

Comparable property data

4. Apply the value approaches

Sales comparison approach

Cost approach

Income approach

5. Arrive at a value conclusion

6. Report the value conclusion

Chapter 9
Analyzing and Adjusting Comparable Sales

Preview   Continuing our discussion of the sales comparison approach in this chapter, we shall consider how and why sales are analyzed. We also describe how to make adjustments for differences between the sales and the subject property. Finally, we will explain how to arrive at a value conclusion using the sales comparison approach.

When you have finished this chapter, you should be able to:

1. Name the four elements of sales comparison.

2. List the three rules for making adjustments.

3. Name the three types of adjustments most commonly used.

4. Explain how a value conclusion is reached.

9.1 PRINCIPLES OF COMPARISON AND ADJUSTMENT

In this section, we discuss the comparison of sales—a key element in the sales comparison approach. Once you have found property sales that are similar to the subject property, you can compare them in several ways. The comparison and analysis process described in this section can lead to an accurate and objective estimation of value.

Elements of Comparison

When the comparable sales have been found, all relevant data about them should be gathered. The next step is to identify and compare the *differences* between the sales and also between the sales and the subject property. Our goal is to identify the differences that cause significant variations in the prices paid in this specific market.

All the information about each sale is divided into four categories, which are known as the four "elements of comparison."

The Four Elements of Comparison

1. Terms and conditions of sale.

2. Time of sale.

3. Location elements.

4. Physical elements.

Terms and Conditions of Sale

The *terms* of the sale can determine the selling price. For instance, favorable financing can logically result in a selling price that is higher than typical. In this circumstance, a price adjustment should be made to reflect the advantage. If unfavorable terms are found, the price should be adjusted to show the disadvantage. In condemnation proceedings, as well as in federally related appraisals, the law requires that appraisals be based on conventional financing at current rates and terms.

Situations that call for financing adjustments include:

1. *Seller financing:* when loans are more favorable than terms of third party lenders.

2. *Assumed financing:* where the assumed loan has terms more favorable than the terms of a new conventional loan.

3. *Seller-paid points:* when points reduce the seller's net receipts in the same way as when the seller sells at a lower price. Sellers usually try to increase the selling price to help cover the amount paid for points.

Techniques for adjusting for terms of sale will be discussed later in this chapter.

The *conditions* of sale must also be taken into account, as outlined in the previous chapter. Conditions of sale include the following:

> 1. Property rights conveyed.
>
> 2. Motives of the parties.
>
> 3. Personal property and/or tenant improvements included.

Time of Sale

Since market conditions and price levels change over time, the time of sale of each comparable should be noted and considered. Where a specific market change can be identified and measured, time adjustments must be made on any sale occurring before such change. Dramatic changes in market conditions since an earlier sale date may invalidate a sale as a useful comparable.

Location Elements

As discussed in the chapters on neighborhood and site analysis, a number of location factors are important elements of the comparison process. Such factors as the condition and quality of nearby properties, the availability of utilities and transportation, and the proximity of nuisances or hazards should be noted. Also, the effects of social, economic, and political forces must be studied to see if any price differences are attributable to them.

Physical Elements

The property and site characteristics that were discussed in Chapter 8 are important elements of comparison to consider. Such sale features include the size, quality, age and condition of improvements, and the degree of modernization, along with the size, shape, topography, and desirability of the land parcel. Any observed problems found among the comparables should also be noted.

Comparing Sales Directly

At the turn of the century, there were no appraisers. Local brokers and/or bankers rode in a buggy to the property, stopped, looked it over, discussed its merits and demerits, and settled on a price. This is the origin of the term *curbstone appraisal.* As appraising evolved, brokers and bankers began to debate the value conclusion by referring to the prices of sales with which they were familiar. In essence, they compared sales directly to the subject property. A knowledgeable broker who is working in a territory that he or she has successfully "farmed" over a period of time often does the same thing. Appraisers have a similar technique, called the direct comparison method.

Technique

First, locate property sales that appear similar to the subject property and are close enough in time and terms of sale. Next, arrange the list of sales so that they are placed in the order of their relative value or desirability. The list could be in price order, that is, from the highest priced sale on the top to the lowest priced sale on the bottom. However, it is usually better to ignore prices at this stage and rank the sales by listing them in the order of their overall appeal.

After completing the list of properties, the appraiser compares the subject property to those on the list. Properties that are judged to be more desirable than the subject property could be identified as "Better," those less desirable as "Worse," and those that are uncertain with a question mark. You would expect to find that properties marked with a "B" are the higher-priced sales and that those marked with a "W" are the lower-priced sales. The sales in between often are a mixture of "Better," "Worse," and question marks. It is within this middle zone or area that the value of the subject property is likely to lie. Example 9.1 shows such a list of sales.

Example 9.1 Direct Comparison of Sales

Sale Address	Time Since Sale (months)	Price	Age	Building Sq. Ft.	Comparison to Subject
991 Arlington Ave.	5	$ 97,000	1925	2,093	W
195 Arlington Ave.	7	160,000	1924	2,427	W
820 Red Rock Ave.	4	180,000	1921	1,519	W
1295 Cougar Ave.	2	190,000	1940	1,776	W
230 Hilldale Ave.	1	192,500	1930	1,645	W
214 Leroy Ave.	5	235,000	1935	3,043	?
319 Hemlock St.	3	255,000	1925	3,300	B
2150 Euclid Ave.	2	255,000	1924	2,152	?
775 Hemlock St.	9	262,500	1936	3,400	B
200 Creston	5	318,000	1937	3,136	B

Note: W=worse; B=better; and ?=questionable.

Limitations

The direct comparison technique has severe limitations. For example, all the sales should be relatively similar to the property being appraised. In addition, this technique relies heavily on the appraiser's intuitive ability to judge which sale property is more attractive to buyers. Since such an ability generally results from experience, beginning appraisers may have trouble using this technique. (See Figure 9.1.)

The Process of Comparing and Adjusting Sales

The process of comparing and adjusting sales involves two steps: (1) the comparison and analysis of the sales elements described above, and (2) the adjusting of sales prices.

The comparison and analysis step (or process) involves identifying the significant differences among the sales and then, in turn, the significant differences between the sales and the subject property. For example, some of the houses among the comparables may be built with slab-on-grade, where others may have a raised floor. Will such differences affect the prices? Some of the houses may be one-story, and others of similar footage may be of split-level or two-story design. Will there be a need for an adjustment for such features? Before you can judge which differences are significant, you must be aware of all the differences.

Figure 9.1
Appraiser's intuition: Which sale property is more attractive to buyers?

In any neighborhood, factors that are most important in affecting market price can often be identified from your own experience in the local market, or by interviewing active sales people who "farm" the area or are otherwise knowledgeable about market preferences here. Clues that can help you identify significant differences can sometimes be found in the sales themselves. For example, you may find two identical sales that sold six months apart. Is there a price difference? If so, perhaps the time difference is the reason. If two similar homes show a significant difference in price, perhaps these sales reflect a difference in interior modernization, or if they are several blocks apart, in location.

The second step in the comparison and adjustment process is the actual sales adjustment. Once you know which property differences are significant, you then estimate the dollar amount needed to adjust the sales price to make the comparable like the subject. However, there are several precautions needed to obtain good results.

First, sales adjustments should be reasonable. In other words, the dollar amount of the adjustment must have a *reasonable relationship* to the feature being adjusted. For example, it would be unreasonable to use a $30,000 adjustment for an extra one-half bath if the cost of building a half-bath is considerably less than that amount. Second, the adjustment amount must be consistently applied to each sale. If there are three sales with similar half-baths, the same amount should be deducted from the sale price of each. Third, the adjustments should reduce the price spread between the sold properties. In theory, if the adjustments are accurate and the sales prices occurred in a perfect market, the prices after adjustment should be identical.

Rules for Making Adjustments

The process of adjusting comparable sales for differences cannot be executed in a haphazard manner. A reliable appraisal will result only from a careful analysis of significant differences and careful application of the following rules for making adjustments.

1. The sale property (and its price) must be adjusted to be more like the subject property, as shown in Figure 9.2. *Adjust the sale to the subject.* For example, if the sale property has extra features, their value must be subtracted to make the sale like the subject. If the sale property is smaller than the subject, the value of the extra space must be added to the sale price. If the sale was made sev-

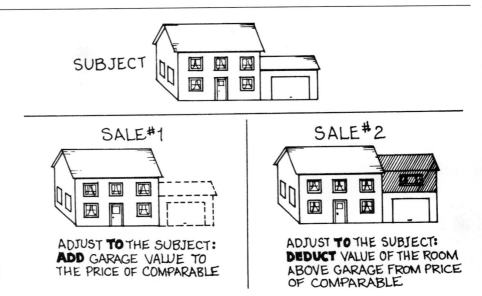

SUBJECT

SALE #1

SALE #2

ADJUST **TO** THE SUBJECT:
ADD GARAGE VALUE TO
THE PRICE OF COMPARABLE

ADJUST **TO** THE SUBJECT:
DEDUCT VALUE OF THE ROOM
ABOVE GARAGE FROM PRICE
OF COMPARABLE

Figure 9.2
The adjustment process.

eral months ago in a rising market and the appraisal is at current value, then the sale price must be raised to account for the increase in prices. Always remember: You must *adjust to the subject.*

2. Use market adjustments. The appraiser's personal reaction to the differences is not what matters. It is the *market's* reaction that is important. You may like modern houses, but are they popular in this market? You might refuse to buy a house located 45 steps above the street, but will others?

3. Make adjustments in the proper sequence. Usually, this means that general adjustments are made first, and adjustments for specific features are made later. A logical sequence of adjustments is: (1) terms and conditions of sale, (2) time and market condition, (3) location, and (4) physical features.

Types of Adjustments

The appraiser can choose from three commonly used types of adjustments: lump-sum dollars, percentage, and units of comparison. (See Figure 9.3.) In practice, these methods are generally used in combination; however, they will be discussed individually here. Details on how to calculate sales adjustments are provided later in this chapter.

Lump-sum dollar adjustments—The first type of adjustment uses a specific dollar amount to adjust each sale for any property difference. Such an amount is added to, or subtracted from, the price of each comparable sale in order to make it more like the subject. For example, one comparable sale might have a swimming pool which the subject property is lacking. If market study suggests that pools generally add about $8,000 to property values in this area, the appraiser can apply the indicated adjustment by subtracting a lump sum of $8,000 from the price of the sale in question. Here is an example:

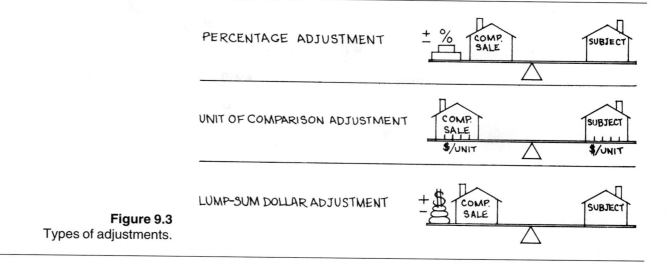

Figure 9.3
Types of adjustments.

PERCENTAGE ADJUSTMENT

UNIT OF COMPARISON ADJUSTMENT

LUMP-SUM DOLLAR ADJUSTMENT

Sale price		$205,000
Less:	Adjustment for swimming pool	−8,000
Equals:	Adjusted price	$197,000

Percentage adjustments—This second type of adjustment uses a percentage of the comparable's sale price to adjust for a difference between the comparable sale and the subject. For example, in a rapidly rising market, a comparable with a sale date that is four months earlier than the date of valuation might be adjusted by 4%, to reflect a 1% per month market price change in the intervening time. If the comparable sold for $310,000, then the adjustment would be 4% of $310,000 or $12,400 (as shown below).

Sale price		$310,000
Plus:	Time adjustment (4%)	+12,400
Equals:	Adjusted price	$322,400

When two or more percentage adjustments are needed for a particular comparable sale, the appraiser has the option of combining the adjustments by (1) the standard plus or minus method, or (2) by multiplying them together, whichever method fits the problem. If reasons for the adjustment are independent, the plus or minus method may apply. For example, a plus 4% time and a plus 3% neighborhood adjustment would combine to a total adjustment of 7%. However, if both neighborhoods have increased in value, the neighborhood adjustment should apply *to the new price levels.* This suggests that the two factors should be multiplied. However, a factor of "one" must be *added* first to each adjustment and then subtracted later. Now, the combined adjustment is calculated as 1.04 × 1.03 = 1.0712. After subtracting "one," the result is .0712, or + 7.12%. When a "minus" adjustment is involved, it must first be *subtracted* from the factor "one." For example, −5% becomes 0.95 (1 − 0.05). When combined with a +7% adjustment (i.e., 1 + 0.07), the total adjustment is calculated as 0.95 × 1.07 = 1.0165. When "one" is now subtracted, an adjustment of plus .0165, or +1.65%, results.

The unit of comparison adjustment—The third type of adjustment is referred to as the unit of comparison method, to be more fully discussed in the next section. To use the unit of comparison, first select an important property unit, such as the square-foot building area, and analyze the sales on this basis. Here you would convert each sales price to the price per square foot. The size adjustment is accomplished when the market-found price per square foot of the comparables is multiplied by the square-foot size of the subject. Then, additional adjustments for features such as age, quality, and appeal may be made, using lump-sum dollars or percentage amounts.

Some authors refer to the unit of comparison as an analysis tool, rather than an adjustment tool. However, when applied properly, the method has the desired result of adjusting for the variable in question.

Calculating a Unit of Comparison

Sale	Building Area	Price	Calculated Price per Sq. Ft.
1	1,877	$311,200	$165.80
2	2,120	320,000	150.94
3	1,795	304,000	169.36

Using a Sales Analysis Grid

It is often difficult to communicate the information in an appraisal report to the reader, especially when a series of sales are involved and a number of adjustments are made. To explain clearly what you have done, it is usually necessary to show your work in the form of a table. Most form appraisal reports have such a table, called a sales analysis or sales adjustment grid. Filling in this grid (Figure 9.4) is a regular part of appraisal practice. Grids offer the advantage of providing a clear comparison of the sales and how they were adjusted. However, it is important to follow current guidelines available for the specific form used (e.g., URAR) when rating the property features to be adjusted.

9.2 SELECTING AND USING UNITS OF COMPARISON

The unit of comparison technique involves the discovery of an important variable aspect of the sale properties that can be objectively measured and used to compare and adjust the sales. For example, if the number of rooms seems to have a significant effect on the prices of the comparables in a residential-income appraisal, the price per room can be calculated for each sale and then compared. In order to calculate the price per room for each sale, divide each sale price by the total number of rooms in the property. Where a consistent pattern is discovered, this unit of comparison can be generalized and then applied

ITEM	SUBJECT	COMPARABLE NO. 1	+(-) $ Adjustment	COMPARABLE NO. 2	+(-) $ Adjustment	COMPARABLE NO. 3	+(-) $ Adjustment
Address	1801 Dona Marta Ventura	1896 Dona Emilia		1821 Don Juan		1932 Via Adobe	
Proximity to Subject		1 block east		2 blocks west		1 block north	
Sales Price	$ N/A	$ 321,500		$ 286,000		$ 280,000	
Price/Gross Liv. Area	$ 141.40 ☑	$ 155.46 ☑		$ 145.18 ☑		$ 155.56 ☑	
Data and/or Verification Sources	Inspection Owner	Doc #182904 Buyer		Doc #014815 CMDC		Doc #097024 Broker	
VALUE ADJUSTMENTS	DESCRIPTION	DESCRIPTION		DESCRIPTION		DESCRIPTION	
Sales or Financing Concessions		Cash		80% Conv.		80% Conv.	
Date of Sale/Time		3/93		2/93		1/93	
Location	Average	Average		Average		Average	
Leasehold/Fee Simple	Fee	Fee		Fee		Fee	
Site	13,068 SF.	14,375	−20,000	11,809		15,246	−12,000
View		Excellent		Min.		Good	
Design and Appeal	Modern	Mod/Good		Mod/V.Good	−2,500	Mod/V.Good	−2,500
Quality of Construction	Good	Good		Good		Good	
Age	22	22		24		24	
Condition	Good	Good		Good		Fair	+5,000
Above Grade Room Count	Total 6 / Bdrms 4 / Baths 2	Total 7 / Bdrms 4 / Baths 2		Total 7 / Bdrms 3 / Baths 2.5		Total 6 / Bdrms 4 / Baths 2	
Gross Living Area	1,768 Sq. Ft.	2,068 Sq. Ft.	−12,000	1,970 Sq. Ft.	−8,000	1,800 Sq. Ft.	
Basement & Finished Rooms Below Grade	None						
Functional Utility	Good	Equal		Equal		Equal	
Heating/Cooling	FAU/No	FAU/No		FAU/No		FAU/No	
Energy Efficient Items	None	None		None		None	
Garage/Carport	2 Car Garage	Same		Same		Same	
Porch, Patio, Deck, Fireplace(s), etc.	Cov. Patio 1 Fireplace	None Same	+500	None Same	+500	None Same	+500
Fence, Pool, etc.	Htd Spa	None	+2,000	None	+2,000	None	+2,000
Net Adj. (total)		☐ + ☒ − $	−29,500	☐ + ☒ − $	−8,000	☐ + ☒ − $	−7,000
Adjusted Sales Price of Comparable		$	292,000	$	278,000	$	273,000

Comments on Sales Comparison (including the subject property's compatibility to the neighborhood, etc.): Comp #1 is same model as subject, enlarged before sale. Has hilltop view. Older Sale #3 used as best closed sale nearby. No time adj. per Realty Board & current escrows. Most weight on Comps #2 and #3.

ITEM	SUBJECT	COMPARABLE NO. 1	COMPARABLE NO. 2	COMPARABLE NO. 3
Date, Price and Data Source for prior sales within year of appraisal	Sold 11/92 for $250k in poor cond.	None	None	None

Analysis of any current agreement of sale, option, or listing of the subject property and analysis of any prior sales of subject and comparables within one year of the date of appraisal: Subject was in poor condition at prior sale. Sale price adjusted for condition supports value indicated by comparables.

INDICATED VALUE BY SALES COMPARISON APPROACH .... $ 275,000

Figure 9.4

A portion of the sales comparison analysis grid of the URAR form.

to the number of rooms in the subject. In this way, the value of the subject property can be related to the most important market factor. The unit of comparison method "eliminates" the major price differences that were caused by the varying numbers of rooms. Once this major property variable is accounted for, you will find it easier to see other influences causing price differences.

Types of Units There are three types of units of comparison commonly used in appraisals. These are: (1) the total property, (2) physical units of comparison, and (3) economic units of comparison. Each of these measures will be now discussed and explained. (See Figure 9.5.)

Total Property Here the total property is the unit of comparison. When all the sales are quite similar to the property being appraised, a total property comparison may be made. Minor differences between the sales can be accounted for by ranking the sales in the direct comparison method previously described, or by using lump-sum dollar adjustments. Techniques for estimating the needed amount of adjustment are outlined in the next section.

Physical Units A physical unit of comparison uses any significant, objectively measurable physical characteristic that varies among the sales. Most often, the size of the property is used as such a unit. When the sale price of each property is divided by its size, the result is the price per unit of size. Highly subjective or unusual property variables, such as view, location, and water orientation, are not readily adjustable using units of comparison.

The most widely used unit of size is the square footage of land or buildings. For buildable lots, prices are usually compared by the square-foot areas. For larger land parcels, the price per acre is commonly used. In some cases, instead of using the land area, you might use the *frontage* of the parcel, for example, the lot dimension facing a major thoroughfare in the case of commercial land. (Commercial rental rates may also be compared by the rent per front foot of land or building.)

For improved properties, many different physical units can be used. For example, homes or apartments are often compared by price per room or price per square foot. Apartments and motels may be compared by price per rental unit. Rooming houses or fraternities can be compared by price per bedroom, or price per bed. Convalescent hospitals are often compared by price per bed and marinas by price per slip or per berth, or by the price per foot of boat dock.

Figure 9.5
Types of units of comparison.   TOTAL PROPERTY   PHYSICAL UNITS   ECONOMIC UNITS

In the appraisal of single-family homes, the most common unit of comparison is the selling price per square foot of living area. When there are only moderate differences in land and building size and the size data are available, the price per square foot method is generally recognized as one of the best ways to compare this type of property.

The use of a size-related unit of comparison has two main advantages. First, it eliminates the price variations that result from differences in size. This makes it easier to see other differences that were not previously apparent. The second advantage is that the calculation of value is easily done by selecting an appropriate unit value and multiplying it by the size measurement of the property being appraised.

Economic Units of Comparison

An economic unit of comparison is some economic feature or characteristic of the property that closely relates to its value. There are many examples of economic units of comparison. One of the most common is used in appraising vacant acreage: Instead of examining land sales in terms of price per acre or price per square foot of land, the land is studied in terms of its usefulness, or what can be done with it. For residential land, for example, this means calculating the price per buildable dwelling unit. Allowable units can be estimated by studying the zoning ordinance in effect.

Zoning ordinances often set restrictions that limit the total size, as well as the number of units for a proposed building. This is because floor-area to land-area ratios, parking requirements, height restrictions, and other restrictions may apply, particularly in the case of commercial property.

Thus, if comparables are in different zoning categories, the allowable building size may vary even when the lot size does not. Here comparing land sales by price per square foot of land may not be useful. Instead try the following: First, examine the zoning ordinance to calculate the amount of floor space that can be developed, considering story-height limits and parking requirements, and so on. Second, take the total calculated potential building floor area and divide it into the price. This result is the price per buildable square footage of floor area. Using this unit of comparison can often automatically adjust for the differences we have cited. Example 9.2 shows how to calculate such a unit of comparison.

What are some other economic units of comparison? The price per convalescent hospital bed has already been suggested as a physical unit of comparison, but it is also economic. When comparing gasoline stations, you could look at the sale price per pump or the price per 1,000 gallons pumped. Since the gallonage is commonly used to establish rent, it is often used to determine the sale price. With retail stores, there generally is a relationship between the rent that is paid and the sales volume the store generates. Consequently, rent as a percent of sales volume is an economic unit of comparison. This applies to restaurants as well. There is also a relationship between the rental income that a property generates and its sale price. This relationship is mathematically represented by gross income multipliers (GIM). Because of the importance of GIMs, they are discussed as a separate topic.

Economic units of comparison are not much harder to apply than physical units of comparison. For vacant parcels, some additional zoning analysis may be necessary. This additional work is worth the effort because economic units of comparison have a big advantage. For complex properties, economic units will give you a clearer understanding of the final price than simple physical comparison. In other words, if you adjust ten sales and use a physical unit of comparison, you can expect to find some remaining variation in the price per unit. If instead, you calculate the economic unit that applies, you can expect to find less remaining variation in the price per unit. In other words, another cause of price variation is eliminated when you use economic units instead of physical units. You will then find it easier to see the factors causing the remaining price variation. Such factors as age, date of sale, and location are much easier to understand when the small differences they cause are not swamped by the larger differences associated with size.

Example 9.2 Physical Versus Economic Units of Comparison

A. Assume that there are four sales of land parcels, all zoned for office use. We first analyze by price per square foot of land area, a physical unit of comparison.

Sale	Price per Sq. Ft. of Land Area
1	$ 44.00
2	150.00
3	62.40
4	33.00

Conclusions: A *wide* range of value indications.

B. The same four sales are next adjusted for differences in the allowable building size to give an economic unit of comparison. The price per square foot of land area is divided by the building-to-land ratio. The answer is the land price per square foot of potential building area.

Sale	Price per Sq. Ft. of Land Area		Allowable Building/Land Ratio		Land Price per Building Sq. Ft.
1	$44.00	÷	1.00	=	$44.00
2	150.00	÷	3.00	=	50.00
3	62.40	÷	1.50	=	41.60
4	33.00	÷	0.75	=	44.00

Conclusion: A *narrow* range of value indications.

Rent or Income Multipliers

Rents, or income multipliers, are also economic units of comparison because they measure an economic characteristic of the property, its income. They are calculated by dividing the price by the rent or income.

The result is called a gross rent (or gross income) multiplier (GRM or GIM). When multiplied by the income of the property being appraised, a GRM will give an indication of property value. Multipliers can be calculated by using either the annual or the monthly income. Traditionally, monthly income has been used for single-family residences, while annual income is most commonly used for apartments or other income property. Any multiplier should be based on all the income that the property commands and not just its rental income. In the case of apartments, such income should include laundry income, parking fees, furniture rentals, and so on.

Note that income multipliers compare the property's income. Why is this important in the sales comparison approach? Income multipliers have traditionally occupied a place somewhere between the income and sales comparison approaches. With single-family homes, multipliers are sometimes considered an acceptable income approach. However, with apartments and commercial property, income multipliers are usually considered as part of the sales comparison approach. The distinction is not important; the multiplier is a tool for the appraiser to use whenever it is suitable. Gross income multipliers will be studied further in Chapter 13.

Applying Units of Comparison

Before applying this technique, it is important to review the unit of comparison selected. Remember that it must be a physical or economic variable that seems to account for the price differences found. If your sales are all 9-room homes, for example, price differences cannot be attributable to the number of rooms as they are not a variable. However, such differences may be explained by square-foot size differences.

Once a valid unit of comparison is selected, the first step is to calculate the unit price. This means the price per square foot, price per bedroom, or price per whatever unit is selected. Once the unit prices for the sales are calculated, these unit prices should be analyzed to identify the causes of any remaining price variation. Are the unit prices for recent sales higher than for older sales? Are the unit prices for the larger properties less than for the smaller properties? Are the unit prices for the older structures lower than for newer structures? It is important for the appraiser to identify such differences and take them into account before the units of comparison are applied. If units of comparison are found to vary significantly among the sales for reasons that are not apparent, there may be a good reason.

It is very common for the price per unit of comparison to decline as the number of units increase. For example, larger structures usually sell for a lower price per physical unit than smaller ones. In the case of larger homes, the lot value and other fixed value components are spread over more square feet of floor space, serving to decrease the value per unit. Also, increased floor size often consists of relatively inexpensive bedroom space or enlarged living rooms. So in a residential sample comparing similar quality homes, we might find prices of $180/SF at 1,000 square feet, $175/SF at 1,500 square feet, and $165/SF at 2,000 square feet in a particular neighborhood. A note of caution: When comparable sales have an extremely wide range of sizes (or other unit of comparison being studied), the sales at each extreme may not suggest a reliable price or value per square foot (or other unit) for the subject.

Graphing the Sales

Variable units of comparison can best be analyzed by graphing the sales. The procedure for preparing a sales graph is first to set up the vertical and horizontal scales on the graph paper. Usually the vertical scale shows the selling price (or the price per unit), and the horizontal scale shows the property characteristic being studied, for example, the square-foot building area. Each sale is plotted on the graph paper by finding the point which matches both the selling price line and the line for the square-foot area. Next, a line is drawn to pass through (or line up with) as many of the sales points as possible. (Statistical techniques that fit a line to these points will be discussed later.) Then the sales that are above and below the line are analyzed. What is causing them to be above or below the line? Finally, the appraiser calculates where the subject property will lie on the line, indicating an estimate of its value.

Figure 9.6 shows a graph of price per square foot versus total square feet of living area. As previously pointed out, the sales prices per square foot often decline as the houses get larger. Based on the graph, the indicated selling price per square foot of building for a house the size of the subject is $167.50. The subject house contains 1,825 square feet, so the indicated price is 1,825 × $167.50, or $305,688, rounded to $305,000.

In some cases, the appraiser might conclude that the subject property is likely to be above the line and in others below it, based on the characteristics of the property as compared with the sales.

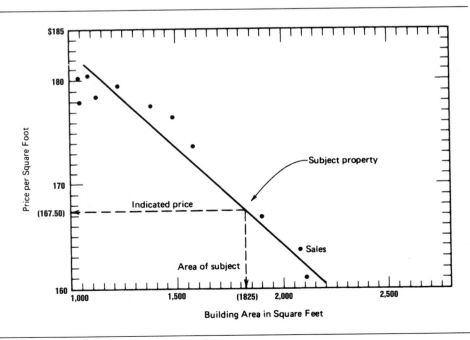

Figure 9.6
Graph shows price per square foot vs. building area.

Perhaps the date of sale or even the age of the building needs to be analyzed. Here the appraiser could graph the price per square foot of living area versus the date of sale or versus the age of the properties. In fact, if the appraiser had plenty of time, he or she could experiment with sales adjustments, graphing the sales after each adjustment to see what the effect is. For example, the appraiser could adjust the sales for time at 4%, 5%, and 6% per year and could, by looking at the three graphs, consider which adjustment appears to be a better match to the market.

The appraiser must recognize that the price per unit of comparison can change in a complex manner. For example, if you are calculating the price per bed in a convalescent hospital, you must consider the licensing requirements of the state. The license law in several states requires a large increase in the nursing staff for a 100-bed building compared to a 99-bed building. Thus the price per bed, instead of changing slowly as the number of beds gradually changes, shifts dramatically at sizes where the licensing staff requirements change.

Remember that a unit of comparison adjusts for only the one variable selected. The price per unit can still vary widely, depending on other differences such as location and quality.

At the present time, graphing has seen limited use in appraisals because its importance has not always been understood. However, wide use of computerized data services may lead to a greater use of graphs.

Methods of estimating the appropriate dollar or percent adjustments for property differences will be the next topic covered.

9.3 HOW TO ESTIMATE DOLLAR AND PERCENT ADJUSTMENTS

The adjustment of the sale prices of comparison properties in a market value appraisal is perhaps the most demanding step in the sales comparison approach. Why? Because, ideally, the adjustments to be made should first and foremost be related to the market. The unit of comparison method described previously has this as its major strength. It relies on "reading" the market reaction to some important physical or economic variables. Of the three additional adjustment methods available, two depend directly on market inputs, and one indirectly.

Direct Market Method

One of the best methods of estimating adjustments is by the direct comparison of sales. The appraiser searches for sales that differ *only* in the single property characteristic being studied. The difference in price between two such properties (sometimes referred to as a "matched pair") can indicate the appropriate dollar or percent adjustment for the feature under study.

Application of Method

This method is simple. First, find at least two sales that have no major differences except the type of difference that you want to examine, say, a large age or size difference. Although these sales need not be completely comparable to the subject, they should be similar enough so that the difference being studied will have the same effect on both the sales and the subject property. The second step is to compare matched pair sales prices to see how big the difference is. This can be expressed either in dollars or as a percentage of the sale price.

The third step is to adjust the sale prices of the comparables to make them more like the subject property, using the amount found by studying the market data. Example 9.3 demonstrates the first two of these three steps, with the ages of the buildings, as well as their sizes, being analyzed.

It is also possible to use the direct comparison method by finding sets of rental comparables. You identify the rental difference that is caused by the feature being studied. This rent difference is then multiplied by the GIM appropriate for that market. The result is the value difference associated with the feature being examined.

Example 9.3 Calculating Adjustments by Matched Pairs

Sales Data Summary

Value Factor	Sale 1	Sale 2	Sale 3
Price	$270,000	$280,000	$256,500
Size (sq. ft.)	2,500	2,700	2,500
Age (years)	20	20	30

Note that sales 1 and 3 differ only in age and that sales 1 and 2 differ only in size.

Analysis Using Matched Pairs

Age Difference

Sale	Age	Price
1	20	$270,000
3	30	256,500
Difference	10 years =	$13,500

Price Difference for Age:

In dollars: $13,500/10 years, or $1,350 per year.
In percent: $13,500/$270,000, or 5% difference.
In percent per year: 5%/10 years, or 0.5 % per year.

Conclusion: An adjustment at 1/2% per year of age difference is indicated.

Size Difference

Sale	Size (sq. ft.)	Price
2	2,700	$280,000
1	2,500	270,000
Difference	200 sq. ft. =	$10,000

Price Difference for Size:

In dollars per square foot:
$10,000/200 sq. ft. or $50.

Conclusion: An adjustment of $50 per square foot of size difference is indicated.

When should the direct market method be used? It is the most reliable method when the appraiser needs to adjust for one single major factor, such as terms of sale, date of sale, location, or physical factors. Adjustments for the date of sale are made by comparing earlier sales and later sales. (Obviously, a resale of the same property might be the most direct evidence of how prices changed with time.)

Here is an example of how this method can be useful in adjusting for location. Assume your subject property is a three-bedroom home and that no three-bedroom homes have sold recently in the subject property's neighborhood but that many two-bedroom homes have. Look for another nearby neighborhood with sales of *both* two- and three-bedroom homes. If you compare prices of two-bedroom homes in the subject property's neighborhood with the two-bedroom homes in the other neighborhood, the percentage difference can be your neighborhood adjustment. If, for example, your neighborhood sold for 9% more, now you can use the three-bedroom comparables from the other neighborhood and adjust their prices up by 9% for the neighborhood difference.

A broad range of physical differences between the subject property and the comparables can be adjusted by the direct market method. The presence or absence of a specific feature such as a swimming pool, basement, or extra bedroom, or physical differences such as size, quality, age, or condition can be measured. The method is also useful in adjusting for remodeled rooms such as kitchens or bathrooms.

Matched pairs of sales are sometimes used in combination with other techniques. For example, you can first adjust your sales for specific differences such as swimming pools; these adjusted sales might then be studied further by using some unit of comparison such as the price per square foot of living area. However, recognize that as more adjustment methods are used, the probability of individual adjustment errors increases.

This direct market method is now being used with very large sets of sales. Such larger sets of sales can be processed easily by using computerized sales data services. For example, a reliable adjustment for time for one area might be obtained by calculating the average price per square foot of all the sales each year, as shown in Example 9.4.

Example 9.4 Analysis of Annual Market Price Changes	Year	Number of Sales	Average Price per Sq. Ft.	Increase (percent)
	1988	147	$138.71	—
	1989	203	146.62	5.7
	1990	191	151.46	3.3
	1991	228	155.09	2.4
	1992	180	157.73	1.7

Depreciated Cost Method

The second method for estimating dollar or percent adjustments is called the depreciated cost method. The adjustment is calculated from an analysis of the depreciated replacement costs for the particular property feature to be adjusted. When costs and depreciation schedules are correctly related to the market, the depreciated cost method can be said to represent an indirect market method.

The depreciated cost method involves the following steps: First, select the particular feature or difference between the properties that is to be adjusted. For instance, you might need to adjust for differences in the size of buildings, the installation of special kitchen equipment, or the absence of a garage. The second step is to estimate the *additional* cost to include that feature when building a new house. (Techniques for estimating new building costs will be covered in Chapter 11.) The third step, after estimating the current construction costs, is to deduct an allowance (called *depreciation*), for the age and condition of the feature being studied. (Methods for calculating depreciation will also be covered later, in Chapter 12.) The final step is to adjust the sale price of the comparable sale by adding or subtracting the depreciated cost amount.

Remember that the purpose of figuring the cost difference is to modify or adjust the price of the comparable so that it will better represent the value of the subject. If the comparable has no garage, for example, and the subject does, then the depreciated cost of this feature would have to be added to the comparable's sale price. Example 9.5 shows how to prepare this adjustment.

The best time to use this method is to adjust for physical property differences. The method is particularly useful when adjusting for a specific building feature, such as a second oven, a swimming pool, a covered porch, and so on.

The depreciated cost method is also useful when a property has some particular problem that must be corrected, such as a leaking roof or termite damage. The total current cost of these repairs (without any deduction for depreciation) would be the price reduction demanded by a knowledgeable buyer.

The depreciated cost method of estimating adjustment amounts is a common tool of the practicing appraiser. Cost manuals are handy and easy to use; the logic of the adjustment process is easily explained. However, it is often difficult to prove the depreciation deduction. Although depreciated cost adjustments are less accurate than they initially appear to be, they remain a common and useful tool in adjusting sales.

Example 9.5 Adjustment by the Depreciated Cost Method

The Problem

The subject property is an eight-room home, new in 1951, with a double garage. Sale 4 is very similar, *except* that it has no garage.

The Solution

Adjust the price of sale 4 upward to reflect the lack of a garage.

The Adjustment Steps

1. Estimate the garage cost new. The area is 20 × 22 feet, or 440 sq. ft. Current replacement cost for this quality and feature from a local cost handbook is $33.50/sq. ft.

2. Estimate depreciation. The garage's actual age is 29 years, and its total economic life is estimated to be 100 years. Depreciation is believed to be nearly straight line, or 29/100, or 29%.

3. Calculation:

Cost new: 440 × $33.50		$14,740
Less:	Depreciation: $14,740 × 0.29	4,275
Equals:	Adjustment amount	$10,465
	Rounded to	$10,000

Adjusting for Sale Terms

As we discussed earlier in this chapter, the sale price of a property is often affected by the type of financing involved. If any of the comparable sales used have unique financing, adjustments must be made. The amount of the adjustment can be calculated from a direct market comparison with similar properties that have conventional financing. However, if such sales are not available, it might be necessary to use a mathematical analysis to calculate an adjustment.

One simple financing adjustment arises when the seller must pay substantial loan points or other loan charges. In conventional loan practice, the *buyer* pays the loan points, or fees, that are charged to set up the loan. However, in some types of loans, the interest rate is fixed for a time period and cannot change as market interest rates change. Lenders compensate for this fixed interest rate by charging an extra loan fee, called *points,* which discount the loan and thus effectively adjust the fixed interest rate to the current market interest rate. When loan points are paid by the seller, the effective or net cost (or price of the sale) to the seller is reduced. To make a proportional adjustment, you might subtract the loan points paid by the seller from the stated selling price, as shown in Example 9.6.

Example 9.6 Adjusting for Points

	Sale 1	Sale 2	Sale 3
Sale price	$210,000	$200,000	$225,000
Loan amount	$168,000	$150,000	$180,000
Loan points (as decimal)	× .04	× .03	× .05
Cost of points	$ 6,720	$ 4,500	$ 9,000
Adjusted price	$203,280	$195,500	$216,000

A more complicated situation arises when a property is sold with unusually favorable financing. This involves a loan that was more advantageous to the buyer than the conventional lender financing available at that time. A desirable loan can substantially increase the selling price of the property. Such loans may be either assumable third-party loans or new loans that are taken back by the seller at the time of sale. The favorable loan may have an interest rate that is lower than normal for the current market. Or the loan could involve a very low down payment (e.g., with a seller take-back loan) or a long amortization period.

It is possible for unfavorable financing to depress the selling price. Sometimes an undesirable loan with an above-market interest rate must be assumed by the buyer or a stiff prepayment penalty paid. In this case, the sale price could well be below the "market value" level.

Estimating the amount of adjustment for favorable or unfavorable loans may be done by studying the discount at which mortgages are being sold in the current finance markets. It is also possible to analyze these mortgages using mathematical techniques similar to those used by lenders to calculate loan points. Such techniques include what is referred to as *discounted cash flow analysis,* to be defined and outlined in Chapter 14.

Unfortunately, it is often difficult to estimate accurate adjustments for terms of sale. Judging what buyers and sellers consider as favorable loan terms in a particular market can be very subjective. Although the mathematical techniques referred to earlier may seem sophisticated and precise, few buyers or sellers understand or use them. As a result, the actual adjustments that occur in the market could differ from what the mathematical calculations suggest.

Statistics—Linear and Multiple Regression

As introduced in Chapter 8, an advanced method of calculating the amount of a sales adjustment uses a statistical technique called regression analysis. There are two techniques of regression analysis currently used in appraising. The first type is called linear regression. This technique adjusts for one difference or variable, such as the date of sale or the age of the house. As the term *linear* implies, the technique assumes that the relationship between the price and variable is a straight line. If the variable is age, then each change in age that occurs shows the same change in price. Thus, if we graph the sales prices versus the ages, we would expect the sales to form a straight line. The linear regression calculation effectively averages the sales to find out what the average change in price is. Figure 9.7 is a graph of the various sale prices; the line represents the results of linear regression.

Although the linear regression technique involves a complex mathematical formula, pocket calculators programmed for linear regression make it relatively simple to apply. If a single variable, like the date of sale, is being studied, the appraiser merely inputs the price of each sale along with its date (or the number of months since the sale). When all the sales are entered, the program computes the price trend. It is also possible to calculate whether such a trend accounts for most of the differences in price. For reliable results, linear regression usually requires larger groups of sales than the other sales adjustment

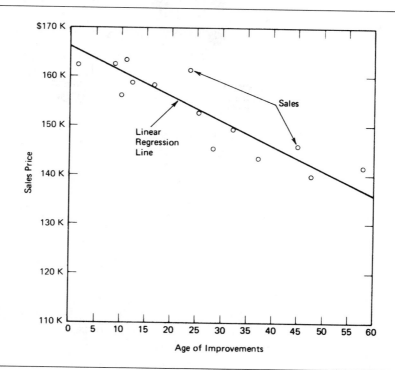

Figure 9.7
Using linear regression to analyze sales.

methods previously discussed. The growing use of computerized data banks lends itself to greater use of simple regression studies to support adjustments for age, sale date, size, and other similar elements of a sale that can change in a continuous linear manner. Other techniques—grouped averages, for example—are better for elements that are of a yes–no nature, such as the presence of a swimming pool.

Multiple regression is the second type of regression analysis. The same process is carried out, but you can look at any number of variables. It is usually done with a programmable calculator or microcomputer. For accuracy, you need to have 20 to 30 sales and at least twice as many sales as the number of variables being studied. Some types of statistical flaws can reduce the reliability of the conclusions without the appraiser being aware of them. However, multiple regression is used increasingly by county assessors and lenders doing appraisal review work. This technique will probably be used more as appraisers become familiar with its application and better understand its limitations. A detailed analysis of this technique is part of advanced appraisal study.

In conclusion, we have discussed thus far in this chapter various topics relating to comparing and adjusting sales. We now turn to the subject of arriving at a value conclusion.

9.4 ARRIVING AT AN INDICATED VALUE

The last step in the sales comparison approach is to arrive at a value conclusion. In order to arrive at such an opinion, you need to follow these four steps:

	The Four Steps to Arrive at a Conclusion
	1. Review the entire approach.
	2. Review the sales data.
	3. Estimate a value range.
	4. Select a final value.

The First Step: Review the Entire Approach

The first step in arriving at a value conclusion is to consider the limitations of the sales comparison approach and how these limitations apply to the particular circumstances of your appraisal. Taking time to review each step taken in the sales comparison approach provides an overall look at the entire process.

Comparability

The sales comparison approach is reliable only when used to appraise property that is commonly bought and sold. If there are no comparable sales, the approach cannot be applied. Similarly, the more unique, specialized, or rare the property being appraised, the less useful the sales comparison approach will be. (See Figure 9.8.)

Figure 9.8
A unique home. (Photograph courtesy of Doug Frost)

Activity Levels In any given community, real estate sales activity will vary from time to time. During a period when no sales are occurring, the sales comparison approach may not be very reliable. Similarly, in an appraisal of a type of property that is rarely sold, such as a major automobile assembly plant, the sales comparison approach is less reliable. Why? Because comparables are few and far between and may require large adjustments for time and location.

Adjustment Accuracy Appraisers often say that no two properties are identical. Almost every comparable needs to be adjusted for some differences. The final appraisal is only as reliable as the adjustment. When the amount of a significantly large adjustment cannot be based on convincing market evidence, the sales comparison approach may not be reliable.

Statistical Limits Statistical techniques that are used as part of the sales comparison approach can have serious technical flaws. This is particularly true of linear and multiple regression. Complex mathematical calculations are needed to judge whether conclusions based on these methods can be relied on in any given appraisal.

Lagging the Market One problem with the sales comparison approach is that the appraiser generally must use sales that occurred prior to the date of the appraisal. If the market is changing, all of the sales have a built-in "lag." If values are going up, then the sales prices of available comparables will likely be lower than current values. If prices are going down, the sale prices will likely be higher than the current values. The appraiser may be able to easily adjust for this time lag, provided that the rate of price change has remained constant through the present time. However, if the rate of change has varied since the last sale, the adjustment will be more difficult. When you suspect that price changes have occurred irregularly, try to solve this problem by looking only for very recent value evidence. Local brokers could be contacted for current listing prices, offers, refusals, and recent sales, as well as opinions on current price trends. When such information is available, the time-lag problem may be resolved.

Motivation The sales comparison approach assumes that the price is the result of vigorous, arms-length bargaining by knowledgeable buyers and sellers. As you know, actual sales prices are not always reached in this way. So, try to understand the motives behind the sales. You should eliminate sales that are within a family, and sales in which there is evidence that suggests a panicky seller or buyer. It is difficult to find out whether a particular sale involves rational and aggressive bargaining over the price. When the appraiser has only a few sales or must rely heavily on one or two, motivation becomes an even more important factor to consider. If a particular sale is critical to your analysis and it is defective, the entire market approach is weakened. Therefore, in this review process, you must consider the extent to which your analysis relies on any one sale.

The Second Step: Review the Sales Data

The next step in arriving at an indicated value through the sales comparison approach is to review the detailed data about the actual sales.

Sales Data

First, consider the reliability of the information. What was the source? How reliable is that source, based on previous experience? If certain data are questionable, would an error lead to an answer that is too high or too low? Can that error be cross-checked against other information? If a particular sale is critical to an appraisal, the appraiser should consider whether enough information about that sale has been collected. Is the evidence or information collected adequate? If not, you should cross-check the information with another source or make a second field inspection. The collection of additional information about one sale may sharpen your understanding of all the sales.

Reviewing the Adjustments

The appraiser must review how the sales were adjusted. What type of adjustment was made? Direct market comparisons are usually more reliable than those from statistics or from a cost approach. However, this reliability could depend on the type of adjustment and the quality of data. At this point, consider the total amount that each sale was adjusted (without regard to plus or minus signs). This gives the best single indication of how comparable a sale is. The less adjustment needed, the more comparable it is. The more comparable it is, the more weight that sale should be given in arriving at a final value conclusion. The more extreme sales are given less weight and might even be eliminated at this point.

The Third Step: Estimate a Value Range

The third step in arriving at an indicated value is to estimate the probable range of value. The upper limit of this range is the *highest* price that can reasonably be concluded, based on the sales study. The lower limit is the *lowest* price that can reasonably be developed or concluded from the sales. When such a bracket is defined, we are one step closer to selecting a final value indication from the sales comparison approach.

Using the Value Range Produced by the Adjusted Sales

In many appraisals, the value range indicated by the sales study can be said to be that range established by the highest and lowest adjusted sales prices. This conclusion is certainly valid where only small, well-supported adjustments have been used in the adjustment process. In such an example, assume that adjusted comparable #1 indicates a market value of $150,750; comparable #2, $160,500; and comparable #3, $165,000. Here, the range of value could logically be suggested at $150,750 to $165,000.

Projecting Upper and Lower Limits for the Sales Adjustments

When the comparables require large, and/or marginally supported, adjustments an unacceptably broad range of value can result. To narrow this range, we can apply upper and lower limits to the individual sales adjustments for each sale, and test the reliability of the value indications.

In arriving at the upper limit for each adjustment, (eg., time, location, size) you should select an amount that leans toward a higher value but still appears to be reasonable for the property feature involved. Estimating the upper limit is a question of giving all the benefit of the doubt in one direction—toward a higher adjustment in each case.

To arrive at the lower limit for each adjustment, give the benefit of the doubt to adjustments that tend to reduce the adjusted price. When estimating both the upper and lower limits, consider any uncertainty that you may have about the amounts of the adjustments. In practice, this process of estimating limits is usually done by intuition. The concept is displayed mathematically in Figure 9.9.

After you total the adjustments used in each sale to reflect both the highest and the lowest reasonable price influence that can be attributed to the differing property features, a range of indicated value is produced for each comparable sale. Observe how wide the range is from the lowest indicated price to the highest indicated price. The narrower this range, the more reliable the value conclusion resulting from that particular sale.

Figure 9.9
Estimating the upper and lower limits of sales adjustments.

Value Adjustments	Estimated Adjustment	Probable Adjustment Range	Upper Limit	Lower Limit
Sales or financing concessions	0			
Date of sale, time	$1,500	$1,300–$1,600	$1,600	$1,300
Location	0			
Site/view	($4,000)	($1,800–$4,300)	($1,800)	($4,300)
Design and appeal	0			
Quality of construction	0			
Age	0			
Condition	($5,000)	($4,700–$5,500)	($4,700)	($5,500)
Above-grade room count; gross living area	($3,000)	($2,300–$3,600)	($2,300)	($3,600)
Basement and finished rooms below grade	0			
Functional utility	0			
Heating/cooling	$5,000	$2,000–$6,000	$6,000	$2,000
Garage/carport	$5,000	$3,000–$6,500	$6,500	$3,000
Porches, patios, pools, etc.	0			
Special energy-efficient items	0			
Fireplace(s)	($1,700)	($1,200–$3,000)	($1,200)	($3,000)
Other (e.g., kitchen equipment, remodeling)	($4,000)	($3,300–$4,800)	($3,300)	($4,800)
Net adjustment (total)	($6,200)		$800	($14,900)
Indicated value of subject	$143,800		$150,800	$135,100
			(Upper limit of value)	(Lower limit of value)

The Range of Value from the Most Comparable Sales

Finally, your estimate of a value range for the subject property should ideally consider only those sales that appear to be the most reliable value indicators. This should be suggested by the upper and lower limits tested for the sales adjustments. If the adjusted prices of the most comparable sales cluster in a particular area within the total range, the value conclusion should be selected from that narrower range.

The Fourth Step: Select a Final Value

Selecting an indicated value from the sales comparison approach is not a science. There is no mathematical formula for it; to a large degree, it requires judgment. There are, however, some sensible rules. First, give the greatest weight to the sale (or sales) that needs the least total adjustment (ignoring the plus and minus signs). This reduces the impact of any errors made during the adjustment process. See Example 9.7.

Example 9.7 Which Sale Needed the Least Adjustment?

	Sale 1	Sale 2	Sale 3	Sale 4
Price	$273,500	$266,800	$278,000	$269,900
Adjustments:				
Time	+7%	+3%	+2%	+5%
Size	−4	+5	−4	0
Location	−3	+3	−3	0
Total	0%	+11%	−5%	+5%
Adjusted price	$273,500	$296,148	$264,100	$283,395

Answer: Sale 4 needed the least adjustment in "absolute" terms.

The second rule is to favor the sales (or the method of adjusting them) that involve the fewest assumptions or the most reliable adjustments. Finally, do *not* average the sales prices or the adjusted sales prices. Averaging assumes that the difference in price from one sale to the next is the result of pure chance and that each sale should have equal weight in the conclusion. With real estate, neither is likely to be true. Instead, it is more likely that the variation in the adjusted sales prices is caused by some problem that the appraiser has not yet found. Since such problems do not occur randomly, averaging will not eliminate the cause. The best action to take is to go back and reconsider why the adjusted sales still vary and try to find a logical explanation. If that is not fruitful, choose the most reliable sales. Using the most reliable sales will reduce the chance that the unknown problem will affect the value conclusion.

In summary, to arrive at an indicated value, make an overall review of the sales comparison approach. Reconsider the data used and verify that they were interpreted in the best manner. Then narrow the adjusted sales prices into a range within which you feel that the value must lie. Finally, within this range, select an appropriate single price based on a careful and thorough analysis of the entire process.

SUMMARY   The comparison of sales is one of the most important parts of the sales comparison approach. Many techniques can be used. One is to make direct sales comparisons. However, direct comparisons are often difficult, so appraisers have developed other methods. These involve two steps: (1) comparison or analysis of sales, and (2) adjustment of sales prices.

In the comparison (or analysis) step, the sales are compared in order to identify differences in terms and conditions of sale, time of sale, and location and physical elements. Next the differences are studied in order to establish which differences may have caused the variations in prices.

In the adjustment step, the prices of the sales are adjusted to account for any differences between the sales and the subject property. Each of the sales is adjusted to make it more like the subject. There are three types of adjustments that can be used, either independently or in combination: the lump-sum dollar adjustment, the percentage adjustment, and the unit of comparison. In order to best explain your adjustment analysis, a special table called the sales analysis grid is included in most appraisal reports. However, the sales analysis grid is only suitable to present a few adjustment techniques.

The amounts of adjustments can be calculated in several ways. One, the direct market method, uses the direct analysis of sales to calculate adjustments. The depreciated cost method calculates adjustments using indirect market information: cost and depreciation. It is especially useful when property differences are mostly differences in the physical improvements or when a property has a defect that needs correction. The kind of financing a property has also may affect its sale price; therefore, adjustments must sometimes be made for the type of financing. A sophisticated statistical technique called regression can be used to calculate the amount of a dollar or percentage adjustment. Appraisers use two types of regression: linear and multiple.

The final step in the sales comparison approach is arriving at a value conclusion. This is achieved by the following four steps:

1. **Review the entire approach.** Consider and try to account for the limitations of your method.

2. **Review the sales data.** Consider the overall reliability of your sales data.

3. **Estimate a value range.** You should identify a lower and an upper limit of value.

4. **Select a final value.** You must ultimately select a single value after completing the above steps.

Important Terms and Concepts

Adjusting sales

Adjustment types
  lump-sum dollar
  percentage
  unit of comparison

Analyzing sales

Elements of comparison

Gross income multipliers

Matched pairs

Price range

Property differences

Regression
  linear
  multiple

Sales analysis grid

Sales graphs

Terms and conditions of sale

Total property comparisons

Units of comparison
  economic
  physical

REVIEWING YOUR UNDERSTANDING

1. The four elements of comparison used in the sales comparison approach include all of the following *except:*
   (a) Terms and conditions of sale
   (b) Direct elements
   (c) Time of sale
   (d) Location elements
   (e) Physical elements

2. The rules for making sales adjustments include all of the following *except:*
   (a) Adjust the sale price toward the subject property
   (b) Use market-related adjustments
   (c) Always use dollar amounts
   (d) Make adjustments in the proper sequence

3. To use the lump-sum adjustment on a sale that is inferior to the subject property:
   (a) Multiply by a percentage of the selling price
   (b) Subtract a lump-sum dollar amount from the price
   (c) Add a lump-sum dollar amount to the price
   (d) None of the above

4. To use the unit of comparison adjustment:
   (a) Select the most consistent feature of the sales
   (b) Select an important property variable and analyze the sales on this basis
   (c) None of the above
   (d) Both (a) and (b)

5. A physical unit of comparison refers to:
   (a) Any significant physical characteristic of the sales that varies
   (b) The largest physical characteristic of the subject property
   (c) Only the building size, expressed in square footage
   (d) None of the above

6. An economic unit of comparison is always:
   (a) The gross rent multiplier
   (b) An economic measure of the property and its value
   (c) The physical characteristic of the property that relates best to the market
   (d) Difficult to use

7. To use the direct market method of estimating the dollar or percent adjustment, you should first:
   (a) Calculate the price difference between two matched pair comparables
   (b) Calculate the price difference between the comparable sale and the subject property
   (c) Select a specific amount and apply it directly to the comparable
   (d) Derive the adjustment from older market sales

8. A comparable should be adjusted for terms of sale when:
   (a) Conventional financing is involved
   (b) It is a cash sale
   (c) There is favorable seller financing
   (d) Financing equivalent to cash is involved

9. Linear regression:
   (a) Adjusts for only one difference or variable
   (b) Adjusts for a number of variables at the same time
   (c) Adjusts for two variables at the same time
   (d) Is used to calculate the replacement cost new for the subject property

10. In the final step of the market comparison approach, the four actions needed to arrive at a value conclusion include all the following *except:*
    (a) Review the entire approach
    (b) Review the sales
    (c) Estimate a value range
    (d) Average the three best sales
    (e) Select a final value

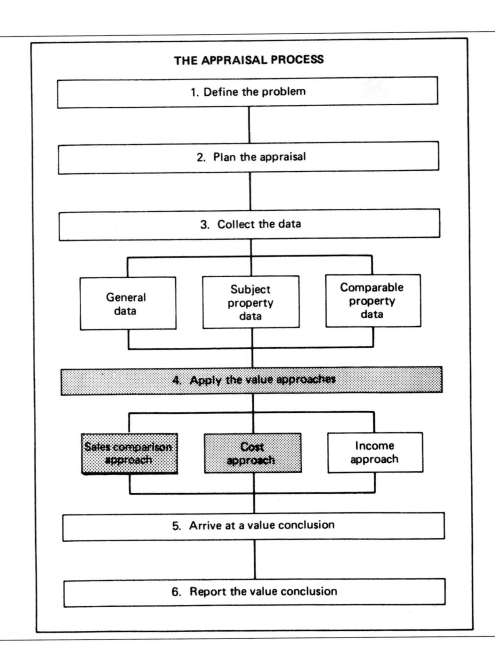

THE APPRAISAL PROCESS

1. Define the problem

2. Plan the appraisal

3. Collect the data

| General data | Subject property data | Comparable property data |

4. Apply the value approaches

| Sales comparison approach | Cost approach | Income approach |

5. Arrive at a value conclusion

6. Report the value conclusion

Chapter 10
Valuing the Site

Preview   In Chapter 6, we discussed the main factors affecting the value of land and the techniques used to physically inspect a site. In this chapter, we shall outline the four methods used to appraise land and explain how they apply to undeveloped acreage, vacant lots, or sites improved with buildings. Since all land appraisal methods rely on property comparison in some form, an understanding of the sales comparison approach techniques covered in Chapters 8 and 9 is essential.

When you have completed this chapter, you should be able to:

1. *Name five different uses of site value appraisals.*

2. *List the four methods of appraising land.*

3. *Name five physical characteristics of a site that affect its value.*

4. *Name three legal and economic considerations in site value.*

10.1 PURPOSE OF LAND OR SITE VALUE ESTIMATES

Land or site value estimates are important not just in the appraisal of vacant or undeveloped land but in other circumstances as well. The site is appraised as if it were vacant whenever a separation of land and building value is necessary for improved properties. Also, a separate site value may be needed in any of the three approaches to value. We shall explore each of these reasons here. In market value studies, we generally appraise land on the basis of its highest and best use, a concept to be reviewed in section 10.2.

Appraisals of Acreage or Vacant Land

The appraisal of vacant land usually requires more specialized experience than the appraisal of improved property. The reason for this is that a very limited percentage of real estate transactions involve vacant land. Bare acreage is also more unique in location, size, or shape than most improved properties. Thus buyers and sellers often require the services of an expert to interpret for them the physical, legal, and economic factors that determine land value.

Land is frequently leased instead of being sold outright. Whether the lease is for agricultural, commercial, or residential purposes, appraisals are often needed to estimate rental value or the equitable return on investment capital. Land leases can be for very long term periods, so correctly estimating the initial rental amounts becomes quite important. Appraisers often base fair rent on a current market value estimate.

Real estate developers, lenders, agricultural interests, government agencies, and courts of law rely on land appraisals to make important decisions on the use and distribution of land. Developers and subdividers need to include the value of land as one of the costs of the finished product. Thus many project feasibility studies incorporate vacant land appraisals. Banks and other lenders often furnish construction financing for real estate developments. Since such loans are often based on the value of the vacant land, formal appraisals are usually needed.

Many government acts, such as taxation, eminent domain, and redevelopment, may require estimates of land value, and frequently require formal appraisals. Also, many court actions concern questions of land value. Such actions may arise out of inheritance settlements, divorce actions, and other types of lawsuits.

Allocation of Value for Tax Purposes

Certain tax laws require that the value of land and improvements be estimated separately for improved properties. First, ad valorem (according to value) property taxes are usually based on separately stated land and improvement values. Some property tax areas even specify different tax rates for land than for improvements. Second, income tax laws generally allow an annual "write-off," or depreciation deduction, when buildings are held for investment purposes. Since such depreciation is allowed only on the value of the structures, an allocation of value or purchase price between land and buildings is required.

Site Value in the Three Value Approaches

Since land and buildings may be regarded as separate economic parts of the property, site value estimates are routinely needed in many improved property appraisals. Even when the defined purpose of an appraisal is to estimate the total market value of an improved property, the particular techniques used by an appraiser may require an estimate of the value of the land.

The cost approach (covered in Chapters 11 and 12) uses an estimate of the site value as a base figure to which the value of the improvements is added. This means that the site must be appraised first. Next, the value of the buildings is estimated as the cost-new-less-depreciation. Note that for *appraisal* purposes, *depreciation* refers to the difference between the present value of the improvements and their replacement cost new.

In the income approach, certain capitalization procedures (to be discussed later) split the net income for the property between the two "production agents": land and building. Hence a separate land value estimate can be required in the income approach, too.

Finally, some sales analysis techniques in the sales comparison approach subtract the land value from the sale price to see what the various buildings "sold for." In order to use this technique, the appraiser must estimate land value for each sale and also for the subject property.

Reasons for Estimating Land Value

1. One Viewpoint
   (a) Sale price
   (b) Rental value
   (c) Feasibility studies
   (d) Loan security
   (e) Property tax
   (f) Eminent domain
   (g) Income tax basis allocation

2. Another Viewpoint
   (a) Cost approach
   (b) Income approach—residual capitalization
   (c) Sales comparison approach

10.2 FOUR METHODS USED TO APPRAISE LAND

Among practicing appraisers, there are four recognized methods of appraising land. These are (1) the market or direct sales comparison method, (2) the allocation or abstraction method, (3) the development method, and (4) the land residual method. (See Figure 10.1.)

As we learned in Chapter 6, the value of land is a function of its highest and best use. Highest and best use is defined as *that reasonable*

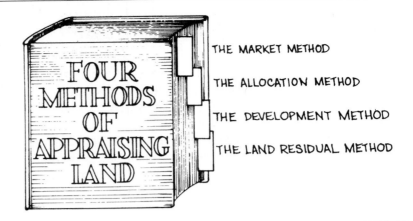

THE MARKET METHOD

THE ALLOCATION METHOD

THE DEVELOPMENT METHOD

THE LAND RESIDUAL METHOD

Figure 10.1

and profitable use that will support the highest land value as of the date of the appraisal. Before we consider the methods of appraising land, a review of the importance of highest and best use is in order.

Importance of Highest and Best Use

Required in market value appraisals by the Uniform Standards of Professional Appraisal Practice, an opinion of the highest and best use suggests an optimum use of the property, both (1) as if vacant, and (2) as presently improved. The first requires consideration of feasible alternative uses, and therefore it provides the basis for land valuation. The second examines the value contribution of any existing improvements. The appraiser may recommend their *interim use* if the improvements do not represent the highest and best use as if vacant. In the latter case, the value assigned to improvements is often referred to as an *interim use value.*

Highest and Best Use Criteria

To be selected as the highest and best use, any suggested use must meet four criteria, or tests. The use must be:

1. Physically possible.

2. Legally permissible.

3. Economically feasible.

4. Maximally productive.

Appraising Land by the Market Method

The most reliable method of appraising land is referred to as the market, or direct sales comparison, method. In concept, it is little different from the sales comparison approach used to appraise improved properties. However, the market method of estimating site value and the sales comparison approach have one important difference, that is, the basis of comparison between parcels.

Figure 10.2
Vacant land for sale. (Photograph courtesy of Doug Frost)

The Basis and Criteria of Comparison

Whether the land is actually vacant or improved, the market method of site appraisal compares the subject property as *if it were vacant.* When this is understood, it follows that all sales comparisons should be sales of vacant land. (See Figure 10.2.)

How are the comparables to be selected? Vacant land sales should be similar to the subject land in location, physical characteristics, and potential use. Location is important for the many reasons discussed in previous chapters. Close proximity to the subject property contributes to the credibility of the sales, since the same value-influencing factors are present. (See Figure 10.3.)

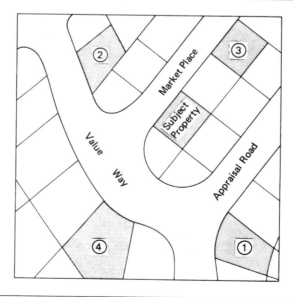

Figure 10.3
Four recent site sales of varying comparability.

Physical features should also be similar. Comparing a steep hillside lot with a flat valley lot would probably require unreasonably large adjustments. Such adjustments might cover higher site preparation costs (for the hillside lot) and also the value difference often associated with a view.

In the market method of land appraisal, vacant land sales should be chosen for their similarity to the subject land in terms of potential use. The most likely use for a parcel is determined primarily by location, zoning (and/or permissible use), and market demand at the time of the appraisal.

Applying the Market Method

Since the market method is the most direct method of appraising land, it is preferred whenever sales of comparable vacant land are available. The method is suitable to appraise sites or to allocate vacant land value for improved sites, whether they are zoned for residential, commercial, industrial, agricultural, or recreational usage.

The application of the market method of site appraisal involves the same sales comparison approach procedures described in Chapter 8. (See Figure 10.4.) The appropriate steps are as follows:

Figure 10.4
Appraisal of land by the market method.

1. Locate vacant land sales that are similar to the subject site in terms of potential use. Gather information as to sale conditions, terms of each sale, and the price paid.

2. Compare each sale with the subject property as to the terms and conditions of sale, the date of sale, location factors, and physical characteristics.

3. Adjust the selling price of each comparable site to reflect any important differences between it and the subject site. Adjustments may be made in either dollar or percentage amounts.

4. Arrive at an indicated value for the subject site, based on the more comparable of the sales analyzed.

Specific techniques of comparison and adjustment will be discussed later in this chapter.

The Allocation or Abstraction Method

When comparable sales of vacant sites are not available, the direct sales comparison or market method cannot be used. As one alternative, land value may be allocated or abstracted from sales of improved property. The allocation or abstraction method typically would be used in built-up areas where little vacant land remains. This method can also be useful in the appraisal of portions of a shared land interest such as those in condominiums, cooperatives, and planned developments.

Since the allocation method is less direct than the market method, it is usually much less accurate. Consequently, if vacant land sales are available, you should not rely on the allocation method of land appraisals.

The first step in the allocation or abstraction method is to find sales of *improved* properties with site characteristics that are comparable to those of the subject property. Next, allocate a proportion of the sales price to the land and a proportion to the buildings. To do this, you might select the value relationship (percent or ratio) that you have found to be typical for similar properties in similar areas. For example, where your research shows that the site represents 35% of the total value, a $250,000 sale of an improved property indicates a site value of 35% of $250,000, or $87,500. Land and building ratios are subject to constant change, so it is important that your research be recent. Ratios also vary between communities and between types of property; therefore, you must be cautious in using them.

When there is no well-defined ratio of land value to total value among the sales, you may select an abstracted site value. You obtain this by estimating the cost of the building less depreciation (discussed in the next two chapters) and subtracting that figure from the total sales price. This would leave a value that is attributable to the land. (See Figure 10.5.) An example is as follows:

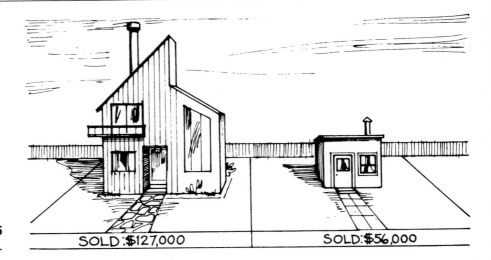

Figure 10.5
Lots may be of equal value.

SOLD:$127,000   SOLD:$56,000

Sale price of the property	$240,000
Less: Depreciated cost of the improvements	−156,000
Equals: "Abstracted" land value	$84,000

Instead of using either of these allocation methods, it is sometimes acceptable to use the land value ratio shown on the local assessment roll. If the roll shows a total value of $260,000, broken into a $60,000 land and $200,000 building value, the ratio is $60,000/$260,000, or 23.1% land. If the property actually sold for $300,000, a land value of $69,300 is suggested by the assessment ratio method ($300,000 × 23.1%).

The site value indicated by the allocation or abstraction method is considered to have a limited reliability. The ratio of land value to total property value usually is different for each location and type of property; therefore, an abstracted site value estimate may be useful only to verify some other value indication. In jurisdictions where current market value assessments are not required, or where market-related allocations are not maintained, using assessment ratios is not reliable.

The Land Development Method

As its name implies, this method is used only to estimate the value of vacant acreage that is ready to be subdivided. It is generally used when there are no sales of comparable acreage or when a detailed analysis of the project is desired. The land development method shows how the raw land value relates economically to its anticipated market value as developed land. Thus this method of estimating value requires that we study current sales of subdivided lots and make a projection of land development costs for the property under appraisal. (See Figure 10.6.)

Figure 10.6
Modern land subdivision.
(Photograph courtesy of
Doug Frost)

To estimate value by the land development method, let us assume a residential subdivision. First, estimate the number of lots to be developed, allowing for zoning, lot size requirements, and the land area needed for streets, parkways, and other open space. Next estimate the typical current price that the lots could be sold for, based on sale prices for comparable subdivision lots. Obtain a total dollar amount to be realized from the gross sales by totaling the estimated prices of the lots. Account for all direct and indirect costs of development, including engineering and government fees. Add costs for promotion, sales, and closing charges. Finally, you must allow for the developer's profit (to cover work effort, overhead costs, and return on capital), typically either as a percentage of gross sales or a percentage of the capital invested in the raw land. After deducting all these development costs and profits from the gross revenues, the remaining amount constitutes the value of the raw acreage. If the project will take more than a year to sell, a further deduction may be necessary to adjust for the time that the developer's capital is tied up in the project. There are a number of different methods of performing subdivision analyses, varying in format and in complexity. Example 10.1 displays one method.

Example 10.1 Valuing Acreage Ready for Subdivision

Suppose that you were appraising a 12-acre parcel of land, approved for development into 50 single-family residential lots. Similar lots nearby, ready to build on, are selling for $60,000 each. You project sales revenues and expenditures as follows. The example allows a developer's return of 30% on the raw land investment, which is both a return on the developer's capital and also payment for the developer's risk, entrepreneurial skills, and overhead costs.

Projected sales: 50 lots at $60,000		$3,000,000
Less: Development costs		
Direct expenses:		
Design and engineering	$ 20,000	
Clearing and grading	100,000	
Utilities and streets	+500,000	
Subtotal		$620,000
Indirect expenses:		
Studies and reports	$ 10,000	
Legal costs and fees	100,000	
Construction financing costs	150,000	
Property taxes	50,000	
Sales and promotion	+150,000	
Subtotal		+460,000
Total deductions from sales		−1,080,000
Equals: Net proceeds before raw		
land and entrepreneurial costs		$1,920,000

These net proceeds represent the land purchase price plus the entrepreneur's costs of 30%, for a total that is 130% of the land value. Therefore:

$$\text{Indicated raw land value} = \$1,920,000/1.30 = \$1,477,000*$$

Note: In this example, the indicated raw land value is just under $30,000 per developable lot, or 50% of the finished value.

*Rounded answer.

The Land Residual Method

This method of estimating the value of the land is based on the principle of surplus productivity, discussed in Chapter 5. The land residual method calculates land value by measuring the amount of income (either actual or potential) that is left after deducting the amount of income that should be attributed to any buildings. Hence the method is one version of the income approach to value.

The land residual method is useful where there are no comparable land sales and newer commercial, industrial, or residential-income properties are being appraised. The techniques used in this method will be discussed in Chapter 14.

10.3 HOW TO USE MARKET COMPARISON TECHNIQUES

The comparison of properties is an essential part of all four methods of appraising land. While the same rules discussed in Chapters 8 and 9 apply to the techniques of site comparison, data and techniques that are unique to site appraisals will be emphasized in this section.

Types and Sources of Data

Although the specific types and sources of data needed for comparison of land sales may differ from those required in the appraisal of improved property, the quality and quantity of data to be gathered are essentially the same.

Criteria for Comparable Sales

For vacant land sales to be used as adequate comparables, they must be competitive with both the subject property and each other. They should be located in the same neighborhood as the subject property, or one like it, and be affected by similar social and economic influences. In fully built-up, older neighborhoods, vacant land sales are usually not available. Therefore, sales from a different location may be considered if the sites are similar in physical and legal characteristics and influenced by the same market factors. Similar prices for comparable improved properties may be convincing evidence of such comparability.

The comparable sales must be open market transactions; distress sales and sales where the buyer gains a unique benefit are not usually considered to be valid comparables. An example of such a special benefit would be a case in which a business buys an adjoining vacant property for much needed expansion. If the alternative to expansion is to relocate to larger premises, the business can often afford to pay a premium to get the adjoining lot.

To be useful, a sale should be recent. This is a relative term, measured from the value date of the appraisal. Depending on the market activity at the time and the type of property being appraised, a sale could be considered recent if it occurred as remotely in time as two or three years before the date of value. However, in an active or changing market, sales more than a few months old may be unacceptable.

Current or Prior Sale of Subject Property

As mentioned in Chapter 8, any known current agreement of sale, option, or listing of the subject property should be considered and analyzed by the appraiser. Also, prior sales of the subject property should be investigated. Industry standards generally require that such a history include all sales that have occurred within one year if one- to four-family residential property is being appraised, or within three years for all other property types. It is important that the appraiser make appropriate comment as to whether or not these historical data are relevant to the current value of the subject property.

What Data to Include

The data collected for each comparable sale should include detailed information about physical, legal, and locational factors. This information helps in judging the comparability to the subject property. Specific physical data usually include lot size, shape, frontage, slope, and topography. Specific legal data, such as zoning, taxes, special assessments, and public and private restrictions, should also be considered. Sales work sheets are often used, providing the appraiser with a convenient means of recording these and other necessary details, such as street address, legal description, name of grantee (buyer), name of grantor (seller), date, price, and terms of sale. All these items will be discussed later on in this chapter.

| Sales History of Comparables | If any of the comparable sales are located in a speculative market area, it would be advisable for the appraiser to include a sales history of these comparable sales. Appropriate analysis and comment on these data should be made. |

Sales History of Comparables

If any of the comparable sales are located in a speculative market area, it would be advisable for the appraiser to include a sales history of these comparable sales. Appropriate analysis and comment on these data should be made.

Sources of Data

Data on vacant land sales may be obtained from public records. For example, ownership records may be discovered by researching recorded deeds in the public recorder's office or the records of the property tax assessor. Checking for demolition and new construction permits or subdivision map applications can also point out parcels where a recent land sale may have occurred, as well as the likely parties to contact.

Buyers, sellers, brokers, land developers, realty board listings, title companies, and lenders are all good private sources of information on recent market activity involving vacant land. Even newspaper advertisements may be a good data source. Also, real estate professionals are usually willing to cooperate in providing data.

Some market data banks accumulate land sales information furnished by participating appraisers. Such groups can be helpful sources of data. Although many of these groups have only limited information on vacant land sales, it can help supplement data from other sources.

Verification of the Data

Any information you collect must be properly verified and interpreted to be of value. Ideally, the total price and terms of the sale should be verified with a principal party or the agent involved in the transaction. This often helps to qualify the sale as an open market transaction. With land sales, it is often especially important to identify the terms of sale. Since institutional loans on vacant land are uncommon, more seller loans are used. When favorable interest rates or terms are provided, the selling price may be significantly increased to reflect the premium value of the loan.

When direct verification of data is not possible, seek out some of the public and private sources already mentioned. As we suggested earlier, data from public records may not accurately indicate the full purchase price. For example, transfer tax charges shown on recorded deeds may reflect only the cash consideration; the amounts for any existing encumbrances assumed by the buyer are usually not included.

Major Land Features Affecting Value

In the comparative process, it is essential that those features of the property that are important in the marketplace be thoroughly understood. Therefore, we shall review here the major factors affecting land value, previously discussed in Chapter 6. In this chapter, the important site characteristics have been divided into physical, legal, and location groupings. (See Figure 10.7.)

Physical Features

Here are some of the most basic physical features to consider (as illustrated in Figure 10.8):

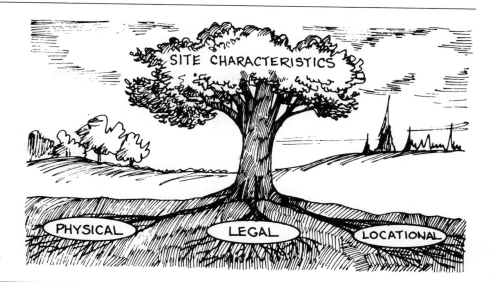

Figure 10.7

1. Size can be measured in square feet, acres, or hectares (the metric land measure—1 hectare is about 2.5 acres), or just by frontage. The size of a parcel is basic to utility and value. Although its relative importance depends on both use and zoning requirements, size is often the best unit of comparison in the analysis of sales.

2. Shape refers to the general parcel configuration and its relative dimensions. An irregular or long and narrow shape, for example, may reduce the utility of a site.

3. Frontage refers to the width of the lot on the access street. Its importance is a function of the land use and specific zoning requirements. This measure affects access to the property. It also affects the exposure of the lot to public notice or view, which is very important in some commercial properties.

Figure 10.8
Major physical features
affecting land value.

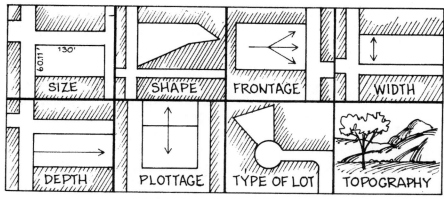

4. Width is important to the *effective* size of a lot. Most zoning ordinances not only regulate minimum lot width, but also require side yard setbacks. Hence, for relatively narrow lots, the side yards have the effect of reducing the net buildable area.

5. Depth of the site is also important. Street setback requirements of local zoning ordinances can considerably reduce the utility of a shallow lot; on the other hand, extra depth may not contribute proportionally to the value of a lot. In urban single residential properties, deep lots may be worth little more than standard depth, or typical lots for the street or neighborhood.

6. Plottage value refers to the added value that is generated when two or more smaller sites can be combined to provide greater utility. For example, two or more commercially zoned lots can sometimes be combined to form the site of a larger, more economically profitable project. However, the assembly of lots does not always result in a plottage value increment; such added value depends on an economic need for the larger unit.

7. The type of lot may affect its relative appeal and marketability. Preference for different lot types (corner, inside, key, flag lot, etc.) may vary from one location to another.

8. Topography refers to the slope and surface features of the site. It can have a dramatic effect on access, drainage, and view, and the cost of construction.

9. Other attributes to be considered include drainage, soil and subsoil features, climate, and view. Such off-site improvements as streets, alleys, sidewalks, and curbs also affect the value of the land itself and are therefore important comparative features.

Legal and Locational Features

Although we are accustomed to thinking of a site as having only physical characteristics, legal and locational features must be compared in appraisals, too.

First, we must consider the legal form of ownership of the land itself. Would it be possible to compare the airspace and common area interests of a condominium site with a conventional detached lot? Probably not. As we learned in Chapter 6, the legal rights associated with condominiums and planned unit developments make them uniquely different from the site we most commonly associate with "conventional" housing. Compare "like with like," whenever possible.

Zoning and other land-use regulations are also critical legal elements to consider in site comparisons. As mentioned before, the highest and best use of land is limited to those uses that are legal under the current zoning (or any probable re-zoning).

Consider the effect of zoning on the typical lot size, for example. As we learned in Chapter 6, zoning often regulates the number of square feet of land required for each living unit. In single-family residence neighborhoods, the minimum lot size may be as little as 4,000 square feet under one zoning designation and as large as 1 acre or more under another. It follows that sales comparisons should generally be made with sales having the same zoning designation.

What effect do new federal, state, and local environmental protection laws have on the use and value of land? Such laws can restrict the legal uses allowable for vacant land but do not usually restrict a use that is already in existence. When new laws are passed, land that is already improved may not be readily comparable with vacant land now selling under restricted-use laws. For example, land developed with apartment buildings prior to open-space laws, which reduced allowable density, might now represent privileged, nonconforming properties. In the case of commercial and industrial properties, state and federal environmental protection laws may require environmental impact reports before any new development or change in usage occurs.

A number of other legal restrictions that limit land use were covered in Chapter 6 and need not all be repeated here. However, it is important to remember that easements, right-of-way regulations, deed restrictions, and private encumbrances can make the affected parcels unique. Hence, such restrictions must be investigated, for they may detract from the comparability of otherwise similar land.

Utilities and other municipal or public services available to the site are largely a function of the site's location. The level of property taxes and other economic factors also should be considered in making land value comparisons. Differences in the quality of schools, fire and police protection, refuse collection, street lighting, and the level of taxation are often so important that it becomes impractical to compare land in different political jurisdictions.

Analyzing the Sales Data

As in the sales comparison approach for improved properties, it is necessary to analyze and compare vacant land sales. We must consider the circumstances of the sale and also compare the properties involved. This process uses four elements of comparison.

Elements of Comparison

Sales should be compared and adjusted by using four elements of comparison: (1) terms and conditions of sale, (2) time of sale, (3) location, and (4) physical characteristics.

It is frequently true that the terms of a sale determine the price. When vacant land is sold for other than cash, it is frequently financed by the seller. If the terms of the seller loan are more favorable than outside lenders offer, the buyer may agree to an inflated price. Low down payments, low interest rates, and subordination clauses are often encountered. (A subordination clause is an agreement by the seller-lender to subordinate this loan to a later development, or construction, loan.) It takes a considerable amount of expertise to adjust vacant land sales prices for the effects of unusual financing. Adjusting for terms of sale was discussed in Chapter 9. The conditions of sale should also be investigated to confirm the real property rights conveyed and to make sure it was an open market transaction.

The time of sale is most often the second element of a sale to be compared and adjusted. Changing market conditions may affect vacant land prices even more quickly and dramatically than prices of improved properties. Changes in zoning, parking requirements, and environmental impact laws are good examples of changing value influences.

Adjustments for location are perhaps the most critical and difficult of the adjustments to make in the appraisal of land. That is why close proximity to the subject property is important so that this adjustment can be minimized.

The physical characteristics of land were referred to earlier in this section. The characteristics of the subject and the comparables should be compared, with priority given to those differences that affect the potential use of the site. How much do size, shape, topography, and so on, affect the value of a site? These questions can be answered only by an analysis of the market's reaction to them. Several techniques help to interpret the market's reaction to these important physical differences. One of these is the direct market method discussed in Chapter 9. This technique makes use of matched pairs of sales. For example, if two lots with only one notable difference, say, standard versus excess depth, have recently sold at different prices, the adjustment for depth might be "read" from the sales. Or it might be possible to locate a depth table that conforms to the sales data and can serve as a guide. (The use of depth tables to suggest how lot value may vary with relative depth was discussed in Chapter 6.) When a large number of sales are available, linear and multiple regression techniques can assist in the analysis of two or more physical differences in the sale properties.

Units of Comparison for Land Appraisals

The appraiser normally compares sales by whatever criteria are most significant in the market. Using a unit of comparison helps you to do this. Appropriate units of comparison are often determined by the type of zoning and potential use. For example, residential lots are usually sold and compared by selling price per lot, square foot, or acre. In the case of lots zoned for multiple-residential or condominium projects, the selling price per dwelling unit to be developed is generally the important unit of comparison. Commercial or industrial land is usually sold and compared by the selling price per square foot, but larger parcels are sold per acre. High-valued commercial property is sometimes sold in terms of price per front foot, where foot traffic is heavy and merchandise display is important.

In the hypothetical sales sample shown in Example 10.2, there seems to be less variability in the price per square foot than in the price per front foot. This implies that the appropriate "market" unit is the price per square foot. In any given study, you may need to make several analyses in order to discover which is the most significant unit of comparison in that market.

Example 10.2 Using Units of Comparison in Appraising Land

Sale	Size	Price	Price per Front Ft.	Price per Sq. Ft.
A	50 × 100	$250,000	$5,000	$50
B	100 × 120	600,000	6,000	50
C	55 × 80	233,200	4,240	53
D	75 × 100	367,500	4,900	49

The Adjustments

Land prices are analyzed and adjusted as part of the comparative process. By way of review, the analysis of sales data usually involves adjusting the comparable sales prices to make the comparables more like the subject property, or as close to a substitute in market appeal as possible. These adjustments can be made by adding or subtracting the lump-sum amounts from the sales price of the comparable, by adding or subtracting percentages, or by accumulating percentages. You can review these adjustment methods in Chapter 9.

A sales adjustment grid, such as that shown in Example 10.3, is a convenient method of displaying the important sales differences, as well as keeping track of all these adjustments.

Example 10.3 Land Sales Adjustment Grid (showing percentage adjustments)

Sale	Price	Time	Location	Size	Total Percent	Indicated Value
1	$50,000	+2	0	−5	−3	$48,500
2	45,000	+4	−5	+5	+4	46,800
3	40,000	+5	+5	0	+10	44,000
4	35,000	+5	+10	+5	+20	42,000
5	60,000	+1	0	−5	−4	57,600

When you have been able to locate a large enough sales sample, sales that require very large adjustments are usually discarded. If valid comparable properties have been used and the adjustments are reasonable, the adjusted prices should now fall into a fairly narrow range.

In reconciling the adjusted sales prices to a value conclusion, it is a good rule to give the greatest weight to the sales requiring the least total adjustment. Both the plus and minus adjustments should be considered in this determination. Averages are rarely justified in appraising.

SUMMARY

Appraisals of vacant or undeveloped land are used for many purposes, including sale and purchase, public actions, and land development. In improved properties, a separation of value between land and buildings is necessary for income and property tax purposes. A separate site value is also required in the cost approach and in several forms of the income approach to value.

Appraisal standards require an opinion of highest and best use in most written appraisals. This optimum use of the land is suggested: (1) as if vacant, and (2) as presently improved. To be selected as representing the highest and best use, any suggested use must meet four criteria or tests. The use must be: (1) physically possible, (2) legally permissible, (3) economically feasible, and (4) maximally productive.

The four primary methods used by appraisers for arriving at land values are:

---

1. The market method.

2. The allocation or abstraction method.

3. The land development method.

4. The land residual method.

The market method is the most reliable for appraising land because it is the most direct. The site is compared to sales of similar parcels of vacant land. The comparison is as if it were vacant and available for its highest and best use. When no comparable sales of vacant land are available for comparison, the site may be appraised by the allocation, abstraction, development, or land residual methods.

The allocation and abstraction methods use sales of improved property and allocate a portion of the sales price to the land. They are useful in built-up areas where little vacant land remains.

The development method of land appraisal relates the value of raw land to its potential market value as developed land. It is used to appraise parcels likely to be subdivided in the near future.

The land residual method is a technique of the income approach and applies mainly to commercial and investment projects. It is an estimate of site value based on the actual or potential income remaining after deducting the income attributed to the improvements.

Each of the four methods of appraising land relies on property comparison in some form. The data needed for land sales comparisons are basically the same as for improved property. For land sales to be considered valid comparables, they must be competitive with the subject property and with each other. They must be qualified as open market transactions, and the sales should be recent.

For the appraiser to compare market sales, it is essential to understand what site characteristics are important. These characteristics are placed in three categories: physical, legal, and locational. The most important physical factors include size, shape, frontage, width, depth, plottage, type of lot, and topography. Legal and locational factors include the most likely profitable use, zoning and other land-use regulations, as well as utilities and public facilities available. The four major elements of comparison used in the analysis of sales data are terms of sale, time of sale, location, and physical characteristics. Sales prices should be compared by what the market considers most important.

In the analysis of vacant land sales, the most common units of comparison are those that compare selling price per lot, per square foot, per acre, per front foot, or per unit developed. The sales prices are adjusted from the comparables *toward* the subject property by adding or subtracting a lump sum or a percentage from the sales price of the comparable. If valid comparables and adjustments have been used, the adjusted sales prices should fall into a fairly narrow range.

Important Terms and Concepts

Abstraction method

Access

Ad valorem tax

Allocation method

Depreciation basis

Development method

Land residual method

Market method

Potential use

REVIEWING YOUR UNDERSTANDING

1. Land or site value estimates are important in the appraisal of both vacant and improved property; thus, such appraisals assist in:
   (a) The sale and purchase of land
   (b) Land development
   (c) Ad valorem and certain income tax situations
   (d) Certain appraisal procedures
   (e) All of the above

2. The market method or direct sales comparison method of estimating site value:
   (a) Does not apply to acreage appraisals
   (b) Is the most reliable method available
   (c) Is considered inferior to other methods
   (d) Is used only when the subject property is a subdivided lot

3. Land value may be abstracted from the sales of improved property. The method is most useful:
   (a) In built-up areas where little vacant land remains
   (b) As an alternative to the market method when comparable sales are not available
   (c) For acreage appraisals
   (d) Both (a) and (b)

4. The land development method in appraisal is used only to estimate the value of vacant acreage that is ready to be subdivided. This method requires:
   (a) The study of current sales of subdivided lots
   (b) The projection of land development costs
   (c) Both (a) and (b)
   (d) Neither (a) nor (b)

5. Many project feasibility studies incorporate vacant land appraisals. If a lot zoned for commercial use is being studied and there are no comparables available, which of the following methods would most probably be applicable?
   (a) The market method
   (b) The subdivision method
   (c) The land residual method
   (d) None of the above

6. The market method is suitable to appraise either vacant or improved sites zoned for:
   (a) Residential
   (b) Commercial
   (c) Industrial
   (d) Any of the above

7. For land sales to be adequate comparables, they must be:
   (a) Competitive with the subject and each other
   (b) Relatively recent
   (c) Open market transactions
   (d) All of the above

8. The unit of comparison for vacant land appraisals is ideally:
   (a) The square foot
   (b) The total lot
   (c) A combination of square foot and front foot units
   (d) The unit considered by the market to be important

9. Land prices are analyzed and adjusted as part of the comparative process. These adjustments could involve:
   (a) Adding or subtracting lump-sum amounts
   (b) Adding or subtracting percentages
   (c) Accumulating percentages
   (d) Any of the above

10. From the land sales adjustment grid shown in the following table, calculate the total adjustment and indicated value for each sale, and then choose a logical market value of the subject. Adjustments are given in percentages. (Give the most weight to the sale requiring the least adjustment, considering both plus and minus adjustments.)

Sale	Price	Time	Location	Size	Total	Indicated Value
1	$38,000	+3	−5	−5	_____	_____
2	40,000	+5	−5	+5	_____	_____
3	35,000	+2	+5	0	_____	_____
4	45,000	+1	−10	−5	_____	_____

(a) $37,450
(b) $35,340
(c) $38,700
(d) $42,000

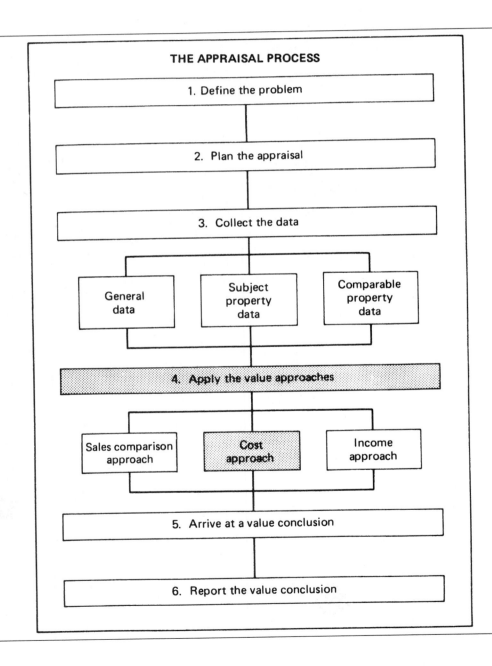

THE APPRAISAL PROCESS

1. Define the problem

2. Plan the appraisal

3. Collect the data

| General data | Subject property data | Comparable property data |

4. Apply the value approaches

| Sales comparison approach | Cost approach | Income approach |

5. Arrive at a value conclusion

6. Report the value conclusion

Chapter 11
Introducing the Cost Approach

Preview One of the three recognized approaches to value, the cost approach provides an estimate of the total land and building outlay (i.e., cost) that would be required to create an equally desirable substitute for the property under appraisal. To introduce the cost approach, this chapter first outlines the approach and explains the difference between reproduction costs and replacement costs. Examples will show how these two different types of costs are used. Next, the chapter covers the four common methods of estimating costs and the direct and indirect elements that make up the total cost of a structure. In the final section, the site, location, and design factors that most directly affect the construction costs of buildings are identified. Chapter 12 will complete the study of the cost approach by listing and describing methods used to estimate depreciation, or loss in value of improvements.

When you have completed this chapter, you should be able to:

1. *List the five basic steps in the cost approach.*

2. *Define the terms* reproduction *cost and* replacement *cost, and explain their use in appraisals.*

3. *Name four methods of estimating costs and explain when each is used.*

4. *List the direct and indirect costs that make up a building's total costs.*

5. *Name the important site, location, and design features that influence the construction costs of a building.*

11.1 USE OF COST ESTIMATES IN APPRAISALS

The principle of substitution suggests that the value of an existing property can be measured by the cost of producing a similar new property as a substitute. The cost approach is based on this principle. Estimating the construction cost is an essential part of the cost approach. Actually, cost estimates of one form or another are used in all three approaches to value. In the cost approach, the value of a property is estimated by adding the land value to the depreciated cost of the improvements. Cost estimates are also used in the sales comparison approach, where they help us adjust sales, a procedure described in Chapter 9. In the income approach, the cost of improvements is a consideration in capitalizing the income of new or proposed investment properties.

The cost estimates that are used in appraisals are what we describe as generalized economic costs. This simply means that they should always reflect:

1. Current cost levels, not "book" costs or historic costs.

2. Typical costs to build a building, rather than the actual construction costs. These two costs could be the same, of course.

3. Costs that include all the charges to the consumer, not just the cost to the developer or builder. All-inclusive costs are sometimes referred to as "turn-key" costs, where all that the first occupant has to do is to turn the key.

Purpose and Outline of the Cost Approach

In practice, appraisers use the cost approach for three main purposes:

1. To estimate the value of new (or nearly new) and economically sound developments. Here, possible depreciation errors will be the smallest.

2. To appraise institutional or special-use properties, such as a church or a government building, not commonly rented or bought and sold in the open market. In this case, the cost approach may be the only approach available.

3. To check the other value approaches. This option is available *whenever* appraising improved properties. Using the cost approach can reduce the chance of making an undetected gross error in the other approaches used.

Steps in the Cost Approach   The cost approach involves five basic steps:

1. Estimating the value of the land as if vacant and available for use. Generally, this is accomplished by market comparison.

2. Estimating the current cost to reproduce or replace the existing improvements.

3. Deciding on appropriate amounts for accrued depreciation (loss in value).

4. Deducting the accrued depreciation from the cost new of the improvements.

5. Adding the depreciated cost of the improvements to the estimated land value to arrive at the property value as indicated by the cost approach.

Since the estimation of accrued depreciation is an important and often complex procedure, all of Chapter 12 has been devoted to this subject. Land valuation was covered in Chapter 10.

Limitations on Using the Cost Approach
The cost approach has certain important limitations. First, some cost elements are difficult to define and estimate, as we shall explain later in this chapter. Second, measuring or estimating accrued depreciation can be difficult and quite subjective. For this reason, the cost approach should *not* be emphasized in the appraisal of unusual or older buildings unless no other method is available.

The Choice of Reproduction or Replacement Costs
Real estate appraisal is basically a process of comparison. The cost approach compares the utility of the structure with its economic cost in today's dollars. It may begin with either an estimate of the *reproduction* cost—the cost of creating a duplicate or identical building—or it may begin with an estimate of *replacement* cost—the cost of constructing a building that would have a similar utility to the subject improvement. Although these two terms are often used interchangeably in casual conversation between appraisers, there is an important technical difference that should be understood.

Using Reproduction Cost Estimates
Since reproduction cost is defined as the cost of a duplicate or approximate replica structure, every physical component must be included. If certain features, such as the intricate design of an out-of-style house, are no longer in demand, their cost is still estimated and included. The reproduction cost estimate is intended to capture the building exactly as it is. It must include the cost of duplicating every peculiarity and feature, whether they contribute as much to the property value as they do to the cost. With reproduction costs, all judgment of the relative marketability or utility of a particular feature is handled in the depreciation portion of the cost approach procedure and not in the cost-new estimate. (See Figure 11.1.)

Figure 11.1
The choice: reproduction or replacement cost. (Photograph courtesy of Doug Frost)

Using Replacement Cost Estimates

Replacement cost is defined as the cost to build a structure of similar utility. In this method, you do *not* include every feature of the building in your estimate of current cost new. Instead, you examine the current utility or usefulness of the improvements and estimate the cost to build a structure that provides similar utility. For example, if the subject property had 9-foot ceiling heights, and you concluded that the market considered 8-foot ceilings to provide equal utility, your replacement cost estimate would be of a structure with 8-foot ceilings. Thus a replacement cost estimate requires a judgment of building utility at the time of estimating cost new, instead of later in the depreciation analysis. Any building features that do not add to the general attractiveness or marketability would not be included in the cost estimate. These features fall into two basic categories:

1. Components of the original building that are no longer being used by builders because of changes in construction and technology. Examples include molded plaster ceilings, hand-carved fireplace mantles, floor furnaces, and hand water pumps.

2. Components that do not add to value because they are not currently in demand at the location. These components could be high-cost features in a low-priced neighborhood, as shown in Figure 11.2, or design features that are not consistent with the highest and best use.

Replacement versus Reproduction

Although there is no clear-cut industry standard, replacement cost estimates are probably used more often than reproduction costs. From the appraiser's point of view, using replacement costs avoids making time-consuming estimates of the cost of old-fashioned materials found in older construction. Also, appraisers argue that using replacement costs provides a direct rating of the market demand for the quality and design and that this makes the cost approach more realistic.

From the client's point of view, however, an appraisal based on reproduction cost is sometimes preferred. Such a cost requires the appraiser to identify and describe specifically the non-marketable features of the building and to explain judgments concerning the amount of utility lost. Any value reductions resulting from such non-marketable features are thus exposed as specific depreciation allowances instead of being hidden as they are in the replacement cost method. Because of these advantages, the standard Uniform Residential Appraisal Report form (illustrated in Chapter 16) requires the use of reproduction cost estimates exclusively. However, if the building components being estimated are no longer available, then replacement cost estimates could be used.

In practice, the choice of cost method to be used depends substantially on the appraisal problem. Examples 11.1 and 11.2 should serve to illustrate common usage of both the reproduction and the replacement cost methods.

Figure 11.2
High-cost features in a low-priced neighborhood.

Example 11.1 Excess
Quality for the Location

The subject is a custom-built 1960 residence located in a neighborhood of lower-quality homes. Market acceptance of the subject is judged to be less than its high quality should command.

Estimated reproduction cost		$98 per sq. ft.
Less:	Loss in usefulness (excess quality)	−28 per sq. ft.
Equals:	Reproduction cost less utility loss	$70 per sq. ft.
	(*Note:* Loss in utility should be estimated by one of the methods outlined in Chapter 12.)	
Secondary Method:		$70 per sq. ft.
Estimated replacement cost		

Example 11.2
Antiquated Materials

The subject building is a 1927 custom residence constructed of hollow-tile walls and other antiquated components not readily available now. It is estimated that construction cost today would be $65 per square foot if we substitute modern construction materials and technology.

Estimated replacement cost		$65 per sq. ft.
Secondary Method:		
Estimated reproduction cost		$80 per sq. ft.
Less:	Estimated loss in utility	−15 per sq. ft.
Equals:	Reproduction cost less utility loss	$65 per sq. ft.

The reproduction cost method is preferred in Example 11.1. Reproduction costs make the actual quality of the house a part of the record and require the appraiser to show how the deduction for the excess quality was handled. The replacement cost method is preferred in Example 11.2 because it saves on the amount of time and effort spent on locating and pricing scarce materials and unusual construction features.

When both excess quality and antiquated materials are found, an optional method used by appraisers combines the two methods shown. First, a modified replacement cost estimate is made, discounting only for the antiquated materials; then a separate allowance is made for the loss in utility that is due to excess quality.

11.2 PRACTICAL COST-ESTIMATING METHODS

Construction cost estimating is considered by many to be a specialized skill requiring a great deal of knowledge about building specifications and construction technology. For routine appraisals, however, reasonable results can be achieved by the appraiser who understands the four basic methods of estimating costs. Although most appraisers use only the first two methods listed, it is important to know the others, for they can be helpful in special situations:

> 1. The comparative square-foot (or comparative unit) method.
>
> 2. The unit-in-place method.
>
> 3. The index (or cost service index) method.
>
> 4. The quantity survey method.

The Comparative Square-Foot Method

The comparative square-foot (or comparative unit) method is the most widely used method of estimating construction costs. It is also the most practical. The appraiser applies this method either by referring to published cost manuals or by citing typical costs that he or she has discovered in the field. Since cost manuals represent the average cost level at any one time, they are generally preferred over the actual costs for any specific project encountered. The cost of a particular building is estimated by applying the average (or typical) square-foot costs of similar buildings. (We note that certain cost-estimating functions performed for government purposes may eventually be using metric measures, eg., meters and centimeters, by the year 1994.) Differences in building specifications and components not included in base costs are adjusted by appropriate multipliers or adjustment amounts. Example 11.3 illustrates the use of this method.

Example 11.3 Comparative Square-Foot Cost Estimate of a Single-Family Residence

Assume that you are estimating the reproduction cost of an average-quality dwelling with three bedrooms and two baths. It has 2,000 square feet and there are six perimeter corners. The general specifications of the most nearly similar house in your construction cost manual match those of the subject except for the built-in kitchen appliances and air conditioning found in the subject house. The adjustments for floor area and shape are obtained from the cost manual. (*Note:* To simplify the example, the local area multiplier has been ignored.) Proceed as follows:

Base cost factor from manual	$80	per sq. ft.
Area and shape multiplier	× 0.973	
Base cost factor, adjusted	$77.84	
Base cost: 2,000 sq. ft. × $77.84 =		$155,680

Plus:		
Refinements		
Built-in appliances	$5,000	
Air conditioning	+6,000	
Total additives		+ 11,000
Equals: Estimated total cost of house		$166,680
Plus: Garage and yard improvements		+ 22,000
Equals: Total cost estimate		$188,680
Rounded		$190,000

The Unit-in-Place Method

The unit-in-place cost-estimating method calculates the separate cost of each component of the building. Typical components would include foundation, walls, floors, roof, ceiling, heating, and so on. The cost estimate for each component includes the cost of attaching or installing the component into the structure. The costs for the various components are added to reach a total cost estimate.

The unit-in-place cost-estimating method is most commonly used to modify or adjust the comparative square-foot method described earlier. Note that in Example 11.3, the basic square-foot cost was refined by using unit-in-place costs for the built-in appliances and air conditioning.

As a primary cost technique, the unit-in-place cost-estimating method is especially well suited for estimating the cost of industrial buildings. Because such buildings often vary widely in size, shape, and height, it is difficult to make an accurate estimate of their cost using comparative square-foot cost calculations.

How It Works

The appraiser refers to one of the various cost-estimating guides available and prices the subject building one component at a time: walls, floors, roof, mechanical, and so on. The figure for each component includes all the necessary costs to fabricate and attach that particular building part to the structure. This means that all the direct and indirect costs of labor, material, design, engineering, and builder's profit are included in the component cost figure.

When applying the unit-in-place method, major structural components are figured first. Floors, walls, and roof structures are typically measured and priced by the square foot of surface area. However, walls can be priced by the linear foot. Costs for interior and exterior extras and roof cover are then added, along with plumbing, electrical, heating and cooling, and other mechanical components. Example 11.4 will illustrate.

Example 11.4 Unit-in-Place Cost Estimate for a Small Commercial Building

Floors	5,000 sq. ft. at $7	=	$35,000
Walls	300 linear ft. at $200	=	60,000
Roof structure	5,000 sq. ft. at $15	=	75,000
Interior partitions	100 linear ft. at $40	=	4,000
Ceilings	5,000 sq. ft. at $4	=	20,000
Doors and windows			5,000
Roof cover			10,000
Plumbing lines and fixtures			5,500
Electrical system			5,000
Heating and cooling			20,000
Hardware and all other costs			10,000
Total direct and indirect costs			$249,500

The Index Method

The index (or cost service index) method is sometimes relied on to estimate costs for unique or unusual structures when the original or historic costs are known. The method adjusts the original costs to the current cost level by a construction multiplier derived from published cost indexes. Year-by-year construction cost information is accumulated and published nationally by a number of well-known companies. Cost records are cataloged by building design and type of construction, and then indexed to a base year such as 1929 or 1940. Regional or area modifiers are also provided to help account for differences in construction costs that relate to location.

The formula for cost estimating by the index method is as follows:

$$\text{Original cost} \times \frac{\text{Current-year index}}{\text{Historical-year index}} = \text{Current cost}$$

To use the index method, follow these steps:

1. Verify that the original cost figure included all the present building components.

2. Find the applicable cost index figures for the current year (or year of appraisal) and for the original or historic year.

3. Divide the current-year index by the historic-year index to derive an adjustment factor.

4. Multiply the original cost by the adjustment factor.

Assume that you are estimating the current cost of a building that cost $80,000 in 1975. You find that no major remodeling has been done since that time. Your cost index chart for this type of building, at this location, shows a current-year index figure of 1754 and a year 1975 index of 726. Current construction cost would then be estimated as follows:

$$\$80,000 \times \frac{1754}{726} = \$80,000 \times 2.42 = \$193,500 \text{ (rounded)}$$

Some published cost services provide charts of pre-computed cost multipliers. In such cases, the factor for the current-year cost update (2.42 in this example) may be taken directly from such a chart.

Although not considered as accurate as other methods of cost estimating, indexing is often used as a secondary value tool. When an estimate of replacement cost new is needed merely to indicate an upper limit of value for a building, indexing can eliminate the time-consuming process of a detailed cost analysis. Indexing is also well adapted to computer-assisted statistical appraisal programs, where the improvement cost new is often a significant variable in the analysis of market sales. Such programs are common in mass appraisal work such as that done in assessment jurisdictions.

The Quantity Survey Method

The quantity survey method is the most detailed and accurate of the construction cost-estimating methods. It involves the listing and separate pricing of all material and labor components of a project, as well as all the indirect costs of construction, such as a survey, permits, overhead, and contractors' profit. Written specifications and drawings are required.

Although the quantity survey method is the most precise method of estimating construction costs, it is rarely used by appraisers. Instead, it is used mainly by building contractors when bidding on unique projects. It is a highly specialized method that requires more technical knowledge of construction than most appraisers have. Also the great amount of time and detail required by the method is seldom warranted (considering that other cost methods produce reasonable answers in less time).

The main features, applications, and requirements of the four methods are listed in Table 11.1.

TABLE 11.1 Cost-Estimating Methods

Method	How It Works	Primary Application	Cost Data Requirements
Comparative square foot	Uses the average cost per square foot (or other unit) of a comparable new building. Most useful method.	Universally used and accepted for most buildings.	Base costs from published or known sources; refinements made by unit-in-place method.
Unit-in-place	Prices building components by "in-place" cost per sq. ft., surface foot, or lump-sum amounts. More accurate and more detailed than the comparative sq.-ft. method.	Primary method for shell-type buildings, unique projects; most often used to refine the comparative sq.-ft. method.	Component costs from published or known sources.
Index	Trends original (historic) costs to current cost level.	Unique buildings; mass appraisal applications.	Trend factor from construction cost index service.
Quantity survey	A detailed cost breakdown by each category of labor, materials, fees, profit margins, etc. most accurate; but least useful for typical buildings because of detail and knowledge required.	Development of detailed construction bid by a contractor.	Current prices and amounts of all materials, wage rates, profit margins.

11.3 UNDERSTANDING DIRECT AND INDIRECT COSTS

Have you ever asked a builder or developer what it would cost to construct a house or some other structure? In all likelihood, the answer you got may have confused as much as helped you because of the different things that people include when they refer to costs. In appraisals, costs should include all the expenditures that are required to produce the structure, make it ready for use, and pay for selling costs at the consumer level. These include not only the builder's direct costs spent for labor and materials but also a number of indirect costs. The latter are not always reported in informal cost discussions. Interest and property taxes during construction and builders' profits are examples of indirect costs. Failure to take into account all direct and indirect costs of building construction often results in an understated cost approach in relation to value.

Direct Costs

All of the items directly involved with the physical construction of the structure are classified as direct cost elements. These include the following:

---

1. Labor.

2. Materials and equipment.

3. Design and engineering.

4. Subcontractors' fees.

Labor Costs

Labor costs include all wages and salaries paid for direct work on the construction project. Such expenditures may be paid either by the builder or by any of the several subcontractors involved in the project. All costs of labor, skilled or unskilled, must be included.

Materials and Equipment

The material and equipment costs include all the items that eventually become integral parts of the structure, whether purchased directly or included in subcontracts: the concrete, steel, and lumber used in the foundation and framework, as well as the appliances, finish hardware, and paint annexed to the completed project. (See Figure 11.3.)

Design and Engineering

Engineering and architectural costs are included in the building cost estimate. However, soil grading, compaction, special soil engineering, and retaining walls, on the other hand, are included in the *site* value.

Some residential structures require little or no engineering, and many are built from standardized plans and specifications. However, design and engineering can involve substantial expense, particularly for custom and/or unusual construction. This is partly because design specialists are often required to supervise the construction work.

Subcontractors' Fees

Much of the construction labor is not provided by employees of the contractor. Instead, subcontractors are used. For example, plumbing,

Figure 11.3
Typical multifamily construction project. (Photograph courtesy of Doug Frost)

heating, and electrical work are commonly performed by subcontractors. Although the amounts paid to subcontractors are not usually broken down between labor, material, and other components, any amount paid for such services is included as one of the four direct construction cost elements.

Indirect Costs

Indirect costs include all of the hidden time and money costs involved in a project. Although they are often somewhat proportional to the direct cost of labor and material, indirect costs can vary considerably from one job to another. Here is a list of indirect construction costs to be included in a cost estimate.

---

1. Legal fees, appraisal fees, and building permits and licenses.
2. Interest and fees for construction financing.
3. Construction liability and casualty insurance.
4. Property taxes during construction.
5. Construction administration and management.
6. Interest on investment, and loss in rental.
7. Builders' and entrepreneurial profit.
8. Selling costs.

Some of the items listed need further definition and discussion.

Interest on Construction Financing

Construction loan funds are usually paid to the borrower in "progress payments," based on the work performed each month during construction. As a result, the amount of principal paid out grows each month, as does the monthly interest payment. Calculating the exact interest amount is quite hard to do. As a rule of thumb, however, interest can be based on one-half of the amount borrowed and then calculated for the entire construction time period. For example, at a 10% interest rate, a $100,000 project that takes six months to develop would incur interest charges of:

$$\frac{\$100,000}{2} = \$50,000 \text{ at } 5\% \text{ (10\% per year for six months)} = \$2,500$$

In addition, the loan fees and points charged for granting the construction financing must be added to the interest charges. For example,

Three points on the loan, or $100,000 × 0.03		=	$3,000
Plus:	Progress inspection fee at 1/2% of the loan		+500
Equals:	Total fees and points		$3,500
Plus:	Interest charges (from above)		+2,500
Equals:	Total loan costs		$6,000

The interest on the construction loan, fees, and points could be paid in cash by the borrower or included as one of the disbursements to be made from the construction loan funds. In either case, it is a valid indirect cost element.

Property Taxes During Construction

Property taxes during the construction period are included in the construction cost estimate. In many jurisdictions, improvements that start construction after a particular date (such as a lien date) are not assessed until the next year. For this reason, property taxes during construction may consist only of taxes on the land itself.

Construction Administration and Management

These costs are generally included in the general contractor's bid and are often referred to as builder's overhead. Office rent, office employee salaries, utilities, and transportation costs are examples of such administrative costs. If the builder's overhead costs have been included in an actual contract cost, they should not be added again.

Interest on Investment and Loss in Rental

The owner's investment in land and buildings is entitled to a fair return during the construction and marketing period. If the owner has a substantial investment beyond the construction loan funds, then some return to that investment must be accounted for here. For example, if the owner had a $100,000 investment in the site, it could be assigned a 5% return rate for a six-month construction period, or $5,000 interest on investment. This represents a 10% annual return. After construction has been completed, sales or rentals provide for a return on investment. However, it often takes from three to six months to sell all the space or to bring a building up to normal occupancy. The lack of return on vacant space during this period is therefore figured as an additional cost.

Builder's and Developer's Profit

These costs are the most variable and difficult to estimate of all the indirect costs of construction. Normal builder's profit represents the payment for professional services paid to the general contractor of a construction job. Typical charges for such services are dependent on competition, the predicted construction progress, and other conditions not entirely controlled by the builder. Charges vary from one project to the next, but most depend on the uniqueness of the undertaking. Some information on prevailing contractor profit margins can be obtained from local builders. At one time, 10% of the total hard costs was a common profit margin for the contractor. Now, there is much variation.

The individual developer who "packages" the project, land, and building is often referred to as the entrepreneur. The entrepreneurial profit is the amount required to pay for the "know-how," incentive, and risk involved in speculative development. The amount to be charged for this element depends on economic conditions and competitive investment opportunities. Many cost manuals try to include a "normal" builder's profit, but very few attempt to suggest the amounts for entrepreneurial profits. However, omitting this amount from a cost approach fails to account for one of the costs that must be paid to get the product into the hands of the consumer.

11.4 IMPORTANT FACTORS AFFECTING BUILDING COST

When you make an inspection and general analysis of the improvements under appraisal, your field notes or inspection check-form should contain the building information needed to estimate the reproduction or replacement cost. This section outlines the site, location, design, and construction features that have the greatest effect on the cost of construction. Clearly, these factors should be noted in your inspection. The section also explains how to use published cost data when you are applying the comparative square-foot or unit-in-place methods.

Site and Location Factors

As discussed in the previous chapter, a number of site and location factors have an effect on the value of a site that directly relates to the cost of development. The size and shape of the site, and its topography, soil, geology, and climate are the most obvious physical factors that affect the cost of construction. Irregularly shaped sites may require special design elements in a building. Uphill, downhill, and sidehill lots as well as those with poor soil or unstable geology conditions generally require more engineering and foundation work, and often more costly utility service connections for the structure. In areas with severely hot or cold climates, expensive insulation and design elements may be involved. Higher costs can also be expected to result in this situation.

Both direct and indirect construction costs are also affected by location. Labor, material, and service costs vary from the East Coast to the West Coast, and up and down the country in much the same way as the cost of living varies from one place to another. Also, as building code requirements for structural, mechanical, electrical, and other components of new construction vary, so will the cost of construction.

Because urban areas usually have relatively stringent building codes, construction costs are often higher in the city limits than in unincorporated areas.

Design and Construction Cost Variables

On a given site, seven different building characteristics affect the total cost of construction as well as the square-foot cost. These can be identified as:

1. Design or use type (type of occupancy).
2. Type of construction (construction classification).
3. Quality of construction.
4. Size.
5. Shape.
6. Height.
7. Yard or site improvements.

Design or Use Type

The design or use category of a structure (sometimes referred to as "type of occupancy") is considered the first cost variable. It defines what features the building is likely to have. For example, single-family homes have entirely different cost characteristics than those of stores or factories. In most construction cost manuals, suggested costs are grouped into the following design or use types:

Auditoriums

Auto showrooms

Banks

Bowling alleys

Car washes

Churches

Farm buildings

Fire stations

Garages

Government buildings

Hospitals

Hotels and motels

Industrial buildings
   factories
   warehouses
   public storage

Lumber yards

Mobile home parks

Nursing homes

Office and professional buildings

Recreation facilities

Residential buildings
   singles, duplexes, multiples

Restaurants

Rooming houses and fraternities

Schools and classrooms

Stores and markets

Theaters

Construction Classification

The second cost variable is the type of construction. Buildings are divided into four or five cost groups by the type of structural frame (supporting columns and beams), walls, floors, roof structures, and fireproofing. Typical building codes identify four such cost groups: A, B, C, and D construction (or Class 1, 2, 3, and 4, as some codes call them). Such classifications are sometimes based on construction categories in the Uniform Building Code. Specifications for the major classifications are outlined in Chapter 7 of this book.

Higher construction costs are typical for the A and B classes of construction because of their greater fire protection, better engineering design, and additional component costs. High-rise and institutional buildings usually are designed to meet class A or B specifications.

Class C and D buildings usually cost less to build than Class A or B buildings. Most residential, commercial, and industrial buildings fit into either the Class C or D category. The frame, floor, roof, and wall structures of the latter buildings may be of masonry, wood and/or sheet metal construction. However, Class C buildings usually feature masonry walls and wood roof structures.

A certain amount of knowledge and experience is needed in order to tell in which construction class a particular building belongs. To assist the inexperienced user, most construction cost manuals define the main characteristics of the building classes. It is important to identify correctly the construction class of a building being appraised because typical cost factors are presented in most cost manuals under the respective construction class headings.

Quality of Construction

For a given use type and construction class, the quality of construction is generally the most important cost variable. In residential appraisal work, quality is usually rated as good, average, fair, or poor. However, in some cost manuals, quality is listed on a scale ranging from "low-cost" to "excellent," with typical specifications usually pegged as "average."

Rating the quality of construction is perhaps the most subjective part of cost estimating. Experience, good building specifications, and some knowledge of construction are therefore essential in making a valid quality rating.

Size and Shape

When estimating construction cost by the comparative square-foot method, it is important to recognize the effect of the size and shape on the square-foot cost.

First, let us examine the effect of size. Most buildings have a floor, a roof, and outside walls; these we can refer to as the building "shell." The cost per square foot of such a building could easily be calculated by adding up the "in-place" costs of these "shell" components and dividing by the number of square feet in the building. Now the effect of the floor area on the square-foot cost can be demonstrated by comparing two shell-type buildings of different sizes. Let us assume that, for both buildings in Example 11.5, the floors cost $7.50 per square foot; roof costs are $15.00 per square foot; and walls cost $262.50 per linear (running) foot of wall (all calculated as "in-place" unit costs).

Note that doubling the dimensions of the building decreased the square-foot cost by $10.50, or 24%. In actual practice, the net effect varies, depending on roof design requirements and the project size. Greater roof spans may increase costs. Generally, however, large projects may often cost less per square foot than smaller ones because of the economies of scale.

In residential buildings (and others that have relatively expensive interior components), the effect of size on square-foot costs may be less predictable than in the examples, but it is still important. The total in-place cost for such things as plumbing, cabinets, and doors is often fairly similar in buildings of different sizes. Consequently, the square-foot cost of such "fixed-cost" components will vary with the size of the building. Thus *increases* in floor area tend to reduce the overall square-foot costs, and *decreases* in floor area generally increase square-foot costs.

Example 11.5 The Effect of Size on Square-Foot Costs (Shell-Type Building)

Floor:
 2,500 sq. ft. at $ 7.50 = $ 18,750
Roof:
 2,500 sq. ft. at   15.00 =   37,500
Walls:
 200 linear ft. at   262.50 =   52,500
   Total cost $108,750

Cost per sq. ft.: $\dfrac{\$108,750}{2,500}$ = $43.50

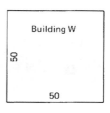

Floor:
 10,000 sq. ft. at $ 7.50 = $ 75,000
Roof:
 10,000 sq. ft. at   15.00 = 150,000
Walls:
 400 linear ft. at   262.50 = 105,000
   Total cost $330,000

Cost per sq. ft.: $\dfrac{\$330,000}{10,000}$ = $33.00

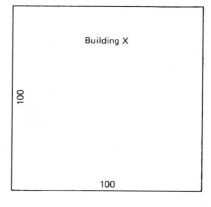

The effect of size on construction cost depends, in part, on building shape. This can be seen if we compare a 50 × 200 foot building with building X in Example 11.5. Let us call this building Y (shown in Example 11.6). Note that buildings X and Y have the same square-foot area despite having different dimensions.

Here, changing the shape from square to long and narrow increases the square-foot cost by $2.62, or about 7.9%. An even more dramatic difference would result if our building Y were scaled down to the square-foot area of building W in Example 11.5.

Example 11.6 The Effect of Shape on Square-Foot Costs

Floor:	10,000 sq. ft. at	$	7.50	=	$ 75,000
Roof:	10,000 sq. ft. at		15.00	=	150,000
Walls:	500 linear ft. at		262.50	=	131,250
	Total cost				$356,250

Cost per sq. ft.: $\dfrac{\$356{,}250}{10{,}000} = \$35.62$

Contrast:
Cost per sq. ft. if dimensions are
100 × 100 ft: $33.00
(per Example 11.5)

In residential buildings, the higher costs resulting from changes in shape can be attributed to several factors. These include:

1. **Increase in the number of corners:** results in increased costs for foundations and wall framing.

2. **Increase in linear feet of the building perimeter:** causes increased costs for walls, doors, windows, insulation, and weather stripping as well as wiring and length of plumbing runs and heat ducting.

3. **Increase in roof framing and overhang:** adds valleys, ridges, flashing, gutters, and downspouts to the costs.

Figure 11.4 shows some of the various shapes that are found in single-residence buildings.

Height The story, or wall height, of a building also influences its cost. We can see how height changes the square-foot cost of a building if we use the size and shape examples previously discussed. With a 20% increase in wall height, the increase in the square-foot costs of the three buildings W, X, and Y would vary from 6.3% to 9.7%.

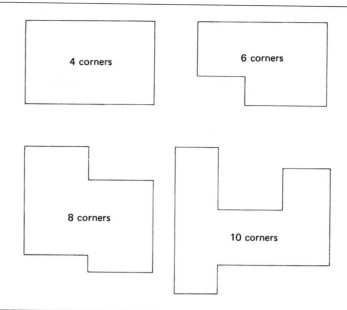

Figure 11.4
Common house shapes.

Yard or Site Improvements

Besides the main building, cost estimates made for appraisal purposes must include any other improvements to the site. This could mean garage or parking structures, walks, driveways, outside lighting, sprinkler systems, fencing, pools, patios, and landscaping. Published cost manuals provide typical unit-in-place costs for many such items.

Landscaping often varies widely in cost; its contribution to value can vary even more. As a result, most appraisers try to estimate how much landscaping contributes to value rather than what it costs. This is both practical and acceptable in single-residence appraisals.

Using Published Building Cost Services

As we have already stated, several building cost services are available to the appraiser—by subscription or purchase. These include the *Marshall Valuation Service* and *Marshall and Swift Residential Cost Handbook,* published by Marshall and Swift Publishing Co., Los Angeles, California; the *Boeckh Valuation and General Estimation Manuals,* published by Boeckh, an operating unit of the American Appraisal Association, Inc., Milwaukee, Wisconsin; and *Building Construction Cost Data* (various editions including Western and Metric), published by R.S. Means Co., Inc., Kingston, Massachusetts. Many of the listed services provide both comparative square-foot and unit-in-place costs. Some also include an index of construction cost changes by year and by class of construction. Most are based on national averages but include local adjustment multipliers. They include all direct cost elements but often exclude entrepreneurial profit, property taxes, interest, and investment return during construction.

General Format of Manuals

As a general rule, the published building cost guides are organized and designed around the major cost variables that were just discussed. The usual handling of these elements is as follows:

1. *Design or use type:* usually the main subdivision of the manual. Up to 40 types of buildings may be described, with photographs and general specifications.

2. *Construction classification:* given as a separate cost schedule within each design type; four or five classifications are typical.

3. *Quality of construction:* interpreted by pictures and typical specifications for each class of construction; includes square-foot cost factors for four to six quality ranges.

4. *Size, shape, and height:* usually handled by corner count or by floor area-shape multipliers and then story-height factors. These are used to adjust the manual's base costs. In multiple-residence buildings, adjustments are often based on the average unit size and number of units. Both are significant cost variables in such buildings.

5. *Cost refinements:* often given as unit-in-place costs for building components; may be broken down into labor and material components.

6. *Yard or site improvements:* referenced in both the main and supplemental cost sections of most guides.

Suggested Costing Procedure

It is very important to read all introductory notes and instructions when using any of the mentioned cost services; they clearly define what costs are included in the manual and how to adjust for cost variables.

Once you have selected the cost section to be used, be sure to read the footnotes that often appear on the individual base cost schedules. Base costs often *exclude* such things as fireplaces and kitchen built-ins, making it necessary to add lump-sum amounts to your initial figure.

Here is a general outline of the steps required in estimating construction costs by the comparative square-foot method, as featured in most of the published building cost services:

1. Select the use-type table appropriate for your building, and determine the building construction class. Choose the quality range with the best-fitting specifications. Determine the base cost factor from the table.

2. Calculate any required floor area, shape, corner, story-height and/or unit size multipliers; multiply (as required) times the base cost factor.

3. Multiply the adjusted base cost times the area of the building.

4. Add the unit-in-place costs for various building components and features.

5. Add lump-sum costs of the various site or yard improvements.

6. Apply a current-cost multiplier and a local multiplier to adjust the published manual costs to the current date and to local costs. Published cost manuals usually provide such multipliers in a supplement or update section.

Computer Costing   The increased use of office computers has influenced cost estimating, too. Several of the cost manual publishers also provide a telephone computer hookup, allowing appraisers to connect their office computers to a central cost data bank and produce complex cost estimates simply and rapidly. Some publishers also provide cost programs to run on the office computer, with periodic cost update disks.

SUMMARY   In this chapter, we discussed construction cost estimates: how they are used in appraisals and how they are made.

Cost estimating plays a significant role in each of the three approaches to value. In appraisals, the concept of cost is related to its economic impact, which means that cost estimates are made at current price levels and reflect the total amount of typical costs passed on to consumers. The cost approach is used primarily to estimate the value of new or special-use properties. It is also an important check against the other value approaches.

There are four methods commonly used to estimate costs. The comparative square-foot method is the most useful because it is the easiest to apply. The unit-in-place method is most often used to refine costs that were estimated by the comparative square-foot method. The index method is useful for costing unique structures or for updating prior cost estimates in mass appraisal applications. The quantity survey method is the most accurate method but is too detailed and technical to be of much practical use in appraisals.

When estimating construction costs, it is important to reflect both direct and indirect costs of construction. The contractor's costs for labor and materials are not the only costs involved. Indirect costs such as building permits, interest on loans and on investment, insurance, property taxes, overhead, and profit must also be included.

A number of site, location, design, and construction features greatly affect construction costs. The size and shape of the site and its topography, soil, geology, and climate are the most obvious physical factors that affect the cost of construction. Both direct and indirect construction costs also depend upon location. Labor, material, and service costs vary with location, as do building code requirements for structural, mechanical, electrical, and other components of new construction.

As reflected in published construction cost manuals, design and construction features affecting construction costs include:

1. Design or use type.
2. Construction classification.
3. Quality.
4. Size, shape, and height of the building.
5. Yard or site improvements.

Appraisers often use cost manuals to make current cost estimates. These manuals provide average cost figures for many types of buildings and include photographs, specifications, and other cost data. Such guides allow appraisers to make reliable cost estimates, using the methods discussed in this chapter.

Important Terms and Concepts

Base costs

Comparative square-foot method

Construction class

Cost approach

Design use or type

Direct costs

Financing charges

Historic cost

Index method

Indirect costs

Insurance costs

Lump-sum costs

Multiplier, cost

Quantity survey method

Replacement cost

Reproduction cost

Shape

Size

Unit-in-place method

REVIEWING YOUR UNDERSTANDING

1. The cost estimates used in appraisals are what we describe as generalized economic costs. This means that they should reflect:
   (a) Wholesale costs
   (b) Current cost levels, not "book" costs or historic costs
   (c) Typical costs to build such a building
   (d) Both (b) and (c)

2. There is an important technical difference between the terms *reproduction cost* and *replacement cost*. Replacement cost refers to:
   (a) The cost of constructing an exact replica building
   (b) The cost of constructing a building that would have a similar utility to the subject property
   (c) The cost of reproducing the subject property
   (d) None of the above

3. From the appraiser's point of view, replacement cost estimates are preferred over reproduction cost estimates because:
   (a) They provide a direct rating of the market demand for the quality and design of a structure
   (b) They are more detailed
   (c) They are less time-consuming
   (d) Both (a) and (c)

4. The cost approach may be emphasized in a number of appraisal situations. Which is not among them?
   (a) Checking the other value approaches
   (b) Appraising institutional or special-use properties

(c) Estimating the value of new or nearly new property

(d) Appraising older homes in an active market

5. The most practical and widely used method of estimating construction costs is:

(a) The comparative square-foot method

(b) The unit-in-place method

(c) The index method

(d) The quantity survey method

6. The cost-estimating method that is often used as a supplement to refine the square-foot method is called:

(a) The quantity survey method

(b) The index method

(c) The unit-in-place method

(d) None of the above

7. Estimating costs by adjusting the original costs to the current cost level with a cost multiplier is a method known as:

(a) The comparative square-foot method

(b) The unit-in-place method

(c) The index method

(d) The quantity survey method

8. Which method of estimating construction costs is the most precise yet seldom used by appraisers?

(a) The index method

(b) The quantity survey method

(c) The comparative square-foot method

(d) The unit-in-place method

9. Which of the following do *not* represent direct cost elements?

(a) Materials and equipment

(b) Interest on investment and loss in rent

(c) Labor and materials

(d) Design and engineering

10. Using the unit-in-place cost factors provided in Example 11.5, calculate the square-foot cost of a shell-type structure that is 25 feet wide and 100 feet long. Compared with the square-foot cost of building W in the illustration, this represents a square-foot cost that is approximately:

(a) $2.00 lower

(b) $5.25 higher

(c) $2.80 higher

(d) The same

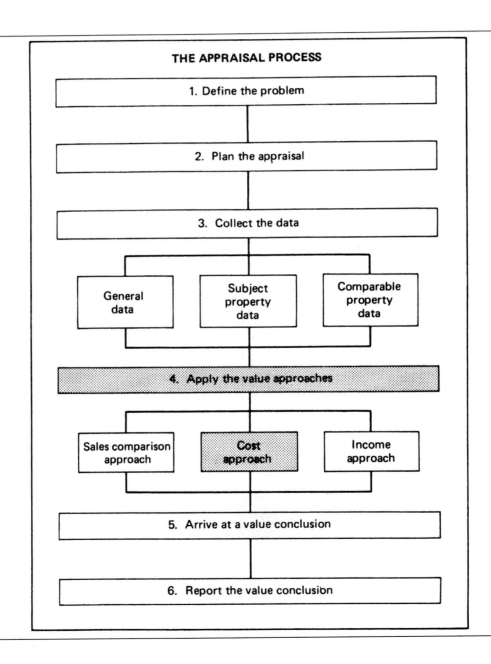

THE APPRAISAL PROCESS

1. Define the problem

2. Plan the appraisal

3. Collect the data

| General data | Subject property data | Comparable property data |

4. Apply the value approaches

| Sales comparison approach | Cost approach | Income approach |

5. Arrive at a value conclusion

6. Report the value conclusion

Chapter 12

Estimating Loss in Value: Accrued Depreciation

Preview   Estimating the relative loss in the value of improvements compared to their costs is a necessary part of the cost approach. Accrued depreciation estimates may also be necessary in the sales comparison and income approaches to value.

What is depreciation? Accountants define it one way, appraisers another. After explaining the difference, this chapter will explore the types and causes of accrued depreciation and explain the major methods appraisers use to measure actual loss in value.

When you have completed this chapter, you should be able to:

1. *Distinguish between the concept of depreciation as it is used in accounting from that used in appraisal.*

2. *Name and give the causes of three types of depreciation.*

3. *Name four methods of estimating accrued depreciation and describe how they may be applied to an appraisal problem.*

12.1 DEPRECIATION DEFINED

Depreciation is a term with two distinctly different meanings, both used by people in real estate. One defines an *accounting* term, used in income tax calculations; the other defines an *appraisal* term, used in the cost approach and elsewhere in the appraisal process.

Depreciation as Used in Accounting

In accounting practice, all capital assets except land are considered to be wasting assets that decline in value over time. These assets may include machinery, vehicles, and other types of equipment as well as buildings. When calculating income for tax purposes, owners of assets held to produce revenue are allowed to deduct annual value loss estimates from income, just as operating expenses are deducted.

Accountants calculate the allowable depreciation deduction by starting with the historic book value of the asset. Book value refers to the original asset cost, plus the cost of any capital additions or improvements, reduced each year by the depreciation deduction taken. Book value is also called cost basis. The important characteristic of income tax depreciation as applied to buildings is that it is determined by the property's cost basis and the allowable depreciation period and does not consider what is actually happening to the building's value. See Example 12-1.

Example 12.1
Accounting Depreciation

Purchase price		$275,000
Less:	Land value	− 65,000
Equals:	Building cost basis	$210,000
Divided by:	Depreciation period	÷ 40 years
Equals:	Annual depreciation claim	$ 5,250

As income tax depreciation deductions are taken, the building cost basis declines. This declining cost basis is often used in reporting the assets of businesses (on balance sheets). When real estate values are increasing, a company with substantial real estate assets can actually have a much higher asset value than that reported to its stockholders. To address this problem, some accountants are now using what is called *current-value* accounting to supplement the more traditional cost-basis accounting procedure.

Accrued Depreciation in Appraisals

The estimate of accrued depreciation that is used in appraisals is governed by an entirely different set of rules than those used in accounting. In appraisals, a dollar or percentage amount is deducted from the estimated *current* cost of the improvements as if new, rather than from their historical cost basis. Second, the amount of depreciation represents the appraiser's best estimate of the actual *market* loss in value as compared to a new building, whereas accounting depreciation is a theoretical loss. Thus an appraiser's estimate of depreciation is not dependent in any way on the property's historical cost basis, the owner's depreciation schedule, or the loss in value allowable for income tax purposes.

As used in appraisals, accrued depreciation is the difference between the current cost new of the improvements and the current market value of those improvements on the valuation date. This difference is sometimes referred to as *diminished utility,* that is, the total loss in value from all causes. As we shall learn in the next section, value loss can be caused by either physical, functional, or economic conditions.

Purpose of Depreciation Estimates in Appraisals

You may recall that the cost approach involves, first, estimating the reproduction or replacement cost new of the improvements; then, deducting the total accrued depreciation from this cost; and last, adding this depreciated improvement value to the land value. An estimate of the total property value is the result. See Example 12.2.

Example 12.2
Appraisal Depreciation

	Reproduction cost new		$150,000
Less:	Estimated accrued depreciation (say, 10%)		− 15,000
Equals:	Reproduction cost less accrued depreciation		$135,000
Plus:	Land value		+ 70,000
Equals:	Total indicated value of the property		$205,000

When *replacement* cost estimates are used instead of *reproduction* cost estimates, note that the amount deducted for accrued depreciation should be only the loss in value *in excess of* any loss in value caused by the loss of utility from antiquated materials, undesirable design features, and the like. The replacement cost estimate would have already adjusted for such factors, whereas reproduction cost estimates do not.

As we learned in the last chapter, estimating accrued depreciation is often the most critical step in the cost approach.

Although depreciation estimates are of the greatest importance in the cost approach to value, they also play an important part in sales comparison and income studies. For example, the sales comparison approach calls for comparing properties, and this may involve an analysis of relative loss in value from age or obsolescence. When the comparables vary in age, the adjustment for age differences can be regarded as the difference in accrued depreciation. Also, in the appraisal of land, the abstraction method of calculating land value from improved sales often involves an estimate of accrued depreciation. In this method, the land value is presumed to be equal to the selling price of the property less the depreciated value of all improvements. Last, depreciation estimates sometimes assist the appraiser in the analysis of income properties. When the total net income for the property must be allocated between land and improvements, the value contribution of each of these agents of production becomes important. As we have seen, the value contribution of improvements can be estimated by calculating their current cost as if new less the total accrued depreciation.

12.2 TYPES AND CAUSES OF ACCRUED DEPRECIATION

Is any one building worth the same as another of the same design type, size, and quality? When the location and site are different, different values should be expected. However, even if the site and location are similar, differences in age, condition, and/or utility usually result in different values. Once differences in these influences have been identified, they can be used to estimate the relative loss in value that they cause. But what are the precise factors involved?

The appraiser's basic task is to recognize specific conditions or features of the property that cause value losses and then to measure the effect of these conditions on value. Two steps are involved. First, the loss in value is categorized by the type and probable cause. Second, the depreciation in each category is classified as either curable or incurable. In other words, the questions are:

1. What is the apparent cause?

2. Can the loss be measured by the cost to correct (or cost to cure) the problem?

Accrued depreciation is classified into three types, or categories, known as physical deterioration, functional obsolescence, and economic obsolescence. We shall discuss the question of whether each is curable as we describe these three types of value loss.

Types of Accrued Depreciation

1. Physical deterioration.

2. Functional obsolescence.

3. Economic (or external) obsolescence.

Physical Deterioration

Regardless of quality or design, all buildings deteriorate physically over the years. The physical deterioration of a structure describes its wear and tear from use, age, weather, neglect, lack of maintenance, or even vandalism. Since each part of a building is affected differently by these conditions, the loss in value is often analyzed component by component. Economically, physical deterioration can prove to be either curable or incurable.

Curable Physical Deterioration

Curable physical deterioration refers to conditions that are economically feasible to correct. This means that correcting the defect would add at least as much to the market value as the cost of the repairs would. For example, if it cost $10,000 to repaint the exterior of a house in a neighborhood where buyers appear willing to pay at least $10,000 more for freshly painted homes, then such repair or renovation would be judged economically feasible. For an otherwise sound building, painting, replacing a worn-out roof or heating system, or simply making the building more presentable by cleaning can often enhance the market value at least as much as the cost of the work. Thus such examples of deferred maintenance or repair would logically fall in the category of *curable* physical deterioration. Examples are shown in Figure 12.1.

Incurable Physical Deterioration

Incurable physical deterioration, on the other hand, describes building conditions that are likely to cost more to repair than the value that would be added to the structure. Such repairs would be considered economically infeasible. For example, slight damage to the foundation or structural framework of a building would usually be considered

Figure 12.1
Examples of deferred maintenance. (Photographs courtesy of Doug Frost)

incurable physical deterioration. This is because the repair cost would be substantial and the resulting increase in market value would be relatively small.

Some other types of deterioration are also considered incurable. They involve some particular part of the building that will need to be replaced in the years ahead but which is too "good" to replace at the moment. An example would be an older air-conditioning system which will need replacement in five or six years but which has too much useful life left to be replaced now. The value loss in such a case is referred to as short-lived incurable deterioration (sometimes also called curable *postponed*). In five years, when the remaining economic life of the air-conditioning system has been used up, we would then consider the value loss as curable. Why? Because replacement of the building component will at that time be economically feasible.

Long-Lived Incurable Physical Deterioration

Value losses attributable to the major components of a building when age is the major contributing factor are called long-lived incurable physical deterioration. These nearly always cost more to repair or renew than the value added by the repairs. Gradual reduction of the value of the foundation, framework, plumbing, fixtures, or electrical wiring, because of age, are examples of long-lived incurable physical deterioration.

Functional Obsolescence

Functional obsolescence describes a type of depreciation that is caused by a relative loss of building utility. Loss of utility means that there is some feature of the building that is not as useful as its cost would suggest. This loss of usefulness could be caused by a faulty building design, outmoded equipment, or some other design defect within the structure. A poorly arranged floor plan and a house lacking a typical side yard are examples of functional obsolescence. (See Figure 12.2.)

Functional obsolescence is often associated with original building design features that are not suitable for the location. A building that is out of place—the wrong type or use for that location—is functionally obsolete (to a degree) and is called a *misplaced improvement*. A building that is too large or lavish for the neighborhood also has functional obsolescence and is labeled an *overimprovement*. Similarly, a building that is too small or of too low quality for the neighborhood and thus suffers from functional obsolescence is called an *underimprovement*.

Functional obsolescence can also be curable or incurable, depending on whether the cost to cure is less than or greater than the value benefits. In some cases, a kitchen can be remodeled, a room added, or a wall knocked out at a fairly nominal cost to bring the building up to current market standards. However, the value loss suffered by a misplaced improvement or overimprovement is usually considered incurable functional obsolescence. (See Figure 12.3.)

Economic (or External) Obsolescence

Also referred to as location or environmental obsolescence, economic obsolescence describes a loss in value that is caused by factors located outside the subject property. Environmental hazards, changes in the highest and best use, zoning of a property, inharmonious nearby land uses, dust and freeway or airport noise are sample conditions that can cause economic value loss. In recent years, such hazards as methane or radon gasses or toxic wastes have been specific environmental problems of great concern. Generally, economic obsolescence is caused by some event that has occurred or has been identified in the neighborhood since the property was built.

Economic obsolescence can be curable or incurable in the same way that physical deterioration and functional obsolescence are. However, the cause of the problem is often beyond the control of any one property owner. The cost to repair is also frequently very large. For example, a very expensive sound barrier wall might be needed to reduce the effects on value created by a noisy freeway. As a result, economic obsolescence is nearly always incurable.

Deciding whether to classify a particular loss in building value as functional or economic obsolescence is sometimes difficult. As the demands, wants, and needs of the market change, buildings that were once considered adequate may no longer measure up to current tastes. For example, in some areas, houses or condominium units with fewer than two baths are now considered out of date. Since the cause of such obsolescence is clearly related to external factors (change in market demand), one might argue that the loss in value should be labeled economic obsolescence. However, the usual practice is to categorize it as functional obsolescence, just as if the defect had been

Figure 12.2
Functional obsolescence: nontypical side yard. (Photograph courtesy of Doug Frost)

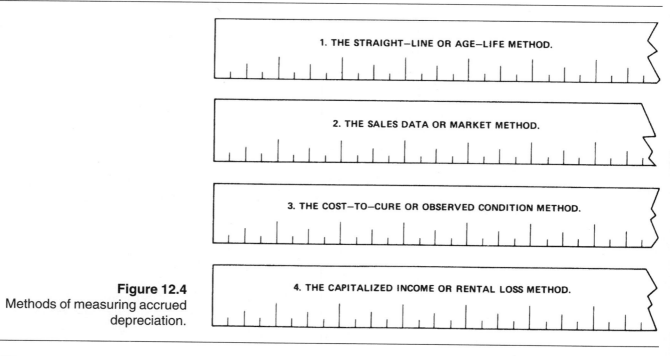

Figure 12.3
A misplaced improvement.
Does it have functional
obsolescence?

present since the time of construction. Changes in public control to address general population needs are credited with causing economic obsolescence (e.g., higher density zoning), whereas changes in specific desires of that same population (e.g., one bath or two, as cited above) are usually explained as causing functional obsolescence. No fine line can really be drawn. However, the appraiser should be careful not to account for the decrease in value twice, by counting the same decrease in value as both functional and economic obsolescence.

12.3 METHODS OF MEASURING ACCRUED DEPRECIATION

There are four basic methods for measuring accrued depreciation. It is important to remember that these methods are not just abstract mathematical calculations. Rather, they are attempts to estimate the actual loss in market value, compared to a new building. Note that, in practice, it is common to use them in combination. The four methods are illustrated in Figure 12.4.

1. THE STRAIGHT—LINE OR AGE—LIFE METHOD.

2. THE SALES DATA OR MARKET METHOD.

3. THE COST—TO—CURE OR OBSERVED CONDITION METHOD.

4. THE CAPITALIZED INCOME OR RENTAL LOSS METHOD.

Figure 12.4
Methods of measuring accrued
depreciation.

Straight-Line or Age-Life Method

The straight-line or age-life method of estimating accrued depreciation is based on the theory that all structures have a total useful life that can be predicted. This is called the *economic life* of the building. It is defined as "the period over which improvements to real estate contribute to the value of the property."* Therefore, at the end of a building's economic life, the vacant land would sell for as much or more than the improved property. Economic life is rarely as long as the physical life of a structure.

In straight-line depreciation, loss in value due to age is assumed to be directly proportional to the so-called age life, or useful life, of the structure. With straight-line depreciation, if a residence is considered to have a 100-year economic life but is now 25 years old, it should be allowed 25% depreciation.

Age		25 years
Divided by:	Economic life	÷ 100 years
Equals:	Accrued depreciation	25%

Buildings of the same age vary greatly in their condition and desirability (because of differences in maintenance, modernization, etc.). For this reason, many appraisers base depreciation estimates on the "effective age" of the building rather than the actual age. The *effective age* of a building is the actual age of other buildings that are in similar condition and of similar utility and marketability. For example, a 40-year-old building that has been modernized and well maintained may be able to compete directly with 20-year-old buildings. Here, the effective age of the 40-year-old building in question would be 20 years. When effective age is used to estimate accrued depreciation, normal functional and economic value loss and some physical deterioration will have been accounted for by the effective age adjustment. If actual age is used in figuring depreciation, however, separate adjustments may be necessary to reflect these factors. Note that the effective age adjustment is largely a matter of judgment and is very difficult to prove.

To estimate the loss in value using effective age rather than actual age, you simply divide the effective age of the structure by the total estimated economic life of the structure. Then, convert this figure to a percent of accrued depreciation as before. For example, let us assume that a 25-year-old building with an effective age of 20 years is judged to have a total economic (useful) life of 100 years. Here the accrued depreciation would be 20%, using a straight-line basis (20/100 = 20%).

*B. N. Boyce, *Real Estate Appraisal Terminology,* rev. ed., Ballinger Publishing Co., Cambridge, Mass., 1981, p. 74.

Age, 25 years, but effective age	20 years
Divided by: Economic life	÷ 100 years
Equals: Accrued depreciation	20%

Many of the published depreciation tables are based on the age-life concept, although they modify the straight-line idea to a more realistic pattern of loss in value. For example, some such tables show a rapid loss of value in early years and then a more gradual loss with age. To use such tables, simply find the correct column for the type of building under appraisal. Then, look up the percent of accrued depreciation for the building's age. Finally, multiply this percent times the building cost new.

Some published depreciation tables claim to be based in part on studies of actual experience with building demolition or major rehabilitation. Others claim to be based on studies of market sales of old and new buildings. In any case, published tables not relating to the specific market conditions surrounding the subject property would give only a generalized result.

There are a few additional drawbacks to the age-life method of estimating depreciation. The economic life of a structure is difficult to predict because the usefulness and value of a building changes, relative to land values, with both market and zoning changes. Neither can be reliably forecast by an appraiser, investor, or broker. Effective age is also subjective. Another disadvantage of the age-life method is that it does not separate curable and incurable loss in value.

Sales Data (or Market) Method

The sales data (or market) method is based on the principle that value loss is determined in the market by buyers and sellers. If old buildings are worth less than new buildings, they will sell for less. In the sales data method, a number of sales are analyzed (subtracting the estimated land value from the selling prices) to obtain the building's contribution to the sales price. In turn, this amount is compared with the current cost of a new building. The difference is the loss in value, or accrued depreciation.

To estimate accrued depreciation of a property by the sales data method, follow these steps:

1. Estimate the reproduction or replacement cost new for the improvements of each comparable sale.

2. Estimate the land value for each comparable, if possible, by using market sales of vacant land.

3. Abstract the building portion of the selling price by subtracting the land value from the selling price.

4. Deduct the abstracted building value from the reproduction/replacement cost new for each sale. The difference is the accrued market depreciation estimated for each comparable sale.

Age differences must be accounted for, however, if we are to compare these data to the subject property. If we divide the accrued depreciation of each property by the estimated cost new for each property, the result is the percentage of value loss for each sale property. Dividing this answer by the age of the improvements translates into an annual percentage loss in value. To complete the analysis, the typical annual percentage loss would be applied to the subject property. Example 12.3 shows how each comparable sale would be analyzed.

Example 12.3 Calculating Depreciation by the Sales Data Method

Reproduction cost new of improvements			$200,000
Less:	Improvement value:		
Sales price		$240,000	
Less:	Land value	−80,000	
Equals:	Improvement value		−$160,000
Accrued depreciation			$ 40,000
Cost new of improvements			$200,000
Percentage of value loss			20%
Age of improvements			20
Equals:	Annual percent depreciation		1%

The sales data method is the most direct method of estimating accrued depreciation from all causes. If an adequate sample is obtained, the results can be studied by plotting them on a chart or by using a simple regression analysis program available for desktop computers. (See Figure 12.5.)

What about the measurement of value loss resulting from unusual property defects or disadvantages? Although it may be difficult to find sale properties with the same defect as the subject, either functional or economic obsolescence can theoretically be measured directly from sales. For example, the loss in value from an obsolete architectural style could be estimated by comparing the sales of two otherwise similar properties in the same neighborhood, one with the same architectural style as the subject and the other with a different style. The difference in price would be the amount of functional obsolescence caused by the poor style, as estimated by the sales data method. (See Figure 12.6.)

Cost-to-Cure (or Observed Condition) Method

This method measures the accrued depreciation by the cost to cure or repair any observed building defects. After inspecting the premises, the appraiser tries to identify each building defect, feature, or condition that reduces value. Each is then classified as either physical, functional, or economic. In addition, each defect must be studied to estimate whether it is economically curable or incurable.

First, the curable physical deterioration is estimated. This means adding up the cost of deferred maintenance work and repairs neces-

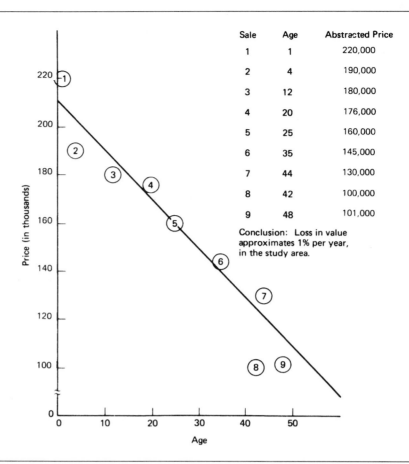

Sale	Age	Abstracted Price
1	1	220,000
2	4	190,000
3	12	180,000
4	20	176,000
5	25	160,000
6	35	145,000
7	44	130,000
8	42	100,000
9	48	101,000

Conclusion: Loss in value approximates 1% per year, in the study area.

Figure 12.5
A study of age and value loss.

sary to restore the structure to normal operating condition. Typical items include repainting peeling exterior paint, repairing broken glass, and repairing inoperative building equipment. Larger repairs might include replacing floor coverings or roofs. Dollar estimates for needed repairs can be derived from contractors' estimates or from cost evaluation services available to the appraiser. The total estimate of painting, fix-up, and repair costs is the estimate of the loss in value due to curable physical deterioration.

Next, any incurable physical deterioration is measured. By comparing the condition of both short-lived and long-lived building components with the same components in a new building, the relative loss in value of each component can be estimated. Here is how it works:

1. Estimate the cost new as of the value date for each building component involved.

2. Calculate the percentage of useful life already used up by dividing the actual chronological age of the component by its total estimated life.

3. Multiply the estimated cost new times the percentage of useful life already used up.

Figure 12.6
Style difference: does it affect price? (Photograph courtesy of Doug Frost)

The result is an estimate of the loss of value caused by incurable physical deterioration. As you can see, this result will be only as reliable as the estimates of total life and cost of replacement for each component.

Last, curable functional obsolescence is estimated. Usually, such value loss results from outmoded equipment such as obsolete plumbing, heating, or lighting fixtures. Here the value loss can be estimated by using the cost to tear out and replace these with modern equipment. Such cost estimates may be based on contractor bids or cost manuals. From the cost to replace with modern equipment, you usually deduct the estimated remaining value of the existing equipment. Only the extra amount is deducted.

Curable functional obsolescence can also be caused by major building deficiencies or inadequacies. For example, a three-bedroom house with a single-car garage (or only one bath, for a different example) may suffer in market appeal compared to one with a double-car garage (or two baths). However, the total added cost for a larger garage (in our example) must not be subtracted as the loss in value because your estimate of current new cost will not have included any costs for the second car space. The accepted procedure is to compare the present cost of adding the extra garage space (or other market-desired components) with the current new cost as if included in the original building. Since remodeling is generally very expensive, the cost of adding space is usually greater. The difference is the measure of curable functional obsolescence in the improvements. See Example 12.4.

Example 12.4 Calculating Curable Functional Obsolescence	Estimated current cost of enlarging garage		$10,000
	Less:	Estimated current cost of added garage area if built as part of the original structure	−6,000
	Equals:	Functional obsolescence	$ 4,000

The cost-to-cure method has some obvious practical limitations. First, individual component life spans that are used to estimate incurable physical deterioration are largely theoretical. Second, unless component costs have already been estimated by using the unit-in-place or quantity survey method to estimate total costs, it is prohibitively time-consuming. Additionally, the cost-to-cure method cannot measure the loss in value from either incurable functional or economic obsolescence. These losses must be measured by the capitalized income method, adding to the complexity.

Capitalized Income (or Rental Loss) Method

The capitalized income method can be used to estimate either the total loss in value from all causes or simply the loss in value from a single cause. To estimate loss in value from all causes, a comparison is made between the current rent of the subject building and the rent of a new or modern building that could take its place. The difference can be called the rental loss attributed to age and/or obsolescence. In practice, a gross rent multiplier is normally used to "capitalize" informally the rental loss. A gross rent multiplier would be the typical ratio found between price and gross scheduled rent for properties in the area.

To illustrate this method, assume that a single-family residence under appraisal suffers from age and functional obsolescence. If its monthly rental is $300 per month less than new competitive properties and a gross rent multiplier of 200 is suggested by a market study, the total accrued depreciation could be estimated by the rental loss method. See Example 12.5.

The amount of value loss attributed to a single cause or factor can also be estimated. The rental or income loss that results from the unique physical, functional, or economic problem with the building is capitalized. For example, if a poor floor plan results in a $150 per month rent reduction, the value loss from that single cause would be $150 × 200, or $30,000 (using the same 200 gross rent multiplier as before).

When typical income property is under appraisal, the loss in value, or depreciation, can be estimated by a more formal capitalized income method, using net income instead of gross income. The first step is to capitalize the net income that can be attributed to the improvements after a return for land is deducted. This provides an estimate of the building value. Subtracting this value from the estimated cost to produce the same building will provide the appraiser with the total amount of accrued depreciation for the building. The capitalized income method is actually part of the income approach to value, to be more fully described in Chapters 13 and 14.

Example 12.5 The Informal Capitalized Income Method			
Monthly rental of new competitive property			$950
Less:	Monthly rental of subject property		− 650
Equals:	Rental loss amount		$300
Multiplied by:	Gross rent multiplier		× 200
Equals:	Accrued depreciation		$60,000

12.4 COST APPROACH SUMMARY

The cost approach is completed when the estimate of land value is added to the depreciated improvement costs for the property under appraisal. Conclusions that might result from the application of the cost approach to a single-family residence are given in Example 12.6.

Example 12.6 Cost Approach Summary

A. Reproduction cost of improvements

Living area:	1,800 sq. ft. × $75	=	$135,000
Covered patio:	200 sq. ft. × $25	=	5,000
Garage:	400 sq. ft. × $30	=	12,000
Yard improvements:			+ 5,000
Total reproduction cost as if new			$157,000

B. Accrued depreciation

Physical deterioration		
curable	$10,000	
incurable	5,000	
Functional obsolescence		
curable (old-style kitchen)	6,000	
incurable (poor floor plan)	5,000	
Economic obsolescence		
(adjacent to commercial)	+ 10,000	
Total accrued depreciation		−$36,000

C. Depreciated cost of improvements

$121,000

D. Estimated land value from sales comparables

+ 70,000

E. Total property value indicated by cost approach

$191,000

SUMMARY

In this chapter, we defined accrued depreciation for appraisal purposes as the estimated loss in value of the improvements compared to their current cost as if new. Such value losses can be caused by physical deterioration, functional obsolescence, and/or economic obsolescence. Physical deterioration is caused by wear and tear, age, and the elements. Functional obsolescence occurs when faulty design or other defects within the property detracts from its marketability. Such loss in value can be evident from the first date of construction, or it may appear when building styles change and the structure can no longer meet the needs of the typical consumer. Economic (or external) obsolescence is caused by factors outside the property. For example, when rezoning makes existing improvements obsolete because a more intensive land use is in demand, the loss in value is categorized as economic obsolescence.

Accrued depreciation may be curable or incurable, depending on whether the value increase resulting from the cure is greater than the cost involved. Many types of physical deterioration, such as deferred maintenance, are curable by painting, fixing up, or doing repair work. However, certain functional and most economic value loss is incurable.

Accrued depreciation may be estimated by the straight-line/age-life method, the sales data method, the cost-to-cure/observed condition method, or the capitalized income method. Sometimes a combination of methods can be used.

The straight-line/age-life method relates the loss in value to the estimated life expectancy of the building. Accrued depreciation caused by physical deterioration and "normal" functional and economic obsolescence is estimated by comparing the age of the structure at the time of the appraisal with its total projected life. Published depreciation tables are usually based on this method.

The sales data (or market) method measures accrued depreciation directly from the market. First, the land value is subtracted from the sales price of a comparable property, giving the building value contribution. Next, the building value is subtracted from its estimated reproduction cost, giving the value loss. Dividing the value loss by the new cost gives the percentage of value loss. In turn, the percentage loss is divided by the age of the building to calculate the annual straight-line depreciation percentage. Functional or economic obsolescence from a single characteristic of a building may also be measured by the sales data method if sales can be found with the same basic defect as the subject property.

The cost-to-cure method equates the loss in value to the cost of repairs or changes necessary to restore the building to a normal operating condition. Incurable physical deterioration is measured by the observed condition of the components involved. Thus the cost-to-cure method may be used to measure all types of accrued depreciation except incurable functional and economic obsolescence.

Lastly, the capitalized income method provides an estimate of value loss by relating the value loss to the loss in gross income. A gross rent multiplier is usually used to calculate the value loss. The total loss in value may also be estimated by comparing an income-derived building value with the reproduction cost new. Loss in value because of a single property defect is often estimated by applying a gross rent multiplier to the estimated rent loss attributed to the particular functional or economic factor involved.

When loss in value from all causes has been estimated, the value of the improvements may be estimated by subtracting the total accrued depreciation from the current cost new of the improvements.

Important Terms and Concepts

Accrued depreciation

Age-life method

Book value

Capitalized income method

Cost basis

Cost-to-cure method

Curable depreciation

Diminished utility

Economic life

Economic (or external) obsolescence

Effective age

Functional obsolescence Physical deterioration

Incurable depreciation Sales data (or market) method

Misplaced improvement Straight-line method

Overimprovement Underimprovement

REVIEWING YOUR UNDERSTANDING

1. In accounting practice, depreciation is treated as:
    (a) A theoretical loss in value
    (b) An expense before taxes
    (c) An asset
    (d) Both (a) and (b)

2. In appraisals, depreciation can be defined as:
    (a) A deduction from value
    (b) Actual loss in value compared to current cost as new
    (c) Diminished utility
    (d) Either (b) or (c)

3. Accrued depreciation is classified into three types or categories. Which of the following should not be included?
    (a) Functional obsolescence
    (b) Economic obsolescence
    (c) Detrimental obsolescence
    (d) Physical deterioration

4. Each category of depreciation can be classified as curable or incurable. This helps the appraiser analyze:
    (a) The economic feasibility to correct the condition
    (b) Whether the value loss can be estimated by the cost of needed repair or remodeling
    (c) Both of the above
    (d) Neither of the above

5. A building that is too large for the neighborhood is an example of functional obsolescence labeled as an overimprovement. Another example of functional obsolescence is:
    (a) A sound building with a worn-out heating system
    (b) A misplaced improvement
    (c) A residence abutting a new freeway
    (d) A building that is likely to cost more to repair than the value added to the structure

6. There are four basic methods for measuring accrued depreciation. Which one of the following would probably be used for estimating the value loss from deferred maintenance?
    (a) The sales data (or market) method
    (b) The straight-line or age-life method
    (c) The cost-to-cure (or observed condition) method
    (d) The capitalized income (or rental loss) method

7. There is a theory that all structures have a total useful life that can be predicted. The method of estimating accrued depreciation based on this theory is:
   (a) The capitalized income (or rental loss) method
   (b) The sales data (or market) method (abstraction method)
   (c) The straight-line or age-life method
   (d) The cost-to-cure (or observed condition) method

8. Some appraisers base depreciation estimates on the "effective age" of the building rather than the actual age. Effective age is best defined as:
   (a) The average age
   (b) The actual age divided by the age life
   (c) The age of other buildings that are similar in condition and utility
   (d) The chronological age

9. A 40-year-old building with an effective age of 20 years has a total life expectancy of 50 years. How much depreciation has occurred?
   (a) 20%
   (b) 50%
   (c) 10%
   (d) 40%

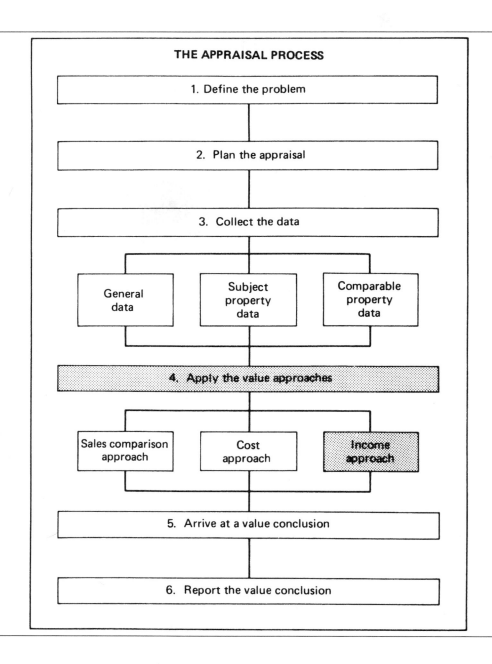

THE APPRAISAL PROCESS

1. Define the problem

2. Plan the appraisal

3. Collect the data

| General data | Subject property data | Comparable property data |

4. Apply the value approaches

| Sales comparison approach | Cost approach | Income approach |

5. Arrive at a value conclusion

6. Report the value conclusion

Chapter 13
The Income Approach

Preview
The income approach is based on the principle of anticipation. This principle states that the value of any property may be defined as the present worth of future benefits. When an owner's benefits are in the form of money, as with investment or income property, the value of such benefits may be measured by the amount of net income the property is expected to produce. With property such as single-family homes, the future benefits of ownership usually consist of such amenities as shelter, security, and pride of ownership. Since these benefits are intangible, they usually cannot be valued by the income approach.

In this chapter, we provide an overview of the income approach and outline how appraisers estimate income and expenses. This discussion of the income approach will be continued in Chapter 14, where we shall also explain how a property's income is capitalized, or converted into an estimate of value.

When you have completed this chapter, you should be able to:

1. *Distinguish between tangible and intangible benefits of property ownership.*

2. *Name the six steps in the income approach to value.*

3. *Explain the use of gross rent multipliers in the income approach.*

4. *Define the terms* contract rent, *and* market (or economic) rent, *as used in appraisals.*

5. *Name the three main categories of expenses and give examples of items in each.*

6. *Outline the procedure used for reconstructing the owner's operating statement.*

13.1 INTRODUCING INCOME PROPERTY AND ITS APPRAISAL

How is income property distinguished from other types of property? What are the motives and benefits of ownership? These are some of the questions we should consider in order to understand how to properly apply the income approach.

Types of Income Property

Any type of real estate may be purchased for income and/or investment purposes. One common reason given for buying a single-family home today is that it can easily be converted to a rental property and retained for the possible benefits of long-term value appreciation. However, the term *income property* traditionally is reserved for property that is purchased primarily for its income. The properties in Figure 13.1 are good examples of income-producing properties.

A multiple-residential property is the most common type of income property. However, income (or investment) property includes commercial and industrial properties as well. Thus a list of property types usually treated as income property should include the following:

---

1. Multiple-residential, including large and small apartment buildings.

2. Commercial buildings, including stores, offices, medical offices, convalescent hospitals, hotel and motel properties, and shopping centers.

3. Industrial properties, such as warehouses and factories.

Motives and Benefits of Ownership

People acquire income property for many different reasons. Some are motivated to invest as a way to "save for a rainy day"; others consider real estate as either an investment made for a profit or a necessary component of a family business. In other words, the real estate investment market is very diverse and consists of both part-time and full-time investors. As in other investment fields, the small, easy-to-manage holdings are normally sought by the casual or part-time investor, and the large and more complex ones by the full-time professional investor. The benefits of owning income or investment property also vary and can be either tangible or intangible.

Figure 13.1
Types of income property
(Photographs courtesy of Doug Frost)

Tangible Benefits   Any investment can be compared to a personal savings account, where the interest earned on the account is the obvious tangible benefit. Since the earnings from the account are not reduced by any expenses, we can describe these earnings as a "net" income. Such earnings are referred to simply as "return on" the investment. What happens when the depositor needs his or her money back for some other purpose? Since the typical savings account deposit is guaranteed returnable, it insures what can be referred to as the "return of" the investment. (See Figure 13.2.)

Following the savings account analogy, the tangible benefits of income property ownership consist of (1) a "return on" investment (which is like interest), and (2) a "return of" investment (allowing the investment funds to be recovered). When prices are stable, the annual net income from an investment property theoretically provides the return on the property's value, with capital return occurring when the property is resold. However, this pattern can be complicated by the effects of financing, income tax, and the inflation or deflation of prices. These two concepts—return on investment and capital return (or recapture)—will be more fully covered in the next chapter.

Intangible Benefits   Relatively small income properties, such as two- to ten-unit apartment buildings, are often acquired for both tangible and intangible benefits. First, retired or semiretired couples, and in recent years younger employed people, purchase such properties, live in one unit, and rent out the others. Expenses can be kept low by the owner-operators doing

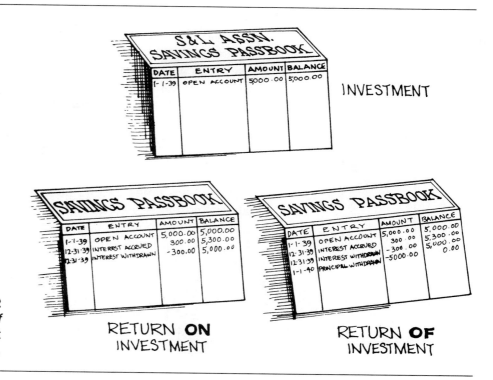

Figure 13.2
Return *on* and return *of* investment—savings account example.

their own building upkeep. Even so, owners of such properties must often be satisfied with a low return on investment. They usually settle for less because of the intangible benefits involved. For example, owners who occupy one unit of an investment property may gain many of the same amenities they would if they lived in a single-family residence. Certainly, pride of ownership and a sense of security can be expected, but there may also be an opportunity for some to develop and apply their management skills.

In summary, the benefits of owning income property may be both tangible and intangible. The mixture of benefits depends on the size and type of the investment. In many cases, the tangible income benefits are enhanced by an opportunity for income tax shelter and for property appreciation. Such advantages will be more fully explored in the next chapter, under the heading, Comparing Investment Property.

The Income–Value Relationships

It is important at this point in our discussion of income property to explore more fully the economic relationship between income and value.

Utility, Income, and Value

Utility is one of the basic characteristics of value. For any commodity to have value, it must have usefulness. Everything else being equal, the greater the utility, the greater the value. In the case of investment property, the utility of a property can best be measured by the rental income it can produce.

What is income? Income may be defined as the annual money received, or as the "return" or flow of funds from an investment. In the case of the savings account mentioned earlier, the expense-free earnings are the income. So are the dividends paid on stocks. With real estate investments, the net rent is the income.

What is value? In economic theory, value can be viewed as the present worth of future benefits. For income-producing properties in particular, value can also be described as the relationship between the amount of net income produced and the rate of return on investment required by the typical investor.

Examples of Monetary Relationships

The savings account example clearly illustrates the direct relationship between value, income, and rate of return. A savings account of $2,000, earning an 8% rate of interest, would earn $160 in one year because 8% times $2,000 equals $160. If someone told us only the annual earnings and the rate of interest, we would still be able to figure out the amount on deposit in the account because of the fixed relationship between the three numbers. The annual income of $160, divided by 8%, equals $2,000.

Let us apply the monetary relationship described here to investment real estate. Assume that the only tangible return on investment is in the form of the annual income. For a property earning $50,000 per year, if a 10% annual rate of return is required, the value would be $500,000. Why? Because $50,000 is 10% of $500,000, or $50,000 divided by 10% equals $500,000.

In both examples, we can again see that value is the relationship between the *amount* of return and the *rate* of return. The amount of value can be expressed by a simple "income capitalization" formula:

$$\text{value} = \frac{\text{income}}{\text{rate of return}}$$

Real estate investments are rarely as simple as deposits in a savings account. For example, the benefits available to the real estate investor are not always restricted to annual income, as we pointed out earlier. For this reason, the relationship between amounts and rates of return is often complex. This topic will be further discussed in the next chapter.

Methods of Appraising Income Property

When the primary benefit of real estate ownership is in the form of monthly or annual rent or income, appraisers most often rely on the income (or capitalization) approach as an indication of value. In the following pages, we shall describe how the income approach is applied and then discuss a second method of appraising property based on its income, which is known as the gross income multiplier. Introduced in Chapter 9, the GIM method is commonly used as the income approach in the appraisal of single-family residential properties.

The Income (Capitalization) Approach

Mathematically, the income approach is based on the relationship between value, income, and rate of return. A property earning $40,000 per year, at a rate of return of 10%, can be said to have a value of $400,000. Dividing the net income by a rate of return is one method of income capitalization. Here are the six basic steps in the income approach:

1. Estimate the annual gross income the property is capable of producing.

2. Estimate typical vacancy and collection losses.

3. Subtract vacancy and collection losses from gross income to arrive at the effective gross income.

4. Estimate annual expenses and subtract them from the effective gross income to calculate the net income (or net operating income).

5. Analyze comparable investments to arrive at a capitalization rate and method appropriate for the subject property.

6. Divide the net operating income by the capitalization rate to obtain the capitalized value.

Let us assume that we are appraising a 20-unit apartment house. It has a projected annual gross income of $150,000 and a predicted vacancy and rent loss amounting to $8,000 per year. Annual expenses of $45,000 can be expected including property taxes. Our analyses indicate that an 8% rate of return is appropriate, and we decide to use the capitalization method already discussed. (Other capitalization methods will be explained in Chapter 14.) Our calculations are shown in Example 13.1.

Example 13.1 Direct Capitalization

Projected gross income		$ 150,000
Less:	Vacancy and collection loss	− 8,000
Equals:	Effective gross income	$ 142,000
Less:	Annual expenses (including property taxes)	− 45,000
Equals:	Net income	$ 97,000
Divided by:	Capitalization rate	÷ .08
Equals:	Value Estimate	$1,212,500

Definition of Terms Used in Income Capitalization

At this stage of our discussion of income property and its appraisal, it is appropriate to define the terms used in the above outline and example.

> *Annual gross income:* scheduled or potential rent plus anticipated service income.
>
> *Vacancy and collection losses:* amounts of gross income that will not be realized because of vacant tenant space and non-collection of rents.
>
> *Effective gross income:* income remaining after subtracting vacancy and credit loss from gross income.
>
> *Operating expenses:* expenses required to maintain the income of the property.
>
> *Net income (or net operating income):* effective gross income less operating expenses.
>
> *Capitalization rate:* the rate of return, percentage, or ratio used to convert income into its value equivalent.

Real estate appraisal by income capitalization depends upon a careful estimate of income and expenses, to be discussed in the last two sections of this chapter.

The Gross Rent Multiplier Method

The gross rent multiplier method is often substituted for the income approach in appraising single-family homes. In the appraisal of multi-family and certain other income-producing properties, the gross rent multiplier is most often used as part of the sales comparison approach.

What is a gross rent (or gross income) multiplier (GRM or GIM)? As described in Chapter 9, the gross rent multiplier is a unit of comparison. It helps the appraiser compare the subject property to the sale properties by using an economic measurement of the property's usefulness—in this case, the rent. Quite simply, it is the ratio of the selling price to the gross income.

$$\text{Gross Rent Multiplier} = \frac{\text{Sales Price}}{\text{Gross Income}}$$

The derivation, analysis and use of gross rent multipliers should follow certain procedures, to be described next.

13.2 GROSS RENT MULTIPLIER ANALYSIS

The gross rent multiplier method is one of the most popular income-related methods in use by the real estate practitioner. Multipliers are easy to understand and often readily available. However, there are some important rules to follow when deriving, selecting, and using gross rent multipliers.

Deriving Gross Rent Multipliers

The recommended procedure for deriving gross rent multipliers is as follows.

---

1. Make an adequate search for comparable sales. At least three recent sales are desired. A larger sample is often preferred.

2. Estimate the market rents for each comparable as of the time of sale (discussed in section 13.3).

3. Divide the selling price (adjusted for any unusual terms) by the gross market rent for each comparable.

4. The result is called the gross rent (or income) multiplier and is abbreviated GRM or GIM.

Gross rent multipliers may be calculated using either the annual or monthly rent. Monthly rent is customarily used in the appraisal of single-family residential property, but the annual rent is customarily used in appraisals of other types of property. One must be careful using the monthly rent if there is much seasonal variation in rents. The GRM using summer rents could be different from the GRM calculated using winter rents.

Usually, the rent schedule should reflect the prevailing market rent (defined in section 13.3). This means that the building's actual rent schedules at the time of sale should be revised to market rents before figuring the gross rent multiplier. However, if the property is under a city or county rent control ordinance, the existing rent schedule would generally be used.

The GRM: Calculated with Market Rents versus Actual Rents

Except where rents are controlled by local ordinance, there is a good reason for calculating the gross rent multiplier using the theoretical market rents rather than the actual rents at the date of sale. When market rents are rising rapidly, some landlords keep their rents moving up with the market, while other landlords lag behind. At the time of sale, then, similar buildings can sell at greatly different multiples of actual rent. Although properties with a lagging rent schedule may sell for less because of the time it takes to bring rents up to market level, GRMs based on their market rents are often more reliable than those based on existing or actual rent.

The gross rent multiplier should be based on the actual selling price of the comparable property, adjusted only for unusual financing and other factors affecting its cash equivalent price. Generally, it is considered improper to adjust property sales prices for time and physical differences before calculating GRMs. However, the calculated multipliers often vary, and the appraiser must seek the reasons for this variation, just as with all units of comparison.

Selecting and Using Gross Rent Multipliers

The gross rent multiplier can be an effective tool for estimating market value when properties are commonly bought and sold on the basis of gross income. Because the GRM is easy to apply, it seems easy to select. However, selecting the appropriate multiplier requires a good understanding of the property characteristics which cause the multiplier to change. Here are the most important of these:

1. *Location and neighborhood.* The buyer's impression of risk relative to other investments and prospects for value appreciation is influenced by the location and neighborhood. Higher multipliers are associated with better locations. Rent control may also be a factor in the considered risk of an investment. Also, if rent control has affected some rents much more than others, causing different expense ratios, GRMs may not be a reliable valuation method.

2. *Intangible amenities.* Multipliers are typically higher for property bought for owner occupancy or other notable intangible benefits.

Examples might be a prestigious address, a famous building, a structure of unusual charm, and so on.

3. *Expense ratio.* Properties with lower operating expenses will normally sell for a higher gross multiplier. Investors are interested in the net, not the gross, income. Example 13.2 demonstrates the effect a change in the expense ratio has on the GRM.

4. *Number of units.* The number of units tends to identify which investment market the property would probably sell in; it also affects operating efficiency. Very small complexes often sell at higher than average multipliers because of the intangible amenities discussed earlier in this chapter.

5. *Size per unit.* Buildings with small dwelling units can have higher operating costs and often higher turnover rates; multipliers are often lower than average.

6. *Services included.* Utilities, furniture, and other services provided by the landlord increase operating costs relative to buildings where tenants pay for them. Hence, lower multipliers often result.

Example 13.2 Effect of Expenses on the Gross Rent Multiplier	Gross Rent	Expenses (%)	Net Income	Capitalization Rate (%)	Price	GRM
	$60,000	.30	$42,000	.07	$600,000	10.0
	60,000	.40	36,000	.07	514,000	8.6
	60,000	.50	30,000	.07	428,500	7.1

Even the most carefully chosen group of sales can produce a wide range of gross rent multipliers. Which is right for the subject property? Estimating the appropriate multiplier can be a problem; however, essentially we apply the same techniques used in the sales comparison approach to select other economic units of comparison. A simple rule is to give the greatest weight to the sales whose characteristics are the closest to those of the subject property. However, where a single factor such as *number of units* or *average square-foot size per unit* varies greatly between the comparable sales, it is a good idea to plot the sales on a graph, or even construct a linear regression equation for the GRM. The GRM can vary with the number of units, as we said earlier, getting smaller as the number of units gets larger. A similar pattern of a declining GRM is sometimes noted as the average apartment unit size declines. In either case, once such a direct relationship between the GRM and the variable is identified, a more intelligent choice of multipliers can be made.

Once you have arrived at an appropriate multiplier for the subject property, merely multiply it times the monthly or annual projected market rent. The result is the indicated value of the subject property. See Example 13.3.

Example 13.3 Gross Rent Multiplier Derivation and Use

Assume that you are appraising a 10-unit unfurnished apartment building with a scheduled annual gross rent of $84,000. A rent survey suggests that the schedule agrees with the prevailing market rents in the area.

Your comparable sales and market rents have been analyzed and established as of the time of sale. The results follow:

Comparable Number	Number of Furnished Units	Number of Unfurnished Units	Price	Scheduled Gross	Gross Rent Multiplier
1	10	—	$729,000	$ 90,000	8.1
2	—	9	800,000	80,000	10.0
3	—	5	544,500	45,000	12.1
4	4	8	977,500	115,000	8.5
5	—	12	950,000	100,000	9.5

Assigning the most weight to comparables 2 and 5 as most similar to the subject, a gross rent multiplier (GRM) of 9.75 is suggested for the appraisal. Comparables 1 and 4 were not stressed since they involved furnished units. Comparable 3 is not considered competitive with the subject since it is a smaller project, which appeals to a different investor market.

Value conclusion:

Annual gross $84,000 $\times$ 9.75 = $819,000 (rounded)

13.3 ESTIMATING GROSS INCOME AND MARKET RENT

The first step in the income approach is to estimate the gross income. This will define the property's potential production, measured in rent dollars. That is why the gross income estimate is sometimes referred to an as "income forecast."

The gross income of a property refers to the total income generated, assuming 100% occupancy. Such income is often composed of two parts: rent for tenant space and service or miscellaneous income. The rent for tenant space is the sum total of all the scheduled rental amounts, including tenant parking space. It is sometimes referred to as the "rent roll" in properties with multiple tenants. Service income refers to money collected for laundry facilities, vending machines, utilities sold to tenants, and other incidental services.

Contract versus Market Rent

Income property is often sold subject to existing leases and other contractual arrangements between the landlord and tenant. We define the rent being paid in such cases as *contract rent.* Selling prices are often influenced by the terms of an existing lease, going up if terms are favorable to the landlord or down if favorable to the tenant. In other words, the price tends to reflect the property rights being sold.

In most appraisals, the property is valued as if it were free from all encumbrances, except for public controls and deed restrictions shown on public records. For this reason, *market rent* is used to estimate the value of all the property rights; then, any adjustments relevant to the specific rights being appraised can be made. Appraisal of leased property will be discussed further in Chapter 17.

Market Rent Defined

Market rent is the rental income the property would most probably command if placed for rent on the open market as of the effective date of the appraisal. This potential gross rent is the most common rent used in appraisals. It not only assumes that the subject property will be available, that is, unencumbered by any lease, but also assumes it is being efficiently managed. Market rent is sometimes referred to as "economic" rent.

Understanding Contract Rent

Technically, contract rent means rent being paid under contractual commitments binding owners and tenants. Such rental agreements range from simple verbal contracts to complex leases beyond the scope of this book. The appraiser's task of seeking out rental information requires a general understanding of common types of rental arrangements.

A tenant's right to occupy space may result from a month-to-month occupancy, short-term lease, or long-term lease agreement. Multiple-residential and commercial tenants most commonly occupy their space under month-to-month agreements or short-term leases ranging from three to five years. Tenants of more specialized properties, such as chain restaurants, office buildings, and department stores, are often willing to sign long-term leases of 10 years or more.

The most common types of leases encountered by appraisers are the straight lease, the step-up lease, and the percentage lease, shown in Figure 13.3. Combinations of these lease forms are common. The straight, or "flat," lease is one in which the monthly or annual rent is a fixed amount that stays the same over the entire lease term. The step-up (or "graduated") lease is a more popular type of lease today because it provides a way to keep up with inflation. Such a lease agreement establishes progressively higher rental amounts for different segments of the lease term. For example, a lease might call for a rental of $750 per month for the first two years, then $850 per month for the third and fourth year, and $950 per month for the fifth and sixth year. Sometimes, the rentals step up with the Consumer Price Index or some other general economic measure of inflation.

The percentage lease fixes the rent as a stipulated percentage, usually of the gross sales of goods and services offered by the tenant. Most percentage leases require a certain base rent regardless of sales volume. Typically, this minimum rent is credited against the percentage rent due. The actual percentage rate generally follows standardized guidelines for each type of tenant, depending on typical profit margins and the volume of business. Percentage rentals range from

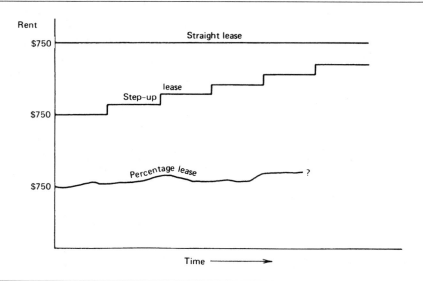

Figure 13.3
Types of leases.

1½% of gross sales for large-volume department store retailers to as high as 50 or 75% for parking lot operators. Most common retail tenancies pay from 2½% to 10% of gross sales under percentage lease agreements.

When existing leases are analyzed and compared with past rent payments, appraisers use special terms to describe the various types of rent payments. "Minimum rent" describes the base rent that is the minimum amount paid under a percentage lease. "Overage rent" describes the amounts paid over and above the base rent, and "excess rent" is the amount by which the total contract rent exceeds market rent. Most of these terms are of concern only to appraisers specializing in commercial-industrial appraisals.

When analyzing a lease, it is important to determine who is responsible for paying the various expenses. In apartment rentals, the usual lease terms hold the landlord responsible for all expenses except for water and gas bills separately metered for the tenant's space. However, in commercial and industrial leases, the landlord and tenant may share many expense costs. The trend is to have the tenants pay the building expenses directly. Operating costs such as maintenance, insurance, and taxes will be discussed later in this chapter.

How to Make a Rent Survey

An estimate of market rent should be based on a survey of the rent charged by competing properties in the immediate neighborhood. When possible, you should choose buildings of the same general age, design, services, and amenities as the subject so that the rentals can be directly compared with those charged for the subject property's space. For many appraisals, the rental schedules of the sales properties used in the sales comparison approach can be incorporated into the rental study. For each property surveyed, the appraiser should record the location and building description, along with the schedule of existing rents and the vacancy history. The number of units and their size, age, condition, and quality should be noted, along with the specific amenities offered to tenants. For multiple-residential properties, it is important to note any units subject to rent control. Also, such features as parking and recreation facilities are important to note and describe. See Figure 13.4.

As shown on the sample rent survey form, apartment units are usually listed by the number of bedrooms and baths, specifying whether each unit is rented furnished or unfurnished. The dates that the spaces were first occupied by the current tenants and the last date of rent adjustment may also be noted. In a rapidly changing market, this infor-

Figure 13.4
A sample rental survey.

Rental Survey

Project Name **Brookvale Manor**   Person Contacted **Grace Schnider**

Number of Units **150**   Position **Assistant Manager**

Address **36163 N. Marcus Blvd.**   Person Surveying **B. Neale**

Watertown   Date of Survey **7-4-92**

PROPERTY DATA:

Age **16 yrs.** Condition **Avg.** No. of Stories **2** No. of Bldgs. **1**

Construction **Lathe and plaster** Land Area **Avg.**

No. of Units **150** Density **Avg.** View **Fair to Good**

Parking **one covered; extra open parking assigned**

AMENITIES: View **some** Pool(s) **one** Recreation Room **large**

Sauna **none** Other Rec. Features **None**

APARTMENT FEATURES: Utilities **All electric--tenant pays**

Furniture **none** Carpets **x** Drapes **x** Patio **none**

Refrigerator **x** Dishwasher **none** Air Cond. **none** Balcony **x**

Range & Oven **x** Fireplace **none** Other Features

RENTAL DATA:

No. of Units	Apartment Type	Area Sq. Ft.	Rental Total	per Sq. Ft.
80	1-BR, 1-Ba	575	$655	$0.97
70	2-BR, 1-Ba	980	$900	$0.92

Concessions **no pets; six months lease**

Deposits **1st & last months rent, plus $135 1-BR or $150 2-BR, Security deposit**

OCCUPANCY

TYPE **Adult---some family** Date Opened **1976**

Total Units **150** No. Occupied **147** % Occupancy **98%**

---

mation is needed to suggest when a rental increase might be practical. If deposits and/or leases are required, record these data, too. Of course, tenant obligations to pay utilities and/or any rent concessions or free rent agreements made by the landlord have a direct effect on the rent schedule and must not be overlooked.

In commercial properties, tenant improvements can have a notable effect on the rent schedules of properties surveyed as well as on the market rent estimate for the subject property. The original rent often depends on who pays the costs of items such as floor covering, lighting, and air conditioning. When these have been installed by the tenant of the surveyed property, the rent may need adjustment before comparing it to a space in the subject property that is ready to occupy.

Industry standards for pricing tenant space usually depend on the type of property. As already indicated, apartment units are usually priced or compared by the number of bedrooms and baths but may be compared by the monthly rent per square foot of living area. Office space may be rented by a monthly or annual price per square foot of net rentable area, or else by the full floor area occupied. Net rentable area usually excludes stairwells and elevator shafts in the building. Stores and industrial properties are most often rented by the gross square-foot area of the building. However, buildings fronting on a busy street or walk may be rented by the front-foot exposure.

Assigning the Market Rent

In most cases, the market rent for the subject property is derived from an analysis of the rentals found in the rent survey and a comparison of these amounts with the existing rent schedule.

Analysis of Survey Rentals

The rental survey provides data on competitive rental rates. After these rates have been analyzed to estimate what factors cause rents to vary, they should then be adjusted to represent rental space more like that of the subject property. The following factors should be considered:

1. *Time:* based on the date the lease was signed or the occupancy began and the observed trend in rental prices.

2. *Location:* if differences are significant.

3. *Physical features:* such as size, age, quality, appeal, amenities offered, and building condition.

4. *Services, utilities, and personalty (personal property) included in the rent:* Note that furnished apartments should not be compared with unfurnished without adjusting. Any furniture or personal property involved in the property under appraisal should be described and the rent allocated separately between real and personal property.

5. *Vacancy rates:* abnormally high vacancy, indicating overpricing; or low vacancy rates, suggesting underpricing of units.

6. *Limitations of any rent control regulations in effect:* imposing artificial limits on tenant rents. Since market rent is commonly understood as the potential *legal* income of the property, some readers may view a market rent survey as an academic exercise in a rent

control situation. However, most rent control ordinances offer some legal opportunity for landlords to appeal rent schedules that are grossly out of line with competing properties. The rent survey might be necessary, therefore, to prepare the appraiser to consider such possibilities.

Construction of Market Rent Schedule

The appraiser's final unit-by-unit rent schedule and gross income estimate should result from the analysis of competing property rentals and the history of rentals for the subject property. However, if the existing management is competent and aggressive in pricing and marketing units, the appraiser might well conclude that the current rent schedule represents market rents. On the other hand, any part of the existing rent schedule that appears to be noticeably higher or lower than the competition should be given a second look and then either adjusted or fully explained.

Current rent schedules may have other defects. For example, rent for the owner's or manager's unit, as well as income from building services such as laundry facilities, are commonly omitted. The appraiser's gross income projection should make corrections for such omissions. If the manager is to be provided free rent, it is more appropriate to include the rent from that unit in the gross income and then deduct the rental amount as part of the management expenses. Example 13.4 shows how to format a market rent schedule.

The appraiser should consider the past history of vacancy rates for the subject property. Unless there are specific problems with the property or its management, abnormal vacancy rates suggest that a rent adjustment is needed. In an area not affected by rent control, the building with the lowest vacancy rates often has the lowest rents. Efficient management can maximize gross receipts by increasing rental rates to "achieve normal vacancy." For example, an apartment building that has a zero vacancy factor could increase actual (effective) gross receipts if rents were increased, say, from $600 to $660 per month (across the board), as long as less than a 10% vacancy factor resulted.

Example 13.4 Market Rent Schedule for a Six-Unit Apartment

Unit Number	Type	Current Rent	Market Rent
101	Two-bedroom	$550	$625
102	One-bedroom	480	550
103	Efficiency	400	450
201	Two-bedroom	575	650
202	One-bedroom	Manager	550
203	One-bedroom	460	520
Total monthly rent roll			$3,345

Total annual rent roll	($3,345 × 12)		$40,140
Plus:	Laundry and miscellaneous income		+ 1,400
Equals:	Total potential gross income		$41,540

Effective Gross Rent

The effective gross rent is defined as the market rent minus the allowance for vacancy and credit losses. It is a projection of the potential income *receipts* of the property before normal operating costs and capital recovery.

Vacancy rates should always be considered separately for each type of unit. Consider the appraisal of a 20-unit apartment building consisting entirely of two-bedroom units. Your rent survey reveals that buildings in the area with one-bedroom units have much lower vacancy rates than those with two- and three-bedroom units. You would conclude that an appropriate vacancy factor for your building would be higher than that of the typical one-bedroom building.

The allowance for rent or credit losses is estimated next to provide for rents not collected because of nonpayment. In making this calculation, we again assume efficient management of the property and follow the typical experience of the neighborhood.

In summary, the estimate of effective gross income should result from a carefully worked-out rent schedule reflecting the rental and vacancy experience of competing properties in its neighborhood. This estimate should *not* be a mere reflection of the existing operation of the property but should be a realistic prediction of what maximum income the property could reasonably produce in the current market under competent management.

13.4 OPERATING EXPENSES AND EXPENSE RATIOS

Annual expenses are deducted from the effective annual gross income to calculate the net income. In turn, annual net income is used in the capitalization process to develop an indicated value of the property.

Expenses to Be Included

For appraisal purposes, expenses are limited generally to current operating costs. These include all property-related expenses necessary to produce the gross income. Owner-related expenses such as loan or interest payments, income taxes, and depreciation deductions are not included. Although such outlays are important to the owner, and significant for accounting and income tax purposes, they relate solely to the debt or tax position of one particular owner rather than to the real estate in question. One exception occurs in equity residual capitalization, where loan payments are deducted to discover the cash flow return on the equity down payment. This procedure is described in Chapter 14.

Operating Expense Categories

Regardless of the type of investment property, operating expenses are formally classified as (1) variable expenses, (2) fixed expenses, and (3) reserves for replacement. There is no requirement that you *must* separate them in this way, but the categories serve as useful reminders.

Variable Expenses

Variable expenses are the day-to-day out-of-pocket expenses required to run the building. These usually include administration and management, maintenance and repairs, and utility costs. Building expenses may be incurred either as payroll items or as contracted services.

In economics, management is considered to be one of the four agents of production. Management cost varies greatly with the type and size of the property. For small apartment buildings, management is often accomplished by the services of a resident manager. Costs vary with the number of units. The resident manager usually collects the rent and takes care of minor maintenance and repair work. Often the manager's compensation is in the form of free rent and perhaps a small salary.

In larger apartment complexes and commercial properties, professional management companies are often needed in order to oversee the on-site property manager and perform all administrative services for the owner. When all legal, accounting, and supervisory costs are included, such companies usually charge from 3% to 7% of the rent collected. In some cases, this includes the payment to the resident manager.

Maintenance and repair costs include all building and grounds up-keep except for the replacement of major building components or equipment. In apartment buildings, monthly maintenance and repair work include grounds and pool maintenance, cleaning, interior painting and decorating, and minor plumbing repairs. Elevator and major equipment maintenance is included and is usually covered by annual service contracts. Outside painting and major building repair is performed at irregular intervals over the years; hence, average annual costs usually should be estimated from the building's history or from industry standards.

Utility costs include water and power, gas, garbage collection, and so on. In most properties, the owner pays for all garbage collection as well as water, power, and gas for the common areas. The latter include parking lots, recreation and laundry facilities as well as central water and space heating. When the rental units have separate meters, tenants usually pay all metered utilities. Appraisers should compare the actual utility costs of a property to those typically experienced by owners of similar buildings. However, it is important to remember that each building is relatively unique. The amount of electricity, gas, and water used, and garbage created, varies with the building design and tenant needs. Utility rates also vary from place to place. Also, leases vary concerning who—landlord or tenant—will pay the utility bill. So, utility cost information from competitive buildings must be used cautiously when being compared to the subject property.

Fixed Expenses

Fixed expenses are those paid on a fairly regular basis and are relatively stable from year to year. Insurance premiums and property taxes are the most common examples.

Insurance coverage on income property usually includes fire, extended coverage, and public liability. Special coverages may also apply. Special coverage could include insurance against rent loss, with one type covering rent loss resulting from fires and similar events and another type insuring or guaranteeing a specified lease (as for a commercial store). Other types of special coverage include earthquake insurance and demolition insurance (insurance against loss resulting from any government order to demolish the property, e.g., because of building code defects). Rates depend in part on the specific coverages. They also vary with the type of occupancy and with the construction classification of the buildings (discussed in Chapter 11). Appraisers often rely on the past costs from the property operating statement to project insurance costs; however, it is a good idea to compare such figures with quotations from local insurance carriers. Note that premiums are sometimes quoted on terms of payment other than on an annual basis; such amounts should be prorated to a yearly cost.

Real property taxes have historically been assessed by an *ad valorem,* or "according to value," formula. However, in some states, including California, current value assessments generally are required only upon change of ownership. For this reason, the existing taxes on a property are not necessarily a good indication of the anticipated tax burden for the property. In market value appraisals, the amount used by the appraiser for the property tax expense should be the amount a new owner would probably be charged under the local tax laws. How is this done?

There are two ways to estimate the property tax expense when the income approach is used in an appraisal. The simplest and most commonly used method is to assign a tentative market value to the property based on the best evidence at hand, say, the value indicated by the sales comparison approach. When this is multiplied by the tax rate showing on the assessment roll, a reasonable estimate of the property tax burden can result. Of course, any special assessments (for local bonded indebtedness, etc.) must be added. These may be found on the latest tax bill for the property.

The second and somewhat more accurate method for estimating taxes within the income approach is to project them as a percentage of value in the capitalization of income. Usually, this can be done simply by adding the tax rate to the capitalization rate and capitalizing the net income *before* taxes with this new rate. Referring to Example 13.1, assume that the net income before deduction of taxes was $112,156 instead of the after-tax figure of $97,000. Assume also that the tax rate is 0.0125. Now, our direct capitalization is:

Net income before taxes		$112,156
Divided by:	(0.08 + 0.0125)	÷ 0.0925
Equals:	Value estimate	$1,212,500

Reserves for Replacement Certain property components wear out from age and usage and must be replaced from time to time. Although inexpensive replacements may be accounted for under maintenance expense, larger costs are most often capitalized (i.e., listed as "capital" improvements). This is why they do not show on building expense statements. An annual *re-*

serve allowance is considered a valid way of accounting for these costs, particularly when the items have shorter useful lives than the main structure.

Reserves for replacement usually include roof and floor coverings, built-in kitchen equipment, water heaters and boilers, heating and air-conditioning units, and other operating machinery and equipment. In furnished offices and apartments, replacement reserves would also be set up to pay for new furnishings as the old ones wear out. However, the expense of furniture reserves is appropriate only if the projected rent includes rent for the furnishings or equipment.

Major capital additions to the structure, such as major remodeling and facility enlargement/expansion do not properly belong under replacement reserves. This is because such work generally alters (increases) the income potential of the property. Replacement reserves are intended simply to maintain the property's condition and income.

How are the dollar amounts for a replacement reserve determined? First, you estimate the current cost of replacing the building component (the roof covering, for example). Next, you divide its replacement cost by the anticipated future useful life of the new item. The result is the annual allocation, or expense, for that component. For instance, if the current replacement cost of a drop-in kitchen range and oven is $900 and its estimated useful life is 15 years, then the annual cost of replacement amounts to $60 per year or:

$$\frac{\$900}{15} = \$60$$

If there are 10 such units in the building, the total annual allowance for ranges and ovens amounts to $600 per year (10 × $60 = $600). When the replacement reserve allowance has been estimated for each of the short-lived building components, the separate figures are added together to calculate the full expense for replacement reserves.

Some authorities argue that the replacement of a building component amounts to a capital addition rather than an operating expense; therefore, such replacement costs should not be deducted in the income approach, except to the extent that they are deducted by typical investors. In practice, appraisers do not use replacement reserves as much as they did in the past. In particular, when the appraiser has derived the capitalization rate from comparable properties without deducting replacement reserves, such reserves should *not* be deducted from the income of the subject property.

Income and Expense Ratios

Used to assist the appraiser in the analysis of income properties, income and expense ratios are the relationships between various income and expense characteristics of income-producing properties.

The *net income* ratio is the net operating income (NOI) divided by the effective gross income of a property. First, the net income is calculated. For example, a property with an effective gross income of $100,000 and expenses of $35,000 has a NOI of $65,000 ($100,000 − $35,000). Now, the net income ratio can be calculated to be .65, or 65% ($65,000/$100,000 = .65).

The *operating expense* ratio is the relationship of the total operating expenses to the effective gross rent. In the example given above, the operating expense ratio is calculated as $35,000/$100,000 = .35, or 35%. The operating expense ratio is the exact complement of the net income ratio. In other words, it can be calculated as *1 minus the net income ratio.* In this case, the operating expense ratio is confirmed as: 1 − .65 = .35, or 35%.

For specific types of properties, operating expenses generally fall within fairly narrow ranges. Thus, a knowledge of typical expense ratios assists in the reconstruction of operating expense statements, to be discussed next.

13.5 RECONSTRUCTION OF THE OPERATING STATEMENT

In written reports, appraisers often include a reconstructed operating statement in the income approach. This statement shows the appraiser's estimate of stabilized income and expenses for the property, listed category by category. By "stabilized," we mean under current economic conditions but adjusted to show current market rents, average collection losses, and normal expenses for this location.

Why We Reconstruct the Statement

The owner's actual operating statement for prior years is important because it is the actual history of the property and usually helps us develop good estimates of many elements of operating income and expenses. (See Example 13.5.) However, owners' statements may contain some items that are improper or that are irrelevant to the appraisal of the property. Quite often, the operating statement is simply an income tax report, reflecting the personal income and expenses of the owner rather than strictly those of the property.

The purpose of reconstructing the operating statement in an appraisal, then, is to set forth an estimate of the current market rents, the

---

Example 13.5 An Owner's Operating Statement

Receipts

Rent	$140,000	
Other	+1,000	
Total		$141,000

Expenses

Management	$4,000	
Utilities	7,805	
Pool service	1,800	
Landscape service	1,700	
Depreciation	10,420	
Building maintenance	5,400	
Property taxes (½ year)	5,000	
Interest	+20,721	
Total		−56,846
Net		$84,154

typical long-term vacancy and collection losses in this location with good management, and the normal annual expenses to operate this property efficiently on a continuing basis.

You should be aware that some advanced capitalization techniques require a year-by-year projection of income, vacancy and collection loss, and expenses. Such a year-by-year series of numbers would probably use different figures from those used in a stabilized statement. As examples, vacancy rates for a new building might be selected to reflect a declining vacancy rate, and replacement reserve deductions could be estimates of the actual replacement amounts for the specific year for which the replacement is anticipated.

Typical Rental and Vacancy Adjustment

Reconstruction of the owner's operating statement must incorporate the findings of the income and expense study already described. Reconstruction nearly always involves some rental adjustments. Example 13.6 is a reconstructed statement based on the owner's statement presented in Example 13.5. One common adjustment arises because owners' statements often fail to list the manager's unit in the rent schedule whereas, in a reconstructed statement, all units would be included. Next, the rental rates usually must be adjusted to market rent levels.

The vacancy and credit-loss allowance must be estimated. Your analysis should consider the vacancy information developed in the rent survey. You should also consider the effect on vacancy of raising rents to your proposed market levels. Usually, the desired vacancy and collection loss rate is one that represents the long-term rate in the area over the years. One year's abnormally high or low rates (perhaps caused by swings in the business cycle) would be converted to a more typical stabilized rate.

Reconstructing Expenses

As noted, there are two typical problems with actual expense statements. The first is the inclusion of expense categories that reflect the owner's particular financing and income tax costs. These expenses must be deleted. Examples include loan interest, loan principal, income taxes, and depreciation. The only exception occurs when you are using equity residual capitalization, as noted earlier.

The second major problem with actual expense statements is the frequent need to adjust the actual expenses reported. One adjustment is to add for expenses not yet paid (e.g., delinquent taxes). Another adjustment is to prorate any actual payments for insurance premiums or service contracts that extend beyond a year's coverage. On occasion, property owners will also prepay property taxes so that the payments in that year cover one and one-half years. Still another reason is to add dollar amounts for expenses that do not involve any dollars in this particular owner's operations. One example is the cost of any free living unit provided for the resident manager, mentioned earlier. Another example involves the owner who performs all the maintenance personally so that the only historical maintenance expense was for materials.

Example 13.6
A Reconstructed Operating
Statement

Scheduled Gross Income

10 units at $600 per month	$6,000	
10 units at $700 per month	+7,000	
Total annual rents		$13,000 × 12 = $156,000

Service Income

Laundry facilities	+2,000
	$158,000

Vacancy and Credit Loss (2.5%)	−3,950
Effective Gross Income	$154,050

Expenses

Operating

Management (6%)	$9,240
Utilities	7,000
Pool service	1,800
Landscape service	1,700
Building maintenance	+7,900
Total operating expenses	$27,640

Fixed

Insurance	$3,000
Real estate taxes	+15,800
Total fixed expenses	$18,800

Reserves for replacement

Carpets and drapes	$4,000
Kitchen built-ins	1,500
Roof	1,900
Other building components	+800
Total reserves for replacement	+$8,200

Total expenses	−$54,640
Net Income Projection	$99,410

Comparing Expenses with
Industry Standards

As reasonable as the owner-reported expenses may seem, it is still advisable to compare them, category by category, with amounts reported for similar properties in the area and with industry "norms." Published expense reports that show typical expense ratios are available from the Institute of Real Estate Management, the Building Owners and Managers Association (BOMA), the Urban Land Institute, and other management groups. Industry experiences are usually reported either as a percentage of the effective gross income or as a cost per square foot of rentable area. After comparing the actual building expenses with those reported in the area, and as with typical industry standards, the appraiser must project realistic expenses for the subject property. The final estimate should reflect not only the prices of labor, material, services, utilities, and taxes in the area but also the unique characteristics of the property under appraisal.

SUMMARY

The income approach is designed to measure the income-production capability of a property or to find what we refer to as the present worth of future benefits. Since the benefits of owning income property may be both tangible and intangible in nature, the method to be used may depend on the size and type of property.

Larger residential-income properties and most commercial or industrial properties are bought primarily for their income-producing ability. In such properties, the income approach is relied on heavily. The income approach consists of the following steps:

1. Estimate the gross annual income the property is capable of producing.

2. Estimate typical vacancy and collection losses.

3. Subtract vacancy and collection losses from gross income to arrive at the effective gross income.

4. Estimate annual expenses and subtract them from the effective gross income to calculate the net income.

5. Analyze comparable investments to arrive at a capitalization rate and method appropriate for the subject property.

6. Divide the net income by the capitalization rate to arrive at the indicated value by the income approach.

The gross rent or income multiplier method is often accepted as a substitute for the income approach in the appraisal of single-family and small investment properties because of the greater importance of intangible amenities or benefits to buyers of such properties. The gross rent multiplier is a simple relationship between the selling price and the gross scheduled rent.

The selection of a specific gross rent multiplier for the subject property should consider the comparability of the location, the building amenities available, and any physical factors that may affect the ratio of income and expenses. Once selected, the GRM is multiplied by the gross scheduled rent of the subject property to estimate the market value.

Income appraisals require an estimate of income and expenses for the property. Gross income consists of rent for tenant space and service income. Since property is most commonly appraised as if "free and clear" of any leases, the rent used should be market rent rather than merely the present rent of the property. Thus, the owner's operating statement serves only as a guide, often requiring both income and expense adjustments. Gross income estimates are based on a rental survey and the past performance of the property under appraisal. Effective gross income takes into account vacancy and rent loss projections.

Operating expenses are customarily estimated in three categories: variable expenses, fixed expenses, and reserves for replacement. Variable expenses include such familiar items as management costs, cost of services and utilities, and building and grounds maintenance. Since major building repairs occur at uneven intervals, average rather than actual annual expenditures are projected under building maintenance. Insurance premiums and property taxes usually make up what are known as fixed expenses. Reserve for replacements is the category to cover annual allocations for the eventual cost to replace short-lived building components such as floor coverings, roof, and mechanical building equipment.

In written appraisal reports, a reconstructed operating statement is often included to support the income approach conclusion. Actual historical numbers for both income and expense may need correcting. The projected rental schedule should reflect the rent level of competing properties in the area, with rent assigned to all units including the owner's or manager's apartment. Expenses must be limited to those necessary to operate the property. Personal expenses, such as interest and depreciation, are deleted for appraisal purposes. A knowledge of typical expense ratios assists in the reconstruction of operating expense statements. For income property, an expense ratio is defined as the ratio between the total operating expense and the effective gross income. In appraisals, expense estimates should be checked against the amounts reported for similar properties in the area or against known industry standards.

Important Terms and Concepts

Contract rent

Direct capitalization

Effective gross rent

Excess rent

Fixed expenses

Gross income

Gross rent or income multiplier

Income capitalization

Income forecast

Intangible benefits

Market rent

Minimum or base rent

Net income ratio

Operating expenses

Operating expense ratio

Overage rent

Percentage lease

Reconstructed operating statement

Rent roll

Reserves for replacement

Return *of* investment

Return *on* investment

Service income

Step-up, or "graduated," lease

Straight, or "flat," lease

Tangible benefits

Vacancy allowance

Variable expenses

REVIEWING YOUR UNDERSTANDING

1. Which of the following might be classified as tangible rather than intangible amenities?
   (a) Pride of ownership
   (b) A sense of security
   (c) Free rent
   (d) Work satisfaction

2. Tom Smith has a savings account that just paid a $700 annual dividend. If the declared interest rate was 7%, which of the following represents the amount of the deposit?
   (a) $1,000
   (b) $10,000
   (c) $17,000
   (d) None of the above

3. An income property renting for $50,000 per year before expenses just sold for $500,000 cash. What was the gross income multiplier?
   (a) $\frac{1}{10}$ or 10%
   (b) 5
   (c) 10
   (d) None of the above

4. Which of the following property features is/are important in the analysis of gross rent multiplier comparables?
   (a) Expense ratio
   (b) Services included in the rent
   (c) Location
   (d) All of the above

5. Market rent can be defined as:
   (a) The potential gross rent
   (b) The contract rent
   (c) The average rent
   (d) None of the above

6. Which of the following is an example of a specific expense item rather than a basic expense category?
   (a) Reserve for replacement
   (b) Property taxes
   (c) Variable expenses
   (d) Fixed charges or expenses

7. The property under appraisal has a 100% occupancy. What conclusion would you probably draw if the typical occupancy rate in the area were only 95%?
   (a) Advertising is superior
   (b) The rents are too high
   (c) The rents are too low
   (d) Management is better

8. A rent survey reveals that buildings offering one-bedroom units have a considerably lower vacancy factor than those with two-bedroom units. If the subject property includes only units with two bedrooms, the appraisal should probably project:
   (a) An average of the vacancy factors for all units surveyed
   (b) A higher factor than found in the one-bedroom units
   (c) A lower factor than found in the one-bedroom units
   (d) The same factor as found in the one-bedroom units

9. An apartment owner spent $4,000 last year to replace five built-in stoves. In a 10-unit apartment house, what annual expense would be projected for replacement if all the units had stoves? Assume a 10-year life for all replacements.
   (a) $800
   (b) $4,000
   (c) $16,000
   (d) $1,600

10. If market rent is less than contract rent, the difference is known as:
    (a) Overage rent
    (b) Excess rent
    (c) Percentage rent
    (d) Capital gain

11. In market value appraisals, which of the following items should be excluded from the expense statement?
    (a) Loan interest payments
    (b) Necessary current expenses
    (c) Projected expenses
    (d) None of the above

12. Painting and redecorating of units is an expense that appraisers normally treat as:
    (a) A variable expense
    (b) A fixed expense
    (c) Unnecessary if you have 100% occupancy
    (d) Overhead

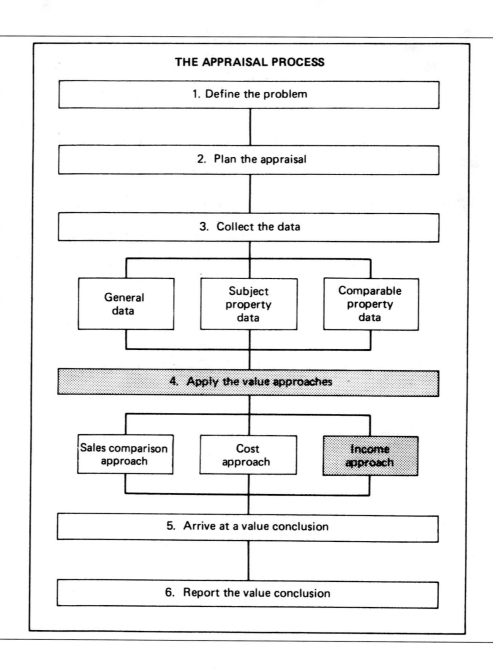

THE APPRAISAL PROCESS

1. Define the problem

2. Plan the appraisal

3. Collect the data

| General data | Subject property data | Comparable property data |

4. Apply the value approaches

| Sales comparison approach | Cost approach | Income approach |

5. Arrive at a value conclusion

6. Report the value conclusion

Chapter 14
Income Capitalization: Rates and Techniques

Preview
In the last chapter, we outlined the basic steps in the income approach and covered the methods used to estimate income and expenses for investment property. This chapter completes our discussion of the income approach by describing the most commonly used techniques of income capitalization.

When you have completed this chapter, you should be able to:

1. *Define income capitalization.*

2. *Name four economic principles on which income capitalization techniques are based.*

3. *List the three methods used to derive interest and/or capitalization rates.*

4. *Explain the concept of capital recovery.*

5. *Name and describe the four techniques for capitalizing income.*

6. *Define discounted cash flow and describe its use in appraisals.*

14.1 PURPOSE AND THEORY OF CAPITALIZATION

We can estimate the value of income property by studying the economic relationship between income and value. Income capitalization is the broad term used to describe this process. A number of income capitalization techniques are available to the appraiser; some are relatively simple and direct, whereas others are more complex. In actual practice, the preferred technique depends on the nature of the appraisal problem and the specific kind of market data available. Commonly used techniques of income capitalization will be described in section 14.3 of this chapter.

Capitalization Defined

Capitalization is the process of converting the net income of a property into its equivalent capital value. We know that a promised future dollar is worth less than a dollar in hand. It follows that income to be received over a number of years is worth less today than the simple total of the dollars to be received. This recognizes a principle known as the "time value of money." The capitalization process reflects the time value of money by reducing or *discounting* future income to its present worth. The actual mathematics of discounting can be a direct or indirect calculation, depending on the capitalization techniques used.

Income capitalization techniques are designed to consider three aspects of the future income, namely, its amount (quantity), its quality, and its duration. What does this mean? Essentially, the concept means that the value of income property does not depend solely on the *amount* of income the property produces. The certainty of the income and the length of time it will last are equally important. For example, a large income from a risky investment can be less valuable than a smaller income from a very safe investment. In either case, the value depends in part on the number of months or years the income can be expected to continue. (See Figure 14.1).

Worded another way, capitalization focuses on the present worth of future benefits. Thus the procedure involves converting the income that is expected over the life of the investment into an estimate of the present value. The choice of capitalization techniques depends on the nature of the property's income and on the types of data that can be collected from the market.

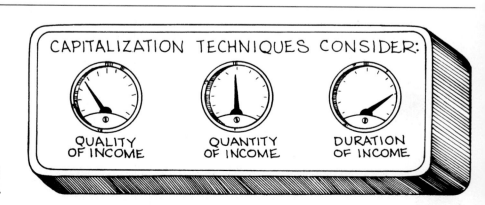

Figure 14.1
Three aspects of future income.

Capitalization Rate Defined

As noted in our introduction to the income approach, value results from the relationship between income and the *rate of return.* Thus the capitalization rate generally is defined as a rate of return, or percentage, used to convert income into its value equivalent. Such a rate directly or indirectly provides for a return on the investment (interest) as well as a return of the investment (capital recovery). The most commonly used capitalization rate is the *overall rate,* or OAR, which is calculated by dividing a property's net income by its sale price. Other types of rates are used in appraisals; the type of rate to be used depends on what capitalization technique is used and how attractive the property and its income are to potential investors.

Comparing Investment Property

Real estate competes with all other types of financial investments. The appraiser's choice of a capitalization technique and rate should consider the investment criteria that motivate purchasers of investment property. Although such criteria are many and varied, the most important are defined as follows:

Investment Criteria

1. Safety.

2. Yield.

3. Liquidity.

4. Management.

5. Appreciation prospects.

6. Property tax burden.

7. Income tax shelter.

8. Size of investment.

9. Hypothecation.

10. Leverage.

Safety

Investment safety refers to the reliability of the net income and assurance of getting the original investment back without loss. Well-located property that is leased to strong tenants is generally considered safe, and therefore it attracts investment funds at a lower rate of return than property of inferior locations and tenancies. (See Figure 14.2.)

Yield

All other things being equal, the investment with the highest yield is the most desirable. Yield refers to the return *on* the investment, such as interest.

Liquidity

The ease with which an investment can be sold is a factor in its value. Common stocks and bonds are considered more desirable than real

Figure 14.2
Which property is the riskier
investment? (Photographs
courtesy of Doug Frost)

estate if everything else is equal because they can be bought and sold more readily and at less expense.

Freedom from Management Burden

Investments that require the least attention and overall supervision are usually the more attractive ones. Real estate generally requires considerably more management effort than financial investments such as securities.

Prospects for Appreciation

When purchasers of either corporate stocks or real estate can anticipate an increase in the value of the investment, they are satisfied with lower current earnings.

Burden of Property Taxes

Ad valorem property taxes decrease the net income of investment property. Thus, such a burden theoretically reduces the attractiveness of real estate as compared with the types of investments not subject to property taxation.

Shelter from Income Taxes

Tax-free municipal bonds sell for a higher price for a given income than similar bonds that have taxable income. This indicates that buyers will accept a *lower* return on income that is sheltered from income tax. Real estate also benefits from certain income tax shelters. The improvement depreciation allowance for investment property is an example.

Size or Denomination

Small investments tend to have broader market appeal and greater liquidity than large ones. Until the advent of limited partnerships and syndications, real estate could not compete with investments of moderate and small denominations. (See Figure 14.3.)

Hypothecation

Using an investment as security for a loan provides a practical substitute for investment liquidity. The relative stability of real estate makes it superior to many other types of investments in this respect.

Figure 14.3
The size of the investment affects
its desirability. (Photographs
courtesy of Doug Frost)

Leverage

Return on investment can often be increased by what is known as "trading upon the equity." When property yield rates are higher than the cost of loan money, an advantage called *leverage* can result. Low equity investments are subject to relatively large loans. In effect, the investor in such cases borrows at a low rate to earn at a higher rate. A similar leverage occurs when low equity is held on property experiencing rapid market appreciation.

Current and Future Returns

In investment properties, current return is the annual (or monthly) flow of net earnings that we refer to in appraisals as the *income stream.* Future, or "deferred," return is the payment of dollars available when an investment is resold. This amount is referred to as the *reversion.* (See Figure 14.4.) When real estate is owned free and clear of any loan, the owner's annual flow of earnings consists of the total net income produced by the property. However, when real estate is encumbered by a loan, the current earnings available to the owner are reduced by the loan payments and are sometimes called *cash flow.*

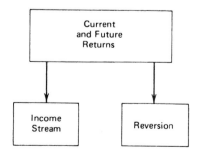

Figure 14.4

In the typical real estate investment, the reversionary returns are the proceeds from the sale of the property. With financed properties, the owner's reversion consists of the selling price less any amount owing on the loan. If any loan principal has been paid off, the owner's reversion will be a greater portion of the sale price. This increase is sometimes called *equity buildup.* The owner's reversion is also increased by any value appreciation that occurs during the holding period. With some investment properties, the loan payments are so large as to eliminate any current cash flow to the owner from the property; in such cases, the return on the equity investment may come entirely from the sale proceeds.

Income and reversion amounts may be calculated on either a pre-tax or post-tax basis, that is, before or after income taxes. For example, the allowable building depreciation in some real estate investments protects some cash flow from income taxation, increasing the post-tax returns. On the other hand, the taxes due on profits made when the property is sold have the effect of decreasing the future return or reversion, when calculated on an after-tax basis. Detailed analysis of income tax aspects of real estate investment is beyond the scope of this book.

Yield versus Recapture

So far, we have pointed out that the financial returns from investments consist of both current income and future reversions. Next, we want to note that such returns consist of various combinations of investment *yield* and *recapture* of capital funds. Although yield is the return on invested capital, it can result from combinations of current income and capital gain. On the other hand, recapture (the return of the invested capital) can also come out of either current income or future reversions. Figure 14.5 shows the various terms used to describe these two types of investment returns. It should be noted that the term *yield* can be used to refer simply to the cash flow return on invested capital, or to the yield-to-maturity, as it is called for bonds. The latter would be a true discounted yield, or *internal rate of return,* as it is often called.

The return of investment capital out of current income can best be illustrated in the field of finance. Lenders are our largest real estate investors: the loan is the investment! In amortized loans, the recapture

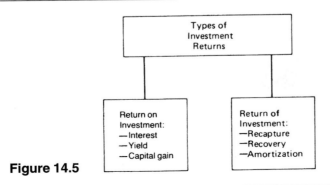

Figure 14.5

of loan funds is provided for as part of the monthly or annual loan payments. The portion of the payment that goes for repayment of the loan principal is providing for loan amortization. Loan amortization (or payoff), then, is the *return of* the lender's investment capital. (See Figure 14.6.)

In real estate equity investments, recapture of investment capital is not always as clearly defined as it is with loans. However, in certain capitalization techniques, recapture is specifically calculated. What portion of real estate is involved? Theoretically, recapture is required for only that part of the real estate whose productive life may be limited, such as the buildings. This means that the recapture of land value is usually unnecessary. When one land use is no longer in demand, another use usually takes its place, supporting a similar or higher value.

What about improvements? Since they are subject to physical deterioration and obsolescence, it is argued that whatever part of the invested capital went for buildings and structures must be recaptured during their productive life. In the mind of the investor, the recapture of such funds invested in wasting assets can come out of the annual net operating income, the proceeds of a future sale, or a combination of the two. When investment recovery comes from the net income, recapture can be thought of either as an expense or as a surcharge on the capitalization rate for the investment. When capital recovery is to come from future sale proceeds, then recapture is a part of the reversion, which was discussed earlier. (See Figure 14.7.)

How is recapture handled in appraisals? It depends on the capitalization technique used. There may be a specific dollar or rate allowance for recapture; or else recapture may simply be a hidden component of the capitalization rate. Section 14.2 will explain this more fully.

Relating Income Capitalization to Economic Principles

The techniques for income capitalization are derived from the economic principles that were covered in Chapter 5. Here is a summary of the more significant principles: anticipation; agents of production; contribution; and highest and best use.

Figure 14.6
Where the loan payment goes.

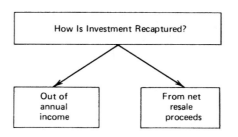

Figure 14.7

Principle of Anticipation	Value is equal to the present worth of future benefits. Income capitalization discounts future income to its present capital worth.
Principle of Agents of Production	All production stems from the use of four agents: labor, coordination, capital, and land. These agents are paid, in the order listed, from available income. Thus land gets paid all the leftover income. In practical terms, all operating expenses (variable and fixed charges and reserves for replacement) are subtracted from the gross income, and the remaining net income must be attributed to the value of the land and improvements.
Principle of Contribution	The value of each one of the four agents of production is proportional to that part of the total income that it contributes. This is also true of any one portion or unit of the property, for example, the land or building. Certain residual capitalization techniques apply this principle by isolating the income attributable to a portion of the property (e.g., the land, the building, or the equity investment) and then capitalizing that income into an estimate of value for that portion of the property.
Principle of Highest and Best Use	The highest and best use of property is that use that produces the greatest income return to the land and therefore develops the highest land value. This is why the land residual technique projects the total income available from the highest and best use of the property and calculates the land value based on the income left after allowing for return on the building investment.

The economic principles reviewed above must be kept in mind throughout the appraisal process. In income capitalization, they influence both the choice of capitalization methods and the selection of capitalization rates.

14.2 SELECTION OF THE CAPITALIZATION RATE

The capitalization rate is the connecting link between an income estimate and a value estimate. Therefore, selecting the appropriate rate is a critical part of the income approach. In this section, we shall define the various rates used in income capitalization procedures and describe the methods for estimating them.

Distinct Types of Rates

For appraisal purposes, there are four distinct types of rates that need to be defined and understood. (See Figure 14.8.) All are important in

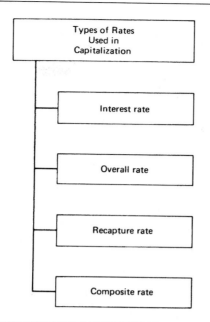

Figure 14.8

the analysis of income properties and the capitalization process. Remember that a rate can be expressed either as a percentage (e.g., 12%) or as a decimal (0.12).

Interest Rate

The interest rate is the rate of return on invested capital. The term is synonymous with yield rate and discount rate. It does not include any provision for the recapture of investment capital.

Overall Capitalization Rate

The relationship between net income and value for the total property (or the ratio of net income to value) is called the overall capitalization rate. Theoretically, this allows for both return *on* investment and recapture *of* investment capital, but the proportions are usually unknown.

Recapture Rate

The rate at which invested funds are being returned to the investor is called the recapture rate.

Composite Capitalization Rate

A rate composed of interest and recapture in separately determined amounts and known proportions is called a composite capitalization rate.

Methods of Estimating Rates

Capitalization rates may be estimated by any of several methods. The direct comparison, band of investment, and summation methods (listed in Figure 14.9) are the ones most commonly used.

The Direct Comparison Method

The direct comparison method (or comparative sales method, as it may be called) is generally the preferred method of deriving a capitalization rate and is also the easiest to understand. To use the direct

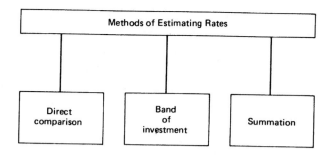

Figure 14.9

Methods of Estimating Rates		
Direct comparison	Band of investment	Summation

comparison method, we simply analyze recent sales of similar properties and, in each case, divide the net income by the sale price (after adjusting for non-market financing). The result is the indicated overall capitalization rate (OAR) for each sale. Here is an example:

Net income		$ 80,000
Divided by:	Selling price	÷800,000
Equals:	Overall rate	.10
		or 10%

For selection of the overall capitalization rate, the direct comparison of market sales is perhaps the most reliable of the methods available. However, considerable effort and skill are required when using it. First, an adequate sample of comparable sales is required. Three or four sales are considered sufficient only if the sample properties are relatively comparable to the subject property. Comparability is as important here as in the sales comparison approach. Location, size, age and condition, number of units (when pertinent), and intensity of land use should be similar to the subject property. Once tentative comparables have been selected, the transaction data for each sale should be screened so that only recent open market sales are used. Unusual financing terms must be analyzed and adjusted. Last, the net income reported for each comparable should be reviewed. Is it based on a current market rent schedule? Have all appropriate expenses been deducted from the scheduled gross? The results of the direct comparison method are only as reliable as the answers to these questions.

In order to extract the *interest* rate rather than the *overall* rate, we must first deduct from the net income the amount required for annual recapture of improvement value before dividing by the sale price. Such a procedure is most valid when property values are declining with age. First, the value of the improvements must be abstracted from the total sale price. Next, the annual recapture amount must be calculated. If it is assumed that recapture will take place at a constant rate over the economic life of the improvements, then the annual amount for recapture may be estimated as follows:

$$\frac{\text{Improvement value}}{\text{Remaining economic life}} = \text{Annual recapture amount}$$

What if we assumed that the improvement in the last example represented 80% of the total value and had a remaining economic life at the time of sale of 40 years? The interest rate could be estimated by the direct comparison method as shown in Example 14.1.

Example 14.1 Interest Rate by Direct Comparison

Total net income			$80,000
Less: Building recapture			
Sale price		$800,000	
Multiplied by:	Improvement ratio	× 0.80	
Equals:	Improvement value	$640,000	
Divided by:	Remaining life	÷40	
Equals:	Building recapture		−$16,000
Equals:	Net income after recapture		$64,000
Divided by:	Sale price		÷$800,000
Equals:	Interest rate		0.08 or 8%

Note that when the interest rate is abstracted from market sales, the appraiser relies on a subjective estimate of economic life and need for recapture. For this reason, the resulting interest rate is generally compared with interest rates calculated by other methods before it is used.

The Band of Investment Method

The real estate market is said to be made up of equity investors on the one hand and lenders on the other. Since both groups may be viewed as investors in income property, they combine to create what is referred to as the "band of investment." The band of investment method produces a capitalization rate that is a weighted average. This means that it is an average of two or more rates, adjusted for the percent of property value each source of money represents. The method combines a rate for mortgage loan money and a rate for the investor's equity. The relative weight, or importance, of each rate depends on the percentage of the purchase price provided by the loan and the equity down payment in typical transactions. There are two separate versions of the band of investment method. One is used to estimate the *interest,* or *risk,* rate for the property; the other is used to estimate the *overall* rate.

To estimate an *interest* rate by the band of investment method, it is first necessary to estimate the required yield rate for equity. Calculations follow the format of this example: Assume that the prevailing loan terms for a particular type of property include 12% interest, with a maximum loan of 75% of the property's value. The equity down payment will accordingly be 25% of the property's value. For this investment, assume that equity yield expectations are found to be 15%.

Loan		$0.75 \times 0.12 = 0.090$
Plus:	Equity	$0.25 \times 0.15 = \underline{0.035}$
Equals:	Property interest rate	0.125
		or 12.5%

In practice, solving for an interest rate by the band of investment method is difficult because good evidence of required equity yields is hard to find. Technically, too, the answer is most valid with an interest-only loan. If amortized loans are typical for the type of property you are analyzing, the procedure shown needs to be adjusted for loan amortization. This adjustment is covered in advanced appraisal courses.

The second type of band of investment method calculates an *overall* capitalization rate for the property. This is the more widely used band of investment method among investors and appraisers. It uses the mortgage constant instead of the mortgage interest rate, and the equity cash-on-cash (or dividend) rate instead of the equity yield rate. By way of explanation, the *mortgage constant* is defined as the total annual loan payment divided by the loan amount, that is, the ratio of the annual loan payment to the loan. The *equity cash-on-cash (or dividend) rate* is the ratio of the equity cash flow to the equity down payment, or investment. Remember that the equity cash flow is defined as the income remaining from the net operating income after deducting the loan payments.

To solve for the overall rate by the band of investment method, follow this example, assuming (1) there is an 80% loan, (2) the annual total of the level monthly payments on the loan amounts to 13% of the original loan amount, and (3) a requirement by the buyer of a 7% first year cash-on-cash return on the down payment.

Loan		$0.80 \times 0.13 = 0.104$
Plus:	Equity	$0.20 \times 0.07 = \underline{0.014}$
Equals:	Indicated overall rate	0.118
		or 11.8%

The Summation Method

The summation method is used most often to estimate an interest rate rather than a note of capitalization. The rate is calculated by combining, or adding up, amounts for the separate theoretical elements that help determine yield rates. Thus, such a rate is sometimes called a built-up rate. The return on a nearly risk-free investment, such as a U.S. government bond, is the starting point and is called the safe rate. Penalties are added to the safe rate for the various ways in which the actual investment property characteristics are less than ideal. (In some models, characteristics judged to be *better* than typical, such as prospects for appreciation, are entered in the formula as *negatives*.) Some of the investment criteria listed earlier in this chapter will be recognized in the following example.

Safe rate	+6.75%
Investment risk	+3.00%
Lack of liquidity	+1.25%
Burden of management	+1.00%
Indicated interest rate	11.00%

The weakness of the summation method lies in the imprecise and subjective methods available for rating the various investment features involved. However, some very large real estate investors now actively use versions of this concept, and it is useful to illustrate the various investment considerations even if the exact component amounts are unknown.

Other Methods of Calculating Rates

Several other methods of estimating rates are worthy of mention. An interest rate can be converted to a composite capitalization rate by adding a component for recapture. Adding a recapture component assumes that the typical investor requires that capital recovery be provided for out of current income. This method should be used only when this assumption is a reasonable one for current markets.

Related to this method is another method, where an interest rate can be converted into an overall capitalization rate by including a component for anticipated future value change. When future values are expected to decline, some capital must be recaptured from income. In this case, a surcharge for recovery is added to the interest rate.

Recently, capitalization techniques have been developed to allow for the return of capital from reversion amounts, that is, out of proceeds from the future sale of the property. For example, the so-called Ellwood method (named after a well-known mortgage banker, author, and lecturer) suggests methods for adjusting overall rates derived from the band of investment to reflect both the equity buildup from loan amortization and/or anticipated changes in property value.

Adjusting Rates to Apply to the Subject Property

When capitalization rates are derived from sales of comparable properties, the rates may need to be adjusted to reflect differences in the physical characteristics of the subject property and the comparable properties as well as differences in the economic conditions as of the valuation date. Although there are no precise methods for adjusting rates, certain techniques of rate adjustment can be borrowed from the rate-finding methods already mentioned. The relevant factors to review when adjusting rates include:

1. Property location.

2. The age, quality, and condition of any improvements.

3. The remaining economic life of the improvements.

4. The ratio of building value to total value.

5. Expenses occurring as a percentage of market value (e.g., property taxes).

Location may have a dramatic effect on interest and capitalization rates because the property's location can affect the relative risk of the investment, the probable future trend of rental rates, and investor motivation in general. The age, quality, condition, and remaining economic life of improvements are important, too. Although small differences may not merit rate adjustments, significant differences may influence the market attitude about the relative safety and durability of the particular property's income stream. Also, the ratio of building value to total value may influence the amount of tax shelter that the investor has available, or it may influence the requirement for capital recovery. As a result, capitalization rates generally should be based on sale properties with building value ratios similar to the subject property ratio.

Market-derived capitalization rates may also be adjusted to reflect the subject property's expenses when they are expected to occur as a percentage of market value. Ad valorem property taxes are the best example. By adding the tax rate to the cap rate, property taxes can often be projected more accurately than by estimating taxes as a dollar amount of expense. Note that the net income *before* taxes is capitalized in this method. An example is given in Chapter 13.

How to Allow for Capital Recovery

There are three recognized methods to calculate a specific provision for capital recovery in income capitalization. (See Figure 14.10.) The straight-line and sinking fund methods specify actual recapture provisions, either in the capitalization rate or in an adjustment to annual income. The annuity method includes recapture within the capitalization technique "automatically." Let us define these three methods and their underlying assumptions. Remember that some capitalization techniques (e.g., the direct-capitalization method) do not specifically provide for capital recovery by any of these three methods. Instead, capital recovery is a hidden component of the overall rate found from analyzing the sales.

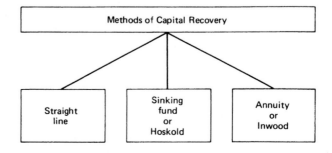

Figure 14.10

| *Straight-Line Recapture* | This method assumes that annual recapture payments must be provided out of the annual net income and should be the same amount each year. In some techniques, the annual payment is treated as an expense in dollars; in others, it is handled as a component of the capitalization rate. The straight-line recapture method has been a common appraisal tool in the past, but it is conceptually flawed and not recommended when reliable overall capitalization rates can be extracted from the market sales. |

The Sinking Fund or Hoskold Method

This method assumes that the annual investment recapture amounts are deposited into a sinking fund or account where they earn interest and compound at a "safe rate" (usually the savings account interest rate or the going rate for long-term U.S. government bonds). The sinking fund method is conceptually valid. It represents what investors actually did at the time the concept was developed in the late 1800s. Now the concept is rarely used either by appraisers or investors. However, managers of some large investment funds use analysis methods that are somewhat similar.

The Annuity or Inwood Method

In this method, invested capital is recovered from the level annual income in exactly the same manner as a loan is paid off. Annual recapture amounts are assumed capable of earning compound interest at the yield, or interest, rate of the property under appraisal (rather than at a safe rate as in the Hoskold method). Because this method also corrects for the flaw inherent in straight-line recapture, a given amount of income recaptures a larger investment than in the straight-line method. Also known as annuity or yield capitalization, the annuity method was in the past reserved for the appraisal of properties under long-term leases to reliable tenants. Now, however, it is considered suitable for any property type if the yield rate is adjusted to reflect the risk involved. (See section 14.3 on income capitalization techniques.)

In any of the three methods mentioned, the recapture of invested funds takes place over a period of time. This period may be either the investor's holding period or the estimated remaining economic life of the improvements, depending on the capitalization technique used. The length of the recapture period depends on such influences as the age and condition of the improvements, the risk of building obsolescence, and the specific requirements of the particular investor.

The Mechanics of Straight-Line Recapture

Some capitalization techniques that will be covered in the next section will require that you know the basic mechanics of straight-line recapture. Two simple steps are involved, as follows:

> 1. The recapture rate is calculated by dividing the capital recovery period into 100%. The result is the recapture rate, expressed as a percentage.

2. The recapture rate is added to the required yield, or interest, rate for the property. The total is the composite capitalization rate used for that portion of the investment involving the wasting asset.

This composite rate can be used to capitalize the portion of the net income that is earned by the improvements. The result is an estimate of improvement value. Here is an example showing how such a rate is derived.

Assume that the market anticipates (1) a 9% average yield, or average return, *on* the total debt and equity funds invested in the property, and (2) that the total capital invested in the improvements is to be recaptured over a period of 40 years. The calculations would be as follows:

Interest rate		9.0%
Plus:	Recapture rate (100% ÷ 40)	+ 2.5%
Equals:	Composite rate	11.5%

It is also possible to calculate an overall capitalization rate if, in addition to the above information, you know the building-to-total-value ratio. If we assume that improvement value is 80% of total value, then the calculation would be:

Interest rate			9.0%
Plus:	Recapture rate: Building rate	2.5%	
	Times: Building ratio	× 80%	
			+ 2.0%
Equals:	Overall rate		11.0%

As we have already pointed out, investment capital may be recovered or recaptured either out of current income or out of proceeds of sale. If investors expect value to appreciate in the future, then investment recapture may not be necessary in the capitalization rate. Remember, too, that in some capitalization methods, the recapture rate is never specifically identified or calculated. Instead, it is simply hidden within the data obtained from the market, as is the case with overall rates derived by the direct comparison method.

14.3 DIRECT AND RESIDUAL CAPITALIZATION TECHNIQUES

As we suggested earlier in this chapter, certain income capitalization techniques are based on the principle of contribution. This implies that any single part of the property can be valued by measuring its contribution to the total net income.

Four income capitalization techniques are presented here. Their current usefulness and/or their historic importance will be discussed as they are described in this section. The names of the techniques suggest their methods: the value of either the total property, or of a specified portion, is measured by the income that is "residual" to, or accountable to, that portion of the property. Here are the four income capitalization techniques:

---

1. Direct capitalization technique.

2. Building residual technique.

3. Land residual technique.

4. Equity residual technique.

Direct Capitalization Technique

The direct capitalization technique is the simplest method of income capitalization, and often the most reliable. In order to apply the direct capitalization technique, the first step is to estimate an overall capitalization rate by one of the three methods described in section 14.2. These were the direct comparison method, the band of investment method, and the summation (built-up) method. The direct comparison method is preferred because it best measures how actual market attitudes affect values. The band of investment technique (using cash-on-cash rates) would be second-best in this regard.

The second and final step in the direct capitalization technique is to capitalize the net income that is projected for the subject property. This is done by dividing the net income by the overall rate you have selected.

The direct capitalization technique is recommended for use when there are adequate numbers of comparative sales to indicate reliably the direct relationship between net income and value. (See Example 14.2.) This means that the sales should be relatively similar to the subject in size, character, and the ratio of land value to building value. Theoretically, the sales and the subject property should also represent or possess similar risks and value trends.

Example 14.2 Direct Capitalization Technique

Net operating income		$100,000
Divided by:	Overall capitalization rate	÷10%
Equals:	Indicated value	$1,000,000

The conclusion reached by direct capitalization is only as accurate as the estimate of income and the overall rate selected. As we learned in the last chapter, income and expenses are not consistently reported by the real estate industry. For example, reserves for replacement are not usually included in the expenses reported in sales and listings. Buildings also differ in the degree of owner management. Appraisal errors can result in both income and capitalization rate analysis when expenses are handled differently for the subject and the comparables. Because of this, it is important to make certain that the net income for the subject was projected on the same basis as for the sales.

Building Residual Technique

This method can be used to capitalize income when there are reliable data to support an accurate estimate of the land value when the building value is unknown. Ideally, the land value would be estimated from recent sales of land parcels that have similar physical characteristics, location, and zoning.

The building residual technique is most useful when you are appraising older buildings, and the sales data are inadequate to estimate overall rates for the direct capitalization technique. Once quite popular, the building residual technique is now considered much less reliable because it rests on two doubtful assumptions: The first is that future land values will be the same as current values; the second is that present building values will decline, so that the investor must recapture the building investment out of annual income. Neither of these assumptions seems warranted in the typical real estate market today.

The building residual technique has five steps if we assume that straight-line recapture is used.

---

1. Estimate the interest rate and recapture rate using the methods described in section 14.2.

2. Calculate the amount of income needed to provide a return on the land investment by multiplying the land value times the selected interest rate. The resulting income is sometimes referred to as the "land charge."

3. Subtract the land return from the total net operating income to calculate the income that can be attributed to the improvements.

4. Capitalize the income to the improvements by using a composite building capitalization rate that combines both interest and recapture.

5. Add the indicated value for the improvements to the value indicated for the land to obtain the total property value.

An illustration of the building residual technique is given in Example 14.3.

Example 14.3 The Building Residual Technique

Assume

Net operating income	$91,000
Land value (estimated from land sales)	$200,000
Interest rate (estimated from sales of leased land)	7%
Recapture rate (estimated from the age and condition of the subject)	4%

Solution

Net income		$91,000
Less:	Return required on land ($200,000 × 0.07)	−14,000
Equals:	Net income to improvements	$77,000
Divided by composite rate:		
	Interest rate	0.07
Plus:	Recapture rate	+0.04
Equals:	Composite rate	÷0.11
Equals:	Indicated improvement value	$700,000
Plus:	Land value	+200,000
Equals:	Property value	$900,000

Land Residual Technique

The land residual technique is useful when the building value can be reliably estimated but the land value is unknown. When the improvements are new or nearly new and are also clearly the highest and best use of the land, the value of the improvements is likely to equal their cost of reproduction. Now land value can be estimated by capitalizing that part of the net income that can be attributed to it. Again, we assume that the superior direct capitalization method cannot be applied. Here are the seven steps in the land residual technique (again, assuming straight-line recapture):

1. Calculate the interest rate and recapture rate as suggested in section 14.2.

2. Add the two rates to calculate the composite building capitalization rate.

3. Estimate the value of the improvements by using their reproduction or replacement cost less accrued depreciation.

4. Multiply the improvement value by the composite rate calculated in step 2. The result is known as the "building charge," or the income needed to provide the desired return of, and return on, the building investment.

5. Subtract the building charge from the net operating income to calculate the net income that can be attributed to the land.

6. Divide the net income available to the land by the selected interest rate. The result is the indicated value of the land.

7. Add the estimated values for the land and building to calculate the indicated value for the total property.

The land residual technique does not have the importance it once had in the appraisal of developed properties because this technique involves the same assumptions as the building residual technique. However, the land residual technique is one of the available methods for the appraisal of land, as described in Chapter 10. Perhaps the major remaining use of the land residual technique, or variations of it, is in studies of the highest and best use and/or project feasibility studies for vacant or under-improved land. The land residual technique is demonstrated in Example 14.4.

Example 14.4 Land Residual Technique

Assume

Net operating income	$70,000
Building cost new	$600,000
Interest rate (estimated from the band of investment or summation method)	6.5%
Recapture rate (estimated from the age and condition of the subject)	2.5%

Solution

Net income				$70,000
Less:	Income to building:			
	Improvement value		$600,000	
	Times composite rate:			
	Interest rate	0.065		
	Plus: Recapture rate	+0.025		
	Equals: Composite rate		×0.09	
Equals:	Income to building			−$54,000
Equals:	Income to land			$16,000
Divided by:	Interest rate			÷0.065
Equals:	Land value (rounded)			$246,000
Plus:	Improvement value			+$600,000
Equals:	Property value			$846,000
	Rounded			$850,000

Equity Residual Technique

The equity residual technique analyzes the cash flow from an investment. This could also be described as the residual-income-to-the-equity investment. This technique can be used whenever financing terms are a major influence on market prices. However, the technique is especially useful for analyzing the buyer's equity position relative to a particular proposed or existing loan. The value of the total property is then estimated by adding the loan amount to the calculated equity value. See Example 14.5.

There are three steps in the equity residual technique.

---

1. Subtract the annual loan payments from the net operating income to estimate the annual cash flow to the investor.

2. Divide the equity cash flow, from step 1, by the estimated equity cash-on-cash rate (equity dividend rate). The result is the indicated value of the equity.

3. Add the indicated value of the equity to the amount owed on the mortgage. The result is the estimated value of the property.

When the equity residual technique is calculated using the typical market financing terms and equity rates, it results in an estimate of market value for the property. However, when it is calculated using unique financing rates (e.g., seller financing), the resulting value is properly described as "value as financed." Similarly, if calculated using the desired equity cash-on-cash rate of a particular investor rather than current market equity cash-on-cash rates, the resulting value is referred to as "investment value."

Example 14.5 Equity Residual Technique

Assume

Net operating income	$100,000
Loan amount	$600,000
Annual loan payments	$70,000
Equity cash-on-cash rate	7%

Solution

Net income		$100,000
Less:	Loan payments	−70,000
Equals:	Equity cash flow	$30,000
Divided by:	Equity cash-on-cash rate	÷0.07
Equals:	Indicated equity value	$429,000
Plus:	Loan amount	+600,000
Equals:	Total value estimate	$1,029,000
	Rounded	$1,000,000

Other Capitalization Theories

Some authorities suggest that all income capitalization techniques fall into two basic groups: direct (or "ratio") capitalization and "yield" capitalization. According to this theory the direct capitalization techniques presented above fall into the first group, where the income attributed to the portion of the property under appraisal is converted into a value estimate by use of a single capitalization rate, or value "ratio." Direct capitalization does not address possible future income and value changes for the property. Therefore, the true investment yield expectations are not known.

Yield capitalization is a more sophisticated method of analyzing an investment. This uses "discount" math instead of direct capitalization to value either the property or the equity income. (For further explanation of "discount math," see section 14.4.) Either short-term or long-term investments can be appraised. Additionally, true investment yield can be analyzed by factoring in anticipated changes in property or equity income, buildup of equity from loan amortization, and/or property value appreciation or depreciation.

Discounted cash flow (often referred to as DCF) is perhaps the most common example of yield capitalization. (Other forms are beyond the scope of this book.) The key feature of DCF is the mathematical discounting of all future income or benefits.

14.4 ESTIMATING, MEASURING, AND DISCOUNTING CASH FLOWS

In appraisals, the value of amounts to be received in the future must be reduced, or discounted, to their present values, recognizing the time value of money. In this section, we will first review the several purposes of cash flow analysis in appraisals, and then cover the subject of discounted cash flows in the context of yield capitalization.

The Analysis of Cash Flow Amounts in Appraisals

The analysis of cash flow lies at the heart of income and investment property appraisal, financing, and management. The cash flow amounts may be in various forms, including investment income or profit, retirement of debt, and/or projected sales proceeds. In the appraisal of new subdivisions or income properties, for example, a common problem facing the appraiser is how to take into account the time period required to sell off units developed, or to rent up new and/or vacant income properties. The solution in both cases is to view the amounts to be received as *cash flows,* and to mathematically discount these amounts in proportion to the time and risk involved.

The discounting of any of the cash flows mentioned involves use of the same mathematical tools as those used in yield capitalization.

Discounted Cash Flows in Yield Capitalization

Whether derived from undivided interests or buyer's equity holdings, discounted cash flows define and measure the present value of ownership benefits. When used to estimate the value of equity, yield capitalization can lead either to an estimate of market value, or to an estimate of so-called investment value of the property involved. The type of value sought depends on whether the cash flows and discount factors are market derived, or instead, unique to the particular investor. What are the types of cash flow returns available to the investor? How are their amounts estimated, measured, and discounted to their present value?

Review of Cash Flow Sources in an Investment

All of the cash flows in a typical investment can be attributed to two sources, *current income* and the *proceeds from the sale* of the property. As we have already suggested, the cash flow amounts in each case depend not only upon the income-producing ability of the property, but the financing involved and the value of the property upon sale. While cash flows can be measured either before or after income taxes, only pretax flows will be discussed here.

Measuring Cash Flow from Current Income

To the equity investor, the cash flow from current investment income can be defined simply as the net income less debt service. However, cash flows can be *even* or *uneven,* depending on the terms of the lease, the amount of expenses, and the amount and type of loan payments.

Even Cash Flow

For an example of even cash flow, assume that an investment property has an annual income of $100,000 from a 30-year net flat lease. There is a $700,000 loan commitment on the property at 9% interest to be amortized with annual payments over 30 years. From this data the expected cash flow is calculated as follows (using a financial table or calculator to solve for the amount of debt service):

Annual net income		$100,000
Less:	Annual debt service	−68,135
Equals:	Annual equity cash flow	$31,865

Uneven Cash Flow

Uneven cash flows can be demonstrated with the same assumptions; except here, we will assume that the lease income steps up after 15 years to $150,000 per year. Cash flows would be as follows:

		Years 1–15	*Years 16–30*
Annual net income		$100,000	$150,000
Less:	Annual debt service	−68,135	−68,135
Equals:	Annual equity cash flow	$31,865	$81,865

When a cash flow from the eventual sale proceeds is added to the annual cash flows, another type of uneven cash flow is created.

Measuring Cash Flow from Sale Proceeds

The cash flow from the eventual sale proceeds is calculated by estimating the value of the property at the end of the holding period and deducting from that amount (1) any loan balance or payoff, and (2) any sale costs expected to be incurred.

Referring to the earlier example, assume that the property can be sold subject to the existing lease after 15 years for cash to a new loan, with the new buyer basing the price upon a capitalization rate of 10% of the net income from the lease. Further assume that there is no prepayment penalty on the loan, and that the broker's fee is 6% of the sale price. We will calculate these amounts as follows, using financial tables for figuring the loan balance:

Sale price:	$150,000 ÷ .10 =	$1,500,000
Less:	Broker's fee @ 6%	−90,000
Equals:	Net price before loan payoff	$1,410,000
Less:	Loan balance	−549,219
Equals:	Cash flow from sale proceeds	$860,781

Discounting Cash Flows

Discounting investment cash flows means estimating a present value for them that recognizes the time value of money and the risk involved. To understand the time value of money, we need to review the theory of discount math.

The Theory of "Discount" Math

A given sum that you have to wait for is worth less to you than the same sum today. Placing money in a savings account and taking it out after it has earned interest is a common example. Let us explain. When you place $1.00 in a 5% account, you are in fact recognizing that the $1.05 promised in one year has only a $1.00 present value. The deposit is less than the future amount. Hence, $1.00 is the present value of $1.05 when discounted for one year to earn 5%.

What is the discount factor in the previous example? Since the ratio of $1.00 to $1.05 is .95238, this is the proven discount factor. The same factor can be used for *any* sum that is due one year in the future when discounted at 5%. For the lump-sum amount of $1.05 due in one year, here are the calculations that show the present value to be $1.00:

Amount due in the future:	$1.05
Times discount factor:	×.95238
Equals:	$1.00

Discount Formula for a Single Payment

Discount factors for a single amount due in one, two, three, or any number of years at any chosen discount or interest rate may be found by the following formula, which is built into discount tables and financial calculators. Note that the single future payment amount is always assumed to be $1.00, so that any dollar amount can be applied against the factor.

$$\text{Present value of } \$1.00 = \frac{1}{(1 + i)^n}$$

where i = discount rate (%)
         n = number of periods

If we use a financial calculator to solve for the single payment discount factor shown earlier, the variables would be entered and the solution found as follows (FV refers to future value and PV to present value):

$$n = 1; \quad \%i = 5; \quad FV = \$1.00$$
To solve: PV = $0.95238

Discounting a Stream of Payments   A stream of payments can be analyzed one at a time with each discounted as a single payment due at a different date in the future, or the entire stream can be discounted at once. Factors for discounting an income stream may be found in financial tables or calculated with a financial calculator.

To demonstrate how to discount a stream of payments, suppose we solve for the present (discounted) value of the first 15-year income stream given in the uneven cash flow investment example cited above. Assuming an investor would require a 12% yield here, we refer to a 12% financial table, in the column referred to as the "present worth of one per period." For 15 years, we find listed the factor of 6.8109. When this present worth factor is applied to the annual income, the present worth of the income stream is found:

$$\$31,865 \times 6.8109 = \$217,000 \text{ (rounded)}$$

Using a financial calculator, the variables are entered, and the problem solved as follows, where *PMT* is the annual cash flow amount:

$$n = 15; \quad i\,(\%) = 12; \quad PMT = \$31,865$$
To solve: PV = $217,000 (rounded)

Discounting the Sale Proceeds   As explained above, the sale proceeds as a single cash flow amount are projected to be available when an investment property is sold. The following example shows how to discount this cash flow:

We refer again to the investment analysis example cited above. There, the net proceeds were projected at $860,781, available in 15 years. To discount to its present value, we refer to a 12% "present worth of one" table at 15 years to find the discount factor and multiply it by the net proceeds, calculating as follows:

$$\$860,781 \times 0.1827 = \$157,250 \text{ (rounded)}$$

Using a financial calculator, the same answer is found, as follows:

$$n = 15; \quad \%i = 12; \quad FV = \$860,781$$

To solve: PV = $157,250 (rounded)

Summary of Anticipated Cash Flows

Let us summarize the anticipated cash flows (a 15-year annual cash flow, and the sale proceeds at the end of 15 years) in the investment example partially solved above.

Annual cash flow:		
Net annual income	$100,000	
Less: Debt service	−68,135	
Equals: Annual cash flow		$31,865
Anticipated sale proceeds:		
Less: Future sale price	$1,500,000	
Less: Sale costs	−90,000	
Equals: Loan balance	−549,219	
Sale proceeds		$860,781

Summary of Discounted Cash Flows

When we summarize the discounted cash flows shown above, we can solve for the present worth of the equity investment, suggesting the amount of down payment that is warranted for the investment in question, assuming the investor's yield requirement is 12 percent:

Cash Flow	Amount	Discount Factor	Present Value
Income stream	$31,865	6.8109	$217,000
Sale proceeds	$860,781	0.1827	157,250
Total present worth of equity			$374,250

SUMMARY

Income capitalization is a process of translating income into value. By selecting capitalization rates that reflect the types and amounts of return sought in the real estate investment market, the appraiser completes the link between income and value.

Rates may be selected by the direct comparison method, the band of investment method, or the summation method. Briefly, the direct comparison method derives an overall capitalization rate from market sales by using the ratio of net income to the selling price. This method often provides the most reliable estimate of overall capitalization rates. The band of investment method can be used to estimate either the property's interest rate or the overall capitalization rate. This method calculates the average of typical loan rates and market equity requirements. Last, the summation method can be used to "build up" a rate, by adding investment risk, nonliquidity, and other investment elements to a base rate or safe rate of return.

Some capitalization techniques require a specific allowance for the return of the money invested in improvements, on the theory that age and obsolescence will limit their economic life expectancy. This allowance is labeled "recapture" or "return of investment." Three methods of recapture are available. All assume that an annual payment for recapture must be paid from the annual income of the property. The straight-line and sinking fund methods make specific annual provisions for recapture, either in the capitalization rate or by a dollar amount subtracted from the net income. The annuity method provides for recapture in the same way that a mortgage is amortized, by use of annuity factors. Selecting the appropriate recapture method depends on the nature, duration, and quality of the income stream. Only straight-line recapture examples are provided in this book because annuity capitalization is only briefly introduced.

Four techniques for capitalizing income are noteworthy. Direct capitalization would be used when a market study shows a consistent relationship between net operating income and sale prices. The net income of the subject property is divided by the overall rate to calculate the estimated value. Good comparable sales and good income data are required for this method.

The building residual technique can be used when the land value is known but the improvement value is unknown. Income attributed to the improvements is capitalized and added to the land value to reach a total value estimate.

The land residual technique can be used when the building value is known but the land value is unknown. Income attributed to the land is capitalized and added to the known improvement value. In both the building and land residual techniques, a specific allowance must be made in order to recapture the improvement investments over their estimated economic life. Because of the controversial assumptions required, neither method is widely used today.

The equity residual technique can qualify as a market valuation technique when typical market loan and equity cash flow figures are used. However, its more common application involves an analysis of a property value from the point of view of a particular investor looking at a specific loan. In either case, the cash flow attributable to the equity investment is capitalized and added to the loan amount.

Some theories suggest that all capitalization techniques can be described as either "direct" or "yield" capitalization. Direct capitalization uses a single capitalization rate, or ratio, to convert the income under study to an estimate of value, whether it is attributed to the total property, the building, the land, or the equity. No yield assumptions are involved. On the other hand, yield capitalization is a mathematical discounting procedure that considers anticipated changes in property or equity income, as well as property value changes projected during the investment period. In this way, true investment yield requirements or expectations can be analyzed.

In appraisals, the market value of amounts to be received in the future must always be reduced or *discounted,* to their present values, recognizing the time value of money. In this chapter we reviewed the several purposes of cash flow analysis in appraisals, and covered the subject of discounted cash flows in the context of yield capitalization.

Important Terms and Concepts

Annuity recapture method

Band of investment method

Building charge

Building residual technique

Capital recovery

Capitalization rate

Cash-on-cash (equity dividend rate)

Composite capitalization rate

Debt service

Direct capitalization technique

Direct comparison method

Discount rate

Discounted cash flow (DCF)

Ellwood method

Equity residual technique

Equity yield rate

Hypothecation

Interest rate

Investment value

Land charge

Land residual technique

Mortgage constant

Overall capitalization rate (OAR)

Property tax rate

Ratio capitalization

Recapture rate

Reversion

Sinking fund (Hoskold) recapture method

Straight-line recapture method

Summation method

Yield capitalization

Yield rate

REVIEWING YOUR UNDERSTANDING

1. Income capitalization is the broad term used to describe the process of estimating the value of income property by studying the economic relationship between income and value. This process:
   (a) Converts the net income of a property into its equivalent capital value

(b) Reflects the time value of money by reducing or discounting future income to its present worth
(c) Focuses on the present worth of future benefits
(d) All of the above

2. The appraiser's choice of a capitalization technique and rate should consider the investment criteria that motivate purchasers of investment property. Which of the following refers to the ability to use the property as loan collateral?
(a) Size or denomination
(b) Hypothecation
(c) Liquidity
(d) Safety

3. The most commonly used capitalization rate is:
(a) The income rate
(b) The composite capitalization rate
(c) The interest rate
(d) The overall rate

4. Capitalization rates may be estimated by any of several methods. Which of the following is generally the preferred method of deriving a capitalization rate?
(a) Summation
(b) Band of investment
(c) Direct comparison
(d) None of the above

5. There are three recognized methods to provide for capital recovery in income capitalization. In which method is invested capital recovered from the annual income in exactly the same manner as a loan is paid off?
(a) The annuity or Inwood method
(b) The straight-line recapture method
(c) The double-declining balance method
(d) The accelerated method

6. The simplest and often the most reliable method of income capitalization is:
(a) The direct capitalization technique
(b) The building residual technique
(c) The land residual technique
(d) The equity residual technique

7. If a $600,000 property has qualified for a 75% loan at a 12% mortgage constant and the buyer wants a 2% annual cash return on his down payment, what net income would the property have to produce?
(a) $3,000
(b) $57,000
(c) $54,000
(d) $12,000

8. If a particular buyer requires a recapture of the building portion of the price in 10 years, what is the indicated recapture rate for the building, assuming straight-line recapture?
   (a) 5%
   (b) 10%
   (c) 20%
   (d) 2%

9. Recapture of the investment capital in real estate finance is that portion of the loan payment that is earmarked for:
   (a) Interest on money due
   (b) Payoff of principal
   (c) Interest and principal payment
   (d) None of the above

10. A new building of 10,000 square feet has just been constructed at a location where no recent vacant land sales have occurred and competitive investments earn 10% interest. The replacement cost is $400,000. Assuming a useful life expectancy of 25 years, an economic rent of $1 per square foot per month, and annual expenses of $30,000 including vacancy, what total property value is indicated?
    (a) $740,000
    (b) $900,000
    (c) $1,200,000
    (d) $400,000

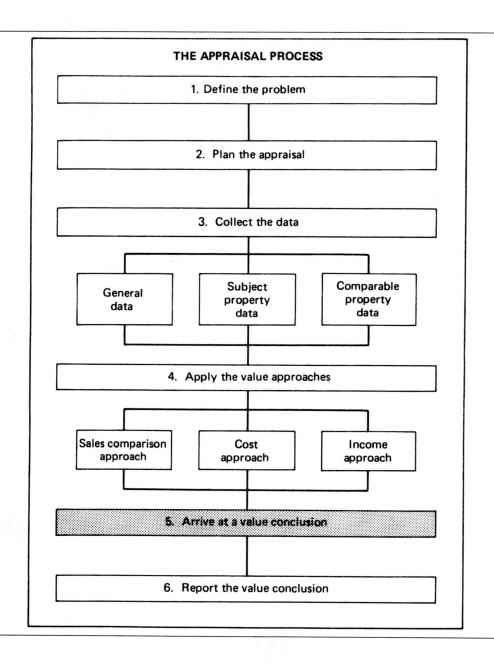

THE APPRAISAL PROCESS

1. Define the problem

2. Plan the appraisal

3. Collect the data

| General data | Subject property data | Comparable property data |

4. Apply the value approaches

| Sales comparison approach | Cost approach | Income approach |

5. Arrive at a value conclusion

6. Report the value conclusion

Chapter 15
Reconciling the Value Estimates

Preview   After the appraiser has processed each of the three approaches, the three value indications that have been developed must be reduced to a single opinion of value. The process that the appraiser follows to do this is called *reconciliation*. This chapter will explain that process.

When you have completed this chapter, you should be able to:

1. *Define the term reconciliation.*

2. *Explain why the appraiser must review each value approach that has been used.*

3. *Explain why the appraiser reviews the data used in each approach.*

4. *Show how to round the final answer.*

15.1 GENERAL REVIEW OF THE APPRAISAL

In order to arrive at a value conclusion, the appraiser must review the appraisal itself. The appraiser must be satisfied that an adequate appraisal was performed before reconciliation begins. This review can be divided into two steps:

> 1. Review the overall appraisal process.
>
> 2. Review for technical accuracy.

Reviewing the Appraisal Process

The first step is to reconsider the overall appraisal assignment. What was the appraisal to accomplish? Have you (1) precisely located and identified the property, (2) clearly defined the property rights to be appraised, (3) pinpointed the date as of which the value estimate applies, and (4) given a formal definition of the type of value stated as the purpose of the appraisal?

In reviewing the data collected and analyzed, have you considered (1) the type of property being appraised, and (2) the purpose of the appraisal? Depending on the property type and the purpose of the appraisal, one of the three value approaches may be most relevant. The appraiser should now go back and apply any important approach that might have been omitted.

Technical Review

The next step in this review process is a clerical check for possible errors. First, all calculations should be checked for accuracy. All critical measurements should be reviewed as well. Second, all data should be checked for completeness and accuracy. Were the data complete and adequate for the purpose for which they were used? Third, the appraiser should check for consistency. Was the highest and best use of the site used as the basis for its value? Is the property age used in the sales comparison approach the same in the cost approach? Were the desirable features rated in the sales comparison approach also considered in estimating rents for the income approach? Was any economic or functional obsolescence in the cost approach also adjusted for in the sales comparison and income approaches? A positive answer to these and similar questions will ensure that the data in the appraisal have been processed in a consistent manner.

Finally, the last step in this technical review is to reconsider any assumptions made during the appraisal. Now that the appraisal has been completed and the appraiser has the benefit of added insight into the market gained from the various approaches used, do the adjustments, judgment, or assumptions used in each approach appear as appropriate, reasonable, and sensible as they did when first employed? This is another way of checking for consistency.

15.2 RECONCILING THE VALUE APPROACHES

Reconciliation has been defined as:

> The process by which the appraiser evaluates, chooses, and selects from among two or more alternative conclusions or indications to reach a single answer (final value estimate). Preferable terminology to the traditional term correlation.*

Appraising the Appraisal

Once an overall review of the appraisal has been made, the process of reconciliation then requires an evaluation of each value approach to estimate its overall relevance and accuracy. The key questions in this evaluation are

1. How appropriate is this approach in this case?

2. How relevant, reliable, and adequate were the data used?

3. What range of values do the three approaches suggest, and what does the value indication of each tell you about the others?

How Appropriate Is the Approach?

Having completed the approaches, how accurate and relevant is each? What does each tell you about the importance of the others? The validity or relevance of each approach to value depends first on the purpose of the appraisal. In this book, our emphasis has been on using appraisals to estimate market value. However, there can be purposes for an appraisal other than estimating market value. For example, appraisals for insurance purposes may call for an emphasis on the cost approach.

The *type* of property plays a role in determining which value approach is used. It usually makes little sense to use an income approach when you are appraising an individual vacant lot. The sales comparison approach would be more logical. Similarly, you would normally use the sales comparison approach when appraising a single-family residence or, for that matter, any property in an area where good comparable sales are in ample supply.

The use of the appropriate approach can also depend on the state of the market. In some markets, for example, single-family homes are rarely bought and sold for their income characteristics. In such markets, an income approach would not be appropriate. In other markets, however, single-family homes may be sought for their income advantages; here the income approach might be the more appropriate.

Finally, you must consider the characteristics of each approach. Each has its strengths. Each has its weaknesses. In a particular case, the strength of one approach may be important; the weakness of another may disqualify it. Your intent throughout is to form an opinion on the relative reliability of each approach in this appraisal.

*B. N. Boyce, *Real Estate Appraisal Terminology,* rev. ed., Ballinger Publishing Co., Cambridge, Mass., 1981.

Evaluating the Data   The next step in the reconciliation process is to consider the relevance, reliability, and adequacy of the data used in each approach. In turn, this step takes you closer to a conclusion about the *reliability* of the approach itself. Each approach must base its conclusions on evidence that is not only pertinent to that approach, but also reliable enough to support its validity. Finally, the quantity of data must be sufficient to have provided a reasonable range of market indicators, and to have supported the techniques used in making the adjustments required. An old appraisal saying is that "One swallow doesn't mark the arrival of spring, nor does one sale make the market."

As part of this review of the data used, the appraiser should consider all the assumptions made in the processing of the data used in each approach. Did the sales require large amounts of adjustment? Were the adjustments well supported? Have replacement costs been based upon consumer-level costs of similar buildings and adjusted to this location? Were the conclusions of market rent, and other critical factors used in the income approach, based on well supported assumptions? These are the kinds of questions that the appraiser needs to ask at this point in the appraisal. And finally, the approach that is deemed the more reliable in the appraisal at hand should be given the greater weight in arriving at a final value conclusion, because that approach is the most relevant, and has in fact been supported by adequate and reliable data.

The Value Range   The last step in reviewing the approaches is to develop a range of values. It is important to note that each approach to value tells you something about the reliability of the other two approaches. Traditionally, experts have said that the cost approach sets the upper limit of value. Most appraisal theoreticians now say that depreciated replacement cost does not set the upper limit. Depending on the types of judgment errors made in the cost approach, it is just as conceivable that, in a particular circumstance, the cost approach will be at the lower limit.

In any one appraisal, the appraiser may have a hunch that one or another approach is likely to result in a value that is high or low. For example, in appraising a home in an area that is primarily owner-occupied, it is possible (but not certain) that the income approach would produce a lower estimate of value than the other approaches. This could depend on how the appraiser came up with the capitalization rate, among other possibilities. Similarly, in appraising a house that may have some economic obsolescence, the cost approach could be higher than the sales comparison approach, particularly if an economic obsolescence deduction had not been calculated. Here is where the appraiser relies on the economic principles that were developed in Chapter 5. By applying these principles to the region, city, and neighborhood, with facts relevant to a particular appraisal, the appraiser can better judge the reliability of each of the three approaches to decide whether they have established a reasonable range of value.

After a review of the three conclusions, you will see that there is a highest number and a lowest number. This suggests the probable range of minimum-maximum value. The reliability of each approach influences the reliability of this range. Sometimes, you may conclude that the approach with the lowest figure probably is a low estimate of value, so your own evaluation of an approach suggests whether it is high or low. Comparing its value conclusion to the conclusions from the other two approaches gives you a cross-check. In addition, two of the three approaches clustering at one end of the range could lead you to pick a value toward that end of the range. At this point, then, the appraiser reviews (1) the reliability of each approach, (2) what value each one indicates, and (3) which values are high and which are low.

Reviewing the Theory of the Approaches

Each approach has its own characteristic strengths and weaknesses. Depending on the type of property and the quality and quantity of evidence considered, a particular approach may deserve more weight or less weight in arriving at a value conclusion. (See Figure 15.1.)

The sales comparison approach, for example, is often considered to be the most direct approach. Because of the usually ample sales data, it often should receive the greatest weight in valuing residences. Depending on the quality of the comparable sales, the sales comparison approach is also considered the best evidence in an appraisal performed for condemnation (eminent domain). However, the sales comparison approach requires that there be comparable sales, that reasonable numbers of sales be available, and that the adjustments to the sales be relatively minor or else fairly well supported.

Figure 15.1
Reconciliation and Value Conclusion.

The cost approach is often cited as being especially useful when new buildings are being appraised. In addition, it is considered as the only way to appraise building types that do not rent *and* are rarely

---

RECONCILIATION AND VALUE CONCLUSION

Indicated Value by the Cost Approach . . . . $ 282,500

Indicated Value by the Sales Comparison Approach . . $ 280,000

Indicated Value by the Income Approach . . . $ 276,500

FINAL RECONCILIATION: In this appraisal, the income approach deserves the least weight because very few homes in the area are rented. While the cost and market indications are fairly close together, the market is the more reliable because of the large depreciation estimate.

As a result of my investigation and analysis, my estimate of Market Value of the subject property as of _____ 7/14 _____ 19 92 is . . . .

$ 280,000

Date 7/20/92 _____ Appraiser Ernest Hemingway III

bought or sold. Examples could include special-purpose or public buildings, certain factories, churches, and so on. Major problems with the cost approach include the difficulty in estimating indirect costs such as the developer's and builder's profit and overhead allowance.

Another problem with the cost approach is in estimating the amount of accrued depreciation, especially with an older building. Depreciation is also difficult to estimate for misplaced improvements or for buildings suffering from other forms of unusual obsolescence. However, even with its weaknesses, the cost approach is still useful as a check on the other approaches.

The income approach is particularly useful when appraising types of properties that are usually purchased as investments, based on their ability to generate income. However, the income approach requires adequate and reliable market data on such factors as rents, expenses, and capitalization rates and techniques. For example, adjusting the capitalization rate for differences between the comparables and the subject property may require documenting changes in rates over time. Other difficult adjustments may be involved. Small errors in the data used in the income approach can cause large errors in the final value conclusion.

Reaching a Final Value Estimate

At the end of this entire process, the appraiser normally reaches a single estimate of value. In a few appraisal assignments, however, a range of value will suffice if specifically called for by the appraisal assignment and the agreement with the client. There is no magic method to reach a final value conclusion. It is rarely a mathematical average of the three value indications, but is sometimes justifiably a weighted average of the three. This means that the three indications are averaged, allotting, for example, twice as much weight to one approach, an average weight to the second approach, and a half a weight to the third approach. However, this often implies a mathematical accuracy that is probably not warranted. In particular, there may be subjective questions that cannot be handled by any weighing process. (See Figure 15.2.)

Of all the steps in the appraisal process, arriving at and explaining the final value conclusion may be one of the most difficult and subjective. However, if the reconciliation process that we have outlined

Figure 15.2
Reconciling the Value Indications on the URAR form.

This appraisal is made [X] "as is" ☐ subject to the repairs, alterations, inspections, or conditions listed below ☐ subject to completion per plans and specifications.	
Conditions of Appraisal:	

Final Reconciliation: Although not weighed heavily, the cost approach tends to confirm the value indicated by the sales comparison approach here. The income approach has not been tested, as inapplicable in this owner-occupied area.

The purpose of this appraisal is to estimate the market value of the real property that is the subject of this report, based on the above conditions and the certification, contingent and limiting conditions, and market value definition that are stated in the attached Freddie Mac Form 439/Fannie Mae Form 1004B (Revised _____).

I (WE) ESTIMATE THE MARKET VALUE, AS DEFINED, OF THE REAL PROPERTY THAT IS THE SUBJECT OF THIS REPORT, AS OF June 24, 1993 (WHICH IS THE DATE OF INSPECTION AND THE EFFECTIVE DATE OF THIS REPORT) TO BE $ _275,000_ .

APPRAISER:	SUPERVISORY APPRAISER (ONLY IF REQUIRED):		
Signature	Signature	☐ Did	☐ Did Not
Name Green Clay	Name	Inspect Property	
Date Report Signed June 24, 1993	Date Report Signed		
State Certification # AR0067** State CA	State Certification #		State
Or State License #	Or State License #		State

Freddie Mac Form 70   6-93
Software by Dynamic Computing (314) 644-1802

PAGE 2 OF 2

Fannie Mae Form 1004   6-93

---

above is carefully followed, the appraiser will have developed a factual basis from which to draw a reliable opinion. The appraiser will then be able to report the factors that were considered, such as the strengths and weaknesses of the approaches and the data that were developed.

15.3 ROUNDING THE ANSWER

Throughout the appraisal process, we are working with numbers, from defining the square footage of an area to estimating the value of a subject property. One of the characteristics of a number is how many significant digits it has. The significant digits are those that go from the first numeral on the left over to the last figure on the right that is not a zero. For example, "10" has only one significant digit, while "111" has three. A number calculated in an appraisal might contain all significant digits, for example, $85,319.27. However, a final value conclusion might be presented with differing numbers of significant digits, depending on the appraisal process and the data used. Thus one appraiser's reconciliation process could lead to a value conclusion of $230,000 (two significant digits). On the same property, another appraiser, perhaps relying on another technique, might conclude a value of $233,495 (six significant digits). To the layman, this difference might suggest that the second appraisal conclusion is more accurate than the first. In fact, the two appraisals may be of *equal* accuracy. Accordingly, it can be misleading for the appraiser to use a larger number of significant digits in the final answer than are warranted. In other words, should that second figure, $233,495, be rounded to $233,500, or to $234,000, or to $235,000, or to $230,000, or even to $250,000?

The General Rule

There is a general rule that the appraiser should follow: The answer to any mathematical step should not be reported with any more significant digits than the smallest number of significant digits occurring in any number used. If $36,312.67 is multiplied by 8.7, the answer, $315,920.22, is only *mathematically* accurate as $320,000. If accrued depreciation in the cost approach is estimated to be 20%, this is a number with one significant digit. It follows that carrying the cost approach conclusion to four significant digits implies greater accuracy than is really there.

In the reconciliation process, however, we are analyzing alternate value indications, usually of differing precision. The cost approach might have only two significant digits, whereas the income approach, say, has three. Because these can be argued to be independent of each other, it is acceptable to round the final value conclusion to an intermediate accuracy.

General Practice

There are no standards of practice for rounding. However, few appraisers report their final conclusion rounded to just one significant digit, for example, $100,000 or $200,000. Instead, appraisers generally round their conclusion to either two, two and one-half, or three significant digits. An answer rounded to two significant digits could be $140,000, $260,000, and so on. When an answer is rounded to two and one-half significant digits, the third digit is either a zero or a five, and no other number. Examples of answers rounded to two and one-half digits would be $145,000, $97,500, and even $220,000. (The last number was rounded from $222,000. Here $220,000 is closer than $225,000.) Answers to three significant digits might be $322,000 or $37,600. Usually, appraisers carry out intermediate answers to more digits than the final answer. Depending on the accuracy of the data, then, appraisers might just round the indicated value of each approach to three or four digits.

SUMMARY

After a value indication has been reached for each of the three approaches, the appraiser must then reduce these values to a single estimate. This process is called reconciliation.

Before reconciliation begins, a review of the overall appraisal process should be made. Such factors as the purpose of the appraisal, the approaches used, and the data collected should be re-evaluated. The question is: Was the appraisal correctly performed? A check for technical accuracy should also be made. Are your figures, sources, data, and other information correct? Now that the appraisal is completed, do you feel that your initial assumptions, adjustments, and use of judgment are still accurate? These are just a few of the questions you could ask yourself before actual reconciliation begins.

The first step in the reconciliation process is to evaluate the reliability of each approach. Carefully review the purpose of the appraisal: Perhaps the intent of the report naturally calls for greater weight on one approach over others. Such factors as the type of property can determine if one approach should be considered over others. It is important to understand the strengths and weaknesses of each approach in order to decide which approach is likely to give the most reliable answer.

The next step in the reconciliation process is to consider if the data used were adequate and reliable. Since each approach is based in part on data, it is the accuracy of each approach that plays a major part in how you select the final value conclusion. Were enough data used to provide reasonable support for the conclusion of the approach? The approach that has the most accurate and adequate data could have the greatest influence on the final value conclusion.

The last step in reconciliation is to develop a range of values. After reviewing all the approaches, you will probably find a high number and a low number. These two figures can *usually* be considered as the maximum-minimum range of value. However, many factors, such as the accuracy of the data collected, can influence these maximum-minimum figures.

At the end of this process, a final value conclusion is normally reached. Arriving at a final conclusion involves many considerations. It usually is not the averaging of the three approaches. It requires the use of judgment—reflection on all of the factors involved in the appraisal and on your subjective or intuitive experience. Combined, these factors should result in a final conclusion.

Once your conclusion has been reached, you may then want to round your answer. There are no set standards for rounding. Most appraisers usually round to either two, two and one-half, or three significant digits. However, the answer for each appraisal assignment should be rounded according to the limits of the data found in that appraisal.

Important Terms and Concepts

Consistency	Reconciliation
Evaluating data	Rounding the answer
Final conclusion of value	Significant digits
Judgment errors	Technical review
Range of values	Value indications

REVIEWING YOUR UNDERSTANDING

1. Before reconciliation begins, the appraiser should:
   (a) Review the overall appraisal process
   (b) Review for technical accuracy
   (c) Both of the above
   (d) None of the above

2. Briefly, reconciliation is defined as:
   (a) An estimate of value
   (b) One of the three approaches
   (c) The process by which the appraiser evaluates, chooses, and selects from among two or more alternative indications to reach a single answer.
   (d) All of the above

3. Reconciliation is important because:
   (a) It is intended to find any possible errors in your appraisal that you may have overlooked
   (b) It can help you to see if the appraisal is accurate and reliable
   (c) It leads to the final value conclusion of the appraisal
   (d) All of the above

4. Appraising the appraisal means asking:
   (a) How appropriate is each approach?
   (b) How much data were used?
   (c) How reliable are the data?
   (d) What range of values do the approaches suggest?
   (e) All of the above

5. In the review of the approaches used, the type of property is:
   (a) Not an important factor
   (b) An important factor
   (c) Important only to the income approach
   (d) The only factor to consider

6. Each value approach has its own strengths and weaknesses. In arriving at a final value conclusion, you should:
   (a) Choose the approach that is the most popular

(b) Emphasize the approach that has the most available data

(c) Weigh the strengths and weaknesses of each approach, as well as the reliability of the data collected

(d) None of the above

7. In evaluating the data you used in each approach, it is important to check and see if:
(a) You have collected enough data
(b) The data are reliable and relevant
(c) The adjustments are well supported
(d) Two of the above
(e) All of the above

8. How many significant digits are there in $135,000?
(a) 5
(b) 3
(c) 6
(d) 2.5

9. Which is the correctly rounded answer to $16,280 divided by 11.3%?
(a) $144,071
(b) $144,070.80
(c) $144,100
(d) $144,000

10. Rounding the final appraisal answer to *three* or more significant digits when the numbers used in all the approaches contained as few as *two* significant digits:
(a) Can be helpful to the client
(b) Is simply a matter of appraisal judgment
(c) Is mathematically justified
(d) Can suggest more accuracy than the data warrants

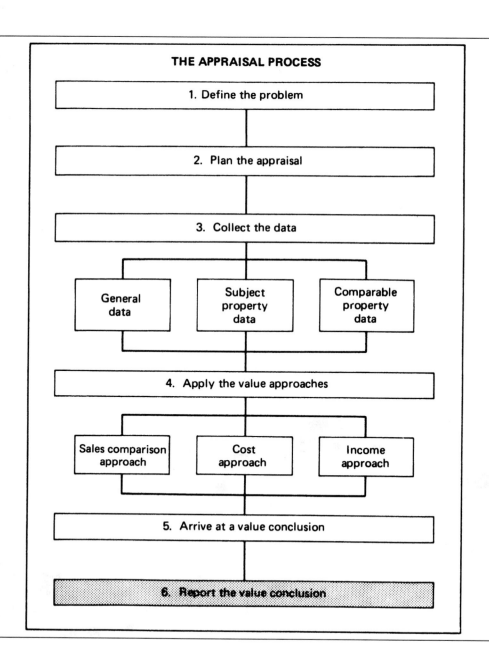

THE APPRAISAL PROCESS

1. Define the problem

2. Plan the appraisal

3. Collect the data

| General data | Subject property data | Comparable property data |

4. Apply the value approaches

| Sales comparison approach | Cost approach | Income approach |

5. Arrive at a value conclusion

6. Report the value conclusion

Chapter 16
Reporting Appraisal Opinions

Preview   The appraisal report is a formal communication that details the investigation the appraiser has made on behalf of the client. Whether oral or delivered as a letter, form, or narrative document, the appraisal report must contain certain minimum elements that are required for practical and professional reasons which have evolved over 50 years of appraisal theory and practice.

In this chapter, we shall cover the basic elements of appraisal reports and describe the three types of written reports most commonly used. The chapter concludes with a detailed outline of the narrative appraisal report and a sample URAR, complete with attachments (see end of chapter).

When you have completed this chapter, you should be able to:

1. *Discuss the twelve essential elements of a written appraisal report.*

2. *Describe the three types of written appraisal reports and suggest whether they meet the requirements imposed on federally related appraisals.*

3. *Outline the contents of a narrative appraisal report.*

16.1 ESSENTIAL ELEMENTS OF APPRAISAL REPORTS

In the past, the form and content of appraisal reports were governed simply by good business practice and appraisal tradition. Now, there are legal and professional considerations as well, particularly for appraisals made in conjunction with federally related real estate financial transactions such as government-insured loans.

Practical Considerations

Written appraisal reports are a form of business communication. This means that every report should be concise, well organized, and easy to read. In particular, the writer must consider the knowledge level of the probable readers, and define technical terms as necessary to ensure comprehension.

All written appraisals should contain only that information which relates to the appraisal problem, yet should be adequate in scope to meet the client's needs. Extraneous data should be omitted, and all pertinent data should be incorporated into the report in a logical order and in nontechnical terms.

Legal and Professional Requirements

Professional standards of leading appraisal groups have long required that most appraisal reports contain the key facts and elements necessary to support the value opinion. Now, Title XI of the Federal Financial Institutions Reform, Recovery, and Enforcement Act of 1989 (known as FIRREA), requires (with certain exceptions to be noted in the next section) that all federally-related appraisals conform to the Uniform Standards of Professional Appraisal Practice (commonly called USPAP).

Now endorsed by all leading appraisal institutions, USPAP requires that each written or oral real property appraisal report 1) "clearly and accurately set forth the appraisal in a manner that will not be misleading", 2) "contain sufficient information to enable the person(s) who receive or rely on the report to understand it properly", and 3) "clearly and accurately disclose any extraordinary assumption or limiting condition that directly affects the appraisal and indicate its impact on value".

It should be noted that professional appraisal standards for both appraising and reporting are in a constant state of change. USPAP in particular is regarded as a dynamic standard, one that is constantly being revised and updated. The standards required for federally related appraisals are also constantly changing. This means that appraisers whose professional affiliation, state license/certification, or work requires them to conform to these standards must make every effort to stay current with the changes.

Outline of Essential Elements

Subject to certain exclusions, the Uniform Standards of Professional Appraisal Practice require that each written, self-contained report contain the following elements:

1. Identify and describe the real estate being appraised.
2. Identify the real property interest being appraised.

3. State the purpose of the appraisal.

4. Define the value to be estimated.

5. Set forth the effective date of the appraisal and the date of the report.

6. Describe the extent of the process of collecting, confirming, and reporting data.

7. Set forth all assumptions and limiting conditions that affect the analyses, opinions, and conclusions.

8. Set forth the information considered, the appraisal procedures followed, and the reasoning that supports the analyses, opinions, and conclusions.

9. Set forth the appraiser's opinion of the highest and best use of the real estate being appraised when such an opinion is necessary and appropriate.

10. Explain and support the exclusion of any of the usual valuation approaches.

11. Set forth any additional information that may be appropriate to show compliance with, or clearly identify and explain permitted departures from the requirements of Standard 1. (The latter requires that the appraiser be aware of, understand, and correctly employ those recognized methods and techniques which are necessary to produce a credible appraisal.)

12. Include the appraiser's signed certification.

In summary, all written appraisal reports should define the appraisal problem and present at least a summary of both the factual data revealed by the study and the analysis that supports the stated opinion of value. With the appraisal report requirements in a constant state of change, all professional appraisers should stay up-to-date in their particular areas of practice.

The required elements of federally related appraisals go beyond those described above, specifically listing certain data requirements and detail that we will cover in the next section.

16.2 TYPES OF WRITTEN APPRAISAL REPORTS

The type of appraisal report to be used should be agreed upon in advance by the client and the appraiser. As a general rule, the type of report depends on the amount of background information and detail required by the client and the written format that best serves the intended use of the report itself. In the case of federally related appraisals, appraisal reports must be presented in a narrative format, or on forms that satisfy specific requirements that will be discussed later on.

There are three general types of written reports: the letter, the form, and the narrative report.

The Letter Report

The letter appraisal report is a short business letter generally defining the appraisal assignment, with a brief summary of the investigation made by the appraiser and an opinion of value for the property in question. Its length is likely to be between three and six pages.

A letter report should contain all the essential elements of an appraisal report. Usually, however, the description of the subject property is brief, and only a summary of the factual data and its analysis is presented. Exhibits such as a plot plan, floor plan, and pictures may be attached to the report if needed.

In most cases, supporting data are included in the letter report only by reference. For example, comparable sales data usually would be summarized in the report itself, with the specific details about each transaction retained in the appraiser's files. However, the assumptions, limiting conditions, and appraiser's value certification must always be included. (Section 16.3 will provide examples.)

It is important to note that letter reports may *not* comply with the full reporting requirements set forth in Standard 2 of the Uniform Standards of Professional Appraisal Practice. Unless they fall below a regulated minimal transaction level, those that depart from the reporting requirements of a complete appraisal are generally not acceptable for government insured loan appraisals, or for government property acquisition.

Among appraisers who are required to conform to USPAP, there is some controversy about the minimum content of letter reports, and whether such reports are acceptable at all. For appraisals that are *not* federally related, some professional groups allow their members to use letter reports, but *only* under the "departure" provision of USPAP. The standards in this area are still evolving.

The Form (or Short-Form) Report

Institutions and agencies that regularly contract for appraisals usually require the use of a standard form appraisal report. Forms are preferred because they are usually designed in a checklist format on a printed page. The types of data commonly required are also presented in a sequence that is easy to review. Most appraisal forms also provide blank spaces for the appraiser to use for additional analysis and comment.

Although designed along similar guidelines, many variations of the form report are available today. Some agencies and appraisal services develop their own forms for each property type. Written instructions for completion are sometimes prepared. Single-family residential, condominium, multifamily residential, and commercial are examples of standard forms currently available.

The increased use of computers to prepare appraisal reports has led to programs that allow easy production of the more common form reports. Some programs check math, store and recall comparable sales or selections of remarks for specific report sections, or prepare plot plans or floor plans. Newer programs print both the form and its contents on a laser printer, simplifying report production.

The URAR Form   The most common form report in use today for loan appraisals is the URAR (Uniform Residential Appraisal Report), also known as the Freddie Mac Form 70 or the Fannie Mae Form 1004. These forms are required by the Federal Home Loan Mortgage Corporation, the Federal National Mortgage Association, the Veterans Administration, and the Federal Housing Agency for single-family appraisals. When properly prepared, the URAR satisfies the form and content requirements of the USPAP and those of federally related appraisals. Most lenders have adopted the URAR form for conventional mortgage loans in order to be able to sell mortgages in the secondary mortgage market.

The URAR contains all the basic elements of an appraisal. The form defines the appraisal problem, presents factual data revealed in the appraisal study, and demonstrates evidence of value through the cost, sales comparison, and income approaches. In federally related appraisals, attachments to the URAR form should include a complete legal description (where too long to appear on the form itself), location and plat maps (the former showing the location of the subject property and the comparables), a diagram or sketch of improvements, and a Freddie Mac Form 439 (or Fannie Mae Form 1004B). The latter attachment contains a formal definition of market value and the appraiser's certification and statement of limiting conditions. Photographs of the subject property as well as of the comparables complete the report. A sample URAR appraisal, with attachments, is shown in Figures 16.6 through 16.11, which follow the review material at the end of this chapter.

The Federal National Mortgage Association publishes written guidelines on how to complete the URAR. The Fannie Mae guidelines present rather definite and concrete information for completing URAR forms. Changes in statutes, case law, market conditions, technology, and appraisal theory will, of course, necessitate periodic revisions in the guidelines. The appraiser should always review current guidelines before attempting to fill out the URAR form.

The Narrative Appraisal Report   The narrative appraisal report is the most formal of the written appraisal reports. Ranging from a dozen to a hundred pages or more in length, this type of appraisal is most often required by large corporations and government agencies. As already indicated, all federally related appraisals must be presented in a narrative format or on forms that satisfy specific requirements.

Narrative reports are preferred when the user needs a self-contained document in which all the pertinent facts discovered in the investigation are presented under one cover. Because of the high standards expected of this type of report, the preparation of a narrative report is often required as a test of competence for the appraiser seeking a professional designation.

What to Include   Over the years, a number of government agencies, lenders, and other users of appraisals have each developed unique requirements for narrative reports. For example, the General Services Administration of

16.2 Types of Written Appraisal Reports   **365**

the Federal Government has a very long and detailed outline that must be followed, as do many municipal, state and federal agencies and courts. Perhaps the most detailed outlines of narrative reports are those issued by the appraisal societies for demonstration appraisals. These are available to the general public in outline form at nominal cost.

Outline of the Narrative Report

One very acceptable format for narrative appraisal reports divides the report into the three main sections that follow. Some appraisers further subdivide the middle section into two parts, separating description from analyses and conclusion.

---

1. Introduction.

2. Description, analyses, and conclusion.

3. Addenda.

The three main subdivisions of the narrative appraisal report include the following items and features:

A. Introduction
1. Title page
2. Letter of transmittal
3. Table of contents
4. Photograph of the subject
5. Summary of salient facts and conclusions

B. Description, Analyses, and Conclusion
1. Identification of the property
2. Sales history of the subject property
3. Objectives of the appraisal
   (a) Property rights appraised
   (b) Date of value estimate
   (c) Purpose of appraisal
   (d) Definition of value sought
   (e) Intended use of the appraisal report
   (f) Standards of conformity (e.g., USPAP)
4. Description of neighborhood and community; current market conditions
5. Description of land, zoning, community services, and taxes
6. Description of improvements
7. Highest and best use analysis
8. Analysis of data by the value approaches
   (a) The cost approach
   (b) The sales comparison approach
   (c) The income approach
9. Reconciliation and final conclusion of value

10. Qualifying and limiting conditions
11. Certification, with the signature of the appraiser
12. Qualifications of the appraiser

C. Addenda or Supporting Material
   1. Maps, plats, and photographs
   2. Plot plan of subject property
   3. Complete legal description
   4. Diagram of improvements
   5. Statistical data
   6. Sales data sheets and sale location maps

Specific guidelines for expanding the narrative appraisal report outline will be provided in the next section of this chapter.

Format Variations

In actual practice, appraisal reports often mix the features of the three types of reports we have described. For example, letter reports sometimes extend in length to become what could be called short narrative-type reports. Other written appraisal reports will often mix the features of the letter, form, and narrative appraisal reports to best suit the needs of the client or the style of the appraisal. Most appraisal offices have developed their own formats as needed for the types of appraisals that their group performs. Where reports are prepared on a personal computer or word processor, a sample or outline will usually be stored in memory. In this way, the headings, subheadings, introductory sentences and definitions will be called up and reused or modified to suit the particular assignment.

Federally Related Appraisals

As already noted, federal regulations require that most real estate appraisals used in connection with federally related transactions be performed in writing, and in accordance with uniform standards that go beyond the requirements of USPAP. Specifically affected agencies include the National Credit Union Administration, the Office of Thrift Supervision, the Office of the Comptroller of the Currency, the Federal Deposit Insurance Corporation, and the Federal Reserve System, as well as all the regulated institutions of each entity. With exceptions to be noted at the end of this topic, the standards of the listed agencies currently require that federally related appraisals performed for institutions under their jurisdiction shall at a minimum:

1. Conform to the Uniform Standards of Professional Appraisal Practice (*without* the Departure provisions).

2. Disclose any steps taken that were necessary or appropriate to comply with the Competency provision of USPAP.

3. Be based upon the definition of market value as set forth in USPAP.

4. Be written and presented in a narrative format or on forms that satisfy all these requirements.

5. Analyze and report in reasonable detail any prior sales of the property being appraised that occurred within one year for one- to four-unit residential property, and within three years for all others.

6. Analyze and report data on current revenues, expenses, and vacancies for the property if it is and will continue to be income producing.

7. Analyze and report a reasonable marketing period for the subject property.

8. Analyze and report on current marketing conditions and trends that will affect projected income or the absorption period, to the extent they affect the value of the subject property.

9. Analyze and report appropriate deductions and discounts for any proposed construction, or any completed properties that are partially leased, or leased at other than market rents as of the date of the appraisal, or any tract developments with unsold units.

10. Include in the certification required by USPAP an additional statement that the appraisal assignment was not based on a requested minimum valuation, a specific valuation, or the approval of a loan.

11. Contain sufficient supporting documentation with all pertinent information reported so that the appraiser's logic, reasoning, judgment, and analysis in arriving at a conclusion indicate to the reader the reasonableness of the market value reported.

12. Include a legal description of the real estate being appraised, in addition to the description required by the USPAP.

13. Identify and separately value any personal property, fixtures, or intangible items that are not real property but are included in the appraisal, and discuss the impact of their inclusion or exclusion on the estimate of market value.

14. Follow a reasonable valuation method that addresses the direct sales comparison, income, and cost approaches to market value, reconciles those approaches, and explains the elimination of each approach not used. If information required or deemed pertinent to the completion of an appraisal is unavailable, that fact shall be disclosed and explained in the appraisal.

Some federally related appraisals need not conform to USPAP standards, or the additional ones cited above, because they involve a type of transaction that is exempted by regulation (for example, low-valued loans). In such cases, federal rules currently allow some reports to be referred to as *evaluations* instead of appraisals. Please note that FIRREA standards are constantly changing in this area.

16.3 WRITING THE NARRATIVE APPRAISAL REPORT

Because of the detail and formality that are characteristic of the narrative appraisal report, this report should have the appearance of a professionally prepared document. It is customarily typed on quality paper and bound in a durable cover. A carelessly prepared report is suggestive of inferior effort put into the appraisal itself. Most narrative reports are now produced on a word processor with a spell checker. This has sharply reduced many typographical errors, but leads to noticeable errors of the types that most spell checkers miss, such as the misuse of *to, too,* and *two.* Word-processed reports also tend to have a better appearance, often with a flush right margin and varied styles of type for headings.

The style of writing, though formal, can be interesting if the writing is succinct and without redundancies. Information on a given topic should be confined to the pertinent subject area and not scattered throughout the narration. To help the client understand, visualize, and remember, topical paragraphs should be sequenced in a logical order. For example, when describing a residential neighborhood, you would cover: the location of the subject; a brief history of the general area; identification of the immediate neighborhood; residential quality; land uses; convenience of the subject property to commercial facilities; and proximity to schools, churches, and parks, approximately in this order.

The contents of the narrative appraisal report should communicate to the client what the appraiser has done, in a step-by-step logical sequence, describing the data gathered and analyzed and explaining the reasoning that leads to the value conclusion.

In this section, we shall cover the major subdivisions of the narrative appraisal report and the recommended content for each section.

Introductory Material

Title Page

The first page of the introductory material is the title page. The typical captions are: Property Address, Type of Property, Date of Value, and By Whom the Property Was Appraised.

Letter of Transmittal

The second page of the introductory material is the letter of transmittal. The form in which the letter is typed should comply with standard business correspondence. The letter is usually addressed to the client unless the appraiser has been instructed otherwise. The purpose of the letter is to present formally the appraisal report and its conclusion to the client. The following elements should be included:

1. Date of the letter.
2. Identification of the person requesting the appraisal.

3. Identification of the subject property.

4. The purpose of the appraisal and the property rights being appraised.

5. A statement that the appraiser has made an investigation and analysis to arrive at a value conclusion.

6. A statement that the letter is transmitting the appraisal report, often with the number of pages indicated.

7. Clear statement of any unusual assumptions or limiting conditions.

8. Reference to other assumptions and limiting conditions set forth in the report.

9. The date of value.

10. The value estimate.

11. The signature of the appraiser. The appraiser's license or certification number, if any, should also be given here.

Figure 16.1 is a sample letter, with each of the elements identified by number. Other pertinent data, such as a brief description of the property, may be included in the letter of transmittal.

Table of Contents

The third page of the introductory material is the table of contents. This lists the major topics as they appear in the report and supplies page numbers. Some report writers recommend that major tables and exhibits also be referenced here.

Photograph of the Subject

Often the introductory material next contains a photograph of the subject property or, perhaps, a map or aerial photograph showing its location.

Summary of Salient Facts and Conclusions

The last page of the introductory material contains a summary of salient facts and conclusions. Items often included are:

1. Location of the property.

2. Present ownership of the property.

3. Summary sales history of the subject property.

4. Date the appraisal was performed.

5. The effective date of value.

6. Type of property.

7. Land size.

8. Improvement size.

9. Age of improvements.

10. Zoning.

① January 19, 1993

Ms. Martha Harris
Senior Partner
Harris, Grimms, and Shelby
5000 Grand Ave., Suite #250
Fresno, CA 93706

Re: Appraisal Report:
③   1836 Alamo Street
              San Antonio, Texas

Dear Ms. Harris,

② In accordance with your request of December 11, 1992, I have personally inspected and made an appraisal of the single family residence referenced above, for the purpose of estimating its market value. A complete legal description of the property, and the definition of market value as used in this appraisal, are provided in the body of this report.

④ The property rights appraised are the fee simple ownership, as if the property were free of any leases, mortgages, or other liens. It is understood that this appraisal is to be used in connection with pending litigation.

⑤⑥ Your attention is invited to the enclosed appraisal report, containing the data and analyses that support the appraiser's opinion of value. The report also includes a statement of the assumptions and limiting conditions that apply to the appraisal. As in all such appraisals,
⑦ damage from wood-destroying organisms, if any, is assumed here to be corrected by the seller, or the repair cost deducted from the stated value opinion. As prepared and presented here, the appraisal and appraisal report are intended to comply with the Uniform Standards of Professional Appraisal Practice.

⑧ Subject to the assumptions and limiting conditions set forth, it is my opinion that the market value of the defined rights to the property commonly known as 1836 Alamo Street, San
⑨ Antonio, Texas, and further described herein, as of January 13, 1993, is the sum of:

⑩ **TWO HUNDRED AND EIGHTY-TWO THOUSAND DOLLARS**

($282,000)

Respectfully submitted,

⑪

George Burgoyne, MAI, SRA

GB:tnp

Figure 16.1
Letter of transmittal.

11. Present use.

12. Highest and best use.

13. Site value.

14. Value indicated by the cost approach.

15. Value indicated by the sales comparison approach.

16. Value indicated by the income approach.

17. Market value estimate.

The appraiser may include in this summary whatever additional information is considered important, such as any special conditions affecting value.

Description, Analyses, and Conclusion

This section follows the introductory material and contains the body of the report. Essentially, it outlines the appraisal process from start to conclusion.

Identification of the Property

The subject parcel should be clearly identified by street address and legal description. If the legal description is lengthy, it may be included in the addenda and simply referred to at this point. A map of the property is desirable if the legal description is difficult to follow.

Sales History of the Subject Property

The sales history should detail the price and terms of any sales or transfers of the subject property that have occurred within one year before the date of value for one- to four-family residential property, and within three years for all other property types. Any current option, listing, and/or offer involving the subject property should also be included. The relevance, if any, of the described information to the appraisal conclusion should be discussed.

Objectives of the Appraisal

The statement of objectives should include the following parts:

---

1. Property rights appraised.

2. The effective date of the appraisal.

3. Purpose of the appraisal and definition of value to be estimated.

4. Intended use of the appraisal report.

5. Standards of conformity (e.g., USPAP).

Description of Neighborhood and Community; Current Market Conditions

Neighborhood and community data should include a brief history of the area and the prominent physical, social, and economic factors. Such a profile should include the type of neighborhood, its growth rate, the trend of property values, an analysis of supply and demand factors, and the typical marketing time for properties like the subject property. To complete the profile, present land uses and land-use changes should be reported as well as predominant occupancies, vacancies, and typical housing prices. The intent is to draw a clear picture of the neighborhood for the reader. Usually, the quality and general appearance of the homes, main community interests, and sources of employment for the residents are included. Other nearby land uses and convenience to shopping, schools, cultural centers, and transportation routes are also described. When important observations and conclusions are made, they should always be accompanied by supporting facts. For example, neighborhood improvement or decline, if asserted, should be documented by reference to specific examples of improved or deteriorated property, or by reference to factual studies.

The amount and kind of detail included in this section depends on the purpose it will serve. Neighborhood and community data that are relevant to the type of property under appraisal should be emphasized. In the appraisal of income and investment properties, the report on neighborhood and community should not only include an analysis of current market conditions and the marketability of the subject property, but should also include all market factors that will directly affect projected income or the estimated absorption period (for rent-up or sell-off). Minimum requirements might include an inventory of existing space, a survey of rent and occupancy levels, and data on new construction in progress.

Land Data, Zoning, Services, and Taxes

Land site data, as discussed in Chapter 6, should present the physical characteristics, site location elements, and private and public restrictions of the subject property. Any easements should also be described and analyzed. Lot size and shape, street improvements, topography, and soil conditions should be described next, with reference to any maps, plats, and photographs included, either in the report or the addenda.

The precise zoning classification of the parcel needs to be identified as well as the municipality that has jurisdiction over the property. (Figure 16.2 is an example of a zoning map.) Also any special building restrictions or regulations must be described.

The availability of public utilities should be noted along with any problems regarding their reliability. For example, if a septic tank is used to dispose of sewage, it should be made known to the client. If there are questions about adequate drainage, they should be referred to the appropriate expert for study.

Based on the latest information available from the assessment roll, relevant property tax information should also be included in this section. When the appraiser has reason to expect a significant change in property taxes, information on the probable change should be provided here. For example, in some states property is reassessed upon property transfer or upon long-term lease agreement.

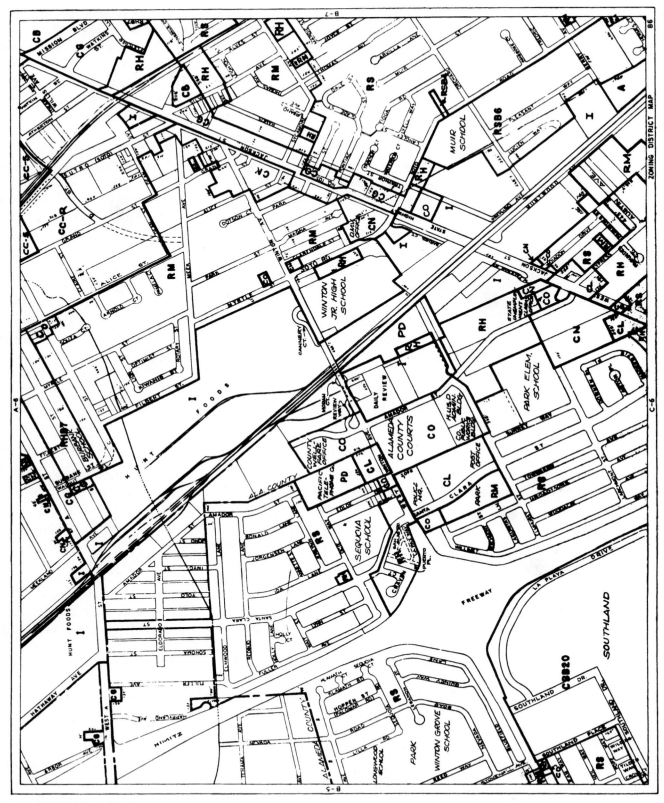

ZONING DISTRICT MAP B6

SEC. 10-1.136

Figure 16.2
Example of a zoning map.

Description of Improvements	Following the inspection guidelines covered in Chapter 7, the description of the improvements should include their physical features and also their condition, general marketability, and appeal. However, if detailed improvement specifications, blueprints, and photographs are to be included, they should probably be placed in the addenda of the report. Any deferred maintenance or apparent structural problems or defects noted during the improvement inspection must be carefully described in the body of the report.
Highest and Best Use	The appraiser's opinion of highest and best use must be stated here. If any use other than the present use is suggested, supporting evidence for such a conclusion should be discussed in detail in the report. The highest and best use statement should cover both the highest and best use of the site as if vacant and the highest and best use of the improved property.
Analysis of Data by the Value Approaches	It is helpful to introduce the value approaches used in the appraisal with a brief description of these methods. Their general strengths and weaknesses and their applicability to the appraisal should be explained. Some appraisers refer to this subsection as "methodology."
The Cost Approach	If structural improvements are included in the appraisal, the cost approach may be presented early or late in the value analysis, depending on its relative importance. The priority of sequence is sometimes interpreted to suggest emphasis. Land or site value should be based on one of the recognized methods of appraisal described in Chapter 10, with a full exposition of the market data leading to the conclusion. Data sheets on each sale are normally placed in the addenda. Improvement value should be demonstrated by an analysis of reproduction or replacement cost new, less the estimated total value loss as compared with the improvement as if it were new. A clear explanation of any deferred maintenance and any functional and/or economic obsolescence allowance should be provided.
The Sales Comparison Approach	The basic data to be included in the sales comparison approach are the pertinent facts about each comparable sale, and each listing used (the latter to show the trend of the market). In the appraisal of **single-family residential properties,** these facts usually include:

1. Names of buyer and seller.

2. Date of sale, date of recordation, and document number. In the case of listings, the type of listing, the date listed, and the dates of any changes in price or terms should be included.

3. Sale price and terms of sale or listing.

4. Lot size and shape.

5. Description of the residence, including square-foot size, number of rooms, number of bedrooms and baths, age and condition, type of construction, and character of outside improvements such as garage and swimming pool.

As already suggested, professional standards also require that the appraiser consider and analyze any current agreement of sale, option, or listing of the property being appraised, if such information is available in the normal course of business. In addition, prior sales must be considered and analyzed when they have occurred within one year for one- to four-family residential property, and within three years for all other property types. If any of the comparables are located in a speculative area, their sales history should be included also, with appropriate comments.

Most narrative appraisal reports present comparable sales in an abbreviated chart form (see Example 16.1) in the body of the report.

Example 16.1 Comparable Sales Chart

No.	Address	Price	Date	Quality	Condition	Lot (SF Size)	Building (SF Size)	Age
1	718 Stonewall	$562,000	1/93	Excellent	Good	8,850	4,811	1978
2	3921 Rose	450,000	7/92	Good	Good	7,250	3,830	1910
3	331 Oakridge	678,000	2/93	Good	Good	28,793	3,461	1952
4	7792 Crestor	477,000	2/93	Good	Average	15,000	3,136	1937
5	1864 Walnut	502,000	10/92	Excellent	Excellent	6,960	2,323	1925
6	8274 Alvarado	585,000	2/93	Excellent	Good	9,200	5,137	1914
7	Subject	—	2/93	Excellent	Very good	8,292	5,409	1907

All the details about the sales are recited in separate sales data sheets in the addenda. A sample sheet is presented in Figure 16.3.

The appraiser should include the following additional data for multiple-family residential sales:

1. Number, type, and size of units.

2. Sale price per unit, per room, and/or per square foot.

3. Gross scheduled rent.

4. Gross rent multiplier.

5. Expense ratio.

SALES DATA

ADDRESS: 1xxx Solano   **PARCEL:** 62-2872-xx

CITY: Berkeley

GRANTOR: Lola G. Smith

GRANTEE: James W. & Lynne H. Jones

DATE SOLD: 1/93   **DATE RECORDED:** 2/9/93

REEL: 2784   **IMAGE:** 26   **DOCUMENT:** 93-149

SALE PRICE: $225,000   **DOCUMENT STAMPS:** $247.50

SALE TERMS: $217,000 mortgage by seller, market rate, 10 year payoff   **CONFIRMED BY:** Seller's attorney and by buyer.

ZONE: Single family   **LOT AREA:** 6225 sq.ft.   **LOT SIZE:** Rectangle, 65 F.F., diagonal rear line.

IMPROVEMENTS: Wood frame residence, 1550 square feet   **STORIES:** 1   **AGE:** new 1926

ANALYSIS:
- Paid $145.16/S.F. of building.
- Rent was $1,000 at sale, raised to $1,125. Another $10 rent increase will go into effect next month because of increased taxes.
- At current rents, sold for 200 times monthly gross income.

Figure 16.3
A typical sales data sheet.

The Income Approach   In the case of income and investment properties, this section in the appraisal report should analyze and report current revenues, expenses, and vacancies for the subject property. Then it should outline and summarize the investigation made to estimate market rent, indicate appropriate capitalization methods, and show how rates of return for the subject property were derived. Specific properties studied should be cited. Then a reconstructed operating statement should be provided, along with a discussion presenting the basis for the expense projections. It is preferred that the income capitalization procedure be clearly demonstrated in formula form, with the process itself explained in a narrative fashion.

Reconciliation and Final Conclusion of Value

This section should describe the extent of the process of collecting, confirming, and reporting data. It should also summarize the information considered, the appraisal procedures followed, and the reasoning that supports the analyses, opinions, and conclusions.

This section should next review for the reader the findings of each value approach explored and should describe their relevance in this appraisal. If any of the usual approaches have been excluded, this should be explained and supported. The appraiser should also discuss the reliability of the data used and the applicability of each approach and, finally, should provide an argument to justify the final conclusion of value rendered.

Qualifying and Limiting Conditions

The statement of qualifying and limiting conditions serves to clarify the assumptions made by the appraiser, limit his or her legal liability, and define the rights of disclosure of information contained in the report. If the appraiser has not employed the recognized methods and techniques necessary to produce a credible appraisal, the reasons for such departure should be set forth and explained. A typical statement includes provisions as follows:

1. The appraiser assumes no responsibility for matters of a legal nature affecting the property.

2. Any sketch in the report may show approximate dimensions; the appraiser has made no survey of the property.

3. The appraiser is not required to give testimony or appear in court regarding the appraisal unless arrangements have been previously made.

4. Any distribution of values in the report between land and improvements applies only under the existing program of utilization and may not apply in other contexts.

5. The appraiser assumes that there are no hidden or unapparent conditions of the property, subsoil, or structures that would render it more or less valuable.

6. Information, estimates, and opinions furnished by others were obtained from sources considered reliable and believed to be true and correct, but no responsibility for the accuracy of such items is assumed by the appraiser.

7. Disclosure of the contents of the appraisal report is governed by the bylaws and regulations of the professional appraisal organizations with which the appraiser is affiliated.

8. Neither all nor any part of the content of the report, or copy thereof, shall be used for any purpose other than the purpose specified in the report without the previous written consent of the appraiser.

Certification   This is a signed statement that gives assurance of the appraiser's neutrality and responsibility. In order to comply with good appraisal practice and the Uniform Standards of Professional Appraisal Practice, each written real estate appraisal report must contain a certification that is similar in content to the following form:

I certify that, to the best of my knowledge and belief:

The statements of fact contained in this report are true and correct.

The reported analyses, opinions, and conclusions are limited only by the reported assumptions and limiting conditions, and are my personal, unbiased professional analyses, opinions, and conclusions.

I have no (or the specified) present or prospective interest in the property that is the subject of this report, and I have no (or the specified) personal interest or bias with respect to the parties involved.

My compensation is not contingent upon the reporting of a predetermined value or direction in value that favors the cause of the client, the amount of the value estimate, the attainment of a stipulated result, or the occurrence of a subsequent event.

My analyses, opinions, and conclusions were developed, and this report has been prepared, in conformity with the Uniform Standards of Professional Appraisal Practice.

I have (or have not) made a personal inspection of the property that is the subject of this report. (If more than one person signs the report, this certification must clearly specify which individuals did, and which individuals did not, make a personal inspection of the appraised property.)

No one provided significant professional assistance to the person signing this report. (If there are exceptions, the name of each individual providing significant professional assistance must be stated, along with a description of each one's contribution.)

For all federally related appraisals, the appraiser's certification should also disclose any steps taken that were necessary to comply with the competency provision of USPAP. Also, the following statement should be added:

This appraisal assignment was not based on a requested minimum valuation, a specific valuation, or the approval of a loan.

Qualifications of the Appraiser	This is usually a one- or two-page biosketch of the appraiser, outlining his or her credentials, education and experience. Any state appraiser license or certification held should be described as well as professional designations. The list of qualifications often cites important appraisals made as well as significant leadership activity, real estate teaching experience, and titles of any published writings. The appraiser's qualifications serve not only to suggest the level of confidence to be placed in the value investigation but also to indicate whether the appraiser would probably be considered by a judge as qualified to testify as an expert witness if such service is ever required. A sample qualifications sheet is shown in Figure 16.4.

Addenda or Supporting Material

The addenda should contain any relevant data not included in the body of the report. Examples include:

> 1. Maps (Figures 16.7 and 16.8) or photographs (Figure 16.11).
>
> 2. Plot plan of the subject property (see Figure 16.5).
>
> 3. Floor plan or diagram of improvements (see Figure 16.9).
>
> 4. Statistical data.
>
> 5. Sales data sheets and maps.

QUALIFICATIONS OF SAMUEL GEORGE

EDUCATION – ACADEMIC
Bachelor of Science and Business Administration Degrees, Real Estate and Urban Land Economics Major, University of Idaho, Moscow, Idaho, 1972 and 1973.

EDUCATION – PROFESSIONAL
Education Seminars and Conferences: University of Idaho Extension; Appraisal Institute, including AI exams or courses 1, 2, 4 & 8; Idaho Real Estate Certificate.

PROFESSIONAL AFFILIATIONS
Member, Appraisal Institute (MAI #CD40); Senior Member, American Society of Appraisers (ASA), in Real Estate.

PROFESSIONAL ACTIVITY
AI: Idaho Chapter Admissions Committee, 1980-82; and other committee memberships
Instructor: Real Estate subjects, University of Idaho Extension Division, Moscow

APPRAISAL EXPERIENCE
Since 1973, appraisals in excess of $100,000.
Expert Witness – Testimony in Shawnee, Clare, and Lowell Counties. Property tax appeals, eminent domain, bankruptcy, income tax, and damage lawsuits.

CLIENTS
Either individually or in association with other appraisers including: Foster City; Bank of Idaho; Union Bank; North Central Bank; First National Bank; Singer Company; SCM Corporation; Newhall Land and Farming Company; Coopers and Lybrand, CPAs; Homequity, Inc.; Executrans; U.S. National Park Service; and numerous private clients.

Figure 16.4
Sample qualifications sheet.

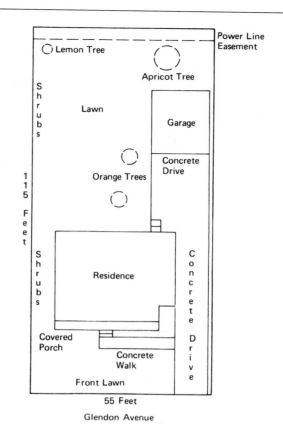

Power Line
Easement

Lemon Tree

Apricot Tree

N

Shrubs

Lawn

Garage

1
1
5
Feet

Orange Trees

Concrete
Drive

Shrubs

Residence

Concrete Drive

Covered
Porch

Concrete
Walk

Front Lawn

55 Feet

Glendon Avenue

Figure 16.5
Plot plan of a residential
property.

SUMMARY

The written appraisal report is a formal business communication from the appraiser to the client. In the tradition of good business standards and appraisal practice, the report should be concise, well organized, and easy to read.

All written appraisals should contain only the information necessary to define the appraisal problem, present the factual data found by the study, and show support for the stated opinion of value.

Every appraisal report, whether written or oral, generally must include the following elements:

1. Identify and describe the real estate being appraised.

2. Identify the real property interest being appraised.

3. State the purpose of the appraisal.

4. Define the value to be estimated.

5. Set forth the effective date of the appraisal, and the date the report was prepared.

6. Describe the extent of the process of collecting, confirming, and reporting data.

7. Set forth all assumptions and limiting conditions that affect the analyses, opinions, and conclusions.

8. Set forth the information considered, the appraisal procedures followed, and the reasoning that supports the analyses, opinions, and conclusions.

9. Set forth the appraiser's opinion of the highest and best use of the real estate being appraised when such an opinion is necessary and appropriate.

10. Explain and support the exclusion of any of the usual valuation approaches.

11. Set forth any additional information that may be appropriate to show compliance with, or clearly identify and explain permitted departures from, the use of recognized appraisal methods and techniques.

12. Include the appraiser's signed certification.

The three main types of written appraisal reports are the letter report, the form (or short-form) report, and the narrative report. The letter report is a short business letter containing all the essential elements but abbreviating the supporting data, often referring to some facts in the appraiser's files. The conditions, assumptions, and appraiser's certification, however, should be included or attached, no matter how short the letter report. Without relying upon the "departure" provisions of USPAP, letter reports do not meet the current content requirements of this standard.

There are many variations of the form (or short-form) report. The most commonly used short-form report is the URAR, also known as the Freddie Mac Form 70 or Fannie Mae Form 1004. This form is required for most single-residential appraisals by the Federal Home Loan Mortgage Corporation, the Federal National Mortgage Association, the Veterans Administration, and the Federal Housing Agency. It contains all the basic elements of an appraisal report and is accompanied by the FHLMC Form 439 (or FNMA Form 1004B), which provides a formal definition of value and furnishes the appraiser's certification and statement of contingent and limiting conditions. When properly prepared, the URAR conforms to the Uniform Standards of Professional Appraisal Practice.

The most detailed, formal, and lengthy appraisal report is the narrative report. This report is preferred when the client wants to follow the appraiser's step-by-step logic in arriving at the value conclusion and needs to have documentation of all the pertinent facts revealed in the investigation performed.

While various government agencies and appraisal organizations have developed their own requirements for the form and content of narrative appraisal reports, one very acceptable format divides the material into three main sections: (1) Introduction; (2) Description, Analyses, and Conclusion; and (3) Addenda. Such an outline or format is not only traditional, but it also makes it easier for the client to follow, visualize, and remember the facts and conclusions presented.

The narrative appraisal report should meet very high standards. The actual writing of this report includes three basic considerations: appearance, form, and content. Obviously, the appearance must be formal, neat, and professional. Narrative appraisal reports should follow a carefully planned outline and form. Of course, the content is the most important of the three considerations. The facts, analyses, and opinions set forth in a narrative report should show the appraiser's best efforts to "leave no stone unturned" in carrying out the appraisal assignment. Thus the narrative appraisal report enables the appraiser to utilize all the knowledge, skill, or training at his or her command and present to the client the information required in a succinct, convincing, and interesting manner.

In practice, appraisal reports tend to mix the features of the basic types of reports, containing some features of the letter report, some of the form, and some of the narrative report. In federally related appraisals, regulations require that all reports be written and presented in a narrative format or on forms that satisfy specific requirements. Such appraisals must also conform to the Uniform Standards of Professional Appraisal Practice, and meet other minimum content standards that are set by each financial institution of the federal government.

Important Terms and Concepts

Assumptions	Letter of transmittal
Certification	Letter report
Fannie Mae Form 1004	Limiting conditions
Federally related appraisals	Narrative report
Form (or short-form) report	Professional standards
Freddie Mac Form 70	Qualifications of the appraiser
Freddie Mac Form 439	URAR

REVIEWING YOUR UNDERSTANDING

1. Written appraisal reports are a form of business communication. Every report should be:
   (a) Concise
   (b) Well organized
   (c) Easy to read
   (d) All of the above

2. The essential elements of written, self-contained appraisal reports:
   (a) Should follow legal and professional requirements
   (b) Need not follow defined standards
   (c) May be abbreviated for the client
   (d) None of the above

3. The type of appraisal report often depends on the amount of background information and detail required by the client. Which of the following types is the longest and most detailed?
   (a) The letter report
   (b) The form report
   (c) The narrative report
   (d) The subdivision report

4. There are three main subdivisions in the typical narrative appraisal report. Which of the following is not one of these subdivisions?
   (a) Introduction
   (b) Letter of transmittal
   (c) Description, analysis, and conclusion
   (d) Addenda

5. Which type of appraisal report requires a statement of the rights being appraised?
   (a) The letter report
   (b) The form report
   (c) The narrative report
   (d) All of the above

6. The letter report:
   (a) Should contain all the essential elements of an appraisal report
   (b) Need not contain the assumptions, limiting conditions, and the appraiser's certification
   (c) Is the most formal written report
   (d) Is required by most institutions and agencies

7. In the form report, it is not usually necessary for the appraiser to:
   (a) Demonstrate evidence of value through one or more approaches
   (b) Describe any physical deterioration or functional inadequacy found in the structure
   (c) Rate the neighborhood employment stability
   (d) Write a letter of transmittal to the client

8. Sales data sheets in the addenda of a narrative appraisal report contain:
   (a) Details about each comparable sale
   (b) An analysis of the data by the value approaches
   (c) An outline of the investigation made to estimate market rent
   (d) All of the above

9. In the reconciliation and final conclusion of value, the appraiser should:
   (a) Describe the relevance of each value approach explored
   (b) Discuss the reliability of the data used
   (c) Provide arguments to justify the final conclusion of value rendered
   (d) All of the above

10. The statement of limiting conditions in the appraisal report:
    (a) Serves to clarify the assumptions made by the appraiser
    (b) Limits the appraiser's legal liability
    (c) Obligates the appraiser to appear in court regarding the appraisal at any future time
    (d) Both (a) and (b)

11. Most real estate appraisals used in connection with federally related transactions must be performed:
    (a) In writing
    (b) In accordance with uniform standards
    (c) By staff appraisers
    (d) To satisfy both (a) and (b) requirements

Sample Appraisal Report

A sample URAR appraisal report, complete with typical attachments, is provided on the following pages.

UNIFORM RESIDENTIAL APPRAISAL REPORT

File No. **SAMPLE1**

SUBJECT

Property Address	1801 Dona Marta — City Ventura — State CA — Zip Code 93003
Legal Description	Lot 68, TR 2505, MB 84-81-01 — County Ventura
Assessor's Parcel No.	009-001-06 — Tax Year 92-93 — R.E. Taxes $ @ .0126 — Special Assessments $ None
Borrower	Robert Burns — Current Owner Same — Occupant [X] Owner [ ] Tenant [ ] Vacant
Property rights appraised	[X] Fee Simple [ ] Leasehold — Project Type [ ] PUD [ ] Condominium (HUD/VA only) — HOA $ /Mo.
Neighborhood or Project Name	N/A — Map Reference 48 C-4 — Census Tract 24689
Sale Price $	RE-FI — Date of Sale N/A — Description and $ amount of loan charges/concessions to be paid by seller None
Lender/Client	Sample Savings & Loan — Address 116 San Luis Blvd., Santa Ventana CA
Appraiser	Green Clay — Address 377 Alameda Lane, Ventura CA

NEIGHBORHOOD

				Single family housing		Present land use %	Land use change
Location	[ ] Urban [X] Suburban [ ] Rural	Predominant occupancy		PRICE $(000) / AGE (yrs)			
Built up	[ ] Over 75% [X] 25-75% [ ] Under 25%			200 Low / 0	One family 60	[X] Not likely [ ] Likely
Growth rate	[ ] Rapid [X] Stable [ ] Slow	[X] Owner		350 High / 25	2-4 family 5	[ ] In process
Property values	[ ] Increasing [X] Stable [ ] Declining	[ ] Tenant		Predominant	Multi-family 5	To:
Demand/supply	[ ] Shortage [X] In balance [ ] Over supply	[ ] Vacant (0-5%)		280 / 17	Commercial 0	
Marketing time	[ ] Under 3 mos. [X] 3-6 mos. [ ] Over 6 mos.	[ ] Vacant (over 5%)			Vacant 30	

Note: Race and the racial composition of the neighborhood are not appraisal factors.

Neighborhood boundaries and characteristics: Generally this quiet rural neighborhood is bounded on north by mountains, south by Main St., east by Foothill Rd., west by San Jon Barranca.

Factors that affect the marketability of the properties in the neighborhood (proximity to employment and amenities, employment stability, appeal to market, etc.): This suburban neighborhood enjoys an above-average prestige factor. Its rural setting and overlook of the city/ocean are the most favorable features of the location. Employment centers are within 2 miles. Parks and recreation areas are within 1 mile.

Market conditions in the subject neighborhood (including support for the above conclusions related to the trend of property values, demand/supply, and marketing time - - such as data on competitive properties for sale in the neighborhood, description of the prevalence of sales and financing concessions, etc.): After a slight decline in value in 1991-1992, market prices have stabilized since January 1993. No vacant houses are in evidence and relatively few houses are for sale. Marketing time has decreased and sales prices average 92% of asking prices per local brokers.

PUD

Project Information for PUDs (If applicable) - - Is the developer/builder in control of the Home Owners' Association (HOA)? [ ] Yes [ ] No

Approximate total number of units in the subject project N/A. Approximate total number of units for sale in the subject project N/A.

Describe common elements and recreational facilities: N/A

SITE

Dimensions 90 X 145.2	Topography Up, Level pad
Site area 13,068 — Corner Lot [X] Yes [ ] No	Size Typical
Specific zoning classification and description R-1-10; Single Family	Shape Rectangular
Zoning compliance [X] Legal [ ] Legal nonconforming (Grandfathered use) [ ] Illegal [ ] No zoning	Drainage Appears Adequate
Highest & best use as improved: [X] Present use [ ] Other use (explain)	View Minimal

Utilities	Public	Other	Off-site improvements	Type	Public	Private		
Electricity	[X]		Street	Asphalt	[X]	[ ]	Landscaping	Average Quality
Gas	[X]		Curb/gutter	Concrete	[X]	[ ]	Driveway Surface	Asphalt
Water	[X]		Sidewalk	None	[ ]	[ ]	Apparent easements	None
Sanitary sewer	[X]		Street lights	Electric	[X]	[ ]	FEMA Special Flood Hazard Area	[ ] Yes [X] No
Storm sewer	[X]		Alley	None	[ ]	[ ]	FEMA Zone —— Map date ——
							FEMA Map No.	Not mapped

Comments (apparent adverse easements, encroachments, special assessments, slide areas, illegal or legal nonconforming zoning use, etc.): No adverse conditions are present. Site has a steep upslope back yard.

IMPROVEMENTS

GENERAL DESCRIPTION		EXTERIOR DESCRIPTION		FOUNDATION		BASEMENT		INSULATION	
No. of Units	One	Foundation	Concrete	Slab	Yes	Area Sq. Ft. None		Roof	[ ]
No. of Stories	One	Exterior Walls	Stucco	Crawl Space	None	% Finished		Ceiling G [X]
Type (Det./Att.)	Detached	Roof Surface	C/Shingle	Basement	None	Ceiling		Walls [ ]
Design (Style)	Modern	Gutters & Dwnspts.	Yes	Sump Pump	No	Walls		Floor [ ]
Existing/Proposed	Existing	Window Type	Sld.Alum.	Dampness	No	Floor		None [ ]
Age (Yrs.)	22	Storm/Screens	Yes	Settlement	None Noted	Outside Entry		Unknown AVG [X]
Effective Age (Yrs.)	17	Manufactured House	No	Infestation	None			

ROOM LIST

ROOMS	Foyer	Living	Dining	Kitchen	Den	Family Rm.	Rec. Rm.	Bedrooms	# Baths	Laundry	Other	Area Sq. Ft.
Basement												None
Level 1	1	1	Area	1				4	2			1,768
Level 2												

Finished area above grade contains: 6 Rooms; 4 Bedroom(s); 2 Bath(s); 1,768 Square Feet of Gross Living Area

DESCRIPTION

INTERIOR	Materials/Condition	HEATING		KITCHEN EQUIP.		ATTIC		AMENITIES		CAR STORAGE:	
Floors	Carpet/Good	Type	F.A.U.	Refrigerator	[ ]	None	[X]	Fireplace(s) # 1	[X]	None	[ ]
Walls	Plaster/V.Good	Fuel	Gas	Range/Oven	[X]	Stairs	[ ]	Patio Concrete	[X]	Garage # of cars	
Trim/Finish	Stock/Good	Condition	Good	Disposal	[X]	Drop Stair	[ ]	Deck Wood	[X]	Attached two
Bath Floor	Ceramic/Good	COOLING		Dishwasher	[X]	Scuttle	[ ]	Porch	[ ]	Detached
Bath Wainscot	Tile Shower	Central	None	Fan/Hood	[X]	Floor	[ ]	Fence Wood	[X]	Built-In
Doors	Wood/Good	Other	None	Microwave	[ ]	Heated	[ ]	Pool	[ ]	Carport
		Condition		Washer/Dryer	[ ]	Finished	[ ]			Driveway Asph

Additional features (special energy efficient items, etc.): Kitchen and bath have skylights. Master bath has double pullman lav. (mirrored). Covered patio and 7 foot heated spa in rear yard.

Condition of the improvements, depreciation (physical, functional, and external), repairs needed, quality of construction, remodeling/additions, etc.: No physical, functional or external inadequacies noted; kitchen and baths redecorated six months ago.

COMMENTS

Adverse environmental conditions (such as, but not limited to, hazardous wastes, toxic substances, etc.) present in the improvements, on the site, or in the immediate vicinity of the subject property: None in evidence.

Figure 16.6
Sample Appraisal Report

UNIFORM RESIDENTIAL APPRAISAL REPORT

File No. SAMPLE1

COST APPROACH

ESTIMATED SITE VALUE .... = $ __150,000__

ESTIMATED REPRODUCTION COST-NEW OF IMPROVEMENTS:

Dwelling	1,768 Sq. Ft. @ $	70.00	= $	123,760
Patio	260 Sq. Ft. @ $	25.00	=	6,500
Heated Spa, Deck			=	9,500
Garage/Carport	484 Sq. Ft. @ $	35.00	=	16,940
Total Estimated Cost New	....		= $	156,700

Less   Physical | Functional | External

Depreciation 26,600   = $ __26,600__

Depreciated Value of Improvements .... = $ __130,100__

"As-is" Value of Site Improvements .... = $ __15,000__

INDICATED VALUE BY COST APPROACH .... = $ __295,100__

Comments on Cost Approach (such as, source of cost estimate, site value, square foot calculation and, for HUD, VA and FmHA, the estimated remaining economic life of the property):

1) See attached for S.F. area computataions and building sketch.

2) No functional or external obsolescence in evidence.

3) Site value abstracted from improved sales.

SALES COMPARISON ANALYSIS

ITEM	SUBJECT	COMPARABLE NO. 1		COMPARABLE NO. 2		COMPARABLE NO. 3	
Address	1801 Dona Marta Ventura	1896 Dona Emilia		1821 Don Juan		1932 Via Adobe	
Proximity to Subject		1 block east		2 blocks west		1 block north	
Sales Price	$ N/A	$	321,500	$	286,000	$	280,000
Price/Gross Liv. Area	$ 141.40 ☑	$ 155.46 ☑		$ 145.18 ☑		$ 155.56 ☑	
Data and/or Verification Sources	Inspection Owner	Doc #182904 Buyer		Doc #014815 CMDC		Doc #097024 Broker	
VALUE ADJUSTMENTS	DESCRIPTION	DESCRIPTION	+(-)$ Adjustment	DESCRIPTION	+(-)$ Adjustment	DESCRIPTION	+(-)$ Adjustment
Sales or Financing Concessions		Cash		80% Conv.		80% Conv.	
Date of Sale/Time		3/93		2/93		1/93	
Location	Average	Average		Average		Average	
Leasehold/Fee Simple	Fee	Fee		Fee		Fee	
Site	13,068 SF.	14,375	−20,000	11,809		15,246	−12,000
View		Excellent		Min.		Good	
Design and Appeal	Modern	Mod/Good		Mod/V.Good	−2,500	Mod/V.Good	−2,500
Quality of Construction	Good	Good		Good		Good	
Age	22	22		24		24	
Condition	Good	Good		Good		Fair	+5,000
Above Grade	Total / Bdrms / Baths	Total / Bdrms / Baths		Total / Bdrms / Baths		Total / Bdrms / Baths	
Room Count	6 / 4 / 2	7 / 4 / 2		7 / 3 / 2.5		6 / 4 / 2	
Gross Living Area	1,768 Sq. Ft.	2,068 Sq. Ft.	−12,000	1,970 Sq. Ft.	−8,000	1,800 Sq. Ft.	
Basement & Finished Rooms Below Grade	None						
Functional Utility	Good	Equal		Equal		Equal	
Heating/Cooling	FAU/No	FAU/No		FAU/No		FAU/No	
Energy Efficient Items	None	None		None		None	
Garage/Carport	2 Car Garage	Same		Same		Same	
Porch, Patio, Deck, Fireplace(s), etc.	Cov. Patio 1 Fireplace	None Same	+500	None Same	+500	None Same	+500
Fence, Pool, etc.	Htd Spa	None	+2,000	None	+2,000	None	+2,000
Net Adj. (total)		☐ + ☒ − $	−29,500	☐ + ☒ − $	−8,000	☐ + ☒ − $	−7,000
Adjusted Sales Price of Comparable		$	292,000	$	278,000	$	273,000

Comments on Sales Comparison (including the subject property's compatibility to the neighborhood, etc.): Comp #1 is same model as subject, enlarged before sale. Has hilltop view. Older Sale #3 used as best closed sale nearby. No time adj. per Realty Board & current escrows. Most weight on Comps #2 and #3.

ITEM	SUBJECT	COMPARABLE NO. 1	COMPARABLE NO. 2	COMPARABLE NO. 3
Date, Price and Data Source for prior sales within year of appraisal	Sold 11/92 for $250k in poor cond.	None	None	None

Analysis of any current agreement of sale, option, or listing of the subject property and analysis of any prior sales of subject and comparables within one year of the date of appraisal: Subject was in poor condition at prior sale. Sale price adjusted for condition supports value indicated by comparables.

INDICATED VALUE BY SALES COMPARISON APPROACH .... $ __275,000__

INDICATED VALUE BY INCOME APPROACH (If Applicable) Estimated Market Rent $ N/A /Mo. x Gross Rent Multiplier N/A = $

This appraisal is made ☒ "as is"   ☐ subject to the repairs, alterations, inspections, or conditions listed below   ☐ subject to completion per plans and specifications.

Conditions of Appraisal: ____

RECONCILIATION

Final Reconciliation: Although not weighed heavily, the cost approach tends to confirm the value indicated by the sales comparison approach here. The income approach has not been tested, as inapplicable in this owner-occupied area.

The purpose of this appraisal is to estimate the market value of the real property that is the subject of this report, based on the above conditions and the certification, contingent and limiting conditions, and market value definition that are stated in the attached Freddie Mac Form 439/Fannie Mae Form 1004B (Revised ____).

I (WE) ESTIMATE THE MARKET VALUE, AS DEFINED, OF THE REAL PROPERTY THAT IS THE SUBJECT OF THIS REPORT, AS OF June 24, 1993 (WHICH IS THE DATE OF INSPECTION AND THE EFFECTIVE DATE OF THIS REPORT) TO BE $ __275,000__.

APPRAISER:

Signature: _Green Clay_

Name: Green Clay

Date Report Signed: June 24, 1993

State Certification #: AR0067**   State CA

Or State License #:   State

SUPERVISORY APPRAISER (ONLY IF REQUIRED):

Signature: ____

Name: ____

Date Report Signed: ____

State Certification #: ____   State

Or State License #: ____   State

☐ Did   ☐ Did Not   Inspect Property

Figure 16.6
Sample Appraisal Report second page

Location Map

1 = Comparable #1

2 = Comparable #2

3 = Comparable #3

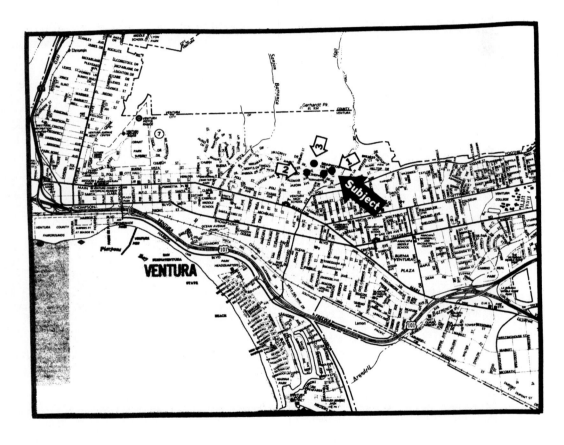

Figure 16.7
Location Map

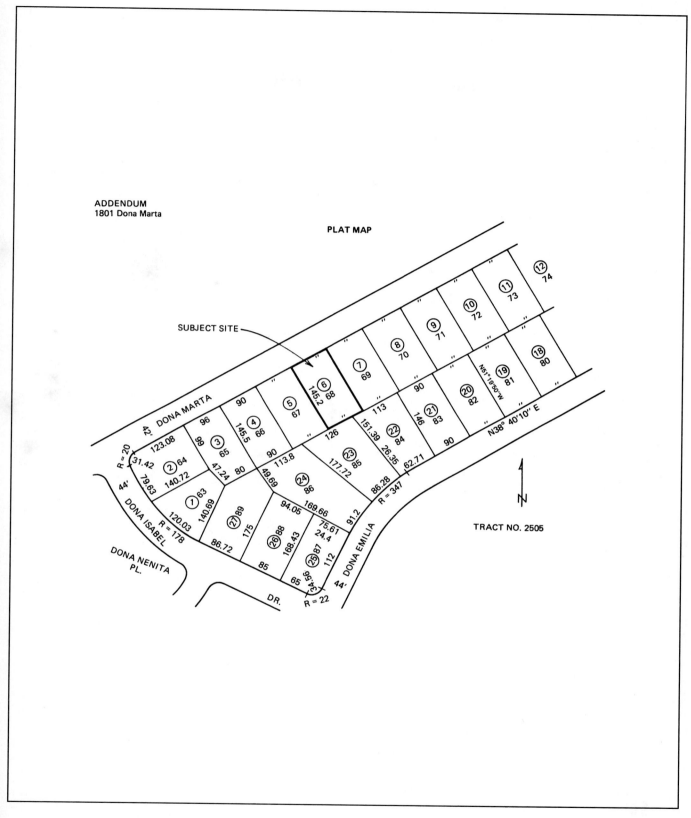

Figure 16.8
Plat Map

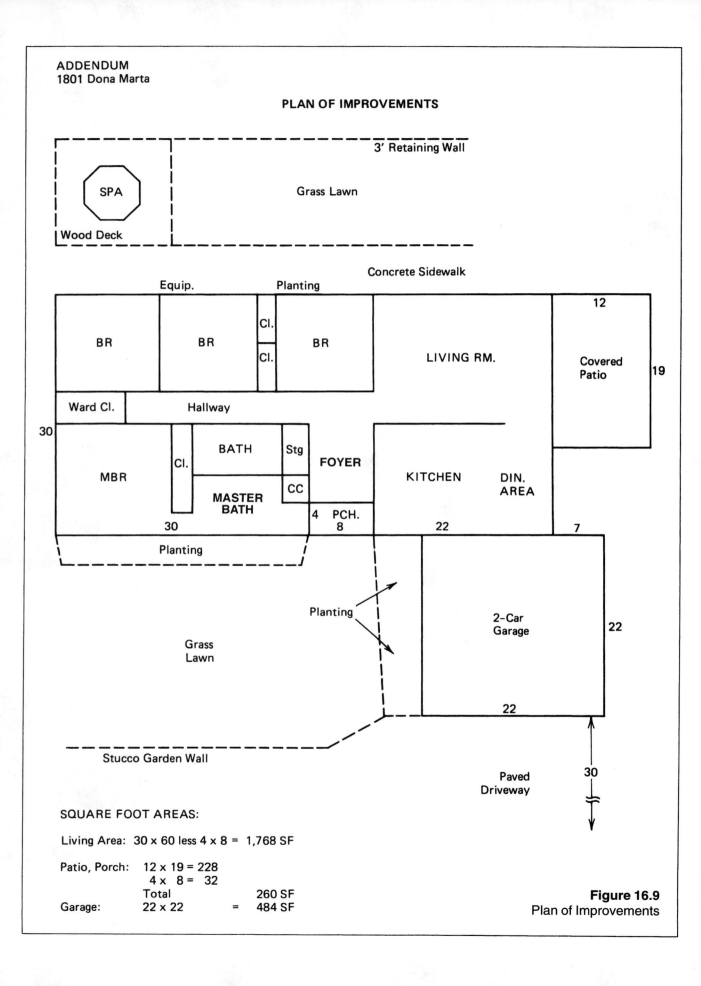

ADDENDUM
1801 Dona Marta

PLAN OF IMPROVEMENTS

3' Retaining Wall

SPA

Grass Lawn

Wood Deck

Concrete Sidewalk

Equip.   Planting

BR   BR   Cl.   BR   LIVING RM.   12

                 Cl.   Covered
                                                    Patio   19

Ward Cl.   Hallway

30   MBR

         BATH   Stg   FOYER   KITCHEN   DIN.
    Cl.   AREA

MBR   CC

         MASTER   4 PCH.
         BATH   8

    30   22   7

Planting

                                                    Planting

Grass
Lawn   2-Car
                                       Garage   22

                                          22

Stucco Garden Wall   30

                                       Paved
                                       Driveway

SQUARE FOOT AREAS:

Living Area: 30 x 60 less 4 x 8 = 1,768 SF

Patio, Porch: 12 x 19 = 228
                 4 x 8 = 32
                Total   260 SF
Garage: 22 x 22   =   484 SF

Figure 16.9
Plan of Improvements

DEFINITION OF MARKET VALUE: The most probable price which a property should bring in a competitive and open market under all conditions requisite to a fair sale, the buyer and seller, each acting prudently, knowledgeably and assuming the price is not affected by undue stimulus. Implicit in this definition is the consummation of a sale as of a specified date and the passing of title from seller to buyer under conditions whereby: (1) buyer and seller are typically motivated; (2) both parties are well informed or well advised, and each acting in what he considers his own best interest; (3) a reasonable time is allowed for exposure in the open market; (4) payment is made in terms of cash in U. S. dollars or in terms of financial arrangements comparable thereto; and (5) the price represents the normal consideration for the property sold unaffected by special or creative financing or sales concessions* granted by anyone associated with the sale.

*Adjustments to the comparables must be made for special or creative financing or sales concessions. No adjustments are necessary for those costs which are normally paid by sellers as a result of tradition or law in a market area; these costs are readily identifiable since the seller pays these costs in virtually all sales transactions. Special or creative financing adjustments can be made to the comparable property by comparisons to financing terms offered by a third party institutional lender that is not already involved in the property or transaction. Any adjustment should not be calculated on a mechanical dollar for dollar cost of the financing or concession but the dollar amount of any adjustment should approximate the market's reaction to the financing or concessions based on the appraiser's judgment.

STATEMENT OF LIMITING CONDITIONS AND APPRAISER'S CERTIFICATION

CONTINGENT AND LIMITING CONDITIONS: The appraiser's certification that appears in the appraisal report is subject to the following conditions:

1. The appraiser will not be responsible for matters of a legal nature that affect either the property being appraised or the title to it. The appraiser assumes that the title is good and marketable and, therefore, will not render any opinions about the title. The property is appraised on the basis of it being under responsible ownership.

2. The appraiser has provided a sketch in the appraisal report to show approximate dimensions of the improvements and the sketch is included only to assist the reader of the report in visualizing the property and understanding the appraiser's determination of its size.

3. The appraiser has examined the available flood maps that are provided by the Federal Emergency Management Agency (or other data sources) and has noted in the appraisal report whether the subject site is located in an identified Special Flood Hazard Area. Because the appraiser is not a surveyor, he or she makes no guarantees, express or implied, regarding this determination.

4. The appraiser will not give testimony or appear in court because he or she made an appraisal of the property in question, unless specific arrangements to do so have been made beforehand.

5. The appraiser has estimated the value of the land in the cost approach at its highest and best use and the improvements at their contributory value. These separate valuations of the land and improvements must not be used in conjunction with any other appraisal and are invalid if they are so used.

6. The appraiser has noted in the appraisal report any adverse conditions (such as, needed repairs, depreciation, the presence of hazardous wastes, toxic substances, etc.) observed during the inspection of the subject property or that he or she became aware of during the normal research involved in performing the appraisal. Unless otherwise stated in the appraisal report, the appraiser has no knowledge of any hidden or unapparent conditions of the property or adverse environmental conditions (including the presence of hazardous wastes, toxic substances, etc.) that would make the property more or less valuable, and has assumed that there are no such conditions and makes no guarantees or warranties, express or implied, regarding the condition of the property. The appraiser will not be responsible for any such conditions that do exist or for any engineering or testing that might be required to discover whether such conditions exist. Because the appraiser is not an expert in the field of environmental hazards, the appraisal report must not be considered as an environmental assessment of the property.

7. The appraiser obtained the information, estimates, and opinions that were expressed in the appraisal report from sources that he or she considers to be reliable and believes them to be true and correct. The appraiser does not assume responsibility for the accuracy of such items that were furnished by other parties.

8. The appraiser will not disclose the contents of the appraisal report except as provided for in the Uniform Standards of Professional Appraisal Practice.

9. The appraiser has based his or her appraisal report and valuation conclusion for an appraisal that is subject to satisfactory completion, repairs, or alterations on the assumption that completion of the improvements will be performed in a workmanlike manner.

10. The appraiser must provide his or her prior written consent before the lender/client specified in the appraisal report can distribute the appraisal report (including conclusions about the property value, the appraiser's identity and professional designations, and references to any professional appraisal organizations or the firm with which the appraiser is associated) to anyone other than the borrower; the mortgagee or its successors and assigns; the mortgage insurer; consultants; professional appraisal organizations; any state or federally approved financial institution; or any department, agency, or instrumentality of the United States or any state or the District of Columbia; except that the lender/client may distribute the property description section of the report only to data collection or reporting service(s) without having to obtain the appraiser's prior written consent. The appraiser's written consent and approval must also be obtained before the appraisal can be conveyed by anyone to the public through advertising, public relations, news, sales, or other media.

Figure 16.10
Certification

Freddie Mac Form 439   6-93   Page 1 of 2   Fannie Mae Form 1004B   6-93

APPRAISER'S CERTIFICATION: The Appraiser certifies and agrees that:

1. I have researched the subject market area and have selected a minimum of three recent sales of properties most similar and proximate to the subject property for consideration in the sales comparison analysis and have made a dollar adjustment when appropriate to reflect the market reaction to those items of significant variation. If a significant item in a comparable property is superior to, or more favorable than, the subject property, I have made a negative adjustment to reduce the adjusted sales price of the comparable and, if a significant item in a comparable property is inferior to, or less favorable than the subject property, I have made a positive adjustment to increase the adjusted sales price of the comparable.

2. I have taken into consideration the factors that have an impact on value in my development of the estimate of market value in the appraisal report. I have not knowingly withheld any significant information from the appraisal report and I believe, to the best of my knowledge, that all statements and information in the appraisal report are true and correct.

3. I stated in the appraisal report only my own personal, unbiased, and professional analysis, opinions, and conclusions, which are subject only to the contingent and limiting conditions specified in this form.

4. I have no present or prospective interest in the property that is the subject of this report, and I have no present or prospective personal interest or bias with respect to the participants in the transaction. I did not base, either partially or completely, my analysis and/or the estimate of market value in the appraisal report on the race, color, religion, sex, handicap, familial status, or national origin of either the prospective owners or occupants of the subject property or of the present owners or occupants of the properties in the vicinity of the subject property.

5. I have no present or contemplated future interest in the subject property, and neither my current or future employment nor my compensation for performing this appraisal is contingent on the appraised value of the property.

6. I was not required to report a predetermined value or direction in value that favors the cause of the client or any related party, the amount of the value estimate, the attainment of a specific result, or the occurrence of a subsequent event in order to receive my compensation and/or employment for performing the appraisal. I did not base the appraisal report on a requested minimum valuation, a specific valuation, or the need to approve a specific mortgage loan.

7. I performed this appraisal in conformity with the Uniform Standards of Professional Appraisal Practice that were adopted and promulgated by the Appraisal Standards Board of The Appraisal Foundation and that were in place as of the efective date of this apraisal, with the exception of the departure provision of those Standards, which does not apply. I acknowledge that an estimate of a reasonable time for exposure in the open market is a condition in the definition of market value and the estimate I developed is consistent with the marketing time noted in the neighborhood section of this report, unless I have otherwise stated in the reconciliation section.

8. I have personally inspected the interior and exterior areas of the subject property and the exterior of all properties listed as comparables in the appraisal report. I further certify that I have noted any apparent or known adverse conditions in the subject improvements, on the subject site, or on any site within the immediate vicinity of the subject property of which I am aware and have made adjustments for these adverse conditions in my analysis of the property value to the extent that I had market evidence to support them. I have also commented about the effect of the adverse conditions on the marketability of the subject property.

9. I personally prepared all conclusions and opinions about the real estate that were set forth in the appraisal report. If I relied on significant professional assistance from any individual or individuals in the performance of the appraisal or the preparation of the appraisal report, I have named such individual(s) and disclosed the specific tasks performed by them in the reconciliation section of this appraisal report. I certify that any individual so named is qualified to perform the tasks. I have not authorized anyone to make a change to any item in the report; therefore, if an unauthorized change is made to the appraisal report, I will take no responsibility for it.

SUPERVISORY APPRAISER'S CERTIFICATION: If a supervisory appraiser signed the appraisal report, he or she certifies and agrees that: I directly supervise the appraiser who prepared the appraisal report, have reviewed the appraisal report, agree with the statements and conclusions of the appraiser, agree to be bound by the appraiser's certifications numbered 4 through 7 above, and am taking full responsibility for the appraisal and the appraisal report.

ADDRESS OF PROPERTY APPRAISED: 1801 Dona Marta, Ventura, CA 93003

APPRAISER:	SUPERVISORY APPRAISER: (only if required):
Signature: *Green Clay*	Signature:
Name: Green Clay	Name:
Date Signed: June 24, 1993	Date Signed:
State Certification #: AR0067**	State Certification #:
or State License #:	or State License #:
State: California	State:
Expiration Date of Certification or License: 3/1/96	Expiration Date of Certification or License:

☐ Did ☐ Did Not Inspect Property

Figure 16.10
Certification
second page

PHOTOGRAPH ADDENDUM

Borrower/Client	Robert Burns
Property Address	1801 Dona Marta
City Ventura	County Ventura State California Zip Code 93003
Lender	Sample Savings & Loan

FRONT OF
SUBJECT PROPERTY

REAR OF
SUBJECT PROPERTY

STREET SCENE

☐ **ADDITIONAL PHOTOGRAPHS ON REVERSE SIDE**

FW 90A

© 1984 Forms and Worms Inc. 315 Whitney Ave. New Haven, Ct. 06511 All Rights Reserved

Figure 16.11
Photograph
Addendum

PHOTOGRAPH ADDENDUM

Borrower/Client	Robert Burns			
Property Address	1801 Dona Marta			
City Ventura	County Ventura	State California	Zip Code 93003	
Lender	Sample Savings & Loan			

COMPARABLE #1

COMPARABLE #2

COMPARABLE #3

☐ **ADDITIONAL PHOTOGRAPHS ON REVERSE SIDE**

FW 90A

Figure 16.11
Photograph
Addendum
second page

Chapter 17
Appraising Special Ownerships and Interests

Preview   Increasingly, unusual ownership concepts and unique types of residential properties have presented new appraisal problems. This chapter provides an introduction to some unusual types of housing—from townhouses to mobile homes.

Next, we review the appraisal of partial interests in real estate. A partial interest consists of an ownership interest that includes less than the unencumbered fee title. The most common example of this is property subject to a lease.

Finally, we introduce you to the appraisal of property for purposes of condemnation under the power of eminent domain. This is one of the most specialized technical areas of appraisal practice. The intent of this section is to point out not only the areas of similarity to other appraisals but the major differences. Performing satisfactory eminent domain appraisals is difficult and generally requires years of appraisal experience and education.

When you have finished this chapter, you should be able to:

1. *List at least four less common types of homes, define each, and explain what special problems each presents to the appraiser.*

2. *Define the several commonly marketed types of partial interests and explain how to value each.*

3. *Explain three ways in which the appraisal process is different for eminent domain appraisals.*

17.1 CONDOMINIUMS AND OTHER SPECIALIZED HOUSING

The typical appraisal assignment is usually to value a detached, single-family home on a fee simple lot. More and more frequently, however, appraisers are working with a number of unusual and different types of housing. Some of these new types of appraisal assignments involve property types that are centuries old; others involve new ideas in housing. A variety of unusual homes will be discussed in this section. We have grouped them by their common elements to emphasize their unusual qualities.

Variations in Housing Design

Several new types of housing are characterized by the lack of side yards. Eliminating side yards reduces the amount of land required per housing unit and lowers the cost of land. The smaller lot also reduces the per-lot costs for roads, streetlights, utility mains, and so on, because the frontage per lot is less. Row houses, townhouses, planned unit developments, and zero-lot-line homes are typical of this type of housing.

Row Houses

What is a row house? It is a house on an individual lot, which is nearly always owned in fee, built without side yards between adjoining houses. The concept of row housing is centuries old and was the tradition in urban housing of the early 1800s in the eastern United States. Many additional row houses were built in San Francisco during the 1920s and in the period following World War II. Lot widths of 25 feet were common. In some areas, lots have been developed with widths of as little as 11 feet. Lot depths of 70 to 100 feet are typical in row house development.

Because of the close proximity of row houses, several housing problems must be given more attention by the appraiser in valuing row houses. One common urban housing problem is obtaining a degree of personal privacy and protection from fire. The limited spacing between neighbors allows row houses less visual privacy than in conventional houses because there is no room for foliage. Fire can be a threat because there is no side yard to function as a firebreak. With row houses, the type of wall between the units may determine the extent of sound insulation and fire resistance. Most commonly, problems arise when two units share a common wall structure, called a party wall, instead of two separate walls. This type of construction is now used less frequently because it is harder to design satisfactorily. In addition, the use of a party wall imposes legal obligations on each owner as to maintenance and repair, which can sometimes lead to conflicts between neighbors.

Townhouses

The townhouse is essentially a modern name for the row house. Most townhouses are in projects built since 1970. They are typically designed as two-story units, on fee lots, without side yards. Townhouses are sometimes built in clusters of four or more, creating end units that are separated by side yards from the next cluster of units. A current trend is toward the small townhouse project (as few as three units) on an existing city lot. These are frequently referred to as "in-fill" developments, since they are "filling in" bypassed vacant lots.

The most noticed townhouse projects are the large ones, which are popular in many parts of the country. Often designed as retirement communities, these developments can offer a type of self-contained living environment, complete with elaborate recreation facilities such as tennis courts and golf courses. The yard areas and recreation facilities are most commonly owned by all the unit owners. Normally, townhouse projects have a homeowners' association, which takes care of the commonly owned areas and exterior maintenance of the buildings. Homeowners pay association fees to cover common expenses. Effectively, the owners' association is a local government, complete with rules, taxing power, and occasional member conflicts.

Notice that each homeowner usually owns the individual lot on which the home sits. Such an ownership is considerably different from condominium ownership (condominiums will be discussed later in this section). In different areas of the country, townhouse projects are called by different names. In California, for example, this type of ownership is usually called a planned unit development and the "townhouse" label usually refers to the architectural styling that is featured.

Planned Unit Development

The planned unit development, or PUD, is a zoning concept that became popular in the late 1960s. Planned unit development zoning allows flexibility in lot size, density, and variety, creating better project designs. Many PUD projects have been built with townhouse styling so that the two terms, *PUD* and *townhouse,* are often used together, as noted earlier. Some newer housing developments mix the types of units: detached houses, townhouses, zero-lot-line homes (discussed below), condominiums, and sometimes rental housing. Commercial buildings can even be a part of the plan.

The unique problems in the appraisal of townhouses and planned unit developments often revolve around handling the recreation facilities and other common areas and recognizing the effects of a good or bad homeowners' association. For example, the cost approach must allocate a proportional part of the total cost of all common area improvements to the unit under appraisal. This cost may add proportionately more to the value of some units than to others. Land value is usually allocated as a percentage of the total property value or abstracted from sales. The sales comparison approach may be troubled by a shortage of adequate recent sales of similar-sized units within the same project. Sales from nearby projects may not be helpful either, if recreation or other amenities are so different that each project forms a different "neighborhood."

At one time, lenders and the Federal National Mortgage Association (FNMA) created a special category of PUDs known as a *De Minimus PUD.* Used mainly to qualify certain projects for insured loans, the term and category was discontinued in 1990, expanding the types of projects that could qualify.

Zero-Lot-Line (Patio) Homes

A zero-lot-line home, also called a patio home, is based on design concepts developed in California in the 1970s. It is an evolution of the no-side-yard idea. Adjacent homes are built without side yards, as in the row house style. Normally, they are one-story buildings. Instead of being rectangular, as row houses or townhouses often are, the homes usually are L-shaped. Each "L" wraps around a courtyard or patio, as shown in Figure 17.1, forming two of the courtyard's four sides. The side wall of the adjacent house forms the third side of the patio. This wall is usually windowless to assure the privacy of the patio. The back of the patio may be the windowless rear wall of the house behind or a high fence or wall. The patio home provides privacy and open space on a very small lot.

In the appraisal of patio homes, it is important to note whether the project design has addressed the sound and fire problems typical of all row houses. The appraiser should examine and note the visual privacy of the outdoor patio, since such privacy is often a major factor to buyers. Because the idea of a patio house is relatively new, it is as yet untested in many markets. The appraiser must consider how it will sell on the local market, usually by comparing the sales prices of patio homes to those of townhouses or detached houses of similar size and amenities.

Varying the Type of Ownership

The second unique housing concept entails a different legal form of ownership. In the regular detached home, the owner's title includes the building and the land under it. Both building and land are owned in

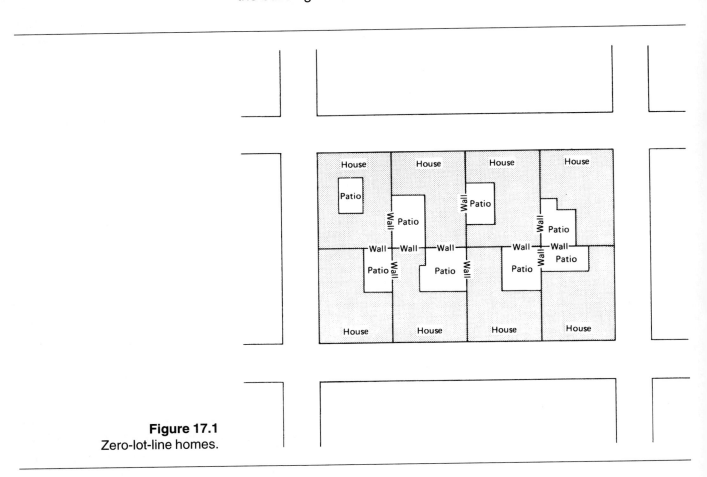

Figure 17.1
Zero-lot-line homes.

fee, that is, owned outright. Of course, such title is subject to the four government restrictions discussed in Chapter 2 as well as to any loans, leases, and so on, that may exist. In the forms of ownership discussed in this section, however, the person who "owns" the dwelling unit holds a different type of title, or ownership right, than with a conventional detached home.

Condominiums   What is a condominium? It is a form of real estate ownership. The dwelling unit itself, or the airspace it occupies, is separately owned, and the land underneath is owned in common with the owners of the other dwelling units. The common example of a condominium is the multistory complex of units, similar to an apartment building. With a three-story building, there could be three identical dwelling units, one on each floor. Obviously, each of the three owners cannot own the land underneath, so they must share its ownership. Beside sharing the ownership of the land, condominium owners share the ownership of the lobby, the halls, parking spaces, recreation facilities, and other common areas. Since the individual units extend between interior wall surfaces, the structural walls are also owned in common. (See Figure 17.2.)

The legal description of a condominium unit, accordingly, is not restricted to just two dimensions on a horizontal plane. Rather, it describes the space as a three-dimensional outline of airspace, to include the height of the unit from some reference point, as well as its length and width. This explains the term *airspace condominium* because each unit consists of a "block" of airspace. The unit description also provides a legal description of the common areas and the percentage of ownership included.

The condominium dates back to ancient Rome. Its active use in the United States is recent, starting with enabling laws passed in the early 1960s. The condominium idea has since been applied to both new construction and to existing buildings. In both cases, a developer must

Figure 17.2
A condominium project.
(Photograph courtesy of
Doug Frost)

subdivide the airspace and offer for sale the right to own individual units separately.

A condominium is usually run by a homeowners' association, similar to that of a PUD or townhouse project. The basic authority given to the association is set forth in the recorded Conditions, Covenants, and Restrictions (CC&Rs) document that is binding on each owner. The association normally runs the project, maintains the exterior and common areas, and adopts rules to minimize conflicts between owners. Some associations also set up recreation, child care, and education programs.

In appraising an individual condominium, the appraiser most commonly emphasizes the sales comparison approach. There are four important aspects to the sales comparison of condominiums. The first is the market itself: Have condominiums sold well in this market area? In some areas, neighborhoods, and price ranges, the condominium concept has sold poorly. In others, market reception has been very good. If the appraiser can identify recent market sales of units in the same project, these sales may provide the best comparables. The second aspect is the unit itself: What size, condition, quality, and amenities are offered? As in the appraisal of townhouses, the appraiser must consider how adequate the sound insulation is, especially in condominium conversions. The third aspect is the scope of recreation facilities, parking, and other common areas. Projects vary greatly. In some states, these common facilities may be owned by the developer and leased to the homeowners' association, so it pays to double-check the ownership of all common areas. These facilities must be reviewed for their quality, condition, and features. In addition, the appraiser must consider whether they are adequate. A single 10×20 foot swimming pool may add little to the value of a 500-unit project in a summer resort area because the pool is far too small for the demand.

A fourth aspect for the appraiser to consider is the homeowners' association. How much is the annual assessment? How does the assessment compare to that of nearby similar projects? Is the budget adequate to maintain the project? Does the association appear competently managed? How stable are the relationships between the association and its members? These questions relate to the continued ability of the project to provide a comfortable place to live.

As you can see, appraisals of condominium projects require first a good understanding of the ownership rights and then a knowledge of the differences that are typical from unit to unit as well as from project to project.

Cooperatives   There are many different types of cooperative ventures in our society. Here, we are interested in the stock cooperative form of ownership for a multiple-unit housing project, somewhat similar to the condominium concept. In a stock cooperative, each owner holds a stated percentage ownership in the cooperative association. The association owns the land and buildings and grants the individual owner the permanent right to occupy the specified dwelling unit as well as the right to the joint use of the common areas.

Cooperative ownership of real estate has existed in the United States for some years. For example, numbers of cooperative apartment buildings were built in New York City during the 1950s and 1960s. A major flaw with the cooperative concept at that time was in the method of financing. One master mortgage covered the entire building. When an individual cooperative unit resold, the buyer had to pay for the seller's equity interest (the total unit value less the unit's proportionate share of the current balance on the master mortgage) in cash or with an unsecured note to the seller. It was not possible to refinance unless a majority of the owners of all of the units agreed to refinance the entire master mortgage. When condominium legislation of the 1960s offered condominiums and other partial ownerships that could be separately financed, the cooperative ownership concept fell into temporary disfavor.

State and federal legislation passed in 1978 and 1979 greatly modified the cooperative housing concept, allowing individual unit mortgages under some circumstances. Consequently, the cooperative offers amenities similar to a condominium. In some markets, value differences between the two types are relatively small. In other markets, however, the value difference between similar condominium and stock cooperative projects may be significant.

Generally, each of the four appraisal considerations that were listed in the discussion of condominiums would apply to the cooperative unit as well. In addition, the appraiser must consider whether the unique loan arrangements of the cooperative are important. Does local law allow individual mortgages? If so, when did it become effective? Do the sales prices for recent cooperative unit sales reflect the amount of equity only, the equity plus master mortgage, or something else? If the appraiser wants to use sales from another building, this information is especially critical. Prior to the cited laws, cooperative units typically sold for substantially less than similar condominium units. Part of the price difference could be explained by the large amounts of cash required to buy a cooperative unit as compared with a condominium. Local refinancing opportunities for cooperatives should be investigated by the appraiser.

Mobile Homes and Prefabs

Another type of unique housing consists of structures that are of unusual construction. Of course, what is unusual construction at any one time may become common a few years later. Two types of similar but unusual construction are of special interest to the appraiser. One is the mobile home; the other, the prefabricated home. The number of each has increased considerably over the past decade. This increased popularity is due to cost advantages but is restrained by some special problems that appraisers need to understand.

Mobile Homes

What is a mobile home? It is a housing unit that is capable of being moved on the highway in one or more sections. The mobile home is different from a travel trailer, which is much smaller and designed for part-time living and frequent moving. A mobile home is also different from a modular home, although both might have the same floor plan and be built at the same factory. Both are described by the label "manufactured housing." However, the modular home has no wheels, undercarriage, or towing arrangement and is designed to be permanently placed on a lot.

Mobile homes are sold in various lengths and widths. Generally, state laws limit the maximum width and length. For many states, 12 feet wide by 60 feet long is a practical maximum. Such units are called a "twelve-wide." Often, the mobile home consists of several units, transported separately and fastened together at the site. Each unit might be the maximum 12 × 60 feet. "Double-wide" units, 24 × 60 feet, are common, and some "triple-wide" mobile homes can be found. Figure 17.3 displays an older "single-wide."

Over the past decade, the number of mobile homes built each year has increased substantially. Mobile homes are built in a factory, which means a major cost savings to the buyer. This advantage has been somewhat ignored because of the poor past image of mobile home communities, relatively unattractive exterior design, and the inability to obtain zoning for new mobile home parks.

The appraisal of mobile homes offers some special problems. As with other housing, the appraiser should consider the age, condition, quality, and features of the mobile home. However, *location* takes on added importance in the appraisal of homes located within rental mobile home parks. In some areas, there are special laws regarding rental rates and occupancy rights in these parks. In addition, most areas have a shortage of spaces, and waiting lists are common. Some park owners also sell new mobile homes and try to reserve vacant spaces for their new customers. As a result, sales prices of used mobile homes can vary, according to whether the buyer gets to rent the space at the park or must move the mobile home. The appraiser must examine sales and try to estimate how much of the total price was paid for the mobile home and how much was paid for the right to occupy the

Figure 17.3
An older mobile home.
(Photograph courtesy of
Doug Frost)

space at the park. A third important element of location is to consider the amenities and market appeal of the particular mobile home park.

Whether the mobile home is located in a mobile home park or situated on a privately owned lot, its appraisal is most commonly based on the sales comparison process. The income capitalization approach is rarely used because very few mobile homes are purchased as income-generating investments. The cost approach is difficult to apply because (1) open market sales of lots zoned for mobile homes are infrequent in most areas, (2) the estimate of accrued depreciation is often more difficult than in conventional homes, and (3) the influence of location on value is difficult to measure when the home is located in a mobile home park.

How is the sales comparison approach applied in the appraisal of mobile homes? When the home is on a privately owned lot, whether in a conventional subdivision or a mobile home park condominium, the process is the same as that used in any appraisal relying on sales of similar homes on similar sites. However, when a mobile home is located in a *rental* mobile home park, and site value is not a factor, some appraisers rely on national publications which list average prices for particular models of mobile homes. This is less accurate than relying on local sales prices but may be adequate for loan purposes because the national data involve a large number of sales. Because of the large numbers of sales, the national publications are also able to present actual average market price adjustments for awnings, utility sheds, and other common mobile home extras.

Prefabricated and Modular Homes

A major portion of the money spent to build a conventional home goes for labor. Traditionally, each board is cut to the desired length at the house site. The use of prefabrication in housing attempts to lower this cost by transferring work from the construction job site to a factory-style operation. See Figure 17.4. The advantages of a factory operation include the use of machines to greatly increase the production per person and an assembly-line style of construction that succeeds with a less skilled, less expensive work force. The influence of the factory-style process on housing has been noticeable in the design of both modular homes and prefabricated components for conventional houses.

Most modular homes are essentially of mobile home design but without the running gear and towing assembly. However, some two-story designs have been offered. The biggest handicaps have been public acceptance, the tendency for a "boxy" look, problems getting building code approval, the high cost to transport units any great distance from the factory, and, occasionally, opposition from construction unions. The advantages are the considerable cost reductions and the reduced construction period compared with other methods. Within the past few years, more attractive designs of modular and prefabricated homes have reduced the resistance to modular homes among building officials as well as among buyers. Thus expansion of modular home construction is anticipated in the years ahead.

Figure 17.4
Modular homes. (Courtesy of the U.S. Department of Housing and Urban Development)

Modular homes, based on mobilehome designs, are not the only form of "factory" housing. A second category is often labeled *prefabricated* housing. Designs are often innovative in both layout and materials. Many experimental ideas have been explored, and some actual buildings have been built. "Habitat," at the Montreal World's Fair in 1967, was a well-publicized example. Unfortunately, the savings in labor costs are usually offset by the high capital costs of the factory. Also, buyers have often reacted to such homes as being either too boxy, too repetitious, or too unusual.

Market acceptance is the biggest question facing the appraisal of modular and prefabricated housing. Of course, the design must be evaluated to consider unit size, features, and especially the layout. The interior and exterior finish materials and the unit's appearance must then be compared with units that are selling in the local area. When the units are quite different from housing sold locally, the appraiser might want to get a consumer panel's reaction to the units if presale appraisals are being made.

As noted earlier, the use of prefabricated components is the second major example of factory-built housing. Roof trusses were an early prefabricated component. As a form of prefabrication, many larger homebuilders now precut and package all the lumber needed for a particular model of a home. Many fireplace–chimney units are prefabricated. Plastic tub and shower combinations are now common; full prefabricated plastic bathrooms are available but less common. Some builders now preassemble nearly all the complex plumbing, drain, and vent pipes into one wall section. Increasing numbers of firms supply preassembled wall panels. Precast concrete floor or wall assemblies are especially common. The use of prefabricated components is clearly a growing element in construction, spurred on by high costs of on-site labor and the appeal of some new energy-saving wall assemblies now being offered.

17.2 VALUATION OF PARTIAL INTERESTS

Concepts and Definitions

Partial interests are created when deeds or other legal instruments divide or limit the fee simple title to the property.

The most familiar partial interests in real estate are those listed here. Brief definitions are included.

---

1. Interests created by a lease:

   Leased fee: the owner's interest in a leased property.

   Leasehold: the tenant's interest in a leased property.

   Subleasehold: the sub-tenant's interest in a leased property.

2. Other partial interests:

   Life estate: consists of an ownership interest that concludes upon the death of the owner or any named person.

   Undivided interests in commonly held property: created when two or more persons share the ownership and each owner has a non-exclusive right of use. Such rights are often coupled with the sole ownership rights of an adjacent property, as in condominiums.

   Mortgaged property: property subject to a mortgage or deed of trust.

   Timeshares: the rights to an exclusive use or occupancy, for a recurrent time period.

   Easements: rights or interests held by one party in the land of another; may be created by grant or other means.

   While appraisals can involve many types of partial interests in real estate, the most common involve undivided interests in commonly held property. These were already discussed in section 17.1 under condominiums and specialized housing. Four other types of partial ownerships will be covered in this section: leased property, life estates, mortgaged property, and time-shared ownerships. Please note that this discussion is only an introduction to the unique appraisal problems these ownerships can present.

Leased Property   A familiar appraisal situation involving a partial interest is the *leased property*. Any lease of real estate subdivides the rights to the property because the tenant gains possession of the property in return for agreeing to pay the owner the contracted rent. If the contract rent is less than the market rent (which can happen in a rising market), the tenant keeps the difference. The benefit of such a rent difference creates a value that belongs to the tenant. The amount of this leasehold value depends on the size of the rent differences as well as how long the lease is to continue.

Defining Leased Property Interests   As you can see, the difference between the contract rent and the market rent divides a leased property into *two* partial interests. The first is the owner's interest (lessor's interest, or *leased fee*), and the second is the tenant's interest (lessee's interest, or *leasehold*). Theoretically, each can be sold; therefore, each can be valued. In the appraisal of partial interests, the combined values of the two interests generally add up to equal the value of the fee simple interest, although there is some question as to whether this is an exact and/or constant rule. Note that leased property interests may involve any type of real property and not just commercial or "income" property. However, for our examples, we shall talk about an income-generating property (such as a store) because we can more easily show how the benefits of ownership are split up by using dollars of income.

Who Gets What?   The primary question in appraising leased property (and every other partial-interest situation) is: "Who gets what?" How are the rights to the property split up? What are the obligations of owner and tenant? The lease conveys possession of the property for a limited time in return for a rental. Thus it is essential to know what property is conveyed. Is the basement included? Does the owner retain use of a locked storeroom? Was the furniture included in the lease?

We must also know what the time period is, that is, the time remaining until the lease expires. This means we must know the exact starting date of the lease. Many leases give the tenant an option to extend or renew the lease when the expiration date arrives. Such options sometimes are at a different rent or even at a rent "to be agreed on." Thus we must read lease option clauses carefully in order to understand their real effect on the owner's and tenant's respective rights.

Finally, we must know what rent terms have been agreed on. The rent could be "flat"—the same amount throughout the lease; or the rent might be projected to vary, as in a step-up lease, where the rent increases by a stated amount at predetermined periods. Some leases set the rent as a percentage of the tenant's business, usually in terms of the gross volume of sales. Percentage rent can be combined *with* a minimum flat rent, or it may be calculated only on sales volumes over a stated amount. Sometimes, percentage rent is reduced by stated categories of expenses paid by the tenant. More and more, we see leases in which it is agreed that the rent is increased as the cost of living index increases. The index used could be the national index or the index for a particular city. The rent increase resulting from increases in the index is sometimes calculated annually, although every five years is also a common interval. There may also be a maximum to the allowable cost of living rent increase. In short, rental terms agreed on between owner and tenant can be almost as varied and complex as the human mind can make them.

The tenant's responsibility for expenses is another factor in the analysis of leased property interests. This is significant because the rental alone may not completely define what amount the tenant pays. Each lease may vary, from a "gross" lease, which stipulates that the landlord must pay all operating expenses, to a truly "net" lease, according to which the tenant pays everything. Indeed, in shopping centers, leases often require the tenants to pay operating expenses, plus a contribution toward a center promotion budget, plus separate payment for all the special partitions, storefronts, and so forth in the store. As a result, the question the appraiser must answer about lease compensation is: "Who pays what?"

Valuing Interests in Leased Property

The lessor's and lessee's interests in leased property usually are appraised by the income approach. Separate valuations of the two interests are typically required. The cost approach does *not* provide a way to separate the interests. When market sales of leased property are available, the sales comparison approach may be used; however, an income analysis is generally required to interpret the sale and apply income criteria to the property being appraised.

The value of the leasehold (the lessee's interest) can be estimated or measured by capitalizing the favorable rent difference over the life of the lease. By favorable rent difference, we mean the difference between the contract rent and market rent. This difference is a net annual benefit, similar to annual incomes from other real estate, and can be capitalized and converted into an estimate of value today. In contrast to other real estate income flows, however, this income benefit is scheduled to end at a known time in the future. For this reason, the capitalization procedure is more complex.

If leasehold estates were commonly bought and sold, the income to the lessee (the net rent savings) could be capitalized by using an overall capitalization rate derived from an analysis of sales. However, only those sales of similar tenant interests would be relevant. In practice, appraisers use annuity capitalization, a technique that was mentioned in Chapter 14 of this text. (The annuity capitalization techniques are more fully covered in advanced appraisal courses.) Briefly, annuity capitalization makes use of special factors, or multipliers, usually available in books of financial tables. The length of the lease and the relevant interest (discount) rate determine the factor selected. The appropriate factor is then multiplied times the annual income to calculate the current value. It is also easy to calculate this number using the present value keys of a financial calculator. If the tenant's rent advantage is not the same each year, more complex methods can be used.

The more common appraisal problem involves the appraisal of the landlord's interest, the leased fee, which could also be labeled the value of the property subject to a lease. As suggested above, the sales comparison approach may sometimes be used here. However, the appraiser using this approach must first determine for each sale what interests were conveyed. If these are similar to the subject property interests under appraisal, the appraiser must still compare the market and contract rents, and the terms of the lease, with those of the subject property, and make adjustments for differences. Even when appraising the fee simple interest in a property, a sale of a property that is subject to a poor lease is *not* the best comparable to use.

The value of the leased fee interest involves analyzing the lease income for a known time period, generally the term of the lease. The present value of this income is estimated in the same manner as is the present value of the leasehold income. However, in addition to the lease income, the lessor gets back possession of the property when the lease is up, and gains the right to sell the fee interest, or rent it at full market rent. This return of the full ownership is called the *reversion.*

To summarize, the value of the leased fee is measured by the economic benefits that the lessor obtains from the lease. These can be described in terms of these two types of cash flows: (1) the annual income from the lease, and (2) the market value of the fee simple rights at the end of the lease. Reworded, the current value of the leased fee equals the present value of the income from the lease, plus the present value of the reversion of the fee simple rights.

How is the present value of the reversion calculated? The first step is to estimate what the fee simple value of the property will be at the time the lease ends. This future value is translated into an estimate of present value using another form of discount factor called the *reversion factor.* This entails looking up the proper factor in the financial tables, using the lease length and the relevant interest/discount rate. Then, the factor is multiplied times the appraiser's estimate of the future value of the reversion. Again, this can also be calculated with a financial calculator rather than with tables. The answer is the present value of the reversion. It is added to the present value of the income stream, and the total is the estimated value of the lessor's interest. (For a review of how to calculate discounted cash flows, refer to Chapter 14, section 14.4.)

Since the combined value of the lessor's and lessee's interests usually equals the value of the undivided fee, some appraisers prefer to value the lessor's interest merely by subtracting the value of the lessee's interest from an estimate of the undivided fee value.

Valuing Other Partial Interests

Life Estates

Another way of breaking up the fee simple interest is to split it into the *life estate* and the *remainder estate.* This unusual breakdown nearly always involves a residence. The owner of the life estate controls the right of possession and use of the property during the lifetime of some specifically named person. While the named person usually owns the life estate, he or she need not. The named person need not occupy the property either, since the owner of the life estate may sell or rent the property. The life estate owner must pay all the operating expenses but does not pay rent. A life estate is different from a lease in that no rent is paid and the term is not a fixed number of years. The owner of the remainder of the estate has no rights to the real property, except the right to gain full fee simple ownership upon the death of the named person by whose life the estate is defined.

No one can reliably forecast when a named individual will die. However, there are studies of the average remaining life for people of various ages. These studies are called actuarial studies and were developed to calculate necessary life insurance premiums. From the actuarial studies, the Internal Revenue Service calculates the breakdown of a property's total value into the life estate and the remainder, based on the age of the person holding the life estate. These calculations are a form of annuity capitalization, dividing the present worth of $1 per year for the remaining life estimate of the holder of the life estate at 10% interest (for gifts or deaths after 1983) by the present worth of $1 per year forever, also calculated at 10% interest. The answer is the total value represented by the life estate.

Figure 17.5 shows the appropriate IRS table for a donor of either sex, with the gift or death after 1983. The donor's age is looked up in column 1, and column 4 shows the value of the remainder interest as a percent of the total market value.

Mortgaged Property

When someone borrows money and signs a mortgage or deed of trust on real property as security for the loan, he or she has split up the fee simple interest into two parts. The lender's interest in the real property is the right to have the real property as security for the amount owing on the promissory note. The borrower's interest is the right to full use of the property less the obligation to make the payments.

In one sense, the current value of the mortgage is its principal balance, or the amount owed. However, if current mortgage interest rates for new loans are considerably different from the interest rate being paid on an existing note and mortgage, then there is a problem. No one would buy the promissory note at its current balance because the interest return they receive would differ from the current rate of interest. Thus the current value of the *note* is a price that will yield for the

(1) Age	(2) Annuity	(3) Life estate	(4) Remainder	(1) Age	(2) Annuity	(3) Life estate	(4) Remainder
0	9.7188	.97188	.02812				
1	9.8988	.98988	.01012	56	7.9006	.79006	.20994
2	9.9017	.99017	.00983	57	7.7931	.77931	.22069
3	9.9008	.99008	.00992	58	7.6822	.76822	.23178
4	9.8981	.98981	.01019	59	7.5675	.75675	.24325
5	9.8938	.98938	.01062	60	7.4491	.74491	.25509
6	9.8884	.98884	.01116	61	7.3267	.73267	.26733
7	9.8822	.98822	.01178	62	7.2002	.72002	.27998
8	9.8748	.98748	.01252	63	7.0696	.70696	.29304
9	9.8663	.98663	.01337	64	6.9352	.69352	.30648
10	9.8565	.98565	.01435	65	6.7970	.67970	.32030
11	9.8453	.98453	.01547	66	6.6551	.66551	.33449
12	9.8329	.98329	.01671	67	6.5096	.65096	.34904
13	9.8198	.98198	.01802	68	6.3610	.63610	.36390
14	9.8066	.98066	.01934	69	6.2066	.62086	.37914

Figure 17.5
Valuation Table A, Internal Revenue Service.

buyer of the mortgage the current market interest rate, given the dollar payments that the borrower has promised to make. Calculating this value involves another aspect of annuity capitalization. First, the annuity factor for the required yield rate and time is looked up. Note that if the loan payments are received monthly, a monthly-payment factor must be used. The factor is then multiplied times the payment amount to find the present value of the promissory note. The value of the note can differ from the value of the lender's interest in the real estate itself. This topic is explored more fully in advanced appraisal courses.

The value of the borrower's interest in the real estate (also called the equity interest) is calculated most accurately by capitalizing the net income that the owner will have left after making loan payments. A number of capitalization techniques are available; one, described as the equity residual technique, is discussed in Chapter 14 of this text.

Time-Shared Ownership

Time-shared ownership is a new example of the increasing complexity of real estate. Most often applied to resort or vacation housing, it is a subdivision of the fee interest into blocks of time, with each time block owned by a different owner. The usual division is made by weeks. Thus owner A might own the right to occupy the property during the second and third week of July. Owner J might purchase the last three weeks of the year, and so on. Most commonly, the project developer not only sells the units but manages them as well. Unoccupied units are rented out, and the unit owners are credited with the revenue after deducting expenses.

The individual time blocks sell for varying prices. In or near ski areas, the Christmas and Easter blocks sell for a large premium, but the summer periods may sell for a discount. The developer's most critical decision is to select a sale price for each block, with these premiums and discounts carefully balanced. The goal is to generate the maximum total revenue and the most rapid sell-out of all the time blocks. Prices for the individual units usually vary as well because of differences in views, exposure, and other locational influences. As a result, there is no fixed formula for valuing individual time blocks. Valuation of the time-block ownership basically involves estimating (1) the value of the unit in fee simple, and then (2) the bonus/discount for each time block. The appraiser must carefully study the locational differences of each unit and the seasonal bonus/discounts found in the market for time-block projects that can be compared with the subject. Only by doing such research can the appraiser hope to value these interesting partial rights in real property.

17.3 VALUATION FOR EMINENT DOMAIN

We said earlier that valuation for condemnation actions under the power of eminent domain is one of the most specialized areas of appraisal practice. The power of eminent domain is one of the four rights to real estate that are retained by the government (see Chapter 2).

Defining Eminent Domain

Eminent domain refers to the government's right to take private property from its owners for public use (whether the owners want to sell or not) upon payment of just compensation. Generally, the term *just compensation* has been interpreted by the courts to mean the fair market value of the property.

From this introduction, you can see that appraisal for eminent domain has the same general purpose as most other appraisals: the estimation of market value. There are other similarities as well as some differences. Valuation for eminent domain is a complex subject; this section is intended to be an introduction.

The Appraisal Process

Eminent domain valuation involves the same appraisal process as we detailed in Chapter 3. The six steps of the appraisal process were listed as:

---

1. Clearly defining the appraisal problem.

2. Formulating an efficient appraisal plan.

3. Collecting and analyzing the pertinent data.

4. Applying the appropriate value approaches.

5. Arriving at a conclusion of value.

6. Reporting the conclusion of value.

Let us explore these steps as they apply to eminent domain appraising. We will not discuss step 2, planning the appraisal, because this step would be essentially the same.

Defining the Appraisal Problem

In Chapter 3, we listed the seven essential elements that are necessary to define the appraisal problem. These elements are also essential to condemnation appraisal.

---

1. Identification of the property.

2. Property rights to be appraised.

3. The purpose and intended use of the appraisal.

4. The extent of the data collection process.

5. Any special limiting conditions.

6. The effective date of the appraisal.

7. Definition of the value being considered.

---

1. Identifying the property to be appraised can be a special problem because the government does not always acquire the entire prop-

erty. However, the appraiser must consider the concept of the "larger parcel," even if only a portion of the property is acquired. The ownership and value of fixtures is also a common problem in condemnation. We shall explore these two topics further under the heading Problems in Condemnation Appraisals.

2. The property rights to be appraised in condemnation are most commonly the fee simple rights. On occasion, however, the governmental agency could be condemning only an easement, a leasehold estate, or some other partial interest. The appraiser will usually be provided with a clear statement of the rights to be taken.

3. The purpose of the appraisal is always the estimation of market value. The intended use of the report could be for the condemnor (the public agency) or the condemnee (the owner). In the case of the former, the report usually will be the basis for the offer to the property owner. Often, the condemnor will furnish the property owner with a copy or a summary of the appraisal report. When the appraisal report is for the condemnee (the property owner), it is most commonly for use in challenging the value assigned by the condemnor.

4. The extent of the process of collecting, confirming, and reporting data should be fully described in appraisal reports intended to be used in condemnation cases.

5. The special limiting conditions surrounding an appraisal made for condemnation may include some unique ones in addition to those usually stated. For example, if the appraiser relied on the opinion of engineers, attorneys, or others in arriving at the value conclusion, such opinions should be specifically documented and cited.

6. The effective date of value can be a significant problem in condemnation appraisals. It will usually be the date that the formal court documents are filed, but it can also be a different date. The appraiser may have to rely on the client's attorney to indicate the date of value. Sometimes, too, the appraiser will have to reappraise the property as of a later date, such as the trial date.

7. The full definition of market value must be included in the appraisal. Various states and the federal courts may follow slightly different legal definitions of value; therefore, the appraiser must use the definition appropriate for the court hearing the condemnation case.

Collecting and Analyzing the Data

In the third step of the appraisal process, collecting and analyzing the data, there is a major difference between condemnation appraisal assignments and others. The difference is that the courts (rather than the appraiser) make the final decision as to what types of data are admissible, that is, can be used in testimony. Indeed, some jurisdictions by law exclude some types of market data that an appraiser might otherwise consider relevant to a particular appraisal. For example, listings and offers are not admissible in some courts. Sometimes, a court will establish its own definition of comparability, as to acceptable limits for date of sale, or distance from the subject property of comparable sales (instead of leaving such matters to the appraiser's judgment). However, the great majority of condemnation appraisals rely on the same kinds of sales, rents, costs, overall rates, and so on that are required for loan appraisals or other common appraisal purposes.

Applying the Value Approaches

Special rules in condemnation appraisal also affect the fourth step in the appraisal process, applying the appropriate value approaches. Certain possible methods of analysis, such as the development method of land appraisal, may not be allowable in some jurisdictions, or are given less weight by the courts. The appraiser will want to know this in planning the appraisal in order not to rely on a method that the court will exclude. However, there are no special approaches to value, just the time-tested sales comparison, cost, and income approaches you have met before. Thus most condemnation appraisals will rely on the same appraisal techniques and methods you would use for any other appraisal assignment.

Arriving at a Value Conclusion

This is the fifth step in the appraisal process. It is no different for eminent domain appraisal than appraising for other purposes, except that the value conclusion may have to be given in several parts, as detailed below under the heading Problems in Condemnation Appraisals.

Reporting the Conclusion

The sixth step in the appraisal process, reporting the value conclusion, is also modified for eminent domain appraisals. The major difference between condemnation and other appraisals is that the format for such appraisal reports varies a great deal. In some cases, as in appraisals made for the condemnee, you might be asked to prepare only an oral report, leaving the expense of preparing a written report to a time closer to trial. If the parties can settle the case without a trial, the written report will not be needed.

In preparing an appraisal for the condemnor, however, a written appraisal report is usually required. The report will often be a long, documented narrative. The condemnee will sometimes be given a copy. A well-written report may play a key role in convincing the property owner to accept the government's offer.

Problems in Condemnation Appraisals

Condemnation law is different for real and personal property. Thus for condemnation appraisals, it is often necessary to identify and appraise *only* the real property.

Fixtures

The problem area is fixtures: objects that were once personal property but have been joined to the real property and may now be either real or personal, depending on a series of complex rules. You may want to review the earlier coverage of this topic in Chapter 2. On occasion, the appraiser will have to prepare sets of values including and excluding particular fixtures and have the court decide which are real property and which are personal property.

The Legal Setting   In condemnation appraisal work, the appraiser may end up as an expert witness, testifying to the judge and jury and being cross-examined about qualifications, comparables, and methods. The appraiser must be aware of this possibility and prepare for it from the first moment of working on an appraisal of this kind. The fixture issue discussed above is one of a number of issues that are decided by the rules of the courts. Eminent domain appraisal is different from most other appraisal work precisely because it is prepared for, and presented to, the courts and is performed according to the special rules established by the courts and legislature.

Often the appraiser will have to rely on an attorney hired by the client (whether condemnor or condemnee) to provide needed legal advice concerning both the appraisal and the testimony. This could involve many issues, such as establishing the probability of re-zoning, what value date to use, what property to appraise, which data and approaches will be admissible in this court, and so on. If the attorney for the other side has a different view of the law, and prevails, your appraisal and your testimony could be tossed out. It is prudent to try to understand the basis for any legal advice and to ask the attorney again if the advice is not understood. A written letter detailing any vital issues is often desirable.

The Partial Taking   Perhaps the most unique aspects of appraising for eminent domain are those that stem from a "partial" taking: when the government agency is acquiring only a portion of the property, called the "take" parcel. The owner is to be left the rest, called the "remainder" parcel. The total parcel is called the "larger parcel." Figure 17.6 portrays such a partial taking.

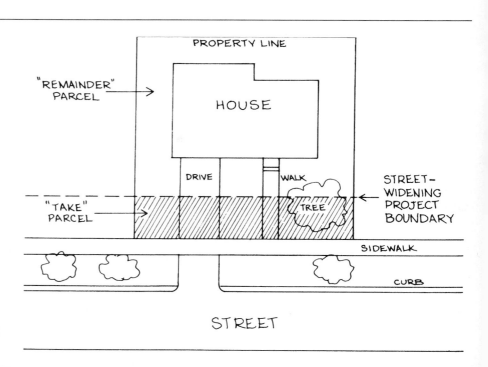

Figure 17.6
A partial taking.

The Larger Parcel   The appraiser must first determine what the larger parcel is. What if the same owner owns the two adjacent houses? What if he or she has a 99-year lease on the warehouse behind? What if her brother and she jointly own the property across the street? This issue is important in evaluating whether the remainder parcel has been hurt (lost value) as a result of the "take." The courts have evolved three tests to determine which parcels make up the larger parcel, based on the theory that the larger parcel consists of a coherent functional economic grouping.

First, the parcels must be contiguous. Increasingly, the courts have interpreted this to include across the street, or even up the street, if economically joined together. Second, they must be under the same ownership. The appraiser may need to review the many court cases examining this issue or else explore the issue with the attorney. Third, the parcels must be put to the same use. The courts have tended to interpret this rule rather strictly. Again, it may be wise for the appraiser to ask an attorney's opinion on this legal issue.

Take, Damages,   The courts have interpreted just compensation in a partial taking to in-
and Benefits   clude the following three elements. Some courts require that each element be calculated in turn. Other courts combine all three elements, appraising the value of the larger parcel and subtracting the value of the remainder parcel. The key is to use the procedure approved by the court involved.

The first element to consider is the value of the part to be taken. The part to be taken is usually valued as if it were a separate parcel. In some cases it is valued as a fraction (by area, for example) of the larger parcel.

The second element is the possible damage to the remainder parcel as a result of the government project, called *severance* damage. For instance, a parcel might no longer front on a road, so that the owner must build a $500,000 bridge over an irrigation canal in order to regain access to the property. The $500,000 cost might be a measure of the damages. A government project could harm property in many other ways. Not all damage, however, are compensated for under the power of eminent domain. Some damages are the result of actions legally authorized under the government's police power, and no compensation or payment to property owners is required. For example, the government, in widening a commercial boulevard from two to four lanes, could also install a center barrier, or median. This would prevent drivers from turning left (in the middle of the block) into shopping area driveways. Customers would have to drive to the next intersection, make a U-turn, and come back. They might shift their business to another store on that side of the street, hurting the business, and the value, of stores on this side of the street. Contrary to certain logic, such limited "circuit of travel" is rarely ruled as a "compensable damage." In many partial-taking appraisals, the appraiser will need to research carefully which damages are compensable and which are not. A legal opinion will often be necessary.

The third element of just compensation in a partial taking is the possible benefit of the government project to the remainder parcel. The courts have defined two kinds of benefits, general and special. Only special benefits affect the calculation of just compensation. General benefits are those that are shared by the community at large or at least by more than just a few adjacent property owners. Special benefits, on the other hand, are those that benefit only the remainder parcel (or perhaps only a few more parcels). An example of a special benefit could arise when a larger parcel is swampy land and too wet to build on. As part of a government project, the low corner of the parcel is taken and extensive drainage put in. After the project, the remainder parcel is well drained, fully developable, and much more valuable. If other land in the area has not similarly benefited, the remainder parcel has obtained a special benefit.

The courts differ on how to apply the value of special benefits. Some courts simply value the larger parcel and then deduct the value of the remainder parcel in its improved state. In this case, extensive special benefits could reduce the total payment by the condemnor to zero. Some states allow recognition of special benefits only to the degree that they offset damages. Thus the appraiser must first decide if the benefits to the remainder exist. Next, are they special benefits? Third, how are they to be appraised? And, fourth, how are they to be applied in calculating the final estimate of just compensation?

SUMMARY   Today, appraisers are faced with a growing variety of appraisal assignments. Many of these assignments now involve unique house designs and unusual concepts in ownership. Such types of housing include:

Condominiums	Planned unit developments (PUDs)
Cooperatives	Row houses
Mobile homes	Townhouses
Modular homes	Zero-lot-line (or patio) homes

The common walls between some of these housing types, such as the townhouse, cause special problems with which appraisers should be familiar. One is the greater possibility of fire spreading from one unit to another. Another is the increased lack of privacy. New trends in ownership should also be noted. New legal forms of ownership, such as the condominium and cooperative, have different ownership rights than the conventional detached residence.

There are many appraisal assignments that involve the appraisal of partial interests or the dividing of the fee title. A common appraisal situation involves estimating the current market value of the lessor's and/or lessee's interests in a given property. Other partial-interest appraisals include those involving the life estate and the remainder estate, the property interests of lender and borrower, and the valuation of time-shared ownerships.

One of the most specialized areas of appraisal practice involves valuing property for eminent domain. This type of appraisal follows the same steps in the standard appraisal process; however, a few areas need special attention. For instance, unlike the regular appraisal process, eminent domain cases often require the appraiser to testify as an expert witness before the courts. Therefore, the data collected and analyzed should be well prepared and documented for such testimony. Eminent domain cases also differ in that the value definition, date of value, and methodology are defined by the courts. The classification of property fixtures is also much more critical.

Finally, eminent domain often involves acquisition of only a portion of the property, called a partial take. Here, the appraiser must consider the concepts of the larger parcel, the remainder parcel, severance damages, and general and special benefits in order to reach a final value conclusion.

Important Terms and Concepts

Airspace

Conditions, covenants, and restrictions (CC&Rs)

Condominiums

Cooperatives

Eminent domain

Fixtures

Homeowners' associations

Just compensation

Leased fee

Leasehold

Life estates

Mobile homes

Modular homes

Mortgaged property

Partial interest

Partial taking

Planned unit development (PUD)

Prefabricated homes

Remainder estate

Row house

Seasonal discount

Subleasehold

Time-shared ownership

Undivided interest in commonly held property

Townhouse

Zero-lot-line home

REVIEWING YOUR UNDERSTANDING

1. Which of the various forms of detached housing are characterized by the lack of side yards?
   (a) Mobile homes, standard detached single-family residential
   (b) Apartment buildings, condominiums
   (c) Row houses, townhouses
   (d) None of the above

2. A condominium is:
   (a) A type of real estate description
   (b) Like a cooperative

(c) A legal concept of ownership
(d) A type of physical design of a building

3. A zero-lot-line home is also known as:
   (a) A duplex
   (b) A modular home
   (c) A patio home
   (d) A condominium

4. Homeowners' associations are often found in:
   (a) PUDs
   (b) Condominiums
   (c) None of the above
   (d) Both (a) and (b)

5. Partial interests are created by:
   (a) Deeds or legal instruments
   (b) Transfer of the fee interest
   (c) The termination of a lease
   (d) None of the above

6. The lessor's interest in leased property is referred to as the:
   (a) Leasehold
   (b) Leased fee
   (c) Fee simple
   (d) Remainder

7. A gross lease is:
   (a) A lease under which the tenant pays for all expenses
   (b) A lease under which the landlord pays for all operating expenses
   (c) A lease that applies only to commercial properties
   (d) None of the above

8. The benefits that belong to the leased fee interest include:
   (a) The lease income
   (b) The reversion
   (c) Both of the above
   (d) None of the above

9. Generally, the courts have determined just compensation in eminent domain cases to mean:
   (a) The fair market value of the property
   (b) Current market value plus compensation for anticipated future benefits
   (c) The market value at the time the property was bought by the current owner
   (d) All of the above

10. Eminent domain cases are commonly referred to as:
    (a) Condemnation
    (b) A take
    (c) Both (a) and (b)
    (d) None of the above

Chapter 18
The Professional Appraiser

Preview   In this last chapter, you meet the appraisers, the people whose craft you have been studying. The first section looks at their education and experience. The second section outlines the typical requirements for state licensing and certification. The third section covers the major professional appraisal organizations: their purposes, membership criteria, and professional designations. In the fourth and fifth sections we examine the standards of appraisal practice and discuss appraising as an occupation.

When you have completed this chapter, you should be able to:

1. *List at least four important courses for an appraiser to take.*

2. *Define the typical state requirements for appraiser licensing and certification.*

3. *List the two major groups of professional appraisers.*

4. *Outline the first two requirements of the Uniform Standards of Professional Appraisal Practice.*

5. *Compare the opportunities of appraisers working for a salary with those of the fee appraiser.*

18.1 THE APPRAISER'S BACKGROUND

What are the backgrounds of people who do appraising? What kind of training is necessary? Are there minimum educational requirements? The qualifications of appraisers vary widely. A few states now require that all appraisers meet minimum requirements of education and experience, and be licensed or certified. However, most state laws require only those involved in federally related appraisals to meet such standards. Typical requirements for licensing and certification will be outlined in section 18.2.

Education

For those not planning to qualify for federally related appraisal work, there are no uniform educational requirements for becoming an appraiser. However, most practicing appraisers have some college-level training, and many have college degrees.

Reasons for Education

Formal education helps the would-be appraiser gain valuable general knowledge and skills. Most college courses help an individual learn to reason clearly, which is an aid in figuring out appraisal problems. The appraiser must also learn to write clearly. The appraisal report, even if on a form, must succinctly communicate the appraiser's findings. Mathematics is also an important skill to master, since all three approaches involve working with numbers. Algebra is helpful in handling formulas in the income approach. Plane geometry is helpful in calculating areas of odd-shaped parcels. These are some of the general skills that are used by appraisers.

Appraisers also need to have a good understanding of the many factors that affect real estate. Taking courses in finance, economics, taxation, city planning, city and county government, real estate law, and urban geography are very helpful in expanding one's understanding of real estate. The series of real estate courses taught at many community colleges is particularly helpful in expanding the appraiser's knowledge of real estate markets and brokerage. Other courses, such as beginning geology, blueprint reading, architecture, accounting, transportation, geography, and statistics may also be helpful.

The third area in which appraisers seek formal education is in their own field. Theories, ideas, and techniques learned in an accredited appraisal course will enable later on-the-job training to be much more meaningful.

General Educational Trends

Increasingly, appraisers have a college degree. The largest professional appraisal group, the Appraisal Institute, requires a college degree for membership. Growing numbers of employers are requiring appraisal trainees to have a college degree, real estate courses, or several years of experience in real estate. Their concern is with making the trainee a productive appraiser in the shortest possible time.

Few people have a degree in real estate, or one with a real estate field of emphasis, because few colleges offer such programs. The University of Wisconsin at Madison and the University of California at Berkeley and at Los Angeles are well known for their real estate curricula. In the absence of a degree specializing in real estate, preferred

Figure 18.1
(Photograph courtesy of
Ken Karp)

fields of emphasis include economics, business administration–finance, urban geography, or city planning.

Real Estate Courses   Many appraisers have taken the series of real estate courses for brokers that community colleges offer. Typically, these includes courses in real estate principles, practices, finance, law, appraisal, and economics. Additional courses may cover real estate investment, exchanges, remodeling, escrows, and other specialized topics. In several states, including California, the student can earn a Certificate in Real Estate by attending a requisite series of courses. Many of these appraisal-related courses meet both the accreditation requirement and the topical content requirements for licensing and certification. Real estate certificates are gaining recognition as a sign of a well-rounded real estate education.

Generally, the appraisal courses sponsored by the major professional societies have also been state-approved for licensing and certification. Such courses may be more advanced than the community college appraisal courses. Some appraisers take the community college course at the very start of their career and the first course of the Appraisal Institute after six months or a year on the job. The second Institute course might be taken six months or a year after that, depending on the course availability and the appraiser's work experience.

Appraisers may also rely on professional societies for specialized education. Appraisal groups offer seminars and courses on such diverse subjects as appraising industrial property or condominiums and introduction to money markets. In addition, there are numerous workshops, special seminars, and dinner speeches that can further the education of appraisers who participate.

Figure 18.2
(Photograph courtesy of Bruce Roberts/RaphoPhoto Researchers)

Do-It-Yourself
By nature, appraisers have to be inquisitive. As a result, casual meetings between appraisers are often filled with shoptalk about this or that new house design, theory, trend, and so on. It is a form of self-improvement.

The body of appraisal theory could be learned by self-instruction. There are numerous texts, journals, books and case studies available. However, appraisal classes offer more than theory. For example, your fellow students in advanced classes may hold different jobs in real estate appraising and have different experiences to share. Shared ideas are a significant part of the learning experience, and often become a springboard for continued learning after the class is finished.

Experience
Education alone will not create a competent appraiser. The second element is applying the ideas and skills learned in class. You will not really know if you understand an idea—the sales comparison approach, for example—until you have tried to use it a number of times. Real estate appraisal involves many bits of knowledge that are learned only through experience. Rating the quality and condition of houses in a field assignment is an example. Despite what we have said on these subjects in this book, you will find that most of your skills in such areas will be gained in the field.

Do not expect to be able to make good appraisals upon completing this book. It usually takes six months of full-time experience before an appraisal trainee can produce reliable appraisals of single-family properties without close supervision. For work requiring a state license, of course, trainee-produced appraisals must usually be supervised and signed by a staff member who is state licensed or certified. With this in mind, the importance of experience in appraising can be understood.

With more complicated appraisals, the appraiser needs more experience than just counting off the number of years. The experience also needs to be varied as to the type of property and the appraisal purpose. The appraiser learns from each new assignment. This accumulated experience is very helpful in preparing complex appraisals.

Knowledge   One measure of an appraiser's qualifications is the extent of his or her knowledge. The general areas of knowledge most important to an appraiser are real estate markets, property operations, and market data.

Markets   Real estate appraisers try to understand how real estate markets function, from the role of the broker to the interaction of supply and demand. This means that appraisers try to be aware of the forces that affect prices and current trends. A practical understanding of markets can be extremely valuable to the appraiser.

Operations   Appraisers have to be somewhat familiar with the characteristics and management procedures of the various types of real estate they appraise. For instance, what are the day-to-day problems of convalescent hospital buildings? What is the current practice in writing tax escalation clauses in office leases? Which lenders customarily make loans on retail store buildings? How common are net-net-net leases on office space? What is the typical depth of an office space from center hall to outside windows? In what locations are walk-up, three-story apartments feasible?

Market Data   One reason for hiring appraisers is that they know how to find market data. On occasion, a client will hire an appraiser solely to work up a list of relevant sales or rents. Market information is not widely circulated. The knowledgeable appraiser will have developed sources for particular kinds of data. Few people realize the amount and variety of data the expert appraiser can uncover.

Judgment   Finally, the most important component of the appraiser's art is *judgment,* an elusive concept. One definition is:

> . . . the operation of the mind, involving comparison and discrimination, by which knowledge and values and relationships are mentally formulated.*

Note that this definition uses the word *discrimination* to mean "recognizing differences." The essential elements in this definition of judgment are to: (1) compare, (2) distinguish differences, (3) recognize relationships, and (4) arrive at opinions. Such a description is so

*Webster's New International Dictionary, 2nd ed.

general, it sounds almost like the appraisal process itself. What makes the use of judgment different from the overall process that appraisers follow?

Judgment for an appraiser means the ability to develop an understanding of the complex relationships among factors, events, and so on. Figure 18.3 suggests the difficult task of weighing and balancing these diverse elements. Judgment is the ability of human intuition to process a mass of data and develop a reliable opinion from it. It is the ability to draw good conclusions. A knowledgeable broker, working in a well-known sales territory with which he or she is familiar, is using judgment when, quickly walking through a home, he or she can judge what it will probably sell for. In short, judgment is what gets us from the market data, and any mathematical or graph analysis of it, to an opinion about market value.

There is no simple method for obtaining good judgment. Taking classes can show what factors to consider. Experience gives you practice in applying analytical techniques to practical situations. Developing good judgment, however, may require a third step: self-review. You may need to follow up on your appraisal to see if your opinions turned out to be true. If not, why not? You may also want to see what others think of your opinion and what reasons they offer for their differences. In a broker's open house tour, for example, how do *your* estimates of probable selling price compare to those of others and, equally important, to the final price? We believe that good judgment is developed by education, experience, and reviewing one's mistakes, and by considering the comments of others.

18.2 STATE LICENSE AND CERTIFICATION REQUIREMENTS

Title XI of the Financial Institutions Reform, Recovery, and Enforcement Act of 1989, generally effective in 1993, requires that most appraisals involved in a federally related real estate financial transaction be performed by a state licensed or certified appraiser. (Certain regulated exemptions apply.) "Federally related real estate transactions" have been interpreted to mean transactions involving federal insurance or assistance (e.g., federally insured loans). While some states

Figure 18.3
Appraisal judgment.

require universal licensing, most require no license or certification for: (1) appraisals *not* involving federally related real estate financial transactions, and (2) opinions given by real estate licensees, engineers, or land surveyors in the ordinary course of business. All state regulations are subject to the approval and oversight of the Financial Institutions Appraisal Subcommittee. Minimum requirements are set by the Appraisal Qualifications Board of the Appraisal Foundation.

Parameters of Practice in Federally Related Appraisals

While federal regulations allow some variation in the levels of licensing and certification established by state law, the typical levels and parameters of practice are as follows:

1. **License:** appraisal of non-complex one- to four-unit residential properties, up to a transaction value of $1 million; complex, up to a transaction value of $250,000.

2. **Certified Residential:** appraisal of all residential properties, regardless of transaction value. Federal guidelines limit this practice to one-to-four units.

3. **Certified General:** appraisal of all real estate transactions, without regard to transaction value or complexity.

Basic Education and Experience Requirements

State and federal laws require specific amounts of education and experience for the licensed and certified appraiser designations. While qualifications are stiffening, those that are typical and current follow.

Education Requirements

Qualifying education must include accredited coursework in subjects related to real estate appraisal. Also, exposure to specific appraisal topics is required.

Minimum education hours required depend upon the qualification level, as follows (*Note:* states may vary.):

a. Licensed	75 hours
b. Certified Residential	120 hours
c. Certified General	165 hours

The following topics must be covered in the aggregate education:

1. Influences on Real Estate Value
2. Legal Considerations in Appraisal

3. Types of Value

4. Economic Principles

5. Real Estate Markets and Analysis

6. Valuation Process

7. Property Description

8. Highest and Best Use Analysis

9. Appraisal Statistical Concepts

10. Sales Comparison Approach

11. Site Value

12. Cost Approach

13. Income Approach
   —Gross Rent Multiplier Analysis
   —Estimation of Income and Expenses
   —Operating Expense Ratios
   —Direct Capitalization*
   —Cash Flow Estimates**
   —Measures of Cash Flow**
   —Discounted Cash Flow Analysis**

14. Valuation of Partial Interests*

15. Appraisal Standards and Ethics

16. Narrative Report Writing*

* Not typically required at the licensed level.
** Typically required only at the certified-general level.

Experience Requirements

Experience in real estate appraisal and/or appraisal assistance is required, as follows (states may vary):

a. Licensed: 2,000 hours (over any time period)

b. Certified Residential: 2,000 hours over at least a two-year period

c. Certified General: 2,000 hours. At least 1,000 hours must be in non-residential work (over four units).

Acceptable appraisal experience may include fee and staff appraisal, review appraisal, appraisal analysis, real estate counseling, highest and best use analysis, feasibility analysis/study, and/or teaching appraisal courses.

Other Requirements	Applicants for appraiser licensing or certification must pass a qualifying exam and pay all appropriate fees. Most states will issue a provisional or trainee license to applicants lacking a critical element of either education or experience. In general, the term of licensing or certification is 4 years, with renewal requiring the completion of 40 hours of approved appraisal-related continuing education courses.
18.3 APPRAISAL GROUPS	The great majority of appraisers are either members or member candidates of one of the various appraisal organizations. Many nonmembers regularly attend appraisal group meetings. What do appraisers gain from being associated with such groups?
Benefits	One benefit is that most groups award professional designations to their members who have achieved the required standards. These designations provide a means for the general public to rate the competency of appraisers. Until recently, licenses have not been generally required for any appraisal activity. When licenses were required, the qualifying education and experience requirements were minimal, compared with those of today. As a result, the public has come to rely on the better-known professional designations as an aid in selecting appraisers.
	A second benefit is that these groups provide a major source of formal and informal training for appraisers. As already mentioned, these groups sponsor regular courses, one-day seminars, afternoon workshops, and dinner speakers for the benefit of members. The various groups also publish periodical journals, texts, research monographs, and newsletters. Beyond this type of formal education, the groups' meetings offer informal education. People ask their peers how to handle a particular problem. They ask who may have recently researched a particular type of property sale. They may ask the group's leaders to arrange for a speaker on some new, troublesome problem (mini-warehouses, for example, when such types of property were first developed).
Major Organizations	There are two nationally recognized appraisal organizations with a membership encompassing all areas of real estate appraising. Both (or their legal predecessors) were founded in the 1930s and now have chapters throughout the country, and offer more than one professional designation. A summary of these designations and their requirements is presented here.
Appraisal Institute	The Appraisal Institute was formed in 1991 when the American Institute of Real Estate Appraisers merged with the Society of Real Estate Appraisers. Both groups had been founded in the 1930s, with original members either real estate brokers or residential lenders. Membership of the Appraisal Institute now includes real estate appraisers of every occupational background. Appraisers first apply and are accepted as candidates for a professional designation. Candidates must then complete courses (or successfully challenge the course exam),

submit written demonstration appraisal reports for grading, and have samples of their actual appraisals reviewed for experience rating.

The Institute has an extensive educational program involving many course titles taught at locations across the country. Courses are taught either in an intensive fashion, lasting for one to three weeks, or else in extended fashion. Courses may be either nationally or local chapter-sponsored. The Institute's publishing program includes the major reference text, *The Appraisal of Real Estate*, as well as a number of other texts, research monographs, video cassettes, and the quarterly journal, *The Appraisal Journal.*

Member, Appraisal Institute (MAI) is the designation granted by this group to an appraiser qualified to appraise income property, complex realty, and all real estate interests generally. Members who earned the similar SRPA designation from the Society of Real Estate Appraisers may still use this designation. The requirements for the MAI designation include at least five years' experience in real estate, five years or more of real estate appraisal experience, and three years of experience appraising a variety of types of income-generating properties. There are approximately 6,000 active holders of the MAI designation. Each designee is given a certificate number. This designation probably has the widest public recognition.

Currently, people who want to receive the MAI designation must attend at least 7 weeks of full-time classes (or successfully challenge the related examinations) and pass seven half-day examinations and one all-day examination. While there are other options, most candidates submit two narrative demonstration appraisal reports, each around 100 pages in length and quite thorough in coverage. At least two oral interviews are required. At the second interview, samples of the candidate's actual work are submitted and critiqued. A college degree is required.

Senior Residential Appraiser (SRA) is the designation granted by the Institute to an appraiser qualified to appraise single-family properties. The Residential Member (RM) designation formerly awarded at this level by the prior group, American Institute of Real Estate Appraisers, may be still used by those who earned it before 1991. The SRA must have a minimum of three years in the real estate field, generally, and at least two years' experience appraising single-family homes. At the time of this writing, a college degree is required. There are about 5,000 holders of the SRA designation and about 1,500 active holders of the previously issued RM designation.

The special education requirements for the SRA designation currently call for either: (1) attending four week-long classes, each followed by a half-day examination; or (2) successfully passing the exams alone. A narrative demonstration appraisal report on a home or an alternate report must be submitted. The alternate can be combinations of actual appraisal reports, plus a demonstration report prepared on an expanded version of the FNMA/FHLMC appraisal form. As with the MAI, candidates for the SRA designation have at least two oral interviews and reviews of their actual work product(s).

The Senior Real Estate Analyst (SREA) designation, formerly granted by the Society of Real Estate Appraisers to an appraiser with substantial experience in real estate analysis and consulting work, may still be used by those Institute members who earned it before the two professional groups merged.

American Society of Appraisers

The ASA differs from the Appraisal Institute in one primary way: Membership encompasses the appraising of all types of property, not just real property. The membership of ASA is composed of appraisers whose individual specialties range from ceramics to chemical plants. The group is headquartered in Washington, D.C. It is the successor, by merger in 1952, of two earlier groups, the American Society of Technical Appraisers and the Technical Valuation Society, which were both founded in the 1930s. The Association of Governmental Appraisers, the Society of Governmental Appraisers, and the Association of Federal Appraisers also merged into ASA in the early 1980s.

The educational program of ASA features a college-degree program developed by ASA and jointly sponsored with various accredited colleges around the country. In addition, ASA publishes a large collection of technical monographs via audio cassettes; the major reference work, *The Bibliography of Appraisal Literature,* first published in 1974; and the monthly journal, *Valuation.*

The ASA awards its professional designations based on competency to appraise a specified type of property; the holder of the designation *must* indicate the property type, in parentheses, on any qualifications list. The three major property headings used are real estate, personal property, and machinery and equipment. There are many possible subheadings. Under personal property are found appraisers of silverware, porcelain, oil paintings, books, antiques, furs, jewelry, household contents, antique automobiles, intangibles, and so on. Under machinery and equipment, appraisers may specialize in sand or asphalt batch plants, in machine tools, or in construction rolling stock. The ASA awards three levels of designation.

1. *AM, or Accredited Member,* is the first professional designation or level. The designation is awarded to appraisers who have a college degree or its equivalent and two years of full-time appraisal experience. An interview, submission of appraisal reports, and an examination are also required. There are about 300 AMs.

2. *ASA, or Senior Member,* is the designation awarded to appraisers who have met the requirements for Member and also have five years of appraisal experience. In addition, Senior Members must be recertified every five years. Some 2,800 people hold the ASA designation.

3. *FASA* stands for Fellow of the American Society of Appraisers. It is awarded to holders of the ASA designation who have distinguished themselves in their appraisal activities. This can be through teaching or writing, or by activity as a National Officer. There are currently 35 Fellows.

Specialized Groups

A large number of other nonprofit appraisal groups exist; some are nationwide, others are regional or local. The national groups tend to have a particular area of interest as opposed to the two general groups that were summarized earlier. Of the large number, several will be mentioned here.

International Right of Way Association

This group, usually abbreviated as IR/WA, is headquartered in Los Angeles and was founded in 1934. As its name indicates, membership orientation is toward those involved in the appraisal and acquisition of rights of way. This includes utility company power lines, oil company pipelines, and public highways. All three involve the acquisition of property by condemnation under the power of eminent domain. As a result, other appraisers active in condemnation appraisals may also join IR/WA. Examples include county public works department employees, city real estate officers, flood control district land representatives, and so on. Fee appraisers who do contract work for all these organizations also join. The IR/WA awards several professional designations.

American Society of Farm Managers and Rural Appraisers

This society is headquartered in Denver, Colorado. Founded in 1929, it awards professional designations for farm managers and for rural appraisers. There are area chapters in most major farming regions.

International Association of Assessing Officers

Membership in the IAAO is made up mostly of governmental property tax assessment staff, private firms who contract in many states to do periodic reassessment work, and private tax representatives for major retailers and manufacturers. The group is headquartered in Chicago and was founded in 1934. There are local chapters in some parts of the country. The IAAO awards two real estate designations: 1) CAE (Certified Assessment Evaluator), denoting competence in all real estate appraisal/assessment work, and 2) RES (Residential Evaluation Specialist). There are also two specialty designations offered: PPS (Personal Property Specialist), and CMS (Cadastral Mapping Specialist). The listed designations are available to all members who meet the requirements of the designation, whether regular members (government-employed), or associate members (privately employed).

National Society of Real Estate Appraisers

Organized in California in 1956, the NSREA is an affiliate of the National Association of Real Estate Brokers and is headquartered in Cleveland, Ohio. Most of the 1,500 members are licensed real estate brokers. The group offers three professional designations: Master Real Estate Appraiser (MREA), Certified Real Estate Appraiser (CRA), and Residential Appraiser (RA).

Society of Auditor-Appraisers

This group, SAA, has as members appraisers who specialize in the appraisal of personal property for property tax purposes. Their job function involves extensive auditing, so many have an accounting background. The group is headquartered in Danville, California, and was founded in 1968. There are three local chapters.

*National Association
of Independent
Fee Appraisers*

The NAIFA accepts as members fee appraisers of real estate, and other interested appraisers. The group was founded in 1961 and is headquartered in St. Louis, Missouri. The NAIFA awards three professional designations: IFA (Member), IFAS (Senior), and IFAC (Appraiser-Counselor). There are local chapters around the country.

*Institute of Business
Appraisers*

Founded in 1978, IBA is headquartered in Boynton Beach, Florida. Its members are involved in the appraisal of businesses. The group awards the designation CBA (Certified Business Appraiser).

18.4 STANDARDS OF PROFESSIONAL APPRAISAL PRACTICE

In a cooperative effort to elevate the standards of professional appraisal practice and to better serve the public, Uniform Standards of Professional Appraisal Practice (known as USPAP) were adopted in 1986–87 by nine leading appraisal groups. Now maintained by the Appraisal Standards Board of the Appraisal Foundation, USPAP standards are by federal law the minimum acceptable standards for most appraisals made in conjunction with federally related financial transactions. All state licensed and certified appraisers are required to follow USPAP.

Ethics and Competency Standards

The ethics and competency provisions of USPAP cover five general areas of practice, with obligations of conformity as follows:

1. **Conduct:** requires that the appraiser perform all assignments with the highest standards of professional ethics, impartiality, objectivity, and independence.

2. **Management:** requires that the appraiser have no undisclosed interest in the appraisal outcome, in the property, or in the appraisal fee; allows no false or misleading advertising.

3. **Confidentiality:** requires that the appraiser not reveal factual data or the value conclusion to anyone except the client and persons authorized by the client (except as authorized by due process of law, or by a duly authorized professional peer review committee).

4. **Record Keeping:** requires that the appraiser prepare and keep written records on all assignments for at least 5 years.

5. **Competency:** requires that appraisers accept only that work that they have the experience necessary to perform (either individually or, if needed, in association with others).

Standards of Practice

The standards relating to the development and communication of a real estate appraisal are broadly stated as:

Standard 1. In developing a real estate appraisal, an appraiser must be aware of, understand, and correctly employ those recognized methods and techniques that are necessary to produce a credible appraisal.

Standard 2. In reporting the results of a real estate appraisal, an appraiser must communicate each analysis, opinion, and conclusion in a manner that is not misleading.

The Uniform Standards of Professional Practice contains additional standards covering appraisal reviews and other specialities. The two standards outlined above, along with Standard 3, "Review Appraisal and Reporting," are provided in detail for your reference at the end of this book. The appraisal practices presented in this text are consistent with these standards.

Impact of Professional Standards

Recognized by government and industry alike, uniform standards of conduct and practice among appraisers serve to protect three distinct groups. First, they protect the interests of the public at large. Second, they specify actions to protect the interests of the appraiser's clients. Third, they establish standards to protect the interests of other appraisers and the profession in general.

The Public

Impartiality

The appraiser should have no financial or undisclosed interest in the results of the appraisal assignment. This has three subcategories:

1. The appraiser should not have an undisclosed interest in the property being appraised.

2. The appraisal fee should not be contingent on the amount of value concluded.

3. The appraiser should neither pay nor receive referral fees, so that referrals will be objectively considered.

Disclosure and Methodology

The appraiser should report his or her findings in full or else in a non-deceptive form. In particular, every report should fully disclose any assumptions relied upon and provide a summary of the value methodology used, a statement as to whether the property was inspected, and identification of who takes the responsibility for the conclusions in the report.

Some codes of practice say the appraisal report should include all the data and reasoning used to reach the value conclusion. Today, the more common view is that the report can be a summary of the total appraisal effort, if specifically requested by the client, as long as the report meets minimum disclosure content.

Support for Conclusion

The appraisal conclusions that are reported should be based on data and analyses rather than solely on judgment or intuition. Supporting data and analyses should be contained in the report or otherwise retained in the appraiser's file for a reasonable time.

The Client

Competency

Appraisers should take on only those appraisal assignments that are within their ability. If necessary, the appraiser should enlist the aid of a more experienced appraiser to be sure that a competent job is being performed. Appraisers should only agree to prepare appraisals that they anticipate can be completed within the agreed-on time period.

Finally, once an appraiser accepts an assignment, he or she should perform it competently and adequately, regardless of whether the agreed-on fee will cover the necessary time. Unexpected problems with property, personality differences, and overtime pressures do not waive this standard, unless clearly covered by the agreement with the client.

Confidentiality

The appraisal report is not a public document. Therefore, the appraiser should keep the value conclusion completely confidential from everyone except as directed by the client, required by order of a court, or required for authorized professional standards review committees. Confidential information provided by the client, or by others, and clearly labeled as such, should also be held confidential.

The Profession

Competitive Activity

The appraiser may compete for business with other appraisers but should do so in a professional manner. This precludes trying to block others from practicing as appraisers. It also precludes attempting to take business away from other appraisers by casting unsupported doubts on their capabilities. The appraiser should base every major appraisal conclusion on the analysis of data, and this analysis should be retained in a file. With this standard of quality, the appraiser offering unsupported opinions should eventually lose favor with the public and be unable to compete.

Cooperative Activity

The appraiser should work with other appraisers to establish a code of behavior agreed to by all. Once established, each appraiser should try to comply with the code. The appraiser should also support and assist any investigation of possible violations of the code of behavior.

The appraiser should share available market data with other appraisers (to the degree legally possible in adversary cases). At the least, the appraiser should not try to hide important market data or misinform other appraisers about the particulars. The appraiser should also indicate when others have played a part in the value analysis of a particular report.

18.5 APPRAISING AS AN OCCUPATION

There are various ways to look at the occupation of appraisal. For example, we could compare people with professional designations to those without, or compare beginning appraisers to experienced appraisers. However, the major breakdown within the industry seems to be (1) those who work for a salary, and (2) those who work for themselves and get paid a fee by the job.

Working for a Salary

The majority of appraisers work for a salary. Nearly all salaried appraisal jobs are with larger government or private institutions. As a result, salaried appraisers are commonly referred to as institutional appraisers. The number of salaried appraisers working for private appraisal firms is small but growing.

Starting Out   Most appraisers start with a salaried job in an institution. The starting position is usually as an assistant or trainee appraiser. The industry rule of thumb is that the first six months of employment are a net loss. After that, the trainee can work alone well enough so that supervision falls off and appraisal production (or assistance) and quality of work climb. Only larger institutions can usually afford this cost burden for an appraisal trainee. Where federally related appraisals are involved, the employee must gain enough experience to qualify for and pass license or certification requirements before full staff status can be awarded.

Another avenue into appraising is to work in a related area and gain valuable experience ahead of the trainee stage. One example is the person who works as an appraisal secretary and gradually learns research skills. Over a period of years, a researcher who is intelligent and interested can develop good appraisal skills. A second example is the real estate broker or salesperson who gradually works into an appraisal career over a number of years.

The Institutional Job   There are many institutions that hire salaried appraisers. Some may have only one or two appraisers on their staff, while others have hundreds. Those with small staffs are usually less known to the public. Nearly all appraisers have worked for an institution during some point in their career.

Among the public institutions with appraisal departments, county property tax assessment offices are well known. Some county schools and county public works departments also maintain appraisal staffs, as do state public works departments and highway or transportation departments. Salaried appraisal staffs are also part of state water, parks, and general services departments, along with state housing and real estate licensing departments, and state bank and savings and loan regulatory bodies. Regional park and transportation districts may have an appraisal staff. At the federal level, appraisal staffs are located in the Corps of Engineers, Navy Department, National Park Service, U.S. Forest Service, Bureau of Land Management, Bureau of Public Roads, Internal Revenue Service, Department of Housing and Urban Development, Federal National Mortgage Association, U.S. Postal Service, General Services Department, and others.

The role of the appraiser in a public institution varies. Establishment of property tax values is the role of the tax appraiser. Another institutional role is to estimate market value of parcels to be acquired by condemnation under the power of eminent domain. This function involves the second largest group of governmental appraisers, after property tax assessment valuation. A third role is to review or audit appraisals made by private parties or institutions such as banks or savings and loans, lenders who submit loans to FHA and FNMA, and individuals making income tax or estate claims based on private appraisals, and so on. In some cases, government appraisers are staffed to value surplus, publicly owned parcels for the purpose of estimating a listing price and probable selling price.

Many private institutions have appraisal staffs. Banks, savings and loans, life insurance companies, mortgage brokers, mortgage bankers, and similar lenders are among the best known. But many appraisers also work for real estate investment trusts (REITs), larger pension funds, and real estate investment management firms (such as Landauer Associates and a number of others).

Many appraisers work as real estate managers for large developers, real estate departments of larger national corporations, and for franchise firms. Major oil companies have appraisal staffs, as do pipeline firms; railroads; electric, gas, water, and telephone utility companies; and major mining companies. Often, such appraisal personnel perform related real estate functions as well, from marketing research to site acquisition negotiations, construction supervision, and property management.

What is it like to be an institutional appraiser? The varied list of institutions reveals that the jobs themselves vary. The majority of the jobs have hours from 9 to 5, five days a week. Because you spend much of your time on the road inspecting properties and sales and confirming market data, it is an out-of-doors job with unpredictable working conditions. Some of these jobs have substantial overtime and travel, but this is usually understood at the start.

Salaries for institutional appraisers tend to be mid-level in the total range of salaried jobs; that is, they are fairly good. Jobs with longer hours and/or more travel tend to be higher paid. Starting salaries for novice appraisers are considerably lower than for experienced persons, and the salary increase for experience is greater than for many other salaried jobs.

The greatest demand is for salaried workers with two or three years of experience, and a state license or certification. Beginning or trainee positions are relatively few; before license and certification were required for federally related work, such positions were usually with banks or savings and loans. Trainees are usually hired when the employer's workload is expanding. However, if there are too few experienced appraisers looking for jobs, trainees are occasionally hired to replace eventually appraisers who have retired or resigned.

Where Does It Lead? Appraisal jobs are relatively secure, although lending institutions tend to hire and fire with changes in the volume of loans. Recently, salaried appraisers have been changing jobs more frequently than in the past. Many leave institutional employment and open their own appraisal businesses. This usually happens after they have accumulated substantial knowledge and industry contacts. Often they wait to obtain a professional designation or an opportunity to contract for appraisal assignments. Some wait for retirement, and soon thereafter open a part-time practice to supplement retirement income.

The Fee Appraiser

The term *fee appraiser* is used to refer to an independent business person who performs appraisals for a number of clients and is paid on a per-job basis. A few institutional appraisal employees are paid on a fee or commission basis, but this is not a common practice and is not considered to be "fee appraising."

Fee appraisers are also commonly referred to as "independent appraisers." However, this description is offensive to some salaried appraisers because to them it implies that only fee appraisers arrive at an independent conclusion, that is, one that is not imposed by the employer.

To be successful, the fee appraiser must be competent both in making appraisals and also in running a small business. This includes managing files, keeping financial records, marketing one's skills effectively, making proposals, collecting money owed, hiring and firing, arranging for space and equipment, and training a staff.

Fee appraisal offices are fairly small. Many consist of just the appraiser and a part-time typist. A smaller office may be operated out of the appraiser's home, with typing hired out or performed by the appraiser. Offices of three (appraiser, assistant, and secretary) or four people are also common. Not too many offices are much larger. An office of 30 people is currently considered very large. Offices of this size are found in large metropolitan areas. Currently, there are probably only a dozen or so offices of this size in the country.

What Is It Like To Be an Appraiser?

The previous discussion has focused on some of the objective aspects of appraisal as a profession. However, the work of appraisers is enjoyable enough for us to offer the reader some additional thoughts about the occupation.

1. Our work is varied. We not only meet people of all ages and backgrounds, but we see the varied and interesting ways that people live and how they decorate their homes.

2. Our work is challenging, since no two properties are alike. There are stimulating problems to solve, even when studying *routine* properties. The more difficult assignments often require a high degree of professional skill and determined effort.

3. Our work involves us with what is going on in our town. We may be making the construction loan appraisal on the large new store in town or an acquisition appraisal for a new redevelopment project. Our education in real estate economics strengthens our ability to understand these events. As a result, we often have a good grasp of current trends.

4. For some of us, appraisal work can be done, to an extent, at our own convenience. Some clients want inspections performed during evenings or weekends, so we can work extra hours if we wish. Because our knowledge will continue to grow as we get older, there will be no mandatory retirement.

5. We know that there are a number of related areas in real estate where our knowledge is also useful. While some appraisers go on to other fields such as property development, mortgage banking, brokerage, and so on, most of us continue to enjoy the challenge and stimulation of professional appraisal work.

SUMMARY   For those not performing federally related appraisals, there are no standard educational requirements for becoming an appraiser. However, having a formal education in real estate can only improve your career options as well as your income. Many employers in real estate require that appraisers have a college degree. Since only a handful of universities offer a degree program in real estate, you can usually do just as well with a degree in a field related to real estate such as economics, finance, or business administration. Many community colleges and appraisal societies offer courses in real estate.

Becoming a competent appraiser requires many different skills. Besides pursuing a formal education, you also need to develop your knowledge of markets and real estate operations. This kind of knowledge is more often gained in the field than in the classroom. Having sound judgment is also an important skill for an appraiser. Developing good judgment usually comes from a combination of experiences: in the field, in education, and most important, as a result of self-review.

Effective in 1993, state and federal laws required that most appraisals involved in federally related real estate financial transactions be performed by state licensed or certified appraisers. Generally, qualifying education and experience requirements vary according to the scope of practice, with 75 to 165 hours of appraisal-related coursework required and at least 2,000 hours of direct appraisal experience.

There is a multitude of appraisal organizations, societies, and groups. Many specialize in particular appraisal areas such as the American Society of Farm Managers and Rural Appraisers. Joining such a group can offer many advantages: the chance to meet and talk to other people in your field, special courses and workshops on important appraisal topics, and professional designations.

The two main appraisal organizations are the Appraisal Institute and the American Society of Appraisers (ASA). Each group offers several designations.

Uniform Standards of Professional Appraisal Practice were adopted in 1987 by leading appraisal groups to maintain a high standard of appraisal practice. Now, the USPAP, as it is referred to, comprises the minimum acceptable appraisal standards for most appraisals involved in federally related financial transactions. Standards codes seek to protect the general public, the client, and the appraisal profession.

Appraisers may be divided into two categories: those who work for a salary and those who work on a per-job basis. Many appraisers begin in a salaried position with an institution. Many private and public institutions hire appraisers. Fee appraisers, on the other hand, usually work for themselves in a small office and must have a good sense of business management to be successful.

Appraising is an interesting and varied profession. It is a field that can offer many benefits to those who enjoy its variety and challenge.

Important Terms and Concepts

Appraiser licensing and certification

Competency

Competition

Conduct

Confidentiality

Designations

Disclosure

Federally related appraisals

Fee appraiser

Formal training

Impartiality

Informal training

Institutional appraiser

Management

Professional societies

Record keeping

REVIEWING YOUR UNDERSTANDING

1. To become an appraiser generally requires:
   (a) A college degree
   (b) A high school diploma
   (c) No specific educational requirements except where licensing or certification is required
   (d) None of the above

2. New state and federal laws require the appraiser to be licensed or certified to perform appraisals that are:
   (a) In support of a loan
   (b) Over $250,000
   (c) Involved in federally related financial transactions
   (d) Not made by a designated appraiser

3. The Certified-Residential appraiser is typically eligible to appraise:
   (a) All residential (one- to four-unit) properties
   (b) Non-complex properties only
   (c) Complex one- to four-unit residential only
   (d) All properties

4. To be qualified to work in the field, a prospective appraiser should be knowledgeable about:
   (a) Economics and advertising
   (b) Professional appraisal groups
   (c) Income and commercial properties
   (d) Sources of market data, real estate operations, and real estate markets

5. Joining an appraisal group or society has many advantages. These include:
   (a) Educational seminars and workshops
   (b) Professional designations

(c) Both of the above

(d) Neither of the above

6. Of the several smaller groups mentioned, which one specializes in appraising personal property for property tax purposes?
   (a) Society of Auditor-Appraisers
   (b) International Right of Way Association
   (c) National Society of Real Estate Appraisers
   (d) None of the above

7. The American Society of Appraisers differs from the Appraisal Institute in one important way:
   (a) ASA members appraise various types of property, not just real property
   (b) ASA members appraise real property exclusively
   (c) ASA members work primarily for the government
   (d) None of the above apply

8. Which professional group offers the "MAI" designation?
   (a) The Appraisal Institute
   (b) Society of Real Estate Agents
   (c) American Society of Appraisers
   (d) None of the above

9. Which of the following areas of appraisal practice is (or are) covered by the ethics provision of USPAP?
   (a) Conduct
   (b) Management
   (c) Confidentiality
   (d) Record keeping
   (e) All of the above

10. A fee appraiser is:
   (a) An appraiser who works for an institution for a fixed salary
   (b) An appraiser who is paid on a per-job basis
   (c) An appraiser who works for a percentage commission
   (d) An appraiser who specializes in the appraisal of leased fee estates

Answers to Reviewing Your Understanding Questions

Chapter 1

1.	(c)	**5.**	(a)	**9.**	(e)
2.	(b)	**6.**	(c)	**10.**	(c)
3.	(a)	**7.**	(a)		
4.	(c)	**8.**	(e)		

Chapter 2

1. (a)

2. (b)

3. Intent, Annexation, Adaptation, Agreement, Relationship of Parties.

4. (b)

5. (c)

6. Building Codes, Coastal Preservation Zones, Master Plans, Rent Control, Subdivision Requirements, Zoning Ordinances, for examples.

7. (a)

8. One square mile, 640 acres.

9. Square of six miles per side; 36 sections of 640 acres each.

10. (b)

Chapter 3

1.	(a)	**5.**	(d)	**9.**	(c)
2.	(b)	**6.**	(b)	**10.**	(c)
3.	(b)	**7.**	(b)		
4.	(b)	**8.**	(d)		

Chapter 4

1.	(d)	**5.**	(b)	**9.**	(b)
2.	(d)	**6.**	(b)	**10.**	(d)
3.	(e)	**7.**	(e)		
4.	(a)	**8.**	(b)		

Chapter 5

1.	(b)	**5.**	(c)	**9.**	(b)
2.	(c)	**6.**	(d)	**10.**	(b)
3.	(b)	**7.**	(d)		
4.	(c)	**8.**	(d)		

Chapter 6

1.	(d)	**5.**	(c)	**9.**	(b)
2.	(a)	**6.**	(b)	**10.**	(a)
3.	(b)	**7.**	(c)		
4.	(a)	**8.**	(b)		

Chapter 7

1.	(c)	**5.**	(d)	**9.**	(b)
2.	(d)	**6.**	(d)	**10.**	(d)
3.	(c)	**7.**	(c)	**11.**	(b)
4.	(d)	**8.**	(a)	**12.**	(c)

Chapter 8

1.	(c)	**5.**	(d)	**9.**	(c)
2.	(a)	**6.**	(e)	**10.**	(d)
3.	(b)	**7.**	(e)	**11.**	(d)
4.	(b)	**8.**	(d)		

Chapter 9

1.	(b)	**5.**	(a)	**9.**	(a)
2.	(c)	**6.**	(b)	**10.**	(d)
3.	(c)	**7.**	(a)		
4.	(b)	**8.**	(c)		

Chapter 10

1.	(e)	**4.**	(c)	**7.**	(d)
2.	(b)	**5.**	(c)	**8.**	(d)
3.	(d)	**6.**	(d)	**9.**	(d)

10. $35,340, $42,000, $37,450, $38,700.

Answer is (a), but median value around $38,000 may be preferred.

Chapter 11

1.	(d)	**5.**	(a)	**9.**	(b)
2.	(b)	**6.**	(c)	**10.**	(b)
3.	(d)	**7.**	(c)		
4.	(d)	**8.**	(b)		

Chapter 12

1.	(d)	**4.**	(c)	**7.**	(c)
2.	(d)	**5.**	(b)	**8.**	(c)
3.	(c)	**6.**	(c)	**9.**	(d)

Chapter 13

1.	(c)	**5.**	(a)	**9.**	(a)
2.	(b)	**6.**	(b)	**10.**	(b)
3.	(c)	**7.**	(c)	**11.**	(a)
4.	(d)	**8.**	(b)	**12.**	(a)

Chapter 14

1.	(d)	**4.**	(c)	**7.**	(b)
2.	(b)	**5.**	(a)	**8.**	(b)
3.	(d)	**6.**	(a)	**9.**	(b)

10. (a) Solution:
Annual gross income:

$1.00 × 10,000 SF × 12 =	$120,000
Expenses (given)	−30,000
Net income before recapture	$90,000
Building charge:	
$400,000 × (.10 + .04)	−56,000
Net income residual to land	$34,000
Land value: Capitalized @ 10% =	$340,000
Add building value	+400,000
Total property value	$740,000 (Answer)

Chapter 15

1. (c)	5. (b)	9. (d)
2. (c)	6. (c)	10. (d)
3. (d)	7. (e)	
4. (e)	8. (b)	

Chapter 16

1. (d)	5. (d)	9. (d)
2. (a)	6. (a)	10. (d)
3. (c)	7. (d)	11. (d)
4. (b)	8. (a)	

Chapter 17

1. (c)	5. (a)	9. (a)
2. (c)	6. (b)	10. (a)
3. (c)	7. (b)	
4. (d)	8. (c)	

Chapter 18

1. (c)	5. (c)	9. (e)
2. (c)	6. (a)	10. (b)
3. (a)	7. (a)	
4. (d)	8. (a)	

Glossary

Absorption Period   The estimated time period required to sell, lease, place in use, or trade the subject property in its marketing area at prevailing prices or rental rates.

Abstraction Method   Method of appraising vacant land. The allocation of the total sale price or appraised value of a property between land and building either by using a ratio or by subtracting a figure representing building value from the total price (or value). Also called Allocation Method.

Access Right   The right of a property owner to have a means of entry and exit from his or her property to a public street.

Accrued Depreciation   Loss in value from current replacement cost of new improvements; the difference between the cost new as of the date of the value and the market value; diminished utility.

Ad Valorem Tax   A property tax based upon value.

Adjustment   In the sales comparison approach, a dollar or percentage amount that is added to or subtracted from the sale price of a comparable property to account for a feature that the property has or does not have which differentiates it from the subject property.

Age-Life Method of Depreciation   *See* Straight-Line Method of Depreciation.

Agents of Production   *See* Principle of Agents of Production.

Allocation Method   *See* Abstraction Method.

Amenities   Qualities that are pleasing and agreeable; generally, intangible benefits of property ownership.

Amortization   The repayment of a financial obligation on an installment basis; also, recovery of any investment over a given period of time.

Annuity   A series of assured payments anticipated over a period of time.

Annuity Capitalization   An income capitalization method providing for "annuity" recapture of invested capital; also referred to as yield capitalization. Discounts future income to an estimate of present value.

Anticipation	*See* Principle of Anticipation.
Appraisal	An estimate or opinion of value as of a certain date.
Appraisal Foundation, The	An entity created by the appraisal profession to regulate its own industry. Empowered by the Financial Institutions Reform, Recovery, and Enforcement Act of 1989 to set minimum standards and qualifications for performing appraisals in federally related financial transactions.
Appraisal Process	An orderly procedure that appraisers use to solve a valuation problem.
Appraisal Report	Communication of a formal appraisal.
Appraiser	One qualified by education, training, and experience to estimate the value of real or personal property based on experience, judgment, facts, and use of formal appraisal procedures.
Appreciation	Increase in the value of property.
Appurtenance	That which has been added or appended to a property and which becomes an inherent part of same.
Appurtenant Right	A right that belongs to the owners of one property that gives them the right to use another property (which they do not own) in a specific way that benefits their property (e.g., an easement).
Area	The space or size of a surface that is defined by a set of boundaries.
Assemblage	*See* Plottage.
Assessment	The valuation of property for the purpose of levying a tax; assessed value. Also, a single charge levied against real estate to defray the cost of public improvements that serve it.
Association Agreement	Set of private conditions, covenants, and restrictions applying to all properties in a planned unit development, condominium, or other community project.
Assumption of Mortgage	The taking of title to property wherein the buyer assumes liability for payment of an existing note secured by a mortgage against the property.
Balance	*See* Principle of Surplus Productivity, Balance and Contribution.
Band of Investment	Method of estimating interest and capitalization rates based on a weighted average of the mortgage interest rate (or other cost of borrowed funds) and the rate of return on equity required.
Base Costs	Average or typical building costs, usually from cost manuals; used, with appropriate refinements, to estimate cost of construction.
Base Rent	*See* Minimum Rent.
Book Value	The capital amount at which property is recorded or listed for accounting purposes; cost basis.
Bracketing	When using the sales comparison approach, selection of market data so that the subject is contained within a range of data.

Building Code	Municipal ordinance that regulates the type and quality of building materials and methods of construction permitted.
Building Residual Technique	Technique of income capitalization; the net income to the building (after deducting the income required for the land) is capitalized into an estimated value for the building.
Bundle of Rights	The rights that accompany the ownership of real estate.
Capital	An agent of production; construction and equipment costs; investment money.
Capital Gain	Profit on the sale of a property.
Capitalization Rate	Any rate used to capitalize income. The rate of return, percentage, or ratio used to convert income into its value equivalent.
Capitalized Income Approach	*See* Income Approach.
Capitalized Income Method of Depreciation	Method for estimating depreciation by comparing the subject's capitalized value to its replacement cost new.
Cash Flow	1) The periodic income or loss arising from an investment; 2) net operating income minus debt service (can be calculated before or after income tax).
Cash-on-Cash	Investment return to cash equity; based on actual cash invested; cash flow as a percentage or ratio to equity.
Cash Return to Equity	Equity dividend; cash flow to equity.
Central Tendency	In statistics, the numeric value that is suggested as the typical value in a sample.
Central Town	A town that performs a variety of services for the surrounding area.
Certification	A signed and dated statement that the appraiser has performed an appraisal in an unbiased and professional manner and that all assumptions and limiting conditions are set forth in the report. *See also* Certified Real Estate Appraiser.
Certified Real Estate Appraiser	An appraiser certified by the appropriate state to value real estate. With de minimus exceptions, federal law allows only licensed or certified appraisers to appraise property in a federally related real estate transaction. Certified Residential real estate appraisers may appraise one- to four-unit residential transactions without regard to transaction value or complexity; Certified General real estate appraisers may appraise all real estate transactions without regard to transaction value or complexity. *See also* Licensed Real Estate Appraiser; Federally Related Transaction.
Change	*See* Principle of Change.
Comparable Sales	Property sales used for purposes of comparison in the appraisal process; ideally competitive, open market transactions, and recent in time of sale.

Comparative Square Foot Method	Method of estimating construction costs using typical square foot costs for the type of construction being estimated.
Competition	*See* Principle of Competition.
Compound Interest	Interest paid on principal and also on the accrued and unpaid interest.
Condemnation	The taking of property by a governmental agency through the power of eminent domain.
Conditions, Covenants, and Restrictions (CC & Rs)	Recorded deed restrictions that run with the land, usually initiated by the original subdivider.
Condominium	A form of legal ownership; each individual owns the airspace in his/her unit in fee simple, plus an undivided interest in the structural supports, building systems, and all common areas.
Conformity	*See* Principle of Conformity.
Consistent Use	See Principle of Consistent Use.
Construction Classification	Type of construction; a system that rates the basic frame, walls, and roof of a structure as to their relative fire resistance (e.g., Class A, B, C, or D construction, Class A being the most fireproof).
Contribution	*See* Principle of Surplus Productivity, Balance and Contribution.
Composite Rate	A capitalization rate composed of interest and recapture in separately determined amounts.
Contract Rent	Amount of rent being paid under contractual commitments binding owners and tenants.
Cooperative	A form of legal ownership; each owner holds a stated percentage ownership in the cooperative association, which owns the land and buildings and grants each owner the permanent right to occupy the specified dwelling unit, as well as the right to the joint use of the common areas.
Coordination	An agent of production; management.
Corner Lot	Lot with frontage on two intersecting streets.
Correlation	*See* Reconciliation.
Cost	*See* Replacement Cost; Reproduction Cost.
Cost Approach	One of the three classic approaches to value. It involves estimating the replacement cost new of the improvements, deducting the estimated accrued depreciation, and then adding the market value of the land.
Cost Basis	Original price paid for a property, plus capital improvements less depreciation. (An accounting term.)
Cost Multiplier	Factor used in adjusting published construction cost figures to estimate current and local costs.
Cost-to-Cure Method of Depreciation	Method of estimating accrued depreciation (loss in value) based on the cost to cure or repair observed building defects.

Courtyard Home	*See* Zero-Lot-Line Home.
Cul-De-Sac Lot	Lot located at or near the end of a dead-end street.
Curable Depreciation	Items of physical deterioration or functional obsolescence that if repaired would add at least as much to the market value of the property as the cost of repairs.
Curbstone Appraisal	A slang phrase implying an informal valuation of a property based on observation and experience.
Debt Service	The periodic interest and/or principal payments required in a loan agreement.
Decline Phase	Third phase in the cycle of a neighborhood, generally marked by delayed repairs and deterioration of buildings.
Dedication	A voluntary giving of private property to some public use by the owner, as in the dedication of land for streets in a subdivision.
Deed Restrictions	Private limitations in the deed to a property that dictate certain uses that may or may not be made of the property.
Demand	The desire to possess plus the ability to buy; an essential element of value.
Demography	The study of human populations (e.g., size, density, growth rate).
Depreciated Cost Method	Method for adjusting comparable sales; adjustments are calculated from an analysis of the depreciated replacement cost for each differentiating feature.
Depreciation	Loss of value in property brought about by age, physical deterioration, and/or functional or economic obsolescence.
Depth	Distance from the frontage of a lot to the rear lot line.
Design Type	Classification of buildings based on the use for which a structure is designed.
Development Method (Land Development Method)	Method of vacant land valuation; development costs are subtracted from estimated gross sales and, finally, developer's profits are accounted for. The results provide an estimate of raw land value.
Development Phase	First phase in the life cycle of a neighborhood, consisting of the initial construction of improvements on vacant land.
Diminished Utility	*See* Accrued Depreciation.
Direct Capitalization Method	Income capitalization technique; value is estimated by dividing net operating income by the overall capitalization rate.
Direct Costs	All of the costs that are directly involved with the physical construction of the structure, including labor, materials and equipment, design and engineering, and subcontractors' fees.
Direct Market Comparison Approach	*See* Sales Comparison Approach.

Direct Market Method	Method of adjusting comparable sales; two or more comparable properties with one differing feature are used to estimate the amount of the adjustment for that feature. (Also called the matched pair method.)
Discounted Cash Flow (DCF)	Technique of income capitalization; estimated future investment returns are mathematically discounted to their present value.
Discount Rate	*See* Interest Rate.
Easement	Right, privilege, or interest that one party has in the land of another, created for a specific purpose by grant, agreement, or necessity.
Economic Base	For a community or defined geographic area, the portion of its economic production that is sold or exported outside its boundaries.
Economic Life	The total number of years of economically useful life that may be expected from a building.
Economic Obsolescence	Loss in value that is caused by factors located outside the subject property; locational or environmental obsolescence.
Economic Rent	*See* Market Rent.
Economic Trend	Pattern of related changes in some aspect of the economy.
Effective Age	Relative age of a structure considering its physical condition and marketability.
Effective Gross Rent	Gross rent minus an allowance for vacancy and credit losses.
Effective Interest Rate	The percentage of interest that is actually being paid by a borrower for the use of money; distinct from nominal interest rate.
Elements of Comparison	Four categories of information about sales: terms of sale, time of sale, location elements, and physical elements.
Elements of Value	Four prerequisites that must be present for an object to have value: utility, scarcity, demand, and transferability.
Ellwood Technique	A mortgage/equity method of capitalization.
Eminent Domain	The power of a government to acquire property for a public purpose by paying just or reasonable compensation.
Environmental Impact Report (EIR)	A formal report designed to assess the results or impact of a proposed activity or development upon the environment. Environmental protection laws generally require EIRs for major public or private developments and other activities posing a potential threat to the environment.
Environmental Obsolescence	*See* Economic Obsolescence.
Equity	Interest or value that an owner has in real estate over and above the liens against it.
Equity Buildup	Increase in the investor's share of the total property value from reduction of debt through regular installment payments of principal and interest and/or through property appreciation.

Equity Capitalization Rate	Factor used to estimate the value of the equity in the equity residual technique of capitalization and other mortgage and equity techniques; the equity cash flow divided by the equity value.
Equity Residual Technique	Technique of income capitalization; the net income remaining to the equity position (after mortgage payments) is capitalized into an estimate of the value of the equity.
Escheat	The right of the state to take back title to property if the owner dies or disappears and leaves no relatives or heirs.
Estate	A person's ownership interest in real property.
Excess Rent	The amount by which the total contract rent exceeds market rent.
Expense Ratio	*See* Operating Expense Ratio.
Export Production	Goods and services produced for sale or use outside the town or area in which they are produced.
External Obsolescence	*See* Economic Obsolescence.
Farmers Home Administration (FHmA)	An agency of the Department of Agriculture that is primarily responsible for providing financial assistance for farmers and others living in rural areas where financing is not available on reasonable terms from private sources.
Federal Home Loan Bank Board (FHLBB)	Former administrative agency that exercised regulating authority over the FHLB system. Its functions are now performed by the Federal Deposit Insurance Corporation and other federal agencies.
Federal Home Loan Mortgage Corporation (FHLMC)	A federal agency known as Freddie Mac that provides a secondary market for mortgages originated by savings and loan associations.
Federal Housing Administration (FHA)	An agency of the federal government that insures mortgage loans.
Federal National Mortgage Association (FNMA)	A quasi-public agency converted into a private corporation known as Fannie Mae, whose primary function is to buy and sell FHA and VA mortgages in the secondary market.
Federal Reserve System	The federal banking system of the United States. Under the control of a central board of governors (Federal Reserve Board), it includes a central bank in each of twelve geographical districts with broad powers in controlling credit and the amount of money in circulation.
Federally Related Transaction	Any real estate transaction involving federal insurance or assistance. *See also* Financial Institutions Reform, Recovery, and Enforcement Act.
Fee Absolute	*See* Fee Simple.
Fee Simple	An estate in real property by which the owner has title limited only by the four government powers (escheat, taxation, police power, and eminent domain).

Financial Institutions Reform, Recovery, and Enforcement Act (FIRREA)	A federal law passed in 1989 to provide guidelines for the regulation of financial institutions. One part of the law requires a state license or certification for the performance of federally related real estate transactions (with de minimus exceptions). *See also* Federally Related Transaction.
Fiscal Policy	Programs by the federal government that are intended to influence economic activity by making changes in government expenditures and taxation.
Fixed Expenses	Operating costs that are more or less permanent and that vary little from year to year.
Fixture	Personal property that, because it has become attached to real estate, is considered part of the real estate.
Flag Lot	Rear lot, behind other houses or lots, with a long, narrow access road (like a flagpole).
Flat Lease	*See* Straight Lease.
Form Report	Written appraisal report presented on a standardized form or checklist.
Formal Appraisal	An estimate of value that is reached by the collection and analysis of relevant data. A formal appraisal is usually reported in writing.
Frontage	Boundary line or lot side that faces a street.
Functional Obsolescence	Loss in value that is caused by a relative loss of building utility or usefulness.
Functional Utility	The combination of the usefulness and attractiveness of a property.
Future Value	The estimated lump-sum value of money or property at a date in the future.
Government National Mortgage Association (GNMA)	A federal corporation known as Ginnie Mae, mainly involved in the administration of the mortgage-backed securities program and in the secondary mortgage market.
Government Survey System	*See* Rectangular Survey System.
Graduated Lease	*See* Step-Up Lease.
Gross Domestic Product (GDP)	The value of all domestic goods and services produced in the country.
Gross Income	Total income from property before any expenses are deducted.
Gross Income Multiplier (GIM)	The ratio of the selling price (or appraisal value) to the gross income of a property. May be multiplied by the gross income of a property to produce an estimate of the property's value. Also known as the gross rent multiplier (GRM).
Gross Lease	Rental agreement under which the landlord pays all expenses.
Gross Rent Multiplier	*See* Gross Income Multiplier.

Highest and Best Use	The reasonable and probable use of a property that will support the highest present value of the land. *See also* Principle of Highest and Best Use.
Historic Cost	Cost of a property at the time it was constructed or purchased.
Improvement	Permanent structure or other development that becomes part of the land.
Income Approach	One of the three classic approaches to value, where the expected net income from the property is capitalized into a value estimate.
Income Forecast	Gross or net income estimate.
Income Property	Property that is purchased for its income-producing capabilities.
Income Stream	Actual or estimated flow of net earnings over time.
Increasing and Decreasing Returns	*See* Principle of Increasing and Decreasing Returns.
Incurable Depreciation	Building defects or problems that would cost more to repair than the anticipated value increase from such repair.
Index Method	Method for estimating construction costs; adjusts original costs to the current cost level by a multiplier obtained from a published cost index.
Indicated Value	Value estimate calculated/produced by an appraisal approach.
Indirect Costs	All of the time and money costs involved in a construction project that are not directly involved with construction itself. Examples are loan fees, interest, legal fees, and marketing costs.
Informal Appraisal	An estimate of value that is reached by using intuition, past experience, and general knowledge.
Intangible Property	Rights to something other than tangible, or physical, property.
Interest	Charge for the use of money for a period of time.
Interest Rate	The rate of return on capital; usually expressed as an annual percentage of the amount loaned or invested.
Interior Lot	Lot with frontage on only one street.
Internal Rate of Return	The rate of return generated by an investment over the holding period; considers all future benefits, discounting them to equal the present value.
Just Compensation	Payment for private property obtained by government by condemnation through the power of eminent domain.
Key Lot	Lot that has several other lots backing onto its sideyard.
Labor	An agent of production; cost of all operating expenses and wages except management.
Land	The surface, the soil and rocks beneath, and the airspace above that the landowner can reasonably use and enjoy.

Land Residual Technique	Technique of income capitalization; the net income remaining to the land (after income attributable to the building has been deducted) is capitalized into an estimate of value for the land.
Landlord	Property owner who rents property to another.
Larger Parcel	Total parcel of property from which a governmental body is acquiring only a portion through condemnation.
Law of Fixtures	Five tests to determine whether an object is a fixture or personal property.
Lease	A written contract between the owner and the tenant setting forth the terms and conditions under which the tenant may occupy and use the property.
Leased Fee	Property owner's interest in leased property.
Leasehold	Tenant's interest in leased property.
Lessee	Tenant; one who rents property under a lease contract.
Lessor	Landlord; owner who enters into a lease with a tenant.
Letter Report	One- to five-page written report summarizing the appraisal and its conclusions.
Leverage	Use of borrowed funds to purchase property with the expectation of increasing the rate of return to equity; sometimes called trading on the equity.
Licensed Real Estate Appraiser	An appraiser licensed by the appropriate state to value real estate. With de minimus exceptions, federal law allows only licensed or certified appraisers to appraise property in a federally related real estate transaction. In general, the licensed appraiser is allowed to perform appraisals only of non-complex one- to four-unit residential properties up to $1 million transaction value, and complex one- to four-unit residential units up to $250,000. *See also* Certified Real Estate Appraiser; Federally Related Transaction.
Life Estate	Holder controls the right of possession and use of a property during the lifetime of some specifically named person.
Linear Regression	Statistical technique for calculating sales price or adjustment; line of "best fit" for two variables.
Liquidity	The ease with which property can be converted into cash.
Local Production	Goods and services produced for sale or use in the town or area in which they are produced.
Long-Lived, Incurable Physical Deterioration	Loss in value attributable to the major components of a building, when age is the major contributing factor and the cost of repair would exceed the value that would be added to the structure by the repair.
Lump-Sum Dollar Adjustment	Type of sales adjustment; specific dollar amount is added or subtracted for each differing feature.
Market Approach	*See* Sales Comparison Approach.

Market Exposure	Making a reasonable number of potential buyers of a property aware that the property is available.
Market Method of Depreciation	*See* Sales Data Method of Depreciation.
Market Rent	The rental income the property could command if placed for rent on the open market as of the effective date of the appraisal.
Market Value	The most probable price in terms of money that a property should bring in a competitive and open market under all conditions requisite to a fair sale, with the buyer and seller each acting prudently and knowledgeably, and assuming the price is not affected by undue stimulus.
Marketing Period	The typical time required to sell or lease a property.
Mature Phase	*See* Stable Phase.
Mean	Measure of central tendency; the average price or numeric value of a statistical sample.
Median	Measure of central tendency; the middle value, that is, the one with as many higher values as lower values in a statistical sample.
Metes and Bounds Description	Legal description of land that describes the length and direction of boundary lines together with their terminal points.
Minimum Rent	Base rent that is the fixed minimum amount paid under a percentage lease.
Misplaced Improvement	A building that is the wrong type or use for its location; an example of functional obsolescence.
Mobile Home	A housing unit that is capable of being moved on the highway.
Mode	Measure of central tendency; the most frequently occurring price or value in a statistical sample.
Modular Home	Building composed of modules constructed on an assembly line in a factory.
Monetary Policy	Programs by the Federal Reserve System that increase or decrease the supply of, or demand for, money in an effort to achieve designated economic goals.
Mortgage	Instrument by which property is used to secure the payment of a debt or obligation.
Mortgage Equity Analysis	A technique used to analyze the debt and equity return requirements, or potential, of an investment.
Multiple Listing Service (MLS)	An association of real estate agents providing for a pooling of listings and the sharing of commissions on a specified basis.
Multiple Regression	Statistical technique for estimating probable sales price, or other variable, using multiple variables.
Narrative Report	A detailed, formal written report of the appraisal and the value conclusion.

Neighborhood	An area whose occupants and users share some common ties or characteristics.
Neighborhood Cycle	The process of neighborhood change involving four phases of change: development, maturity, decline, and renaissance. *See also* Principle of Change.
Net Area	*See* Useful Area.
Net Income	Gross annual income less income lost due to vacancies and uncollectible rents less all operating expenses.
Net Income Ratio	Net income divided by the effective gross income.
Net Lease	Lease under which the lessee pays all property expenses.
Net Operating Income	*See* Net Income.
Nominal Interest Rate	A stated (or contract) rate of interest. May not correspond to the true or effective annual percentage rate (e.g., when payments are made monthly).
Observed Condition Method of Depreciation	*See* Cost-to-Cure Method of Depreciation.
Obsolescence	Loss in value from a reduced desirability or usefulness of a structure. *See* Functional Obsolescence; Economic Obsolescence.
Open-Market Transaction	Transaction in which both buyer and seller act willingly, with full knowledge of all details of the property and the transaction, and under no pressure.
Operating Expenses	Expenses required to run a property (i.e., to maintain its income). Includes fixed, variable, and reserves for replacement.
Operating Expense Ratio	The ratio of total operating expenses to the effective gross rent in an income property.
Operating Statement	Written record of a property's gross income, expenses, and resultant net income for a given period of time.
Overage Rent	Amounts paid over and above the base rent, under a percentage lease.
Overall Rate (OAR)	The relationship between the net income and value of the total property; used to capitalize income.
Overimprovement	A building that is too large or has excess quality for its neighborhood and therefore suffers from functional obsolescence; also called superadequacy.
Partial Interests	Interests in real estate that represent less than the fee simple estate (i.e., a leased fee or leasehold estate).
Partial Taking	Governmental agency acquiring only a portion of a property through condemnation.
Patio Home	*See* Zero-Lot-Line Home.

Percentage Adjustment	Type of sales adjustment; the estimated difference between the comparable sale and the subject is first calculated as a percentage of the sale price of the comparable, and then applied as an upward or downward adjustment to the price.
Percentage Lease	Lease agreement by which the tenant pays a stipulated percentage, usually of the gross sales of goods and services offered by the tenant; most percentage leases require a certain base rent regardless of sales volume.
Personal Property	Property that is movable; any property that is not real property.
Physical Deterioration	Wear and tear from use, age, the weather, neglect, lack of maintenance, and/or vandalism.
Planned Unit Development (PUD)	A project consisting of individually owned parcels of land with a common area and facilities owned by an association of which the owners of all the parcels are members.
Plottage	The combining of two or more parcels together for increased utility. Also referred to as assemblage. The term plottage is also used to denote plottage value. *See* also Plottage Value.
Plottage Value	The increase in utility or unit value that is created by joining two or more parcels together into one large ownership.
Points	Amounts paid by the borrower or the seller that increase the effective yield for a lender; each point equals 1% of the loan amount.
Police Power	Power of a governmental body to regulate property for the health, safety, morals, and general welfare of the public.
Prefabricated Home	House manufactured and sometimes partly assembled before delivery to the building site.
Present Value	Current value or the discounted value of some future income or benefits.
Principle of Agents of Production	All production or income can be said to be the result of the four factors of labor, coordination, capital, and land.
Principle of Anticipation	Value is the present worth of future benefits, both income and intangible amenities.
Principle of Balance	*See* Principle of Surplus Productivity.
Principle of Change	Real estate values are constantly changed by social, economic, and political forces in society. *See also* Neighborhood Cycle.
Principle of Competition	Market demand generates profits; profits generate competition; and competition stabilizes profits.
Principle of Conformity	Maximum value results when properties in a neighborhood are relatively similar in size, style, quality, use and/or type.
Principle of Consistent Use	Requires that land and improvements be appraised on the basis of the same use.
Principle of Contribution	*See* Principle of Surplus Productivity.

Principle of Highest and Best Use	Maximum market value of a given parcel of land, vacant or improved, is created by development or utilization at its highest and best use.
Principle of Increasing and Decreasing Returns	Income and other benefits available from real estate may be increased by adding capital improvements only up to the point of balance in the agents of production beyond which the increase in value tends to be less than the increase in costs.
Principle of Progression and Regression	Lower-valued properties generally benefit from close proximity to properties of higher value, and higher-valued properties tend to suffer when placed in close proximity with lower-valued properties.
Principle of Substitution	When a property can be easily replaced by another, the value of such property tends to be set by the cost of acquiring an equally desirable substitute property.
Principle of Supply and Demand	Prices and rent levels tend to increase when demand is greater than supply and tend to decrease when supply exceeds demand.
Principle of Surplus Productivity, Balance and Contribution	Income that is available to land after the other economic agents have been paid for is known as the surplus of productivity; a proper balance of the agents maximizes the income available to land; the value of any agent is determined by its contribution to the whole.
Promissory Note	An agreement signed by the borrower, promising to repay the loan under stipulated terms.
Quality of Construction	Classification or rating based on basic structural integrity, materials, finishes, and special features.
Quantity Survey Method	Process for arriving at a cost estimate for new construction involving a detailed estimate of the quantities of raw materials used, the current price of each material, and installation costs.
Range	Measure of central tendency; the difference, or spread, between the highest and lowest value in the sample.
Ratio Capitalization	Describes any capitalization method that uses the typical ratio of income to value to convert projected income into a value estimate for the property (or property component) under appraisal. Includes direct capitalization as well as land, building, and equity residual capitalization methods when sales price–income ratios are used.
Real Estate	The land and everything that is permanently fastened to the land; real property.
Real Estate Cycle	Periodic pattern of changes in the amount of construction and volume of sales in the real estate market.
Real Property	Real estate.
Recapture	The return of investment capital. May come out of current income or future reversions (e.g., resale).
Reconciliation	The process by which the appraiser reviews and considers the indicated values developed by the applied approaches to arrive at a final value conclusion.

Recorded Lot, Block and Tract	Legal description of a parcel of land by means of reference to the recorded plat of a subdivision.
Rectangular Survey System	System for legal description of property based on principal meridians, base lines, and a grid system.
Regression Analysis	*See* Linear Regression; Multiple Regression.
Remainder Estate	An estate that takes effect after the termination of a life estate.
Remainder Parcel	The portion of a property left to the owner when there has been a partial taking by eminent domain.
Renaissance	Fourth phase in the cycle of a neighborhood; the transition to a new cycle through the demolition, relocation, or major renovation of existing buildings.
Rent	Consideration paid for the use of real property.
Rent Multiplier	*See* Gross Income Multiplier.
Rent Roll	Total of all scheduled rental amounts for tenant space, services, and parking.
Rental Loss Method of Depreciation	*See* Capitalized Income Method of Depreciation.
Replacement Cost	Cost of constructing a building or structure that would have a similar utility to the subject improvement but constructed with modern materials and according to current standards, design, and layout.
Reproduction Cost	Cost of a near duplicate, or replica, structure.
Reserves for Replacement	Annual allowances set up for replacement of building components and equipment.
Residual Techniques of Capitalization	Income approach methods that separate income amounts attributed to a component of the property, such as land or building, or debt or equity, for purposes of analysis of its value contribution to the total property.
Return of Investment	Recapture or conversion of the investment in real estate to cash or other valuable assets.
Return on Investment	Profits produced by the investment in real estate.
Reversion	Return of capital and/or added profits through sale or through return of rights in real estate to a lessor at the expiration of a lease.
Row House	*See* Townhouse.
Sales Analysis Grid	Table of relevant data on comparable properties.
Sales Comparison Approach	One of the three classic approaches to value. It involves comparing similar properties, that have recently sold, to the subject property.
Sales Data Method of Depreciation	Method of estimating depreciation wherein building values abstracted from sales are compared to current costs new.
Scarcity	A condition where demand exceeds supply. One of the four elements of value.

Severance Damage	Damage to the value of the remainder parcel as a result of a partial taking by eminent domain.
Special-Function Town	A town whose employment concentrates on one special service or purpose.
Stable Phase	Second phase in the cycle of a neighborhood, marked by stability of the existing buildings and occupants.
Standard Deviation	A measure of the extent of variability in a sample, that is, whether the observations are clustered near the mean or scattered throughout the range. The square root of the sum of the squared differences between each observation and the mean of all observations, divided by the total number of observations. In an appraisal, each sale price, for example, could be considered an observation.
Step-Up Lease	Lease agreement that establishes progressively higher rental amounts for different segments of the lease term; graduated lease.
Straight Lease	Lease agreement in which rent is a fixed amount that stays the same over the entire lease term.
Straight-Line Method of Depreciation	Method of estimating depreciation in which the loss in value of a building is assumed to be the ratio of its age (or effective age) to its total useful or economic life.
Subdivision	A legal definition of those divisions of real property (for the purpose of sale, lease, or financing) that are regulated by law; typically, a tract of land that has been divided into lots or plots, with streets and other improvements suitable for development.
Summation Approach	*See* Cost Approach.
Superadequacy	*See* Overimprovement.
Supply and Demand	*See* Principle of Supply and Demand.
T-Intersection Lot	Lot facing the dead-end street at the T-intersection.
Take Parcel	The portion of a property acquired in a partial taking by a governmental agency by eminent domain.
Tangible Property	Physical objects and/or the rights thereto.
Tax	A levy under legal auspices for governmental purposes.
Tenant	One who occupies and/or leases property.
Terms of Sale	Financing arrangements and conditions of a sale.
Time-Shared Ownership	Subdivision of the fee interest of a property into blocks of time, with each time block owned by a different owner.
Time-Value of Money	The financial principle that a dollar in the present is worth more than a promised dollar in the future because of the present dollar's interest-earning capability.
Topography	Nature of the surface of land.

Townhouse	Row house; a house on an individual lot, owned in fee; usually built without sideyards between adjoining houses; an architectural style.
Transferability	Capable of change in ownership or use. One of the four elements of value.
Transportation Service Town	A town that is selected to provide services along a transportation route, usually located at transportation nodes.
Turn-Key Costs	Costs that include all of the charges to the consumer, not just the costs to the developer or builder.
Type of Construction	Building classification based on a structure's basic frame, wall, and floor construction.
Type of Occupancy	*See* Design Type.
Undivided Interests in Commonly Held Property	Interests involving two or more persons sharing the ownership, each having non-exclusive rights of use. Undivided interests are often coupled with the sole ownership rights of an adjacent property, as in a condominium.
Uniform Standards of Professional Appraisal Practice (USPAP)	A set of standards and ethics originally developed by nine appraisal associations to guide members in the development and reporting of appraisals. Now maintained by the Appraisal Standards Board of the Appraisal Foundation.
Unit-in-Place Method	Method of estimating the reproduction cost of a building by estimating the installed cost of each component part.
Units of Comparison	*See* Unit of Comparison Adjustment.
Unit of Comparison Adjustment	Sales analysis tool wherein sales prices of the comparables are converted to price per total property, or a physical or economic unit that is found to be closely related to selling price or value. The value of the subject property is suggested by multiplying its number of units by the price per physical or economic unit of comparison found to be typical or appropriate.
Use Type	*See* Design Type.
Useful Area	That portion of the gross area of a site that can be built on or developed.
Utility	Usefulness; in economics, one of the four elements of value.
Variable Expenses	Operating expenses that vary with occupancy level or intensity of use of a property (e.g., utility costs and maintenance).
Variance	In zoning, a legal exception to the use, type, density, or other allowable feature of the normal permitted development or use of a specific site. In statistics, a measure of variability or deviation from the mean.
Value	The worth, usefulness, or utility of an object to someone for some purpose.
Value Conclusion	The final estimate of value in an appraisal.

Value in Exchange	The value of an item or object to the general public; an objective view of value.
Value in Use	The value of an item or object to a particular user; a subjective view of value.
Veterans Administration (VA)	A federal agency which, among other things, guarantees approved lenders against financial loss on loans made to eligible veterans.
Volume	Measurement of the amount of space that a three-dimensional object occupies. In real estate, volume is normally measured in cubic feet or cubic yards.
Yield	Total net profit earned by an investor on invested capital.
Yield Rate	*See* Interest Rate.
Yield Capitalization	Capitalization method that mathematically discounts future benefits at appropriate yield rates, producing a value that explicitly reflects the income pattern, value change, and yield rate characteristics of the investment.
Zero-Lot-Line Home	House built without a sideyard; may be wrapped around two or more sides of a courtyard or patio.
Zoning	Under the police power of government, local laws that control the use of land. Zoning regulations apply to the type of use (e.g., residential, commercial), density, height of buildings, parking requirements, etc., permitted in a specific jurisdiction.

Excerpts From the Uniform Standards of Professional Appraisal Practice

---

To Include

1. **Outline and Table of Contents**
2. **Excerpts Applicable to Federally Related Real Estate Appraisals, and to General Real Estate Appraisal Practice by Conforming Appraisers**

Preview of this Excerpt

The Uniform Standards of Professional Appraisal Practice (USPAP) are promulgated and maintained by the Appraisal Standards Board of The Appraisal Foundation. State and federal laws require conformity to USPAP in most appraisals involved in federally related real estate financial transactions. **In such appraisals, the departure provisions of USPAP *do not apply*.**

   USPAP Standards and Rules have been adopted by, and define the required Standards of Practice for, members of all major appraisal groups.

OUTLINE AND TABLE OF CONTENTS OF USPAP

APPLICABLE EXCERPTS OF USPAP

Of the total of 10 Standards listed in the Table of Contents, only the Introductory material and Standards 1 through 3 apply to federally related appraisals, and to general real estate appraisal practice and review. All the Standards as well as the integral comments are subject to ongoing review and revision by the Standards Board of The Appraisal Foundation.

INTRODUCTORY MATERIAL

PREAMBLE

It is essential that a professional appraiser arrive at and communicate his or her analyses, opinions, and advice in a manner that will be meaningful to the client and will not be misleading in the marketplace. These Uniform Standards of Professional Appraisal Practice reflect the current standards of the appraisal profession.

The importance of the role of the appraiser places ethical obligations on those who serve in this capacity. These standards include explanatory comments and begin with an Ethics Provision setting forth the requirements for integrity, objectivity, independent judgment, and ethical conduct. In addition, these standards include a Competency Provision which places an immediate responsibility on the appraiser prior to acceptance of an assignment. The Standards contain binding requirements, as well as specific guidelines to which a Departure Provision may apply under certain limited conditions. Definitions applicable to these Standards are also included.

These standards deal with the procedures to be followed in performing an appraisal, review or consulting service, and the manner in which an appraisal, review or consulting service is communicated. Standards 1 and 2 relate to the development and communication of a real property appraisal. Standard 3 establishes guidelines for reviewing an appraisal and reporting on that review. Standards 4 and 5 address the development and communication of various real estate or real property consulting functions by an appraiser. Standard 6 sets forth criteria for the development and reporting of mass appraisals for ad valorem tax purposes or any other universe of properties. Standards 7 and 8 establish guidelines for developing and communicating personal property appraisals. Standards 9 and 10 establish guidelines for developing and communicating business appraisals.

These Standards include Statements on Appraisal Standards issued by the Appraisal Standards Board for the purpose of clarification, interpretation, explanation, or elaboration of a Standard or Standards Rule.

These Standards are for appraisers and the users of appraisal services. To maintain the highest level of professional practice, appraisers must observe these Standards. The users of appraisal services should demand work performed in conformance with these Standards.

> *Comment:* Explanatory comments are an integral part of the Uniform Standards and should be viewed as extensions of the provisions, definitions, and Standards Rules. Comments provide interpretation from the Appraisal Standards Board concerning the background or application of certain provisions, definitions, or Standards Rules. There are no comments for provisions, definitions, and Standards Rules that are axiomatic or have not yet required further explanation; however, additional comments will be developed and others supplemented or revised as the need arises.

ETHICS PROVISION

Because of the fiduciary responsibilities inherent in professional appraisal practice, the appraiser must observe the highest standards of professional ethics. This Ethics Provision is divided into four sections: conduct, management, confidentiality, and record keeping.

> *Comment:* This provision emphasizes the personal obligations and responsibilities of the individual appraiser. However, it should also be emphasized that groups and organizations engaged in appraisal practice share the same ethical obligations.

Conduct

An appraiser must perform ethically and competently in accordance with these standards and not engage in conduct that is unlawful, unethical, or improper. An appraiser who could reasonably be perceived to act as a disinterested third party in rendering an unbiased appraisal, review, or consulting service must perform assignments with impartiality, objectivity, and independence and without accommodation of personal interests.

Comment: An appraiser is required to avoid any action that could be considered misleading or fraudulent. In particular, it is unethical for an appraiser to use or communicate a misleading or fraudulent report or to knowingly permit an employee or other person to communicate a misleading or fraudulent report.

The development of an appraisal, review, or consulting service based on a hypothetical condition is unethical unless: 1) the use of the hypothesis is clearly disclosed; 2) the assumption of the hypothetical condition is clearly required for legal purposes, for purposes of reasonable analysis, or for purposes of comparison and would not be misleading; and 3) the report clearly describes the rationale for this assumption, the nature of the hypothetical condition, and its effect on the result of the appraisal, review, or consulting service.

An individual appraiser employed by a group or organization which conducts itself in a manner that does not conform to these standards should take steps that are appropriate under the circumstances to ensure compliance with the standards.

Management

The acceptance of compensation that is contingent upon the reporting of a predetermined value or a direction in value that favors the cause of the client, the amount of the value estimate, the attainment of a stipulated result, or the occurrence of a subsequent event is unethical.

The payment of undisclosed fees, commissions, or things of value in connection with the procurement of appraisal, review, or consulting assignments is unethical.

Comment: Disclosure of fees, commissions, or things of value connected to the procurement of an assignment should appear in the certification of a written report and in any transmittal letter in which conclusions are stated. In groups or organizations engaged in appraisal practice, intra-company payments to employees for business development are not considered to be unethical. Competency, rather than financial incentives, should be the primary basis for awarding an assignment.

Advertising for or soliciting appraisal assignments in a manner which is false, misleading or exaggerated is unethical.

Comment: In groups or organizations engaged in appraisal practice, decisions concerning finder or referral fees, contingent compensation, and advertising may not be the responsibility of an individual appraiser, but for a particular assignment, it is the responsibility of the individual appraiser to ascertain that there has been no breach of ethics, that the appraisal is prepared in accordance with these standards, and that the report can be properly certified as required by Standards Rules 2-3, 3-2, 5-3, 6-8, 8-3 or 10-3.

The restriction on contingent compensation in the first paragraph of this section does not apply to consulting assignments where the appraiser is not acting in a disinterested manner and

would not reasonably be perceived as performing a service that requires impartiality. This permitted contingent compensation must be properly disclosed in the report.

Comment: Assignments where the appraiser is not acting in a disinterested manner are further discussed in the General Comment to Standard 4. The preparer of the written report of such an assignment must certify that the compensation is contingent and must explain the basis for the contingency in the report (See Standard Rule 5-3) and in any transmittal letter in which conclusions are stated.

Confidentiality

An appraiser must protect the confidential nature of the appraiser-client relationship.

Comment: An appraiser must not disclose confidential factual data obtained from a client or the results of an assignment prepared for a client to anyone other than: 1) the client and persons specifically authorized by the client; 2) such third parties as may be authorized by due process of law; and 3) a duly authorized professional peer review committee. As a corollary, it is unethical for a member of a duly authorized professional peer review committee to disclose confidential information or factual data presented to the committee.

Record Keeping

An appraiser must prepare written records of appraisal, review, and consulting assignments including oral testimony and reports and retain such records for a period of at least five (5) years after preparation or at least two (2) years after final disposition of any judicial proceeding in which testimony was given, whichever period expires last.

Comment: Written records of assignments include true copies of written reports, written summaries of oral testimony and reports (or a transcript of testimony), all data and statements required by these standards, and other information as may be required to support the findings and conclusions of the appraiser. The term written records also includes information stored on electronic, magnetic, or other media. Such records must be made available by the appraiser when required by due process of law or by a duly authorized professional peer review committee.

COMPETENCY PROVISION

Prior to accepting an assignment or entering into an agreement to perform any assignment, an appraiser must properly identify the problem to be addressed and have the knowledge and experience to complete the assignment competently; or alternatively:

1. disclose the lack of knowledge and/or experience to the client before accepting the assignment; and

2. take all steps necessary or appropriate to complete the assignment competently; and

3. describe the lack of knowledge and/or experience and the steps taken to complete the assignment competently in the report.

Comment: The background and experience of appraisers varies widely and a lack of knowledge or experience can lead to inaccurate or inappropriate appraisal practice. The competency provision requires an appraiser to have both the knowledge and the experience required to perform a specific appraisal service competently. If an appraiser is offered the opportunity to perform an appraisal service but lacks the necessary knowledge or experience to complete it competently, the appraiser must disclose his or her lack of knowledge or experience to the client before accepting the assignment and then take the necessary or appropriate steps to complete the appraisal service competently. This may be accomplished in various ways including, but not limited to, personal study by the appraiser; association with an appraiser reasonably believed to have the necessary knowledge or experience; or retention of others who possess the required knowledge or experience.

Although this provision requires an appraiser to identify the problem and disclose any deficiency in competence prior to accepting an assignment, facts or conditions uncovered during the course of an assignment could cause an appraiser to discover that he or she lacks the required knowledge or experience to complete the assignment competently. At the point of such discovery, the appraiser is obligated to notify the client and comply with items 2 and 3 of the provision.

The concept of competency also extends to appraisers who are requested or required to travel to geographic areas wherein they have no recent appraisal experience. An appraiser preparing an appraisal in an unfamiliar location must spend sufficient time to understand the nuances of the local market and the supply and demand factors relating to the specific property type and the location involved. Such understanding will not be imparted solely from a consideration of specific data such as demographics, costs, sales and rentals. The necessary understanding of local market conditions provides the bridge between a sale and a comparable sale or a rental and a comparable rental. If an appraiser is not in a position to spend the necessary amount of time in a market area to obtain this understanding, affiliation with a qualified local appraiser may be the appropriate response to ensure the development of a competent appraisal.

DEPARTURE PROVISION

This provision permits limited exceptions to sections of the Uniform Standards that are classified as specific guidelines rather than binding requirements. The burden of proof is on the appraiser to decide before accepting a limited assignment that the result will not confuse or mislead. The burden of disclosure is also on the appraiser to report any limitations.

An appraiser may enter into an agreement to perform an assignment that calls for something less than, or different from, the work that would otherwise be required by the specific guidelines, provided that prior to entering into such an agreement:

1. the appraiser has determined that the assignment to be performed is not so limited in scope that the resulting appraisal, review, or consulting service would tend to mislead or confuse the client, the users of the report, or the public; and
2. the appraiser has advised the client that the assignment calls for something less than, or different from, the work required by the specific guidelines and that the report will state the limited or differing scope of the appraisal, review, or consulting service.

Exceptions to the following requirements are not permitted: Standards Rules 1-1, 1-5, 2-1, 2-2, 2-3, 2-5, 3-1, 3-2, 4-1, 5-1, 5-3, 6-1, 6-3, 6-6, 6-7, 6-8, 7-1, 8-1, 8-3, 9-1, 9-3, 9-5, 10-1, 10-3 and 10-5. This restriction on departure is reiterated throughout the document with the reminder comment: *Departure from this binding requirement is not permitted.*

Comment: Before making a decision to enter into an agreement for appraisal services calling for a departure from a specific appraisal guideline, an appraiser must use extreme care to determine whether the scope of the appraisal service to be performed is so limited that the resulting analysis, opinion, or conclusion would tend to mislead or confuse the client, the users of the report, or the public. For the purpose of this provision, users of the report might include parties such as lenders, employees of government agencies, limited partners of a client, and a client's attorney and accountant. In this context the purpose of the appraisal and the anticipated or possible use of the report are critical.

If an appraiser enters into an agreement to perform an appraisal service that calls for something less than, or different from, the work that would otherwise be required by the specific appraisal guidelines, Standards Rules 2-2(k), 5-2(i), 8-2(h), and 10-2(h) require that this fact be clearly and accurately set forth in the report.

The requirements of the departure provision may be satisfied by the technique of incorporating by reference.

For example, if an appraiser's complete file were introduced into evidence at a public hearing or public trial and the appraiser subsequently prepared a one-page report that 1) identified the property, 2) stated the value, and 3) stated that the value conclusion could not be properly understood without reference to his or her complete file and directed the reader to the complete file, the requirements of the departure provision would be satisfied if the appraiser's complete file contained, in coherent form, all the data and statements that are required by the Uniform Standards.

Another example would be an update report that expressly incorporated by reference all the background data, market conditions, assumptions, and limiting conditions that were contained in the original report prepared for the same client.

JURISDICTIONAL EXCEPTION

If any part of these standards is contrary to the law or public policy of any jurisdiction, only that part shall be void and of no force or effect in that jurisdiction.

SUPPLEMENTAL STANDARDS

These Uniform Standards provide the common basis for all appraisal practice. Supplemental standards applicable to appraisals prepared for specific purposes or property types may be issued by public agencies and certain client groups, e.g. regulatory agencies, eminent domain authorities, asset managers, and financial institutions. Appraisers and clients must ascertain whether any supplemental standards in addition to these Uniform Standards apply to the assignment being considered.

DEFINITIONS

For the purpose of these standards, the following definitions apply:

APPRAISAL: (noun) the act or process of estimating value; an estimate of value.

(adjective) of or pertaining to appraising and related functions, e.g. appraisal practice, appraisal services.

APPRAISAL PRACTICE: the work or services performed by appraisers, defined by three terms in these standards: appraisal, review, and consulting.

Comment: These three terms are intentionally generic, and not mutually exclusive. For example, an estimate of value may be required as part of a review or consulting service. The use of other nomenclature by an appraiser (e.g. analysis, counseling, evaluation, study, submission, valuation) does not exempt an appraiser from adherence to these standards.

BUSINESS ASSETS: tangible and intangible resources that are employed by a business enterprise in its operations.

BUSINESS ENTERPRISE: a commercial, industrial, or service organization pursuing an economic activity.

BUSINESS EQUITY: the interests, benefits, and rights inherent in the ownership of a business enterprise or a part thereof in any form (including but not necessarily limited to capital stock partnership interests, cooperatives, sole proprietorships, options, and warrants).

CASH FLOW ANALYSIS: a study of the anticipated movement of cash into or out of an investment.

CLIENT: any party for whom an appraiser performs a service.

CONSULTING: the act or process of providing information, analysis of real estate data, and recommendations or conclusions on diversified problems in real estate, other than estimating value.

FEASIBILITY ANALYSIS: a study of the cost-benefit relationship of an economic endeavor.

INTANGIBLE PROPERTY (INTANGIBLE ASSETS): non-physical assets, including but not limited to franchises, trademarks, patents, copyrights, goodwill, equities, mineral rights, securities, and contracts, as distinguished from physical assets such as facilities and equipment.

INVESTMENT ANALYSIS: a study that reflects the relationship between acquisition price and anticipated future benefits of a real estate investment.

MARKET ANALYSIS: a study of real estate market conditions for a specific type of property.

MARKET VALUE: Market value is the major focus of most real property appraisal assignments. Both economic and legal definitions of market value have been developed and refined. A current economic definition agreed upon by agencies that regulate federal financial institutions in the United States of America is:

> The most probable price which a property should bring in a competitive and open market under all conditions requisite to a fair sale, the buyer and seller each acting prudently and knowledgeably, and assuming the price is not affected by undue stimulus. Implicit in this definition is the consummation of a sale as of a specified date and the passing of title from seller to buyer under conditions whereby:
>
> 1. buyer and seller are typically motivated;
> 2. both parties are well informed or well advised, and acting in what they consider their best interests;
> 3. a reasonable time is allowed for exposure in the open market;
> 4. payment is made in terms of cash in United States dollars or in terms of financial arrangements comparable thereto; and
> 5. the price represents the normal consideration for the property sold unaffected by special or creative financing or sales concessions granted by anyone associated with the sale.

Substitution of another currency for *United States dollars* in the fourth condition is appropriate in other countries or in reports addressed to clients from other countries.

Persons performing appraisal services that may be subject to litigation are cautioned to seek the exact legal definition of market value in the jurisdiction in which the services are being performed.

MASS APPRAISAL: the process of valuing a universe of properties as of a given date utilizing standard methodology, employing common data, and allowing for statistical testing.

MASS APPRAISAL MODEL: a mathematical expression of how supply and demand factors interact in a market.

PERSONAL PROPERTY: identifiable portable and tangible objects which are considered by the general public as being "personal," e.g. furnishings, artwork, antiques, gems and jewelry, collectibles, machinery and equipment; all property that is not classified as real estate.

REAL ESTATE: an identified parcel or tract of land, including improvements, if any.

REAL PROPERTY: the interests, benefits, and rights inherent in the ownership of real estate.

> *Comment:* In some jurisdictions, the terms *real estate* and *real property* have the same legal meaning. The separate definitions recognize the traditional distinction between the two concepts in appraisal theory.

REPORT: any communication, written or oral, of an appraisal, review, or analysis; the document that is transmitted to the client upon completion of an assignment.

> *Comment:* Most reports are written and most clients mandate written reports. Oral report guidelines (See Standards Rule 2-4) and restrictions (See Ethics Provision: Record Keeping) are included to cover court testimony and other oral communications of an appraisal, review, or consulting service.

REVIEW: the act or process of critically studying a report prepared by another.

STANDARDS AND STANDARDS RULES

STANDARD 1

In developing a real property appraisal, an appraiser must be aware of, understand, and correctly employ those recognized methods and techniques that are necessary to produce a credible appraisal.

> *Comment:* Standard 1 is directed toward the substantive aspects of developing a competent appraisal. The requirements set forth in Standards Rule 1-1, the appraisal guidelines set forth in Standards Rule 1-2, 1-3, 1-4, and the requirements set forth in Standards Rule 1-5 mirror the appraisal

process in the order of topics addressed and can be used by appraisers and the users of appraisal services as a convenient checklist.

Standards Rule 1-1

In developing a real property appraisal, an appraiser must:

(a) be aware of, understand, and correctly employ those recognized methods and techniques that are necessary to produce a credible appraisal;

Comment: Departure from this binding requirement is not permitted. This rule recognizes that the principle of change continues to affect the manner in which appraisers perform appraisal services. Changes and developments in the real estate field have a substantial impact on the appraisal profession. Important changes in the cost and manner of constructing and marketing commercial, industrial, and residential real estate and changes in the legal framework in which real property rights and interests are created, conveyed, and mortgaged have resulted in corresponding changes in appraisal theory and practice. Social change has also had an effect on appraisal theory and practice. To keep abreast of these changes and developments, the appraisal profession is constantly reviewing and revising appraisal methods and techniques and devising new methods and techniques to meet new circumstances. For this reason it is not sufficient for appraisers to simply maintain the skills and the knowledge they possess when they become appraisers. Each appraiser must continuously improve his or her skills to remain proficient in real property appraisal.

(b) not commit a substantial error of omission or commission that significantly affects an appraisal;

Comment: Departure from this binding requirement is not permitted. In performing appraisal services an appraiser must be certain that the gathering of factual information is conducted in a manner that is sufficiently diligent to ensure that the data that would have a material or significant effect on the resulting opinions or conclusions are considered. Further, an appraiser must use sufficient care in analyzing such data to avoid errors that would significantly affect his or her opinions and conclusions.

(c) not render appraisal services in a careless or negligent manner, such as a series of errors that, considered individually, may not significantly affect the results of an appraisal, but which, when considered in the aggregate, would be misleading.

Comment: Departure from this binding requirement is not permitted. Perfection is impossible to attain and competence does not require perfection. However, an appraiser must not render appraisal services in a careless or negligent manner. This rule requires an appraiser to use due diligence and due care. The fact that the carelessness or negligence of an appraiser has not caused an error that significantly affects his or her opinions or conclusions and thereby seriously harms a client or a third party does not excuse such carelessness or negligence.

Standards Rule 1-2

In developing a real property appraisal, an appraiser must observe the following specific appraisal guidelines:

(a) adequately identify the real estate, identify the real property interest, consider the purpose and intended use of the appraisal, consider the extent of the data collection process, identify any special limiting conditions, and identify the effective date of the appraisal;

(b) define the value being considered; if the value to be estimated is market value, the appraiser must clearly indicate whether the estimate is the most probable price:

 (i) in terms of cash; or

 (ii) in terms of financial arrangements equivalent to cash; or

 (iii) in such other terms as may be precisely defined; if an estimate of value is based on submarket financing or financing with unusual conditions or incentives, the terms of such financing must be clearly set forth, their contributions to or negative influence on value must be described and estimated, and the market data supporting the valuation estimate must be described and explained;

Comment: For certain types of appraisal assignments in which a legal definition of market value has been established and takes precedence, the Jurisdictional Exception may apply to this guideline.

When estimating market value, the appraiser should be specific as to the estimate of exposure time linked to the value estimate.

(c) consider easements, restrictions, encumbrances, leases, reservations, covenants, contracts, declarations, special assessments, ordinances, or other items of a similar nature;

(d) consider whether an appraised fractional interest, physical segment, or partial holding contributes pro rata to the value of the whole;

Comment: This guideline does not require an appraiser to value the whole when the subject of the appraisal is a fractional interest, a physical segment, or a partial holding. However, if the value of the whole is not considered, the appraisal must clearly reflect that the value of the property being appraised cannot be used to estimate the value of the whole by mathematical extension.

(e) identify and consider the effect on value of any personal property, trade fixtures or intangible items that are not real property but are included in the appraisal.

Comment: This guideline requires the appraiser to recognize the inclusion of items that are not real property in an overall value estimate. Additional expertise in personal property (See Standard 7) or business (See Standard 9) appraisal may be required to allocate the overall value to its various components. Separate valuation of such items is required when they are significant to the overall value.

Standards Rule 1-3

In developing a real property appraisal, an appraiser must observe the following specific appraisal guidelines:

(a) consider the effect on use and value of the following factors: existing land use regulations, reasonably probable modifications of such land use regulations, economic demand, the physical adaptability of the real estate, neighborhood trends, and the highest and best use of the real estate;

Comment: This guideline sets forth a list of factors that affect use and value. In considering neighborhood trends, an appraiser must avoid stereotyped or biased assumptions relating to race, age, color, religion, gender, or national origin or an assumption that racial, ethnic, or religious homogeneity is necessary to maximize value in a neighborhood. Further, an appraiser must avoid making an unsupported assumption or premise about neighborhood decline, effective age, and remaining life. In considering highest and best use, an appraiser should develop the concept to the extent that is required for a proper solution of the appraisal problem being considered.

(b) recognize that land is appraised as though vacant and available for development to its highest and best use and that the appraisal of improvements is based on their actual contribution to the site.

Comment: This guideline may be modified to reflect the fact that, in various legal and practical situations, a site may have a contributory value that differs from the value as if vacant.

Standards Rule 1-4

In developing a real property appraisal, an appraiser must observe the following specific appraisal guidelines, when applicable:

(a) value the site by an appropriate appraisal method or technique;
(b) collect, verify, analyze, and reconcile:
    (i) such comparable cost data as are available to estimate the cost new of the improvements (if any);
    (ii) such comparable data as are available to estimate the difference between cost new and the present worth of the improvements (accrued depreciation);
    (iii) such comparable sales data, adequately identified and described, as are available to indicate a value conclusion;
    (iv) such comparable rental data as are available to estimate the market rental of the property being appraised;
    (v) such comparable operating expense data as are available to estimate the operating expenses of the property being appraised;

(vi) such comparable data as are available to estimate rates of capitalization and/or rates of discount.

Comment: This rule covers the three approaches to value. See Standards Rule 2-2(1) for corresponding reporting requirements.

(c) base projections of future rent and expenses on reasonably clear and appropriate evidence;

Comment: This guideline requires an appraiser, in developing income and expense statements and cash flow projections, to weigh historical information and trends, current market factors affecting such trends, and anticipated events such as competition from developments under construction.

(d) when estimating the value of a leased fee estate or a leasehold estate, consider and analyze the effect on value, if any, of the terms and conditions of the lease(s);

(e) consider and analyze the effect on value, if any, of the assemblage of the various estates or component parts of a property and refrain from estimating the value of the whole solely by adding together the individual values of the various estates or component parts;

Comment: Although the value of the whole may be equal to the sum of the separate estates or parts, it also may be greater than or less than the sum of such estates or parts. Therefore, the value of the whole must be tested by reference to appropriate market data and supported by an appropriate analysis of such data.

A similar procedure must be followed when the value of the whole has been established and the appraiser seeks to estimate the value of a part. The value of any such part must be tested by reference to appropriate market data and supported by an appropriate analysis of such data.

(f) consider and analyze the effect on value, if any, of anticipated public or private improvements, located on or off the site, to the extent that market actions reflect such anticipated improvements as of the effective appraisal date;

Comment: In condemnation valuation assignments in certain jurisdictions, the Jurisdictional Exception may apply to this guideline.

(g) identify and consider the appropriate procedures and market information required to perform the appraisal, including all physical, functional, and external market factors as they may affect the appraisal;

Comment: The appraisal may require a complete market analysis (See Standards Rule 4-4).

(h) appraise proposed improvements only after examining and having available for future examination:

(i) plans, specifications, or other documentation sufficient to identify the scope and character of the proposed improvements;

(ii) evidence indicating the probable time of completion of the proposed improvements; and

(iii) reasonably clear and appropriate evidence supporting development costs, anticipated earnings, occupancy projections, and the anticipated competition at the time of completion.

Comment: The evidence required to be examined and maintained under this guideline may include such items as contractors' estimates relating to cost and the time required to complete construction, market, and feasibility studies; operating cost data; and the history of recently completed similar developments. The appraisal may require a complete feasibility analysis (See Standards Rule 4-6).

(iv) All pertinent information in items (a) through (h) above shall be used in the development of an appraisal.

Comment: See Standards Rule 2-2(k) for corresponding reporting requirements.

Standards Rule 1-5

In developing a real property appraisal, an appraiser must:

(a) consider and analyze any current agreement of sale, option, or listing of the property being appraised, if such information is available to the appraiser in the normal course of business;

(b) consider and analyze any prior sales of the property being appraised that occurred within the following time periods:

(i)   one year for one-to-four family residential property; and

(ii) three years for all other property types;

Comment: The intent of this requirement is to encourage the research and analysis of prior sales of the subject; the time frames cited are minimums.

(c) consider and reconcile the quality and quantity of data available and analyzed within the approaches used and the applicability or suitability of the approaches used.

Comment: Departure from binding requirements (a) through (c) is not permitted. See Standards Rule 2-2(k) Comment for corresponding reporting requirements.

STANDARD 2

In reporting the results of a real property appraisal an appraiser must communicate each analysis, opinion, and conclusion in a manner that is not misleading.

Comment: Standard 2 governs the form and content of the report that communicates the results of an appraisal to a client and third parties.

Standards Rule 2-1

Each written or oral real property appraisal report must:

(a) clearly and accurately set forth the appraisal in a manner that will not be misleading;

Comment: Departure from this binding requirement is not permitted. Since most reports are used and relied upon by third parties, communications considered adequate by the appraiser's client may not be sufficient. An appraiser must take extreme care to make certain that his or her reports will not be misleading in the marketplace or to the public.

(b) contain sufficient information to enable the person(s) who receive or rely on the report to understand it properly;

Comment: Departure from this binding requirement is not permitted. A failure to observe this rule could cause a client or other users of the report to make a serious error even though each analysis, opinion, and conclusion in the report is clearly and accurately stated. To avoid this problem and the dangers it presents to clients and other users of reports, 2-1(b) requires an appraiser to include in each report sufficient information to enable the reader to understand it properly. All reports, both written and oral, must clearly and accurately present the analyses, opinions, and conclusions of the appraiser in sufficient depth and detail to address adequately the significance of the specific appraisal problem.

(c) clearly and accurately disclose any extraordinary assumption or limiting condition that directly affects the appraisal and indicate its impact on value.

Comment: Departure from this binding requirement is not permitted. Examples of extraordinary assumptions or conditions might include items such as the execution of a pending lease agreement, atypical financing, or completion of onsite or offsite improvements. In a written report the disclosure would be required in conjunction with statements of each opinion or conclusion that is affected.

Standards Rule 2-2

Each written real property appraisal report must:

(a) identify and describe the real estate being appraised;
(b) identify the real property interest being appraised;

Comment on (a) and (b): These two requirements are essential elements in any report. Identifying the real estate can be accomplished by any combination of a legal description, address, map reference, copy of a survey or map, property sketch and/or photographs. A property sketch and photographs also provide some description of the real estate in addition to written comments about the physical attributes of the real estate. Identifying the real property rights being appraised requires a direct statement substantiated as needed by copies or summaries of legal descriptions or other documents setting forth any encumbrances.

(c) state the purpose of the appraisal;
(d) define the value to be estimated;
(e) set forth the effective date of the appraisal and the date of the report;

Comment on (c), (d) and (e): These three requirements call for clear disclosure to the reader of a report the "why, what and when" surrounding the appraisal. The purpose of the appraisal is used generically to include both the task involved and rationale for the appraisal. Defining the value to be estimated requires both an appropriately referenced definition and any comments needed to clearly indicate to the reader how the definition is being applied [See Standards Rule 1-2(b)]. The effective date of the appraisal establishes the context for the value estimate, while the date of the report indicates whether the perspective of the appraiser on the market conditions as of the effective date of the appraisal was prospective, current, or retrospective. Reiteration of the date of the report and the effective date of the appraisal at various stages of the report in tandem is important for the clear understanding of the reader whenever market conditions on the date of the report are different from market conditions on the effective date of the appraisal.

(f) describe the extent of the process of collecting, confirming, and reporting data;

Comment: This requirement is designed to protect third parties whose reliance on an appraisal report may be affected by the extent of the appraiser's investigation; i.e. the process of collecting, confirming, and reporting data.

(g) set forth all assumptions and limiting conditions that affect the analyses, opinions, and conclusions;

Comment: It is suggested that assumptions and limiting conditions be grouped together in an identified section of the report.

(h) set forth the information considered, the appraisal procedures followed, and the reasoning that supports the analyses, opinions, and conclusions;

Comment: This requirement calls for the appraiser to summarize the data considered and the procedures that were followed. Each item must be addressed in the depth and detail required by its significance to the appraisal. The appraiser must be certain that sufficient information is provided so that the client, the users of the report, and the public will understand it and will not be misled or confused. The substantive content of the report, not its size, determines its compliance with this specific reporting guideline.

(i) set forth the appraiser's opinion of the highest and best use of the real estate, when such an opinion is necessary and appropriate;

Comment: This requirement calls for a written report to contain a statement of the appraiser's opinion as to the highest and best use of the real estate, unless an opinion as to highest and best use is unnecessary, e.g. insurance valuation or value in use appraisals. If an opinion as to highest and best use is required, the reasoning in support of the opinion must also be included.

(j) explain and support the exclusion of any of the usual valuation approaches;

(k) set forth any additional information that may be appropriate to show compliance with, or clearly identify and explain permitted departures from, the requirements of Standard 1;

Comment: This requirement calls for a written appraisal report or other written communication concerning the results of an appraisal to contain sufficient information to indicate that the appraiser complied with the requirements of Standard 1, including the requirements governing any permitted departures from the appraisal guidelines. The amount of detail required will vary with the significance of the information to the appraisal.

Information considered and analyzed in compliance with Standards Rule 1-5 is significant information that deserves comment in any report. If such information is unobtainable, comment on the efforts undertaken by the appraiser to obtain the information is required.

(l) include a signed certification in accordance with Standards Rule 2-3.

Comment: Departure from binding requirements (a) through (l) above is not permitted.

Standards Rule 2-3

Each written real property appraisal report must contain a certification that is similar in content to the following form:

I certify that, to the best of my knowledge and belief:

—the statements of fact contained in this report are true and correct.
—the reported analyses, opinions, and conclusions are limited only by the reported assumptions and limiting conditions, and are my personal, unbiased professional analyses, opinions, and conclusions.
—I have no (or the specified) present or prospective interest in the property that is the subject of this report, and I have no (or the specified) personal interest or bias with respect to the parties involved.

—my compensation is not contingent upon the reporting of a predetermined value or direction in value that favors the cause of the client, the amount of the value estimate, the attainment of a stipulated result, or the occurrence of a subsequent event.

—my analyses, opinions, and conclusions were developed, and this report has been prepared, in conformity with the Uniform Standards of Professional Appraisal Practice. I have (or have not) made a personal inspection of the property that is the subject of this report. (If more than one person signs the report, this certification must clearly specify which individuals did and which individuals did not make a personal inspection of the appraised property.)

—no one provided significant professional assistance to the person signing this report. (If there are exceptions, the name of each individual providing significant professional assistance must be stated.)

Comment: Departure from this binding requirement is not permitted.

Standards Rule 2-4

To the extent that it is both possible and appropriate, each oral real property appraisal report (including expert testimony) must address the substantive matters set forth in Standards Rule 2-2.

Comment: In addition to complying with the requirements of Standards Rule 2-1, an appraiser making an oral report must use his or her best efforts to address each of the substantive matters in Standards Rule 2-2.

Testimony of an appraiser concerning his or her analyses, opinions, and conclusions is an oral report in which the appraiser must comply with the requirements of this Standards Rule.

See *Record Keeping* under the ETHICS PROVISION: for corresponding requirements.

Standards Rule 2-5

An appraiser who signs a real property appraisal report prepared by another, even under the label of "review appraiser," must accept full responsibility for the contents of the report.

Comment: Departure from this binding requirement is not permitted.

This requirement is directed to the employer or supervisor signing the report of an employee or subcontractor. The employer or supervisor signing the report is as responsible as the individual preparing the appraisal for the content and conclusions of the appraisal and the report. Using a conditional label next to the signature of the employer or supervisor or signing a form report on the line over the words "review appraiser" does not exempt that individual from adherence to these standards.

This requirement does not address the responsibilities of a review appraiser, the subject of Standard 3.

STANDARD 3

In reviewing an appraisal and reporting the results of that review, an appraiser must form an opinion as to the adequacy and appropriateness of the report being reviewed and must clearly disclose the nature of the review process undertaken.

Comment: The function of reviewing an appraisal requires the preparation of a separate report or a file memorandum by the appraiser performing the review setting forth the results of the review process. Review appraisers go beyond checking for a level of completeness and consistency in the report under review by providing comment on the content and conclusions of the report. They may or may not have firsthand knowledge of the subject property of or data in the report. The COMPETENCY PROVISION applies to the appraiser performing the review as well as the appraiser who prepared the report under review.

Reviewing is a distinctly different function from that addressed in Standards Rule 2-5. To avoid confusion in the marketplace between these two functions, review appraisers should not sign the report under review unless they intend to take the responsibility of a cosigner.

Review appraisers must take appropriate steps to indicate to third parties the precise extent of the review process. A separate report or letter is one method. Another appropriate method is a form or check-list prepared and signed by the appraiser conducting the review and attached to the report under review. It is also possible that a stamped impression on the appraisal report under review, signed or initialed by the reviewing appraiser, may be an appropriate method for separating the review function from the actual signing of the report. To be effective, however, the stamp must briefly indicate the extent of the review process and refer to a file memorandum that clearly outlines the review process conducted.

The review appraiser must exercise extreme care in clearly distinguishing between the review process and the appraisal or consulting processes. Original work by the review appraiser may be governed by STANDARD 1 or STANDARD 4 rather than this standard. A misleading or fraudulent review and/or report violates the ETHICS PROVISION.

Standards Rule 3-1

In reviewing an appraisal, an appraiser must:

(a) identify the report under review, the real estate and real property interest being appraised, the effective date of the opinion in the report under review, and the date of the review;
(b) identify the extent of the review process to be conducted;
(c) form an opinion as to the completeness of the report under review in light of the requirements in these standards;

Comment: The review should be conducted in the context of market conditions as of the effective date of the opinion in the report being reviewed.

(d) form an opinion as to the apparent adequacy and relevance of the data and the propriety of any adjustments to the data;
(e) form an opinion as to the appropriateness of the appraisal

methods and techniques used and develop the reasons for any disagreement;

(f) form an opinion as to whether the analyses, opinions, and conclusions in the report under review are appropriate and reasonable, and develop the reasons for any disagreement.

Comment: Departure from binding requirements (a) through (f) above is not permitted.

An opinion of a different estimate of value from that in the report under review may be expressed, provided the review appraiser:

1. satisfies the requirements of STANDARD 1;
2. identifies and sets forth any additional data relied upon and the reasoning and basis for the different estimate of value; and,
3. clearly identifies and discloses all assumptions and limitations connected with the different estimate of value to avoid confusion in the marketplace.

Standards Rule 3-2

In reporting the results of an appraisal review, an appraiser must:

(a) disclose the nature, extent, and detail of the review process undertaken;

(b) disclose the information that must be considered in Standards Rule 3-1 (a) and (b);

(c) set forth the opinions, reasons, and conclusions required in Standards Rule 3-1 (c), (d), (e) and (f);

(d) include all known pertinent information;

(e) include a signed certification similar in content to the following

I certify that, to the best of my knowledge and belief:

—**the facts and data reported by the review appraiser and used in the review process are true and correct.**

—**the analyses, opinions, and conclusions in this review report are limited only by the assumptions and limiting conditions stated in this review report, and are my personal, unbiased professional analyses, opinions and conclusions.**

—**I have no (or the specified) present or prospective interest in the property that is the subject of this report and I have no (or the specified) personal interest or bias with respect to the parties involved.**

—**my compensation is not contingent on an action or event resulting from the analyses, opinions, or conclusions in, or the use of, this review report.**

—**my analyses, opinions, and conclusions were developed and this review report was prepared in conformity with the Uniform Standards of Professional Appraisal Practice.**

—**I did not (did) personally inspect the subject property of the report under review.**

—no one provided significant professional assistance to the person signing this review report. (If there are exceptions, the name of each individual providing significant professional assistance must be stated.)

Comment: Departure from binding requirements (a) through (e) above is not permitted.

Index